WOMEN'S WORKS IN STALIN'S TIME

WOMEN'S WORKS IN STALIN'S TIME

On Lidiia Chukovskaia and
Nadezhda Mandelstam

BETH HOLMGREN

INDIANA UNIVERSITY PRESS
Bloomington and Indianapolis

© 1993 by Beth Holmgren

All rights reserved

No part of this book may be reproduced or utilized in any form or by
any means, electronic or mechanical, including photocopying and
recording, or by any information storage and retrieval system, without
permission in writing from the publisher. The Association of American
University Presses' Resolution on Permissions constitutes the only
exception to this prohibition.

The paper used in this publication meets the minimum requirements of American
National Standard for Information Sciences—Permanence of Paper for Printed
Library Materials, ANSI Z39.48-1984.

Manufactured in the United States of America

Library of Congress Cataloging-in-Publication Data

Holmgren, Beth, date.
   Women's works in Stalin's time : on Lidiia Chukovskaia and
Nadezhda Mandelstam / Beth Holmgren.
     p.   cm.
   Includes bibliographical references and index.
   ISBN 0-253-32865-9 (cloth).—ISBN 0-253-20829-7 (paper)
   1. Russian literature—Women authors—History and criticism.
2. Chukovskaia, Lidiia Korneevna—Criticism and interpretation.
3. Mandel'shtam, Nadezhda, date —Criticism and interpretation.
I. Title.
PG2997.H65 1993
891.709'9287—dc20   92-46343

1 2 3 4 5   97 96 95 94 93

For my parents,
Virginia and Kenneth Holmgren

CONTENTS

ACKNOWLEDGMENTS ix

Introduction 1
1. Women's Works in Stalin's Time 5

Lidiia Chukovskaia

2. Father and Daughter 29
3. Alternative Scripts and Novel Therapies 44
4. *Notes on Anna Akhmatova* 68

Nadezhda Mandelstam

5. Husband and Wife 97
6. *Hope against Hope* 114
7. *Hope Abandoned* 139

The Post-Stalin Legacy

8. The Widows' Might 171

NOTES 181
WORKS CITED 213
INDEX 222

ACKNOWLEDGMENTS

This book was written by a Slavist about subjects traditionally located in Slavic studies, but it owes its existence to a heterogeneous group of interlocutors, well-wishers, and supporting institutions. My project formally began with a talk I delivered on Lidiia Chukovskaia and Nadezhda Mandelstam at the 1989 Western Association of Women's Historians conference in Asilomar, California; the response of that audience of non-Slavists made me realize the power of Chukovskaia's and Mandelstam's life stories and the importance of relating their lives and works to a more general, particularly a feminist readership. Funded by a short-term research grant from the International Research and Exchanges Board (IREX) and a University of California Faculty Career Development grant, I made my own sort of pilgrimage to the Soviet Union in fall 1989 to recover these stories; the first interlocutors for my project were in many ways its sources. I owe an immeasurable debt of gratitude to Lidiia Chukovskaia for meeting with me informally and sharing her reflections on her own work in conversation and correspondence. I am deeply grateful to Iurii Freidin (Nadezhda Mandelstam's legal heir), Nina Belosinskaia, Varvara Shklovskaia and Nikolai Panchenko, Liudmila Sergeeva, Mikhail Polivanov, and Alla and Leonid Latynin for their interest, insights, and extraordinary generosity; my interviews and conversations with them fundamentally stimulated and shaped my analysis. I also thank the expert staffs at the Central State Archive of Literature and Art, the State Literary Museum, and the library of the Institute of World Literature in Moscow for their efficiency and accessibility.

I was able to complete the manuscript with the continuing financial support of the University of California in the form of a second Faculty Career Development Grant and grants from the UC-San Diego Dean of Arts and Humanities. I wrote and rewrote the text in dialogue with differently seeing, but uniformly helpful groups of readers. In the Slavic field Steven Cassedy, Caryl Emerson, Helena Goscilo, Michael Heim, Madeline Levine, Don Ostrowski, Stephanie Sandler, and Jurij Striedter helped me ground my analysis more thoroughly and rigorously in its specific literary and historical contexts. My non-Slavist colleagues in the Department of Literature at the University of California, San Diego—Stephanie Jed, Nicole Tonkovich, Susan Kirkpatrick, Kathryn Shevelow, Pasquale Verdicchio, and Judith Halberstam—read my manuscript for clarity in content and style and suggested theoretical connections with non-Russian literatures and contexts. Whatever appeal this book holds for a broader audience stems largely from their questions, suggestions, and requests for further explanation.

Thanks are also due to Iurii Freidin and Princeton University Library for permission to publish materials from the Osip Mandelshtam papers housed in Princeton University's Firestone Library and to M.E. Sharpe for permission to publish chapter 5, which appeared (in slightly altered form) in *Fruits of Her Plume: Essays on Contemporary Russian Women's Culture*, edited by Helena Goscilo (New York: M.E. Sharpe, 1993). The photo of Nadezhda Mandelstam is reprinted here courtesy of Ardis Press; the photo of Lidiia Chukovskaia appears on the cover of the second volume of *Notes on Anna Akhmatova*, published by YMCA Press.

Any finished book represents the collective effort of the author's family; the particular subject of this book made me keenly appreciative of my family's support. My husband, Mark Sidell, was my mainstay in all things—a generous and exceedingly patient partner, tireless morale booster, and computer expert *extraordinaire*. My sister, Janet Holmgren McKay, was my most important reader; her belief in and understanding of my project sustained me from prospectus to final draft. My nieces, Elizabeth and Ellen McKay, helped me keep my work in the proper perspective. And my parents, Virginia and Kenneth Holmgren, supported me at all times, through all the hard places. This book is dedicated to them because, as I see more and more clearly, it is founded on the spiritual education they gave me—their model of abiding love, strong religious faith, and spirited partnership.

WOMEN'S WORKS IN STALIN'S TIME

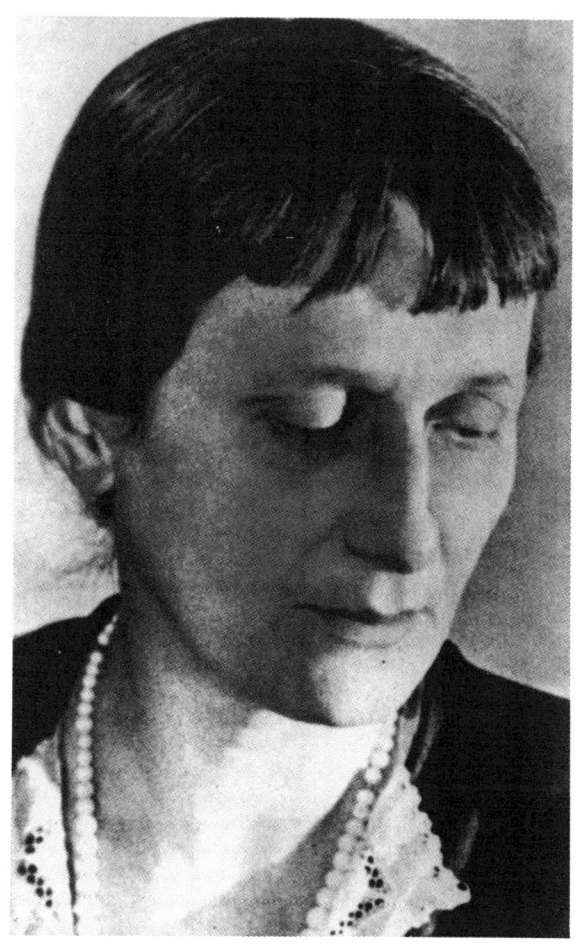

Anna Akhmatova

INTRODUCTION

> In the fearful years of the Yezhov terror I spent seventeen months in prison queues in Leningrad. One day somebody identified me. Beside me, in the queue, there was a woman with blue lips. She had, of course, never heard of me; but she suddenly came out of that trance so common to us all and whispered in my ear (everybody spoke in whispers there): "Can you describe this?" And I said: "Yes, I can." And then something like a shadow of a smile crossed what had once been her face.
>
> Anna Akhmatova, *Requiem*[1]

In the course of the vital, complex relationship long cultivated between Russian writers and their society, no period has been more disruptive than the decades of Stalin's rule. During that time the Soviet literary establishment was collectivized into a conforming body supported and controlled by the government; its output was largely dictated by socialist realism—a state-sponsored literary doctrine that severely restricted writers in their choice of subjects and techniques. Those who resisted this regimentation largely disappeared from public view, silenced by the new means of production or imprisoned and sometimes executed for their deviance.

Writers and critics since have attempted to mend this ruptured relationship by rehabilitating the silenced and the dead, recovering lost biographies and hidden texts, and thereby reconstituting the rich variety of themes and poetics long suppressed in twentieth-century Russian literature. Under Gorbachev, these efforts were officially sanctioned through the campaign for *glasnost'*, but they had been risked even as the destruction was taking place under Stalin and were accelerated after Stalin's death. Indeed, a striking feature of this recovery was its spontaneous, unsponsored progress. Begun without official approval, it soon overwhelmed the program of the post-Stalin official establishment during the "thaw" (the authorities had not intended so thorough a critique) and eventually spilled over into the relatively new unofficial venues of *samizdat* (clandestine self-publishing) and *tamizdat* (publishing abroad). Its forms were often improvised and unconventional: In the absence of long-awaited scholarly biographies and academy editions there appeared a veritable flood of autobiographical writing—memoirs, testimonials, diaries, documentary prose.[2] In a sense, these nonfictional, unscholarly texts assayed a most immediate healing of the rupture. Testifying from an eyewitness perspective, they sought to authenticate and so reify lives, works, and creative practices verbally, and sometimes literally, obliterated by the Stalinist regime.

Just as these forms and venues of publication had to supplement and circumvent the literary establishment, so many of the participants in this process had to work outside official literary channels. Given the restrictions placed on professionals, one could say that this process *depended*, to an important degree, on the covert labor of professionals and even amateurs—that is, the loyal relatives, friends, and admirers of proscribed artists.[3] It is perhaps predictable, then, and certainly significant that women figured prominently as these unofficial memoirists, especially in contrast with their minority in the literary establishment; for this kind of writing and circulation they required no credentials or institutional support. To some extent these women became writers because they were survivors charged to bear witness. In many cases they were "literary widows" who bravely assumed responsibility for their husbands' forbidden archives and biographies.[4] Moreover, in composing autobiographical texts, these women were working in a medium traditionally accessible to Russian women—one that, ideally, afforded them unmediated self-definition and, at the same time, justified what the reading public perceived as the audacity of their authorship because they wrote to commemorate political victims.[5]

Yet, as I demonstrate in this book, other important reasons exist for these women's authorship and influence. It is my contention that Stalinist society paradoxically generated a productive artistic and political moment for women involved in unofficial culture. These women were not merely articulate survivors, but eventual powerbrokers enabled by a peculiar overlap of neglect and opportunity. The Stalinist system was intent on building up heavy industry and defense and so regressed to a more or less traditional sexual division of labor and leadership; women bore the double burden of work and home and exercised little political clout. Consequently, during the waves of political purges women were less liable to be arrested and more often were left to maintain the home front—that precarious site of unofficial culture and potential political resistance. As the custodians of this sphere, some women were drawn into the production and maintenance of unofficial culture. It fell to them to preserve the cultural artifacts—the texts, images, and practices—produced in this place. And once the terror and deprivations eased in the post-Stalin era, they could claim a sort of privilege of experience and involvement; they frequently resurfaced as the guardians and even co-producers of buried artistic treasure.

To begin assessing the contributions of these women memoirists to the recovery of Russian culture, I examine the creative development and major works of two of the most powerful writers to emerge from the Stalinist experience—Lidiia Korneevna Chukovskaia (1907-) and Nadezhda Iakovlevna Mandelstam (1899–1980). The Stalinist purges victimized both women, destroying their husbands and many of their friends, driving them from their homes, and, in Mandelstam's case, forcing her to live as a fugitive for twenty-five years. These traumas compelled both to a kind of writing distinct from their professional work. Nadezhda Mandelstam literally became a writer through her volumes of memoirs, and Lidiia Chukovskaia, trained as a critic and editor, created fiction, poetry, and a stunning journal of her meetings with Anna Akhmatova *during* the

Introduction

Stalinist period. Both Mandelstam's memoirs and Chukovskaia's journal offer remarkably similar testimony: Their texts re-create the life of a proscribed artist (or artists) and chart the different stages and features of the unofficial creative process. Through this writing, in turn, both Mandelstam and Chukovskaia articulated the extraordinary works of women in unofficial Soviet culture. In the post-Stalin era their writings, joined with their personal example, helped found and influence a new dissident society.

I have chosen these subjects in large part because of their impressive achievements as writers and their influence as cultural activists, although I am certain that neither Chukovskaia nor Mandelstam would feel they deserved particular attention. Both women tended to project themselves as adjunct to more important figures—Nadezhda Mandelstam was ever the wife of the great poet Osip Mandelstam, and Chukovskaia deferred to a host of other greats, including her father, the famous critic and children's writer Kornei Ivanovich Chukovskii. I respect their humility, but it does them and Russian culture a disservice to dismiss them at their word. As I will elaborate, Chukovskaia and Mandelstam seemed to be fulfilling duties traditionally assigned women in Russian culture, and while this service earned them glory (and approval) from a male-dominated consensus (among dissidents, émigrés, and Western observers), it tended to obscure their distinction *as writers*. Apart from reviews of their work (which almost inevitably foreground their courage and fidelity), there exists little secondary literature on either one. Their work is appropriated (very often uncritically) as useful information, not carefully constructed literature; we have not yet formalized our evaluation of such "behind the scenes" texts.[6] On the other hand, if assessed from some feminist perspectives, Chukovskaia and Mandelstam run the risk of being judged for their willing performance of a patriarchally approved role. In the case of Russian and Soviet Russian women, it is essential that any feminist project of reclamation and interpretation (especially one conducted by a Western scholar) situate its subjects within their distinctive conditions and traditions and develop a nuanced, critical reading rather than a prejudgment based on a set of presumably "universal" political and/or theoretical assumptions. Heeding the call of some feminist scholars for a "new history . . . encompass[ing] the complexity of women's past," I have tried to navigate between these kinds of traditional and theoretical hazards, drawing on different types of Russian and feminist literary criticism and historiography to provide an analysis that is both contextually grounded and sensitive to the problems, issues, and possibilities engaging a Russian woman writer.[7]

What is more problematic, perhaps, is my comparative framework, a juxtaposition that would likely discomfit both women. As I learned in the course of my research (which included interviews with their friends and associates), their profound temperamental and behavioral differences informed their approach to the literary world and writing and served in the long run to alienate them from each other. Yet I opted to compare the two precisely because they demonstrate what I consider to be a paradigmatic opposition for Russian women writers from Stalinist times into the present. Chukovskaia might be said to represent a conservative position; she respects and inscribes traditional hierarchies, rituals, and symbols. Mandelstam embraces some of this traditional sensibility, but in her writing manner she very often plays the iconoclast, unmasking the symbols and violating the hierarchies and forms that Chukovskaia carefully observes. That is, Chukovskaia in large part realizes socially and culturally accepted roles for a female *intelligent*, whereas Mandelstam begins to discern new, unorthodox models of female behavior and identity. This contrast is best illustrated in their relationship to a recognized female artist, the great poet Anna Akhmatova. Both women were inspired and educated by this female mentor, yet they evoked strikingly different creative models from their observations and interaction. They discovered in her the very different writers they themselves were proving to be.

In sum, this book is designed to evaluate and historicize two important writers and their most influential texts. As is customary for any act of literary reclamation, it attends to the writers' "lives" and "works" or, as I amend these categories, their creative biographies and the larger works of their writing, actions, and examples. And because my subjects are women who seemed compelled and equipped to write under extraordinary circumstances, my analysis entails a more general inquiry into the position and roles of women in Stalinist society and the distinctive works they produced. I begin, therefore, by discussing the various political, social, and cultural factors that enabled the phenomenon of these women memoirists, mapping the relationship between the exercise of power, the conditions of writing, the situation of women, and the projected constructs of gender and the domestic sphere in official and unofficial writings of the Stalinist period.

1.
WOMEN'S WORKS IN STALIN'S TIME

Power relations and authorship

After a decade of diverse experiments in political and economic programs, social legislation, and artistic trends, Soviet society underwent a colossal transformation in the first few years of Stalin's rule (1929–33). According to most observers, Stalin built his dictatorship on the bedrock of enforced and rewarded conformity, mass entertainment, and pervasive government control. The Soviet state became seemingly monolithic; in the words of one historian, "it substituted itself for society, to become the sole initiator of action and controller of all important spheres of life."[1] Whatever his strategies for gaining power (and these have been well debated elsewhere), Stalin took strong measures to ensure the state's dependence on his personal rule and vision.[2] He performed drastic surgery on his party elite, purging potentially "hostile" elements and recruiting personnel who were, above all, demonstrably loyal to him. He implemented a command economy that operated according to a vertical hierarchy and entailed forced collectivization of agriculture, the use of forced labor, and the imposition of unrealistic work quotas in agriculture and industry. He encouraged loyalty and patriotism, on the one hand, by awarding material privileges to his new elite and engaging the rank and file with an uplifting, accessible popular culture. On the extreme other hand, he extorted compliance from Soviet society by expanding his secret police force and unleashing waves of political terror against "suspect" segments of the population—first violent collectivization and the "terror-famine" against the peasantry (1929–33) and then successive purges conducted against various groups (party and army personnel, the cultural and technical intelligentsia, different nationalities). Historians may never be able to determine the exact number of victims, but it is estimated that at least twenty million died as a result of Stalinist repressions and about forty million were victimized.[3]

With this uniform system patronized and terrorized into place, Stalin succeeded in fostering a tremendous cult of his own personality. His opinions on every topic and in every discipline were cited as sacred scripture; his image proliferated as the icon of the great Leader, the father of the nation, even (during the Second World War) the Generalissimo.[4] At least on the public surface of Soviet society an almost religious, enraptured atmosphere prevailed in which "[t]he social consciousness of the people took on elements of religious psychology: illusions, autosuggestion, the inability to think critically, intolerance towards dissidents, and fanaticism."[5] Under these conditions, the state-controlled press was equipped to enthrall readers with its black-and-white version of reality. Even during the worst years of the purges (1937–38) most citizens could take comfort in the romantic fictions "reported" in the news:

> If one looks at the Soviet press of the period one senses the currents of fear and exhilaration that ran through the whole society. . . . There it is set in vivid colors: the kingdoms of light and darkness. From the yellowed pages of *Pravda* and *Izvestia* the smiling heroes peer at us: those very Russian faces of the record-breaking pilots, the Arctic explorers under Professor Schmidt who sent a message of homage to the Leader, as well as a resolution approving the execution of the army traitors. . . . How could one believe that the Leader hailed so continuously by these brave and handsome young men — shown clasping them to his bosom, inquiring solicitously about the details of their feats — was a bloody tyrant, who after a triumphant reception sat down and signed another list of victims to be murdered and deported? . . . Against the world of heroes exuding strength, resolve, and gaiety was the murky realm of traitors and enemies. Stories about them appear as often as those about the heroes.[6]

This cult, atmosphere, and supporting fictions have led several literary critics to comment on the peculiar aesthetic properties of Stalin's dictatorship. Boris Grois argues that Stalinist culture represented the culmination of the avant-garde movement, for it succeeded in aestheticizing all of Soviet life, transforming the population into "extras" and "stagehands" and Stalin himself into its "single author and spectator."[7] The writer Abram Tertz (the provocative alter ego of the critic Andrei Siniavskii) has pondered Stalin's "artistry" for most of his career. In his very first essay *What Is Socialist Realism?* he identifies the "magical night" of Stalin's dictatorship and ironically laments the Leader's fall from magnificent hyperbole into mortality. In a later essay he characterizes the Stalinist period as a time when art

> was totally replaced by the games of a single Magician, who for a lengthy period was able to lend history itself the power and appearance of fairy-tale fantasy. Art vanished and rotted away so that for a while life (if one looks at it from a standpoint that is detached and tolerant of evil) might acquire the aesthetic savor of nightmarish and bloody farce played out according to theatrical and literary rules. One only has to consider the detective-novel conception of history which the leader managed to inculcate in millions of people, or his love of realizing metaphors. . . . The pathos of 1937 lay not only in the extent to which the country was gripped by a Bacchic frenzy, nor in the fact that the purges destroyed the most loyal party zealots, but also in the extraordinarily vivid, novelistic way in which metaphors came to life — when the whole country was suddenly crawling with all kinds of invisible (and therefore especially dangerous) reptiles, snakes and scorpions with such terrible names as "Trotskyite" or "wrecker" . . . Stalin had brought into play (without possibly suspecting it) the magic powers contained in the language and Russian society, ever susceptible to a graphic perception of words and the mirac-

ulous transformation of life into the plot of a novel (from which, incidentally, stem the beauty and grandeur of Russian literature), submitted to this terrifying illusion of living in a world of miracles, sorcery, and artifice. These elements were visibly in control of reality and produced a certain intense theatrical pleasure, even as they sent shivers down everybody's spine.[8]

Whether or not Stalin was the artist Siniavskii/Tertz senses him to be, it is clear that the ruler conceded art extraordinary power—at least according to his own value system; he seemed ever wary of the danger of uncontrolled words and images.[9] Under his general direction, fiction writers and journalists carefully determined and recycled plots, characters, and metaphors that would legitimize state power and rationalize the irrational atrocity of the state's actions. An artist who wrote otherwise would be subverting an ontology thoroughly inscribed by the regime, committing an act of political sabotage and so incurring the punishment of oblivion (being written out) or obliteration (the link between literary and literal in Stalinist "aesthetics").

Stalinist conditions of authorship, then, interestingly manipulated the general historical schema Michel Foucault posits in his famous essay "What Is an Author?" Whereas Foucault dates the recognition of authorship to its "punishability" and charts its shift from "the bipolar field of the sacred and profane" into a commercial "circuit of ownership," official authorship under Stalin effectively blended these religious and commercial phases.[10] In these conditions authorship derived from the politically sacred, yet was incorporated in a modern bureaucratic system of ownership and distribution; with the institution of a single Union of Soviet Writers in 1932, different literary groupings and publishing ventures all came under uniform government control and patronage.[11] If a writer wished to be published (and be identified and maintained as a state-approved author), then he or she had to employ the "language," "syntax," and themes prescribed under the state doctrine of socialist realism.[12] The publicly recognized, materially privileged author was one who accepted this complex disciple/client contract with the state, writing what the state deemed sacred and enjoying the material support the state provided its loyal workers.[13]

Writers who would not abide by the terms of this contract could not simply turn their backs on the literary establishment, for it was their single source of employment. Yet their official status as author clearly eroded as they worked out forms of partial dependence. Not wishing to write according to the dictates of socialist realism, they tried to earn money by translation or, in some cases, scholarship focused on pre-revolutionary subjects and thus were sidetracked from the high position of the artist in Russian culture. If their works were denied publication in the most visible (and therefore most closely censored) forums, then they were forced to resurface in the margins (e.g., the provincial press) or adjunct spheres (film, radio) of this vast centralized network. In sum, if a writer refused to harness his or her power to the state's machinery, then he or she was deprived of the means to exert it in any other service and effaced as a cultural presence. Under Stalin there could be no public recurrence of writerly authorities like Lev Tolstoi or, for that matter, the political philosopher-turned-novelist Nikolai Chernyshevskii. In nineteenth-century Russia such authors had functioned as spiritual and moral leaders beyond government control. In the Stalinist state writers were always suspected of harboring this ambition, and once "proven guilty," they were demoted further to the status of criminal.[14] In these cases, the state ruthlessly maintained its pronounced ontology: It expelled such writers from Soviet society, concealed them in the invisible underworld of the prisons and camps, and rewrote their images and life stories to conform to the official fictions about "enemies of the people."

In spite of these dangers, a number of writers continued to produce work they knew was unpublishable and "criminal" and consequently improvised their own means of production, preservation, and (very restricted) circulation. In place of professional editors, proofreaders, and printers, they had to rely on the volunteered service of family and friends and all these enlisted parties had somehow to cope with the risks of the material text. During the 1930s, the decade of Stalin's most virulent purges, Soviet citizens learned to evaluate written documents and private archives according to government practice. In the assessment of Marietta Chudakova, a renowned Soviet archivist, "documents were no longer potential or actual monuments of culture—they were perceived in large part as potential material evidence incriminating their owner."[15] With very few exceptions, writers could not hope to save their work from state impoundment by depositing it in state-controlled archives.[16] Nor could the participants in unofficial literary production venture to "publish" a manuscript—even on a very limited scale. At best, writers and readers struggled to preserve a text without alerting the authorities to its existence and endangering the lives of all those contaminated by their contact with it. These pieces of "material evidence," then, were cautiously dispersed, concealed, and even de-materialized. Several copies of a poem might be distributed among trusted friends for safekeeping and manuscripts were secreted in the homeliest places—stuck in saucepans, carted around in old suitcases and trunks and baskets, even buried in jars in the garden.[17] In other instances, texts were committed to memory rather than paper. The text was thus preserved as a domestic or oral artifact and the archive transposed from physical plant to private household or human body.

These desperate, ingenious modes of production and preservation complicated and intensified the relationship between writer and reader. Given the terrible penalties involved, their interaction resembled nothing so much as a conspiracy. The writer put the reader at the same risk he or she had assumed in creating; both had to rely on mutual trust and maintain a fervent belief in the high value of uncensored art.[18] Yet because responsibility for the text was shared, the reader was empowered as well as endangered. He or she became, in effect, a joint owner of a manuscript, even a joint archive for memorized texts. In a few cases, regrettably, this joint responsibility and ownership deviated into a kind of embezzlement when unscrupulous readers sold the materials entrusted to them. More often, however, this writer-reader collaboration resulted in a dispersion of creative authority and an intriguing confusion of literary roles. Charged so long with the care of a dangerous text, a reader could absorb the roles of editor and textologist, especially if the writer had perished. Even if the writer survived, the reader-depository of a memorized text could easily disagree with its author about its final form. And whether or not the writer was dead or alive, the reader was implicated as potential biographer, for the unofficial artist had been unnamed or misnamed by the authorities. Thus, the reader of unofficial literature was invested with a tremendous privilege — the authority to re-create and interpret the writer's text as well as the writer's image and life story.

The domestic sphere and the situation of women

If Stalinist society was so well-controlled and policed, where could this unofficial production and maintenance take place? What space existed outside the institutions and organizations in and through which the government exercised its power? The "total" notion of "totalitarian" would seem to preclude a discrete part in the whole, an overlooked underground. Yet, as a result of Bolshevik and then Stalinist policy (as well as traditional Russian attitudes toward women), the state never fully colonized the domestic sphere. It was never subject to the same degree of scrutiny and control applied to the workplace and spaces for public use. The writing, reading, and hiding of unofficial literature, therefore, was chiefly managed in the not altogether private Soviet home.

As in so many other cultures, this sphere was recognized as the domain of women, but it was not conceded the special significance it projected in Western European capitalist societies. Scholars like Nancy Armstrong, Gillian Brown, and Anita Levy have argued that English and American literatures, in tandem with the emergence of capitalism, privileged the domestic sphere and the domestic woman as a means of legitimizing and universalizing middle-class authority and concepts of selfhood and individualism.[19] Under Stalin, the domestic sphere and its official literary depiction were certainly manipulated to support state policies, but never moved into the foreground; the workplace held that position. Indeed, the Bolsheviks had instituted this ranking from the very outset. The new Soviet state granted absolute legal equality to women and initially recognized women's double burden of work and home. Its remedy, however, was to elevate professional labor over domestic work and, at least in its early dreams of a communist utopia, to replace this sphere with collective services — day-care centers, communal kitchens and households.[20] To a great extent, this program mirrored the party's general policy on women: It lobbied to recruit women for the work force and involve them politically in establishing the new Soviet state. A special organization, the *Zhenotdel* (Women's Section), had been created to address their specific developmental needs — particularly as workers and public citizens. Their domestic roles did not hold the party's attention.

These somewhat limited organizations and projects were then discarded in the Stalinist period because, as the press kept insisting, Soviet women had already achieved full equality. In order to ensure a stable work force, the government legislated a retreat to more conservative social policies; in public discourse "[d]omestic labour, self-determination, and sexuality became non-issues."[21] That is, while the state restored the ideal of the nuclear family and urged women to become Heroine Mothers (as well as shock workers in industry and agriculture), it simply ignored their domestic burden and made no pragmatic investment in the domestic sphere. Unlike the explicitly conservative programs of fascist Germany and Italy, the Stalinist system emphasized labor over all. It agitated to retain and recruit female workers—especially after the devastation wrought by collectivization and the purges.[22] Therefore, although Stalinism "assigned a set of functions and roles to women that in some respects intensified the sexual division of labor," it never exclusively vaunted the domain of the family hearth and the image of the female homemaker.[23] This limited focus on the home resulted in material neglect but also a kind of political reprieve. Because women were treated (if not acknowledged) as secondary in society—the rank and file in industry and politics and the invisible homemakers—they were less targeted for party approval or censure.[24]

I argue, then, that despite significant restrictions and deprivations, the domestic sphere under Stalin benefitted from this political neglect, and women acquired a valuable low profile along with their secondary status.[25] The neglected domain of women furnished the most likely site for venting difference and creating other-than-official works of testimony or art. In a variation on Western European practice, the domestic sphere and its creative possibilities under Stalin could be conflated as readily with an alternative society as with the status quo. Here lay both the symbolic potential for opposition (a potential this space sometimes afforded in American and European literatures) and a real arena for dissident acts. And this sort of conflation had long been exploited in Russian society. In the nineteenth century, the exclusionary structure of the tsarist government relegated any opposition to the domestic sphere (reading circles and study groups), a developing underground, and the lone public forum of literature, through which different philosophical and political views could be coded (e.g., by Aesopian language), if not openly stated, for the Russian audience. Hence writers and readers in the Stalinist period were historically trained to activate this link between private life, political resistance, and the written word. In their more controlled context, however, writing and reading had to be more closely guarded and the domestic sphere had to serve as shelter, a place of furtive rather than open exchange.

This historic conflation of the domestic sphere and political dissent also established patterns of women's involvement in the opposition. Of course, during the tsarist period women were more confined than liberated within the domestic sphere; for much of the nineteenth century they were largely prevented from entering public life and the skilled labor force. Yet because women were exposed to radical and liberal ideologies mainly through reading and discussion in the home, the domestic sphere furnished them an inadvertent connection with the political underground. While they could not leave home for an assured university education or government service, they could run away from home to join the makeshift households of the underground—its fictitious marriages and actual communes. The reform agenda emerging in the wake of the Crimean war (1855) already included the cause of women's emancipation, and very early on, women of the gentry and the intelligentsia enlisted in the service of this and other more subversive causes.[26] In fact, these other causes diverted many women from what they perceived to be the narrow interests and middle-class privileges of feminism. They seemed more readily attracted to the movements (nihilist, populist, socialist) which at least claimed to serve the whole of society, or, more urgently, the oppressed masses of peasants and workers. It seemed, too, that when women managed to escape the strict confines of home and surmount the educational and professional restrictions placed on them, they were propelled further in their dedication and self-sacrifice.[27] Their participation became noteworthy: By the second half of the nineteenth century, "women constituted a substantial and influential minority in the Russian radical intelligentsia."[28]

Their evident altruism often led women to disregard their specific needs in favor of "generic" (i.e., tacitly male-oriented) goals, but it garnered them a special prestige among their male cohorts. Assessing women's involvement in the populist movement, one historian observes:

> The women's moral fervor, their "spiritual beauty," earned populists the sympathy of a sector of the educated public . . . [These qualities] also contributed to the creation of a sort of mythology, which defined the revolutionary woman as limitlessly devoted and endlessly self-sacrificing, a martyr heroine. A myth with enormous appeal to women as well as men of the left, it would remain alive in every subsequent revolutionary movement and war.[29]

Read from the public performance of the revolutionaries, this myth amplified and capitalized on the idealized image Russian male writers had ascribed to their female characters.[30] Women would never achieve the same leadership positions as men in these underground movements, but their demonstrated "feminine virtues" (e.g., moral fervor, self-sacrifice, a capacity for caretaking) were highly valued and *generally* prescribed. Women had enacted and were recognized for a culturally defined "female" heroism that was bound to political resistance. Passing almost directly from the domestic sphere into the underground, women indicated that certain traits and behaviors learned in the home could be spectacularly adapted to oppositional (and even terrorist) work. As Barbara Engel surmises in her study *Mothers and Daughters: Women of the Intelligentsia in Nineteenth-Century Russia*, the dedication and success of these women stemmed from what they themselves defined as a female legacy—the religious beliefs and practice of their mothers, the "family" support of other female revolutionaries, and their ideal of femininity as "the capacity for feeling, for suffering, and for self-sacrifice."[31]

By the Stalinist period many of these revolutionary women had been appropriated as official heroines and their successors welcomed into public life and government service. Nevertheless, their model of response, divested of any terrorist elements, proved useful under rather different oppositional circumstances. In the Stalinist state there could be no active underground—certainly not the sweep of nineteenth-century reading and study circles. The secret police apparatus was too well-invested and empowered to miss such "loopholes." But there were vast numbers of people—and of these more women than men—who had been victimized by the regime and left at large in society. In a small, exceedingly brave group of this mass of victims the traditions of literary protest and certain aspects of female-ascribed political resistance coalesced and produced new scenarios of heroism and opposition. For at this point even personal and textual survival were construed as forms of political dissidence; the virtues of self-sacrifice and caretaking could therefore be reapplied to the preservation of these "criminal" lives, texts, and biographies. After Stalin's death, these survivor-caretakers and their new brand of heroism would help to shape a far more comprehensive mode of political dissidence against the totalitarian state.

The gender scripts of socialist realism

This relationship between writing, dissidence, and the domestic sphere is very interestingly refracted in the literary texts of the Stalinist period. For that reason, before I turn to the works of Lidiia Chukovskaia and Nadezhda Mandelstam, I want to consider their textual as well as contextual framework, their empowering points of departure from or contiguity with contemporary works of fiction. With their development in mind, I find it significant that many unofficial texts from this era highlight the particular domain and feats of women. This becomes especially apparent against the normative background of socialist realism. Official and unofficial works contrast in their privileging of different cultural constructs of gender which, in turn, convey different political and philosophical worldviews. The signifying of gender (and by this I mean the cultural and creative construction of gender, not an essential biological category) becomes a complex indicator of one's position vis-à-vis the state.

Socialist realist literature, on the one hand, developed certain gender constructs in a rigid hierarchy, projecting a reductive and powerful standard that laid down the terms of debate for both official and unofficial writers. As sanctioned expression of the state, these works necessarily took their cue from Stalin himself, who symbolized military and industrial strength and embraced the martial, elitist, and authoritarian in his governing and self-display.[32] The combined elements of physical might, technical and industrial prowess, and military style were promoted in all aspects of public life and suggested a cult of stereotyped, hyperbolized masculinity, although they did not interfere with official rhetoric about equality between the sexes.[33] Rather, these properties—along with an all-consuming work ethic and loyalty to the state—were to be inculcated in men and women alike.[34] This generated very interesting effects in official literature. Especially in the period of "high Stalinism" (the pre-war decade), socialist realist works staged the most important action in the public world or the workplace—in the factory or at a construction project or on the collective farm—and featured heroes of great physical courage and generally martial bearing. In her analysis of the socialist realist novel, Katerina Clark provides an implicit catalogue of these "masculine" heroes and their plots. As culled from real life (i.e., for newspaper portraits) and created for fiction, the socialist realist hero echoed the figure of the *bogatyr'*, the mighty warrior in Russian folklore, and was "all 'struggle,' 'vigilance,' heroic achievement, energy and another cluster of qualities rather like the 'true grit' of the American frontier: 'stickability' (*vyderžka*), 'hard as flint' (*kremen*), and 'will' (*volja*)."[35]

Plots, too, were built around conventionally masculine images and themes that fictionalized political lessons. By the early 1930s, "Soviet society's leaders became 'fathers' (with Stalin as the patriarch); the national heroes, 'sons'; the state, a 'family' or 'tribe.' "[36] The state was figured as master patriarchy, extending lines of qualified patrilineal inheritance and inspiring the "sons" to the quests and trials that comprised both essential service to the state and a prerequisite rite of passage (from "spontaneous" to "conscious" commitment). The plot, then, very often inscribed the warrior son's dynamic development: It depicted a young man who proves himself to his symbolic "father" by various physical feats—flying planes, exploring new territories, defending the nation, overfulfilling five-year plans. Typical heroes from this period of high Stalinism emerged from the ranks of aviators, explorers, border guards, athletes, and Stakhanovites (shock workers).[37] Their most significant relationships were played out with the state and its "fathers," while other ties of love and kinship were relegated to secondary plots.[38]

With this predominance of male heroes, male lines of authority, and conventionally male professions and plots, female characters blended into the foreground; their difference was lost or dismissed. At least in the first edition of Fiodor Gladkov's *Cement* (1925), a prototype for the socialist realist novel, the figure of Dasha occasionally steals the limelight from her hero-husband, Gleb Chumalov. A product of the less hierarchical 1920s, she had earned a peculiar sort of hero status along with her separate-but-equal leadership in *Zhenotdel*: Her work as a Party activist is accorded special attention in the text, and she is depicted besting her warrior husband in terms of discipline and Party literacy. Yet Dasha's model did not become productive. While women did write socialist realist fiction and female characters did appear as protagonists, these heroines wore the straitjacket of male role models. They, too, had to subordinate the personal to the political, invest themselves wholly in their professional labors, and perform Herculean physical feats in service to the state. In effect, they won equality through conformity, playing surrogate "sons" to unchanged "fathers."

Any display of presumed "feminine" traits and duties shunted them into the role of supporting player. In her study of female characters in official Stalinist literature, Xenia Gasiorowska reiterates that "the introduction of proper femininity into the characterization of the woman comrade may be responsible for her having never developed leadership, the distinguished quality of the hero."[39]

What most often obtained in female characters was a mélange of Stalinist masculine ideals and careful signals of a conventional wholesome femininity—"modesty" and "a sweet naivete" (for girls), marital fidelity, and abiding maternal instincts.[40] Whatever her marital state or class background (Gasiorowska itemizes peasant, worker, and intelligentsia categories), the female character usually and willingly ceded place of importance to the male. She equalled the average male, but was "seldom allowed to be anything more than average."[41] If married, she almost invariably worked and also served as her husband's helpmate and faithful follower; if single, she could attain the position of esteemed worker (even "Stakhanovite"), but never that of innovator or leader. And although female characters were lauded as mothers in socialist realist fiction, their more or less exclusive domain of childrearing and homemaking remained conveniently out of focus.[42]

Erected in the 1930s, these rigid hierarchies of setting, plot, and characterization set a standard of public conduct that endorsed the features and behaviors of an outsized masculinity and projected the domain and "feminine" traits of women as subordinate; women appeared as leaders neither in Stalinist society nor in Stalinist fiction. It is important to recognize, however, that even official writers began to dismantle some of these hierarchies in response to postwar conditions. By the end of World War II, Soviet military and industrial might had been proved, and accordingly, authors could transform their heroes from warriors to white-collar workers and transfer them from building sites to the family circle. Love and family relations were more fully integrated into the hero's development; indeed, the role of hero was often conferred on a wife or mother who struggled to keep her family intact.[43] While these changed emphases did not fundamentally alter the secondary status of women, they forecast certain preoccupations central to the post-Stalin era and indirectly productive of women's greater role in unofficial Soviet society.[44]

Just as these texts cautiously anticipated the concerns and values of the thaw period—for example, a call for greater "sincerity" and a focus on emotional development and family life—they faintly echoed a much stronger, earlier backlash in unofficial literature against the warrior ethos. The domestic world they began to claim for the state was already in the process of being staked out and interpreted—much more boldly and eloquently—by unofficial writers. We cannot gauge the scope of this prior exploration, for we never will know how many manuscripts were lost or destroyed. But I propose to consider this phenomenon on the evidence of several important writers and their texts—specifically, the works of Osip Mandelstam, Mikhail Bulgakov, Boris Pasternak, and Anna Akhmatova. Composed and preserved in the Soviet Union during the Stalinist years, their texts generated significantly different plots and heroes and posited alternative constructs of gender. To understand the place of Lidiia Chukovskaia and Nadezhda Mandelstam in this company, I first review the gender scripts that male artists assigned them in their function as helpers and then I consider how the poetry of Akhmatova equipped them with a complementary enabling script written from a woman's perspective.

Alternative scripts

In a richly complex way, the poetry and essays of Osip Mandelstam (1891–1938) prepared this different focus; as we shall see, the roles he devised for men and women encouraged his wife in part to become one sort of writer. Mandelstam already sensed and meditated on the cataclysmic effects of revolution in *Tristia*, his second collection of poems (1916–20), and this "eschatological vision" consequently informed much of his life work.[45] Enacting his self-styled role as the "preserver of cultural continuity," he countered the revolution's disruption of culture with the evocation of a composite underworld—one that interspersed classical imagery of the afterlife with the utensils and artifacts of a multicultural domesticity.[46] Stocked with images of honey, wine, clay jugs, a loaf of bread, yarn, and spinning wheels, this underworld seemed to incarnate the "domestic Hellenism" that Mandelstam subsequently prescribed for Russian poetry in his 1922 essay "On the Nature of the Word":

> Hellenism is the conscious surrounding of man with domestic utensils instead of impersonal objects; the transformation of impersonal objects into domestic utensils; and the humanizing and warming of the surrounding world with the most delicate teleological warmth. Hellenism is any kind of stove near which a man sits, treasuring its heat as something akin to his own internal body heat. And finally, Hellenism is the Egyptian funerary ship in which the dead are carried, into which everything required of man's earthly wanderings is put, down to perfume phials, mirrors, and combs.[47]

Already in the first years of the Soviet state, Mandelstam had defined a set of important, connected oppositions: the revolution's disruption of culture versus cultural continuity maintained in a domestic underworld; a culture in which words are enslaved for "liturgical use" (at this point he is attacking the Russian Symbolists) versus a "man-centered" culture that cherishes the crafts and materials of its own home (that is, the ideal of his own poetic group, the Acmeists). It was as if he were prophesying his response to the disruptive violence and restriction of Stalinism; in both oppositions, he privileged his own peculiar, elastic vision of the domestic sphere. In this early period, however, Mandelstam still hoped that his views could be incorporated into the new social order.[48] A decade later, when he reasserted his "organic poetics" and the "sacralization of everyday life" in the travel essay "Journey to Armenia" (1933), he had become a pariah in the literary establishment and was having great difficulty publishing his work.[49] It would seem that Mandelstam's "man-centered" values and poetics inexorably cast him as an opponent in the Stalinist system. (Indeed, the exceptional appearance of "Journey to Armenia" in the magazine *Zvezda* cost its editor, Tsezar Volpe, his position.)[50] His defamatory poem about Stalin then made him a palpable criminal, and he was arrested, exiled, and officially repressed as a writer.

Although Mandelstam's complex assignments of gender (particularly to the formation of the poet) developed throughout his writing life, I would argue that they are also essentially connected to the vision of *Tristia*.[51] While Mandelstam wished to inculcate "a perfect manliness" in Russian poetry by way of responding to a new "heroic age," his *Tristia* poems had already imaged this "manliness" in a series of noble, doomed gestures.[52] The manly hero of socialist realist fiction was inadequate for Mandelstam's purpose; he anticipated and displaced the victorious warrior with portraits of a courageous, vanquished, dying brotherhood who "shall remember even in the Lethean cold / That the cost of this earth was ten heavens."[53] In coping with the tragic defeat he first evoked in *Tristia*, Mandelstam located, among many other mythologies, a model of the kenotic Christ which could embody the tragic and the manly along with a capacity for transcendence. In his book, *A Coat of Many Colors: Osip Mandelstam and His Mythologies of Self-Presentation*, Gregory Freidin analyzes this and other mythologies in Mandelstam's work with great perspicacity and erudition; what I want to consider here, therefore, is not the specific application of the model, but the androgynous possibilities it contains.[54] According to Christian scriptures, Christ was incarnated as a man and called only men to be his disciples. But, as interpreted by Mandelstam and several other Russian writers, he eschewed a martial ideal for a martyrdom/heroism permeated with the traditional "feminine" traits of gentleness, compassion, and utter self-sacrifice. By appropriating this model for his own self-image as a poet, Mandelstam was extending, perhaps, his own very early definition of the lyric poet as a "two-sexed creature" (*"dvupoloe sushchestvo"*).[55] Most certainly he posed the figure of the suffering, redemptive poet—particularly the poet Mandelstam—as the true hero of his age.[56]

In the tradition of many poets, Mandelstam developed an androgynous model of the creator which nonetheless was to be assumed by himself and other men.[57] Yet, among the various images he ascribed to female subjects and addressees, he reiterated one important role for women that engendered its own heroism and, in some cases, creative personae. Once again, his *Tristia* poems set the pattern: They project enduring images of women as the "blessed wives" (*"blazhennye zheny"*) who can divine the future and "will gather the light ashes" of the dead.[58] In his vision, women were not magnified as surrogate "sons," but valued and symbolized in the more traditionally female vocations of mourner and seer.[59] The final lines of the poem *Tristia* make this assignation: "Not for us conjectures about Greek Erebus, / wax is for women what bronze is for a man, / Only in battles do we learn our lot, / but they are granted death in the act of divination."[60] And once again, Mandelstam's vision functioned as a sort of prophecy. Foretold in *Tristia*, this role, in a sense, was commemorated in his last poem "Toward the empty earth" (*"K pustoi zemle nevol'no pripadaia"*). As Jane Gary Harris notes in her biography of Mandelstam, this poem was begun as a tribute to Natasha Evgen'evna Shtempel', a young schoolteacher who befriended the Mandelstams in their Voronezh exile and helped Nadezhda Mandelstam in the dangerous, difficult task of preserving Osip's work.⁶¹ Mandelstam's poem beautifully defines and generalizes her heroism:

> There are women kin to the damp earth
> And their every step is a resonant sobbing.
> To escort the resurrected and be first
> To greet the dead is their calling.
> To demand caresses from them is criminal,
> And to part with them is unendurable.
> Today—an angel; tomorrow—a graveyard worm,
> And the day after that—only an outline.
> What had been her step will become unrecognizable.
> Flowers are immortal. Heaven is whole.
> And what will be is only a promise.⁶²

Mandelstam's prescience was distinctive, but his basic views on the domestic sphere and male and female roles coincided to a remarkable extent with the visions of other writers forced to work unofficially. In particular, I have in mind the two major fictions of Mikhail Bulgakov and Boris Pasternak—*The Master and Margarita* and *Doctor Zhivago*. While these texts are set in different historical periods (only Bulgakov's novel takes place in a carefully manipulated version of Stalinist times), their portraits of the Soviet artist resemble each other in their response to and deviance from the Stalinist model.

Both texts stem from their authors' own experience, although neither Bulgakov nor Pasternak suffered the extreme persecution of Mandelstam. Despite bans put on his plays, Bulgakov (1891–1940) managed to keep working as a playwright and a librettist in various theatres for most of his life; in one of the most curious episodes in Soviet literary history, Stalin himself interceded to return Bulgakov to his post. Pasternak (1890–1960) was not severely attacked in the Stalinist years, but he had to take refuge in translation during the waves of pre- and postwar purges. Nevertheless, both men were aware that their novels would be deemed criminal by the regime.⁶³ They worked (more or less) in secret on their texts, shared them only with friends and close associates, and did not try to publish them while Stalin lived.⁶⁴ Within that sustaining network of friends and family, both writers especially relied on the support of the women they loved—Pasternak on his second wife, Zinaida Neigauz, and his mistress, Olga Ivinskaia, who maintained a separate household for him and suffered imprisonment largely on his account; Bulgakov on his third wife, Elena Shilovskaia, who preserved his novel after his death and eventually saw to its publication in the 1960s. Perhaps in consequence, their novels—whatever their historical setting—highlight the conditions and parties involved in the unofficial literary process.

Both novels focus on the experience and reception of an independent artist. The literary establishment plays little or no part in their protagonists' creative development. It is simply absent in *Zhivago*. In *The Master and Margarita* it is the object of extravagant satire: The Union of Soviet Writers (renamed

MASSOLIT) is exposed as an organization of hacks and bureaucrats who scramble for the material privileges of official writers—special villas, paid vacations, entrance to the "best restaurant in Moscow." The artist-heroes in these works therefore rely on other, nonliterary means of support and the creative workspace of home. The poet Zhivago, for example, earns his living as a doctor and writes poems in catch breaths from his work and the onrush of history—especially when he finds himself in the right domestic environment. When his family flees Moscow for the remote Ural town of Varykino, Zhivago keeps a journal in the winter evenings when everyone relaxes around a warm stove, the women sewing or knitting and the men reading aloud. Later, when he returns to Varykino to make a temporary home with his mistress, Lara, he is once again inspired to write by "the warm, well-lit room," the writing utensils on his desk, the clean linen on the beds, and the pure faces of the sleeping Lara and her daughter. He christens his last lodging, a studio specially provided him for work, a "banqueting room of the spirit, a cupboard of mad dreams, a storeroom of revelations" (489).[65] And as he savors his first home in Varykino, Zhivago articulates a definition of art which spurns the "high-flown rhetoric" of revolutionary literature and echoes, on a purely Russian scale, Mandelstam's ideal of "domestic Hellenism":

> Only the familiar, touched by the hand of genius, is truly marvelous. The best object lesson in this is Pushkin. What a hymn to honest labor, duty, the customs of everyday life! Today "bourgeois" and "petty bourgeois" have become terms of abuse. Pushkin anticipated this criticism in his "Family Tree":
>
> "I am middle-class, I am middle-class."
>
> And in "Onegin's Travels":
>
>> "Now my ideal is a housewife,
>> My greatest wish, a quiet life
>> And a big bowl of cabbage soup." (285–86)

Bulgakov's Master, on the other hand, is a professional historian who wins one hundred thousand rubles in a lottery, quits his job, and devotes himself to writing a novel about Pontius Pilate. The prize money furnishes him with income and, much more important, two basement rooms in a small house with a garden—"an altogether private apartment with a foyer, and a sink in it" and "small windows just above the pathway leading to the gate" (155).[66] This is the sanctum in which he and his mistress, Margarita, become completely absorbed in the creation of his novel. After many fantastic events, when the Master and Margarita have been spirited away into the afterlife by a peculiarly beneficent Satan, they are granted the final refuge of a secluded country home with a Venetian window, a "vine climbing to the very roof," and a babbling brook nearby. As one critic has remarked, Bulgakov envisions a "Romantic destiny" for his hero—

> a cozy home, domestic peace and security in the company of his beloved, and a

life furnished with all the appurtenances of cultured society in the late eighteenth and early nineteenth centuries, including music, goosequills for his lucubrations, Goethean scientific investigation, and the harmonious beauties of domesticated nature.[67]

Thus, Pasternak and Bulgakov figure the domestic sphere as the birthplace (and perhaps guiding spirit) of art and the artist's ideal workplace. Their heroes feel most comfortable in this sphere and seem both reluctant and ill-equipped to assert themselves in a public role; they contrast with the socialist realist hero in body as well as spirit. Zhivago possesses a snub nose and an "unremarkable face" (125), while the Master appears dressed in shabby hospital garb. They do not metamorphose into warriors or important bureaucrats or even official authors. Zhivago is esteemed as a doctor and an artist, but he effectively shuns professional glory and material status. Bulgakov's hero has renounced his job, his past, and even his name in order to be identified, in a half-ironic homely way, as a "master"; the only emblem of his lofty vocation is a greasy skullcap Margarita has embroidered with the letter "M." Neither achieves public fame as a writer. Zhivago's works are published through the good graces of friends and are highly valued by friends and "collectors." The Master does submit his novel for official publication, but the resulting wave of vicious condemnation (directed at a text that is never published) terrorizes him into burning his manuscript and committing himself to a mental hospital.

Unimposing by socialist realist standards, Zhivago and the Master instead reiterate certain features of Mandelstam's heroism, evincing comparisons with the figure of Christ. Curiously enough, the parallels in the Master's case apply to his frail humanity as well as his conception of himself as an artist—that is, his commitment to express his intuition of the truth. The Yeshua (Christ) he depicts in his novel is no powerful deity, but an itinerant, well-meaning young man who seeks to elicit the good in people through his own "good words." Yeshua explicitly discounts the myths that are being ascribed to him, and when he seems to demonstrate a superhuman power (divining the physical suffering of Pilate), he explains his ability as a simple process of human deduction. Wise and compassionate, this version of Christ is nonetheless earth-bound and physically unheroic. He is eager to avoid torture and in no way seems prepared for the meaningful self-sacrifice of a kenotic Christ.

For Zhivago the association is more self-conscious and self-styled, a fundamental theme in the narrative and the poems carefully displayed at the novel's end. Zhivago's Christ, connected to the figure of Hamlet in his first poem, is the epitome of self-renunciation, receptivity, and inner freedom or, in the words of his philosopher uncle, the ideas of the "free personality" and "life as sacrifice" (10).[68] Zhivago, in turn, manifests these qualities in his capacious nature—his unwillingness to commit to a partisan cause or a public persona, his great sensitivity toward others and his love of life (his surname derives from the Russian root *zhiv* or "live"), his aversion to mortal combat and what one critic identifies as "an almost complete lack of male aggressiveness."[69] Moreover, Zhivago's model of a nonaggressive, receptive, self-sacrificing Christ clearly joins the dissident and the domestic.[70] The Christ theorized in the narrative of *Doctor Zhivago* overturns the beastliness and corruption of all previous empires with his "emphatically human, deliberately provincial" image, his birth to a simple girl, his truths taken from everyday life. Both Pasternak and Bulgakov, then, use the figure of Christ to develop a heroism which is oppositional and "emphatically human"—if not an implicit synthesis of masculine and feminine traits, then a nonaggressive, self-sacrificing model of masculinity.

Of course, this "emphatically human" Christ and the heroes he inspires are all men; as in so many Russian novels, only male characters seem endowed with the gift of artistic creativity. But, perhaps more than ever before, the male creators are depicted here as dependent, frail creatures whose creations inevitably overshadow and transcend them. Their unpublished or marginally published works are boldly highlighted in narratives which merely include the story of the artist; within the novels, the reception of these texts is of first (or final) importance. The closing narrative scene of *Doctor Zhivago* portrays the doctor's friends in the act of communing with his book. One could argue that the whole of *The Master and Margarita* constitutes proof of the text's transcendence, for it is related by the Devil and written, read, and dreamed by mortals. Although Pasternak and Bulgakov do not describe the actual maintenance of these texts (instead the manuscripts are saved by mysteriously powerful figures—Zhivago's half-brother Evgraf and Satan himself), they do designate a few faithful readers who value the hero's work and at the very least facilitate its creation and preservation. The most important of these are the mistresses of the two artists, Lara and Margarita. Like Mandelstam's "blessed wives," they do not break with the stereotype of the female helpmate attached to the male creator, but given the prescriptions of Stalinist society and culture, it is highly significant that these female characters are allotted a special emphasis, role, and value in their respective texts.

As one might guess from her absence in the title of *Zhivago*, Lara emerges as the more conventional man-made character. Raised in a petty bourgeois family, she works as a governess and then a teacher, serves as a nurse in the first world war, and becomes the most beloved and influential of Zhivago's three "wives." All three share the "common denominator of domesticity," but Lara especially incarnates and articulates it as an ideal.[71] Lara's beauty most enthralls Zhivago when she is "busy at her domestic chores"—cooking, washing, cleaning, ironing (407). Although she is initially sympathetic to the revolution, she expresses primary allegiance to her home and daughter. Her first household—with her husband Pavel Antipov—had been destroyed by the sloganizing and conformist ethos of the times; this artificial atmosphere misled Antipov into military service, first in the tsarist army and then in the Red Army. For Lara, Antipov's feats of military valor are beside the point, an obstacle to her real goal: "If by some miracle, I could see the window of our house shining, the lamplight on Pasha's desk and his books, even if it were at the end of the earth—I would crawl to it on my knees" (404).

Therefore, while Lara reiterates the stereotype of the domesticated woman, her domesticity may also be read as a source of alternative power in a regimented, politically invasive society.[72] It is important that her equally stereotyped feminine capacities for attracting, nursing, coping, and facilitating are idealized in the novel, not demoted to a secondary plot. While it might seem that Pasternak is simply resurrecting the traditional nineteenth-century Russian plot of the superfluous man and the beautiful woman who symbolizes a "higher Purpose," he has filled both Purpose and symbol with material, human content.[73] The ideals he opposes to the status quo are not visions of a new social order, but the tangible Lara and the domestic refuge she creates—in short, Pushkin's "housewife" and "bowl of cabbage soup." And unlike the superfluous antihero, who always proved incapable of appreciating and committing himself to his beloved, Zhivago avidly pursues a relationship with Lara until political circumstances force them to separate.

Lara never fully assumes charge over Zhivago's texts, although she performs other essential roles. As I have already noted, she maintains the environment in which he can write; she inspires many of his poems. One of the designated spokescharacters in the novel (she, Zhivago, and several others extend and confirm the philosophizing of the narrator), Lara, a self-proclaimed "ordinary woman," engages the hero in conversations "as full of meaning as the dialogues of Plato" (396). She is scripted as a self-styled Mary Magdalene to Zhivago's self-styled Christ and her disciple's gift of understanding is rendered exceptionally important. She is neither writer nor philosopher, but she is granted the ultimate honor of eulogizing Zhivago and their love; in his final absence, *she* must interpret his and their meaning. Lara does begin the task of sorting Zhivago's papers, yet her work (like her relationship with Zhivago) is interrupted by cataclysmic events. In the end, her death is just as ennobled (if not so amply memorialized) as Zhivago's consciously sacrificed life. Zhivago dies before he assumes his proper place in Soviet culture and society, untried by Stalinism; Lara, embarked on a tragic search for her child by Zhivago, is sacrificed as a victim of the purges.

Compared with Lara, the figure of Margarita is much more devoted to her supportive literary role. But she, too, embodies yet another variant of conventional femininity. Whereas Lara actively keeps house and mothers her daughter, Margarita is a childless lady of leisure—a woman married into the Soviet equivalent of the upper middle class (her husband is a "very prominent specialist"), who does not work, lives in a luxurious apartment, and even keeps a maid. In lieu of the order and stability Lara so gracefully labors to achieve, Margarita pursues a quite different domestic ideal remarkably undiffused by concerns for family or material welfare. Her privileged status frees her from the duties of wife, mother, and working woman; her intermittent life with the Master constitutes a further rarefaction, a secret (even underground) household that conspires in romantic love and artistic creation. For the Master and Margarita both, domestic bliss rests on the convenient juncture of financial security, illicit love, and idealistic desires.[74]

But when this secret home is lost and the Master languishes in an asylum, Margarita finds she cannot return to the world of material comfort. Instead, she charts a new, actively heroic, wholly fantastic course for her character. Margarita emerges as the stronger partner in their relationship, avenging the Master's persecution and displaying extraordinary courage and determination in her attempts to recover him. Of all the residents of Moscow, she alone eagerly cooperates with the Devil—on blind faith that he will lead her to the Master. In a striking departure from Goethe's *Faust* (to which this novel frequently and playfully alludes), Margarita navigates between Gretchen's passive suffering and Faust's overweening ambition as she strikes her own deal with the Devil.[75] Her pact results not in the acquisition of creative power, but in a kind of quest-romance with the gender roles reversed. Here Margarita is the bold hero who braves fantastic adventures in order to rescue her beloved (the "bride-figure" in traditional romances).[76] The female helper thus plays the role of active hero and undergoes both metamorphosis and death to achieve her goal. In yet another reversal, the demonic figures she meets in her quest are not her enemies; rather, she invokes their supernatural aid (and standards) against the evils of Stalinist society. We saw in *Zhivago* how the artist and the domestic sphere were allied with and sanctified by the figure of Christ. In *The Master and Margarita* the home and persons of writer and reader are guaranteed by Satan—albeit beyond the limits of Stalinist reality. As in Mandelstam's vision, the locus of unofficial culture is once again figured in a benevolent underworld.

In Bulgakov's version of the underworld, then, Margarita considerably exceeds the figure of "blessed wife." Rather than enduring as mourner or seer, she is transformed into a witch, a woman possessed by supernatural powers and outcast because she reverses "normal and socially accepted behavior."[77] She enjoys the most fantastic sights and adventures in the novel as she flies over Moscow, attends a witches' sabbath, and presides over Satan's ball; just as the Master is named for his work, so she earns the underworld title of Queen. Although her powers derive from Satan, she—like her mentor—intends evil and works good within the inherently immoral system of Stalinism. In effect, Margarita embraces and wields the criminality assigned her and the Master by Stalinist society. Transformed into a fantastic criminal, she finds that she has real power to act—to break with the corrupted world, to wreak vengeance on the literary establishment (she destroys the home of the Master's chief persecutor), and to rescue her beloved and their treasure.

Nevertheless, the impulse of the "blessed wife" lies at the heart of her witchery. Margarita's thrilling metamorphosis does not alter her fundamental concerns with the writer and the text. She does not plead to remain a witch (as does her capricious maid, Natasha). Before, during, and after her bewitchment, Margarita remains uniformly devoted to the Master and, more particularly, to his manuscript. It is Margarita who eagerly reads and rereads the text as it is composed, who rakes out the remains of the burned manuscript with her bare hands, who cherishes and keeps these charred pages as one of her most treasured possessions. (In this story, the blessed wife literally tends the ashes of the destroyed manuscript.) Her avid interest, reverence, and devotion suggest that she perceives the novel as common property, even a collective divination. After all her exertions, it is only fitting that Margarita—the female helpmate elevated to active hero—is iconically portrayed as the one Reader of the text:

> After crying her fill, Margarita picked up the intact manuscript and found the place she had been reading before her meeting with Azazello by the Kremlin wall. Margarita was not sleepy. She stroked the paper lovingly as though it were a favorite cat, and turned it in her hands, examining it from all sides, now looking at the title page, now opening the end. She was suddenly chilled by the thought that all of this was only witchcraft, that in a moment the manuscript would vanish from sight, that she would find herself in her own bedroom, and she would have to go and drown herself when she woke up. But this was the last frightening thought she had—an echo of her past ordeals. Nothing disappeared. The omnipotent Woland [Satan] was indeed omnipotent, and Margarita could go on turning the pages of the manuscript as long as she wished, even till dawn, and look at them, and kiss them, and read and reread the words:
> "The darkness which had come from the Mediterranean shrouded the city hated by the Procurator. . . ." (310–11)

As I have attempted to show, the works of Mandelstam, Pasternak, and Bulgakov all delineate different versions of the same basic scenario: the domestic (and seemingly middle-class) refuge of the artist in a repressive, controlling state; the roles of the Christ-like self-sacrificing creator and his loyal, self-sacrificing female helpmate; the final transcendent promise of the text. In describing this alternative creative process, they fit writer and helpmate with gender constructs that tend to privilege conventional feminine traits: The male artist becomes more domesticated and the feminine qualities of the helpmate are accorded power and value. While not directly referential, these fictional characters and themes explore and embellish on the actual situation of their male creators. In life Mandelstam, Pasternak, and Bulgakov all depended on the ministrations of the women closest to them to produce and maintain their work. The autobiographical texts of real-life "blessed wives" like Nadezhda Mandelstam then tell this story from the other side and with the supposedly greater authenticity and lesser imagination of nonfiction.

In telling their story, however, these "wives" confront a culturally imposed gender gap between preserving and creating; men have already scripted their noble images, acts, thoughts, and speech in the roles of helpmate and reader, not writer. As I will explore on their individual examples, Chukovskaia and Mandelstam came to write out of a complexity of influences and sanctions, but it is important to note here that they were specifically empowered by one unofficial female artist—that is, the poet Anna Akhmatova (1889–1966). Under Stalin, Akhmatova earned a martyrdom similar to that of Mandelstam: Although she did not die in the camps, her third husband and only son were imprisoned, her first husband was executed, and she herself was expelled from the Union of Soviet Writers after World War II. She lived in poverty and fear for most of her life. Yet throughout the Stalinist years she produced unofficial poems that reflected on and generalized from her terrible experience—most often through a female persona. Akhmatova, therefore, demonstrated the possibility of a woman writing about these times from her own perspective.

More specifically, Akhmatova does not rewrite the scenario of the unofficial male creator; rather, she explores the special capacity and experience of those left in charge of the domestic sphere and shows how a woman writer can achieve the status of an unofficial bard, a true heroine of her age. In striking contrast to her male associates, she does not idealize the domestic sphere but uses it as a resonating place of torment—a private space where women agonize over their victimized loved ones and cope with the dual reality of Stalinist life. Akhmatova, unlike Bulgakov and Pasternak, addresses the horrors of Stalinism as they occur. In her famous poetic cycle "Requiem" (written from 1938 to 1940) she chronicles the anguish of a female "I" (what seems to be an autobiographical persona) whose son has been arrested. Alone in her room, the woman endures waves of illness, alienation, guilt, madness, and a longing for death. Her home provides no comfort, only a place for confronting the truth. When the woman receives word of her son's sentence, she registers its impact in chilling domestic terms—in the incongruity of "that bright day and deserted house."

Furthermore, Akhmatova connects this anguished domestic sphere with yet another kind of underworld—the silent and silenced world of prison queues where petitioners wait to receive word about their imprisoned loved ones and to send them packages, letters, and money. Women largely people both of these spheres; the poetic "I" bears witness to the different women who stand there and quotes one beautiful girl who comes to the queue "as if it were home." With its cast of women and alternating settings of prison line and domestic interior, Akhmatova's text suggests that the prison queues comprise an inevitable extension of the domestic sphere. Charged to maintain the home and family, women are compelled there—to the very threshold of the prisons and camps—out of concern for their missing family members and friends. Given the impossibility of a political underground, this threshold world ventures the one collective site where the bereaved and victimized can gather together and observe among themselves "how faces fall apart, / How fear looks out from under the eyelids, / How deep are the hieroglyphics / Cut by suffering on people's cheeks."[78]

Thus, while Mandelstam, Pasternak, and Bulgakov posit an idealized or metaphysical refuge and opposition, Akhmatova chooses to focus on this real space and potential community of women's experience. She even binds her image as artist to the prison queues. In the prose foreword to "Requiem" (quoted at the beginning of this chapter) she consoles a woman with her promise to write this experience; in the "Epilogue" she directs future generations to erect her monument before the prison gates "where I stood for three hundred hours / And where they never, never opened the doors for me." Through the sequence of "Requiem" Akhmatova projects herself undergoing a crucial transformation from the capricious "sylvan-princessly" personae of her early poetry (poetry which marked her as poet "for women") into the impressive monument of a female poet who stands with and mourns for all the tyrant's victims.

In this way, Akhmatova does educe a writing role for the "blessed wife," but this persona is no helpmate to a male creator. In lieu of the Christ-like traits of male artists, she enhances her role through other historical and religious analogies—the Russian boyars' wives lamenting over their slain rebel husbands and, in direct complement to the Christ figure, the mother of Christ suffering unimaginably at her son's crucifixion. According to the scenes of "Requiem," Akhmatova's gender constructs very much echo those of Mandelstam, although they reverse his assignment of speaking roles. In her rendering, men are depicted as the silenced, unseen victims, while the mourning women are empowered to lament and commemorate.

The works of Lidiia Chukovskaia and Nadezhda Mandelstam

For Lidiia Chukovskaia and Nadezhda Mandelstam, Akhmatova therefore functions as an authorizing point of departure—a female creator who reveals the important vantages of women in Stalinist society and creates the speaking persona of the female mourner. Both would adapt this writing role for their own use; both would turn to her as special mentor and catalyst. Yet they dared not appropriate Akhmatova's culturally rooted sense of poetic birthright. Chukovskaia and Mandelstam were educated women and professionally linked with the arts, but they did not establish themselves as writers before the Stalinist period. They willingly served and conceived of themselves as caretakers for repressed artists—Nadezhda Mandelstam for her husband and Chukovskaia most notably for Akhmatova herself. Their most distinctive writing, then, truly seemed to be engendered by their experience and loss under Stalin.

In this sense, their texts resemble a different literary model, one that informed many unofficial memoirs about Stalinist times and especially those written by women. Rather than projecting themselves into the ranks of high culture, Chukovskaia and Mandelstam approached their writing as moral duty, political resistance. They were *acting* to name the silenced and invisible victims; to expose the tortures and hardships papered over by official writing; to effect, through this dispersal of unofficial knowledge, a moral and perhaps political renewal in their society. Heeding this moral imperative, Chukovskaia and Mandelstam availed themselves of the highly productive Russian tradition of memoirs by political activists and martyrs. Like the enterprise of Russian fiction, the writing of Russian autobiography has often served as a more or less covert platform for different philosophical, political, and social agendas. In the case of known political activists, these agendas clearly fuelled the writing impulse and often displaced or reshaped any writerly designs; their memoirs were produced to inform and enlighten, not to prove their credentials as writers. This model afforded a special advantage for women in the opposition: Because the state construed and punished their personal experience as political, their lives, otherwise deemed secondary, provided valuable and necessary documentation of "greater" political campaigns and injustices. In consequence, this model encouraged a phenomenal number of texts written by women—not only the memoirs of important "widows" (women close to repressed literary and political figures), but the prison and labor camp writings of women like Evgeniia Ginzburg and Mariia Ioffe.[79] As we shall see, both Chukovskaia and Mandelstam respond to this imperative and benefit from this sanction and then articulate quite different interpretations of their writing "duties."

Thus, along several different lines, the works of Lidiia Chukovskaia and Nadezhda Mandelstam emerged from the dangerous, potent overlapping of unofficial "criminal" culture and the situation of women under Stalin. Through various traditional and familial mediations, the two women inscribed their own positions of writing privilege wherein the domestic sphere is recognized, utilized, and valued as a locus for the unofficial, alternative, and even oppositional; and the "feminine" virtues of its caretakers are deemed heroic and at times normative. By recording their experiences and actions in life practice, Chukovskaia and Mandelstam produced a vital extension of the unofficial scripts written *for* female caretakers. Their enactment is important in and of itself; exploiting the presumed authenticity of nonfiction, they volunteered more extensive proof of a lost culture's existence. But I am particularly intrigued by the ways Chukovskaia and Mandelstam reclaimed and revised and, especially in Mandelstam's case, overwhelmed these scripts. I selected their texts out of a pool of works by female caretakers—including the diary of Bulgakov's wife, Elena Sergeevna, and the memoir of Pasternak's mistress, Olga Ivinskaia—because Chukovskaia and Mandelstam, more distinctly than the others, undertook their task with a deep awareness of its historical, moral, and literary significance and, in the process of fulfilling it, realized their own specific power and authority as writers and activists.[80] In short, they moved from the position of self-declared caretakers to (undeclared) creators of influential cultural/political texts *and* a new kind of dissident community. For through the texts and acts of their works, Chukovskaia and Mandelstam reflected and facilitated the prominent roles women and the domestic domain came to play in unofficial post-Stalin society.

In the following two sections, devoted respectively to Lidiia Chukovskaia and Nadezhda Mandelstam, I analyze in greater detail their creative development and richly influential works. The first chapters of each section focus on how these two women depict their path to writing through childhood experience and family life, and especially through their relationship with powerful male mentors—in Chukovskaia's case, her famous father, and in Mandelstam's, her father and her husband. The ensuing chapters then offer close readings of their texts, with particular attention to their evolution as writers as well as to their scripts of the unofficial literary process and the roles and capacities of women in Stalinist times. In conclusion, I consider their works in a broader sense of influence, assessing their legacy within the multiple frames of Russian literature, Soviet politics, and women's history.

Lidiia Chukovskaia

Lidiia Chukovskaia

2.
FATHER AND DAUGHTER

By the time Lidiia Chukovskaia began keeping *Notes on Anna Akhmatova* in 1938, she had happily embraced the *maintenance* of literature as her vocation. She felt inspired and fulfilled by her first job as apprentice editor in the children's literature section of the Leningrad State Publishing House.¹ It is characteristic that she was driven from this post by outside persecution, not by any urge to abandon editing for more explicitly creative endeavors. Throughout most of her life, in fact, Chukovskaia overtly pursued a career of enthusiastic deference to others, discovering and celebrating their superior talents and good works.² She makes this pattern of service, self-effacement, and hero worship autobiographically definitive in *Pamiati detstva* (*To the Memory of Childhood*) (1970–83). Here Chukovskaia outlines the core truths of her personal and professional self-perception through a portrait of her father, the famous literary critic and children's writer, Kornei Ivanovich Chukovskii.* Begun as an extended eulogy to her parent, *To the Memory of Childhood* nonetheless offers her closest approximation of a childhood memoir, a curiously other-directed narrative of her own formation.³ If we are to understand Chukovskaia's genesis as a writer and an artist, therefore, we must first read the daughter as she chooses to write her early self—in absolute, enabling connection with her father.

Magnifying and exploring this connection in *To the Memory of Childhood*, Chukovskaia expresses what some critics identify as a characteristic of women's autobiography in Western European traditions: She attempts self-definition through important relationships rather than progressive separations and, specifically, through her bond with an empowering, endorsing male figure.⁴ In Chukovskaia's case, self-definition may even be beside the point, for she never

---

* Kornei Ivanovich Chukovskii, pseudonym for Nikolai Vasil'evich Korneichukov (1882–1969), was an enormously versatile artist—poet, critic, literary historian, editor, and translator. He first established himself as a literary critic and publicist in the prerevolutionary period, when he began composing the keen analyses of contemporary literature and portraits of contemporary writers that became his trademark. Yet he is most renowned as a writer of works for and about children; these include famous verse tales like "The Crocodile" (1917) and "The Telephone" (1926) as well as a seminal study of children's linguistic and literary development *From Two to Five* (1928). On the basis of his writings and active work among children, Chukovskii has long been heeded as an authority in children's literature and even a kind of cultural parent for generations of Soviet boys and girls. For a fine account of Chukovskii's contribution to children's literature, see Elena Sokol's *Russian Poetry for Children* (Knoxville: University of Tennessee Press, 1984).

highlights the importance of her own development. With her unwavering focus on Kornei Ivanovich and her careful reference to his writings, Chukovskaia would seem to be substituting biography for autobiography. She reviews her memories to enforce his impact; she pledges her life story as a confirmation of her father's legend, as a daughter's irrefutable proof of her father's ability to play cultural parent for all Russian children.

Writing to serve and connect, eschewing self-reflection for deferential tribute, Chukovskaia echoes a common orientation and practice of other women authors. Yet within the closer context of Russian women's autobiographies (particularly of the nineteenth and early twentieth centuries) her text is quite distinctive—both in its oblique focus on the author's self and its representation of the father. For the most part these autobiographers—educated women of the aristocracy and the intelligentsia—convey their childhood as a lonely, disorienting period, a painful catalyst to self-awareness. Often deprived of a close bond with either parent, raised by servants, discouraged by their limited prospects as women, these writers claim an acute self-consciousness from an early age and express a great longing for close relationships and positive role models. Of all the members of their distanced families, their fathers are frequently portrayed as the most remote—ranging in type from inaccessible tyrant to a kind of benign cipher. The famous mathematician Sofia Kovalevskaia (1850–1890), characterizing her childhood on a provincial estate, remembered her father as a disgruntled, bewildered patriarch. The great modernist poet Marina Tsvetaeva (1892–1941), overwhelmed by her musical mother, mentioned her father as an incidental, unconnected, and unhearing figure. Even Nadezhda Durova (1783–1866), who emulated her beloved father when she ran off to join the tsarist cavalry, admitted that she was raised by a military adjutant; her closest childhood companion was her horse.[5]

In apparently positive contrast, Chukovskaia's life story takes shape from very different familial, psychological, and social conditions. She spent her formative years in a close family circle, in the cloistered environment of Kuokkala, a Finnish community where Russians built their summer homes and her father chose to live and work year-round. Parents, children (Lidiia and her two brothers),[6] and servants formed a harmonious, self-reliant household. Their happy home, in turn, served as a center for visiting artists and friends, a modest domestic retreat from the nearby cultural capital of Saint Petersburg. In Lidiia's memory, Kuokkala functions as a sort of arcadia, a first blessed place of family happiness and natural beauty. At its center she locates her father; he was its founder and general master of ceremonies, a man who discovered "his spiritual homeland" in Kuokkala and came to energize and direct its social life.[7] Within his own household he emerged as an engaging, active, creative, primary parent. Working mainly at home, Chukovskii truly presided over his children's lives, supervising and supplementing their education, training them to help him in household tasks, and devising regular family outings. He even contrived a professional bond with his children: Lidiia and her brothers became firsthand sources for his writing about children, the first "readers" of his writing for them.[8]

Father and Daughter 31

If we accept her testimony, it is understandable, perhaps, that Chukovskaia would renounce self-analysis for a loving evocation of this wonderful (and forever lost) childhood world.[9] As she explains it, even her focus on Chukovskii depends on the touchstone of her Kuokkala childhood: "I am not writing Kornei Ivanovich's biography. I am writing about my childhood, and he was its creator. He and my childhood—no matter how old he was or I was—were inseparable" (121). Nevertheless, it is the portrait of the involved creator that overwhelms her narrative; her father looms large as the first, most important, most powerful artist of her life, the Prospero of her childhood paradise. As she depicts her formative years, Chukovskaia does not create herself, but inherits herself as her father's creation. *To the Memory of Childhood* thus aims to reveal and analyze the author of her text, to write autobiography as a kind of critical study of her creator-parent.

Yet in naming her father sole "creator," Chukovskaia implies some alarming limitations. Can a father "create" a daughter's childhood without restricting or distorting her—even in the harmonious environment of Kuokkala? How can a daughter benefit from a paternal role model which, inadvertently or otherwise, might echo larger social prejudices and relegate women to a secondary status, to a belittled or silenced difference? And what does this "creation" imply about the bonds between mother and daughter? In the case of this father-daughter relationship, such questions elicit a particularly complex accounting of restrictions and benefits. Given the focus of her text, the restrictions appear to be categorical: Chukovskaia effaces any identification with her mother. In his daughter's view, Chukovskii simply eclipses his wife, assuming what would traditionally be the maternal duties of cultural and spiritual instruction in the home.[10] From the opening pages of the text, Lidiia emphasizes her father's figurative and literal prominence: She names him as the very measure of the natural world, judging the ocean to be twelve "papas" deep, a tall pine tree to be ten "papas" high (1). Her mother Mariia Borisovna, on the other hand, hovers in the unlit background, intimated by all the domestic chores her husband "cannot" perform, unobtrusively maintaining the comforts of home (along with a female servant, Nanny Tonia), endeavoring—in her rare speaking appearances—to facilitate her husband's work or rest. It is only when her husband acts most irresponsibly and "childishly" that she merits a distinct maternal presence in the text. Chukovskii takes his own and other neighborhood children out boating in bad weather, and after a near disaster, they return to find the anxious mothers "clinging together on the beach and weeping in the darkness" (44). Even here Mariia Borisovna appears in a symbolic configuration of unspeaking, passively suffering women.[11]

Whatever the reasons for this focus (and Chukovskaia volunteers none), the mother's absence tends to enhance and intensify the father-daughter bond in the text and suggests a dangerous conformity in the daughter's development. Chukovskaia's few specific reflections on being a girl intimate that this indeed may be the case. As she recalls parenthetically:

(Before our move to Petrograd I didn't have a single girl friend. Kornei Ivanovich told me that until I was three I talked about myself like Kolya, in the masculine:

himself, he ate. With my dolls, I'd usually conscientiously sit them up in the morning in chairs, telling them that, "Mama was going to the city on business," and then not touch them again for the rest of the day. . . .) (125)

In both role-playing and language, the young Lidiia casts herself as male, unconsciously renouncing the social signs of her sex for what she perceives as the masculine norm.[12] Offered dolls (which, she notes, were not family gifts, but presents from unknowing acquaintances), she substitutes absence for the playing out of any sort of maternal role. In much the same way, Lidiia senses no support for her occasionally "girlish" preferences in reading. She remarks that her father tolerates, but does not really approve of her penchant for books like *The Little Princess* and *Little Women* (96–97). As reflected in his daughter's testimony, Chukovskii's presumably "objective" model of childrearing may in fact be too unconsciously male-centered to encourage a daughter's different tastes. Perhaps in consequence, Chukovskaia reports that she longed to be an accepted, undifferentiated member of her father's exclusive group—to be one of those lucky enough to be "invited along" with him (10). She seems to accept and approve his generic devotion to all children, explaining that Kornei Ivanovich—unlike most "mamas, papas, and uncles"—never expressed his love through ostentatious caresses, indulgent gifts, or favoritism (even for his own offspring) (127–28).

These restrictions are significant ones; they indicate how Chukovskaia absorbed a worldview that privileges father over mother and explicitly dismisses notions of valued female difference.[13] Yet the specific contents of her paternal inheritance also afford her some surprising accommodations—especially in the context of her times. First of all, the very conformity that Chukovskii instilled constituted a progressive upbringing in fin-de-siècle Russian society. In the early 1900s educated young men and women still tended to espouse the goals the nihilists proclaimed in the 1860s: an absolute and undifferentiated social, political, and economic equality, regardless of women's particular needs. Chukovskii, in fact, proved to be more discerning than many of his contemporaries when he focused on the specific interests of children. With his efforts to compile or create quality reading for children, his instructions for their literary development, and his common treatment of boys and girls, Chukovskii was aiming to realize a most advanced ideal—an excellent, standardized "poetic education" for all young people, whatever their sex or class.

In her own mind and according to the standards of her Russian contemporaries, therefore, Chukovskaia received a most equitable education. Secondly, our full assessment of her "creation," like her account of her childhood, necessarily hinges on the remarkable person of her "creator." Although Chukovskaia establishes her father as the dominant authority in her world, she does not portray him as a conventional patriarch. Under his influence, her upbringing was intensely emotional, physical, familial—an unmediated interaction with her father as both subject and object.[14] Indeed, her portrait reveals some surprising advantages; in effect, she reads in Kornei Ivanovich an unusual synthesis of traditional gender roles and qualities—a synthesis that in certain ways validates her as a well-rounded, creative child and a female literary professional.

What emerges first in Chukovskaia's text is her awed *physical* depiction of her father—his great height, huge feet, and outsize actions. Evoked from a child's perspective, Chukovskii strides into the text like a benevolent fairy-tale giant "expressly designed 'for younger children' and produced in a special one-of-a-kind edition" (2). Kornei Ivanovich allowed children to use him as a marvelous "toy"; they could walk under him, climb up him, jump from him, ride on his shoulders. He would sit for hours in his study, immersed in his writing, but he spent his free time actively, physically, in projects that did not distinguish work from play and invariably enlisted his eager children. In the process Chukovskii taught them how to use their bodies (specifically for "rough, manual labor" [5]) and initiated them into the natural world. His daughter portrays him as a Russian version of a Renaissance man—as intellectual and outdoorsman, accomplished writer and skilled laborer, bibliophile and nature lover. Her portrait of her father thus resists the traditional problematic split between spirit and flesh; in the absence of a close mother-daughter relationship, he performed the important service of approving and encouraging his daughter's physical nature—at least as a sexually immature child. He also trained her to find emotional comfort and renewal in the physical world, to indulge in nature as a healthy, ever-available therapy. It is significant that Chukovskaia very often renders her father's complex influence as a physical effect, a sensory impression of his power and goodness. Perhaps most of all, she locates his multiple powers in the synecdoche of his beautiful hands—the hands of a laborer, writer, and father:

> You can trust his hands completely. They always catch you in time, never drop you or hurt you. . . . Flying or falling, don't be afraid; they will always catch you and hold you. . . . Those big, reliable hands, full of fun, with their round, shining clean nails. And even in the coldest weather, hot as can be. (4)

Just as her father's model enabled Chukovskaia a positive connection with the physical world, so his behavior encouraged her, in an unprecedented way, to value her childish experience and, consequently, her "fundamental" creative ability. Kornei Ivanovich did play the role of exacting parent, setting standards and enforcing rules, but his daughter generally depicts him in a less formidable (and more childish) guise—as "our leader, the commander of our games, our studies, our work, our captain of seagoing excursions" (2).[15] Kornei Ivanovich, she notes, was temperamentally closest to children; she cites his diary to prove that he felt most natural, renewed, and "in love" when he was playing with them (129). Among children Chukovskii conducted his greatest scholarly and artistic experiment, analyzing them and creating from them. As a child, therefore, his daughter enjoyed a most privileged status—as her father's kindred spirit, preferred companion, and the source of his artistic and intellectual inspiration. Applying his own conclusions, she could value herself as a member of an innately creative, artistically sensitive group. And this conception of herself as typically gifted, a sample product of her father's farsighted experiment, came to fuel all of her writing endeavors.[16]

As a professional woman, however, Chukovskaia probably benefitted most directly from her father's painful sense of his own difference. It seems that although Lidiia instinctively played boy to be admitted to his children's games, she did not need to play man (at least overtly) to follow in his adult footsteps. As she gradually discloses, her father's professional and familial roles evolved, on the one hand, from what he perceived as his marginal status and class inferiority and, on the other, from the most positive figure in *his* childhood—his mother. In fact, his peculiar development partly reenacted the dilemma and adaptive strategies of growing up female in tsarist patriarchal society and, as such, outfitted his daughter with a surprisingly usable sense of self-esteem and vocation.

Chukovskaia underscores her father's difference early in the text. In terms of class and family, he was doubly outcast: He and his younger sister were the illegitimate children of a student (presumably from the gentry) and a peasant woman. Chukovskii literally had to work his way from the ranks of the lower middle class into the intelligentsia, training himself by reading and supporting himself by writing:

> He saw the people who despised his mother, his sister and himself; the world which took pleasure in excluding "cook's children" from gymnasium education, the world which he (its *antipath* as one young Odessa Miss called him), a stoop-shouldered, clumsy, unfortunate, fatherless boy in worn boots and tattered student cap with its insignia torn off, had left forever for a life of work, literature, and poetry, for Tyutchev and Walt Whitman. (22)

Chukovskii's self-education (and the individuals who helped him learn) necessarily replaced the institutions that refused to accept and qualify him. His literary aspirations saved him from being absorbed into the petty bourgeoisie of his native Odessa—what he deplored as "the philistine factory." By dint of personal effort, Chukovskii eventually secured the position of *literator* (a man of letters) but was forever scarred and driven by a sense of his own unworthy status as a self-made intellectual. Even while consorting with great artists, he consistently denied his talent and pledged his writing as mere service (58). In his initial confinement and extreme dedication, then, Chukovskii presents an intriguing parallel to the many Russian women who left home in the latter half of the nineteenth century to pursue otherwise forbidden educational opportunities or to join the political underground. Like these women, he was deemed undeserving of educational and professional training. Like these women, he overcame conservative family and social restrictions, found acceptance in oppositional circles (in his case, among artistic rather than political groups), and devoted himself utterly to the cause.[17] Yet, in contrast, Chukovskii's revolt eventually could conclude in a return to the family where he, as a man, could assume uncontested authority. It was the family—not the political cell or the literary salon—that provided the base for his unorthodox operations.

Returning to her father's difference in a later chapter, Chukovskaia posits its formative influence on his writing and parenting:

> And he, the sort of person he was and the kind of childhood he created for us, was created by his own abandonment. . . . It was a fundamental aspect of the way he related to children, his own and others', the source of his insatiable desire to enrich children, to endow them so that they would never, under any circumstances, become "poor, poor." . . . It inspired his constant efforts to insure that we grew up surrounded by culture, not cut off from it. English, poetry, skiing, books.
>
> Everything he had been deprived of as a child, he bestowed upon his children when he became a father. (121–22)

According to his daughter's analysis of his life and work, Chukovskii was motivated by the "insatiable" need for emotional compensation and reparation. He set himself the recuperative goal of correcting his father's negative example, molding himself as a parent who is present and involved.[18] Yet Chukovskii's notion of fathering was not strictly his own invention. His one positive family role model (and the only female figure highlighted in Chukovskaia's text) was his handsome, vigorous, and likewise deprived mother.[19] Ostracized by a patriarchal society, "robbed" and "spat upon," he repelled his father "as an enemy" and felt the greatest tenderness for his mother—a wronged peasant woman, the ultimate victim in tsarist Russia.[20] Chukovskii, therefore, manifested a maternal attachment that his daughter does not see or inscribe in her own case: He endorsed his mother's particular virtues and reembodied them as both father and writer. Chukovskaia confirms the legacy of industriousness, energy, solicitude, and adoring love that passed from mother to son (123–24). Next in succession, the daughter thus inherits from her father a rather encouraging model—that of a man who, although degraded and nearly silenced by his marginal status, managed to achieve legitimacy in a less conventional world and continued to cherish and apply the skills and values he received from his mother.[21]

Perhaps most notably, his mother's orthodox piety (respected but not practiced in his home) was reincarnated in Chukovskii's fervent devotion to culture. In *To the Memory of Childhood*, Chukovskaia identifies and elaborates her father's "religion":

> He believed that art could not only forge a new soul, not only endow a person with happiness, it could also renew the physical self. . . . He believed that the happiness bestowed by art was contagious, that this happiness could and should be shared with other people, that it could make the lame to walk, and the blind to see. . . . He believed in the omnipotence of literature as others believe in the omnipotence of religion. (81)

Chukovskii's articles of faith, recapitulated by his daughter, echoed general Christian concepts—the notion of the soul, a belief that faith can renew the spirit and actually heal the body. His religion, too, depended on the power of sacred texts, although his scriptures were authored by any person with the "halo" of talent and could dispense an unspecific, nonprescriptive godliness. Yet however diffuse the content of his revered art, Chukovskii proved most strict in his religious observance. His daughter notes his high standards for reading, studying, and writing about art and his related criteria for salvation (aesthetic sensitivity) and damnation (obtuseness, tastelessness) (91). At rare moments, he even punished those who showed insufficient respect—by interrupting a poetry recitation or breaking the silence crucial for his own meditations on art.[22] Above all, Chukovskii enforced the worship of art (mainly through reading and recitation) as daily practice, a ritual to be observed by his entire household.

Chukovskaia also provides examples of his "religious instruction"—most particularly, their "game of games" when Kornei Ivanovich took the children out rowing on the Gulf of Finland. Cast off from shore, they eagerly waited for their father to begin reciting:

> At sea, he allowed himself free rein. The rhythm of the waves and of the rowing naturally called forth a rhythmic response.
>
> I have never heard poetry recited more beguilingly. It was as if, at these moments, every aspect of his being was concentrated in voice, inflection, lips, and sounds, sounds seeming to cling to lips, and lips to sounds. As a little girl, I first noticed how beautiful his hands were one day when I was listening to him recite poetry at sea. . . .
>
> There was a kind of sorcery in his voice when he read great poetry which bewitched both him and us. He often wrote that from childhood on he was accustomed to "get drunk" on poetry. Ecstasy was contagious. We undoubtedly grew drunk listening to him grow drunk on what he was reciting. And all the poetry I ever learned later, on my own, without him, the sound of any sort of poetic line, no matter who recited it, was always connected in my mind to my childhood and his voice. (29)

The scene is paradigmatic: In the enraptured perception of his daughter, Chukovskii permanently binds together an inspiring nature, the happy community of Chukovskaia's childhood, the "intoxication" of poetry, and his own beloved person. Chukovskaia credits her father with devising a "poetic education" that makes poetry a means of connecting with the physical world, a sensible delight rather than an academic subject. She reports little or no alienation from the symbolic order of the text which, according to some psychoanalytic theories, proves to be an obstacle in girls' development.[23] In fact, associating poetry at an early age with her father's presence and recitation, Chukovskaia initially presumed its existence as a natural phenomenon. She highlights yet another important revelation when her father shows her an original manuscript. He stages a reverent approach—leading her "the way one would lead a small child to a lighted Christmas tree" to a desk which is "more a pulpit or a shrine" (73). There she is allowed to see a yellowed manuscript of Nekrasov's poetry and she vividly remembers the shock of recognition:

> But strangest of all was the discovery that verses I'd heard recited and read in

> books had actually been composed and written down first! A discovery? Of course I didn't really understand it until that moment. Kornei Ivanovich named some year—some mythically long ago time, which I instantly forgot; the date was crowded out by the thought that, necessarily, *before* that date, the poem did not exist, had simply never existed, in the same way that Boba, say, had not existed before June 1910. Unlike the sea, the sand and the stars, these verses hadn't always been on earth; a human being, Nikolai Alekseevich Nekrasov, had written them. (73–74)

For the first time, Chukovskaia learns to distinguish literature from nature, to analyze what her father had fused into a single experience. Yet her memories surrounding this first sacred text still resist disembodiment; they emphasize, instead, the human touch. She describes her father's "long, suntanned fingers" on the yellow pages and recalls his explanation that a blank manuscript sheet could not be thrown away because Nekrasov "touched it, looked at it" (74). Even after her "fall" into knowledge, her notions of the text seem firmly bound to its human making and use—its feel, sight, sound, and emotional impact. Just as important—her admission into a world of made texts and read poetry seems neither to strain her enjoyment nor diminish her ability, systematically exercised by her father, to use poetry as an oral art form.[24]

Her father's example conditions her further initiation into this literary world. In a fascinating sequence, she depicts herself acquiring a sudden emotional maturity and conditional power when she learns to read. The opening sentences in chapter 12 herald this development: "I learned to read uncommonly early. This chance circumstance played a large role in my life and a not unimportant role in the Kuokkala part of my father's life" (85). Chukovskaia recalls that she taught herself to read at the age of four, during a period when she was ill and her father was away on a brief lecture tour. Her accomplishment is potentially rich in significance: She competes successfully with her older brother; she first asserts her autonomy; she gains access to the most precious possession in their household. But she mainly values her achievement because of the *service* she could now provide her father. Chukovskaia devotes two chapters of her memoir to the treatment of her father's insomnia by reading aloud—a task that she mainly performed in Kuokkala between the ages of six and ten. Although many others assumed this responsibility in Chukovskii's lifetime, Lidiia, because of her age and position, was perhaps most cognizant of and affected by her role.

In chapter 13, she reenacts a typical session of what she dubs her "favorite game." As with all the activities orchestrated by and around Chukovskii (and remembered from a child's viewpoint), this game observes a prescribed, ritualized pattern. Lidiia ascends the stairs, waits for her father's summons, and marks its beginning with a rhyme recited to the household. Yet once admitted to his study and faced with the critical task of ensuring her father his rest, Lidiia must play the game in earnest. The usual relationship between father and daughter is upset, recast. Although Chukovskii still attempts to impose himself as teacher, correcting Lidiia's mispronounced words, restoring the rhythm sacrificed by her hurried reading, he depends terribly on her help and submits, under a playful guise, to her authority. For a brief time, Lidiia becomes the most important, most powerful member of her family:

> Our mama, Maria Borisovna, was too nervous a woman to calm his agitation. Kolya could not hide his yawns, and Kornei Ivanovich would soon send him off to bed. I not only loved reading out loud, but was ready to appear wide awake the whole night through if it would let him sleep. This also was a game, and what a game: first, it was just between him and me, no one else; secondly, it wasn't really a game, but the most important of all jobs—I was putting Papa to sleep!; and thirdly, I was his commander, not he mine. I was putting my own father to bed, the way other little girls put their dolls to bed. I played "doll-mother" with him, and not only that, he listened when I gave him orders. That was very flattering. (89–90)

Through the act of reading for her father, Chukovskaia develops, in an unusually intense way, a maternal role she has dismissed elsewhere. Her father, the primary parent, not only legitimizes certain maternal functions and responses in his own behavior, but enables and authorizes her own attempt at mothering—as long as this involves specifically literary service. In her attempts to nurse her insomniac father with books, Lidiia performs most admirably, even teaching herself to read (or improvise reading) in the dark (104). And it is significant that when she chooses a happy ending for her reenactment, Chukovskaia cites this exchange with her mother:

> The lamp which hangs over the dining room table shines brightly. Boba and Kolya have long ago gone to bed.
> "He's asleep!" I say in answer to Mama's questioning look. (105)

Lidiia reports in response to her still silent mother that she has successfully replaced her in this duty, that she can do what her mother wants to but cannot. She has absorbed a potent lesson: She first positively distinguishes herself as female in her role as literary mother, a girl who earns a kind of caretaking power through her service to her "mock-son" father and her facility with literary texts. In this case, her father does not directly train her for her future role but elicits her own more deferential version of his cultural parenting.

Through her father's example and influence, Chukovskaia was thus raised to perceive and engage with the literary text as religious practice, family devotion, and a way to complex emotional fulfillment. Conditioned by her father's judgments on the talented and the obtuse, a devotee of his cult of the great artist, a witness of his practice, Chukovskaia also learns to equate talent with virtue and believes that each text manifests its author's spiritual and ethical nature.[25] Her interpretation of great literature, in consequence, unfolds as a procession of (largely) great men, with her father leading the way. In *To the Memory of Childhood* she narrates his life and works as a seamless whole: His literature for children reflected his unabating love for them; the good cheer and kindness of his work expressed his basic character; the vast scope of his writings demonstrated his enormous appetite for the new, the "diversity of [his] interests and attachments." She matches praise for his literary service with proof of his good deeds. She depicts him as eager intercessor on behalf of family, friends, and even mere acquaintances—a man who exploited his hard-won celebrity for the benefit it could bring to others.

Chukovskaia also finds in her father a model for professing this worship of great men:

> He thought of himself as a natural-born critic, an instrument created to respond to art, and in fact he was such an instrument, responding as it were to poetry and prose, both classical and modern, not only with eye and ear, but with the tips of his fingers and every inch of his skin. He was a fanatic about literary work. He was obsessed by art. (132)

Once again, Chukovskaia depicts her father's involvement as physical, even sensuous, implying an absolute link between profession and person. As reconstructed by his daughter, Chukovskii naturally possessed the responsive, facilitating traits most often presumed and cultivated to exist in women. Although he took for granted the primary importance of his work at home and easily assumed the function of writer (Lidiia remembers the times when "papa was not to be disturbed in his study"), he conceived of his professional status as secondary. Departing from the traditional assignations of male creative genius and female helpmate, Chukovskii perceived and represented himself as the willing assistant of great artists—as their admirer, interpreter, and conservator. He not only threw himself into the supporting roles of critic, translator, editor, literary historian, textologist, and portraitist, but systematically promoted this service with semi-scholarly monographs—works on the principles of translation (*The Art of Translation* and *The Lofty Art*) and children's acquisition of language and literature (*From Two to Five*). Chukovskii pursued the caretaking and sharing of literature as a respectable, essential profession.

Perhaps even more important, the daughter infers creative value in this service, declaring her father to be "an artist." In the last chapters of her memoir, she defines the interactive character of his art, asserting that his critical articles were composed like "poetry" and "were intended to be read in a strong voice in an auditorium full of people who, hearing them, were not for one minute to grow bored, yawn, or whisper to their neighbor" (133). She interprets his critical function as fundamentally re-creative of the life that makes the text and quotes his letters in support: "I understood (maybe too late) that the foundation of my calling is description, literary portraits, and I was happy working on them." For father (and consequently for daughter), critical analysis necessarily involves biography and both are enhanced by art in an attempt to recover the true image of the artist. Biographical sketches, contemporary portraits—these were the forms Chukovskii wrote to convey his devotion most powerfully and "infectiously."[26]

Despite the professional opportunities Chukovskii approved for himself and his children, it is important to remember that he was able to excel in his supporting roles by relying on the unnamed support of others—mainly, during the Kuokkala period, his wife and domestic help. (In later years, Chukovskaia herself figured as one of his female caretakers.[27]) The women of his wife's generation were only beginning to enjoy the fruits of their mothers' labors—the acceptance of women's equality among most members of the intelligentsia, reforms of women's education, limited admission of women into various professions—but it was his daughter's generation that moved, on a massive scale, out of the home into the workplace.[28] As never before in Russian history, a daughter was more or less free to pursue her father's career.

As a work of biographical criticism, *To the Memory of Childhood* clearly realizes this father-daughter legacy, but it offers very little information about Chukovskaia's professional life. The daughter's adult career must be traced elsewhere—in a composite of her other works of tribute, service, and oblique self-reference. After formal studies in literature at the Institute for the History of the Arts, she took her first job in the Children's Section of the Leningrad State Publishing House in 1927 and apprenticed, under the caring tutelage of Samuil Marshak, to be an editor of children's books. To a striking degree, Marshak—a poet, editor, occasional writer for children and friend of her father—reinforced Chukovskii's poetic education in the professional sphere. Marshak functioned as paternal mentor to his staff, seeking to infect others with his love for the classics of Russian literature and cultivating in them his sensitivity and industry. Ever the dutiful daughter, Chukovskaia repays him with a written testimonial—chapters in her own book of training essays *V laboratorii redaktora* (In the editor's workshop) (1960). Summing up his work, she implies the same fusion of domestic, professional, and spiritual practice that enriched her childhood:

> According to Marshak, the publishing house was to become a home where there took place—again and again—the fruitful meeting of new material and tradition. . . .
> And in [our] daily work together he instilled in his assistants these views and taste and sensitivity; with time his assistants developed into fellow believers (*edinomyshlenniki*) and the master, the editor-in-chief, could entrust only them—not cultural co-workers, but fellow believers and comrades-in-arms—with the study and selection of submitted manuscripts. (224, 226)

The purges of the 1930s literally destroyed Chukovskaia's professional and private homes. Her section was shut down and most of her co-workers arrested; her second husband, Matvei Petrovich Bronshtein, an astrophysicist and author of science books for children, was arrested in August 1937 and summarily executed in February 1938 (although Chukovskaia was not officially informed of his fate until 1957).[29] She herself managed to escape arrest twice—in 1938 when she was to be implicated in her husband's "case" and in 1941 when the secret police had learned of her "criminal" writing. Along with her daughter Elena (1932–) and her daughter's nanny, Chukovskaia more or less maintained a household in Leningrad until the World War II blockade forced their evacuation to Central Asia. Yet the combined horrors of war and political terror did not dispossess her of her inheritance. From the 1930s until the early 1970s she continued to devote much of her critical and editorial expertise to the cause of children's literature, carrying on her father's campaign to provide children with an appropriate, enduring "poetic education." In the name of children, she fought for standards then denied all official Soviet literature—intellectual rigor, a natural language, a respect for the truth. This specialization, moreover, sanctioned her own first efforts at biography; she was unveiling wholesome models for children to admire. During Stalin's lifetime, she tended toward subjects safely ensconced in the nineteenth century and representative of many of the values her father upheld: creative ability, a great intellectual curiosity, an extraordinary work ethic, an abiding commitment to freedom and justice, a life that reflected a consonance of belief and action. In particular, she located in the exiled Decembrists—the Borisov brothers and Nikolai Bestuzhev—both appropriate models and an encouraging paradigm for the intelligentsia under Stalinist siege. Persecuted by the tsar-tyrant Nicholas I (who "was distinguished by an innate, crude, narrow-minded [*skalozubovskii*] disrespect for talent"),[30] these aristocrats ("the intellectual flower of the nation" [7]) devoted their lives in Siberian exile to scientific research, creative work, and the instruction of indigenous peoples. In her sketches of the Decembrists, Chukovskaia seemed to be claiming her ideal forefathers:

> However, the exiles—even when they were separated from each other and cast to remote corners of Siberia or fettered by constant police surveillance—proved stronger than the authorities. In both penal servitude and exile, they did not cease their educational and pedagogical activity for a single day.[31]

A bibliography of Chukovskaia's other official writing lists a series of similar instructive tributes: critical introductions to *The Collected Works of Taras Shevchenko* (1946) and the diaries of the nineteenth-century Russian explorer Nikolai Miklukho-Maklai (1947); "critical-biographical sketches" of children's writers Susanna Georgievskaia and Boris Zhitkov (a persecuted friend of her father). Her consideration of Aleksandr Herzen's memoir *My Past and Thoughts* (1966) represents perhaps her best and most elaborate critical effort in the series. Here, in great measure, she follows her father's guidelines, divining the particular art of an essayist like Herzen, analyzing his text, and amplifying its meaning through individual and cultural biography. Reflecting on the genre of Herzen's voluminous memoir, she eventually conflates author and work, reasserting what her father had shown time and again:

> Very likely *My Past and Thoughts* is no less a self-portrait than an autobiography. Here is the complete Herzen—revolutionary, thinker, man. Here is the whole man—full of love, indignation, and oppressive thoughts; mocking, sorrowful, and angry; shown with his own voice, laugh, and walk. This work not only describes

his spiritual personality as a fighter and thinker but presents him in the flesh, with all the power of his charm.[32]

Even after her expulsion from the Union of Soviet Writers in 1974 (the culminating "punishment" for her writings and actions in defense of dissidents like Joseph Brodskii, Andrei Sakharov, and Aleksandr Solzhenitsyn), Chukovskaia continued in the role of morally enlightening literary critic and caretaker, a champion of the great good men (and sometimes women) she had read or met.[33] That is, throughout her writing life, Chukovskaia adhered to the self-perception, core values, and professional practice that she delineates in her father's example in *To the Memory of Childhood*. Both memoir and self-conception thus developed through her subtly nuanced re-creation of her father's presumed "creation." Narrating a portrait of "her" artist from his years as a young father up until his death, Chukovskaia reinscribes Kornei Chukovskii as a model rooted in important connections—of the physical and the intellectual, the child and the adult, the realm of literature and the natural world, the making of an artistic text and the spiritual conduct of a life, even (to a more limited extent) paternal and maternal lines of inheritance. She lays out the tenets and practices of his own acquired faith in art and artist—a faith in which he raises his children. Beyond the creation of her childhood, she implies his role in facilitating her professional development and thereby smoothing her particular passage from childhood to adulthood. Socially restricted as a poor "cook's child," Chukovskii fulfilled a quest for emotional compensation, social legitimacy, and professional standing through a career of diligent literary service. If she kept to the path her father had blazed for his children, Chukovskaia could become a *literator* while remaining a good and dutiful daughter.[34]

According to his daughter's testimony, Chukovskii exerted a remarkably constructive influence on her development. As a self-made intellectual—a member of a cultural intelligentsia that rebelled against the political repression and social conventions of the tsarist state—he outfitted her with a fundamentally positive socio-political and psychological orientation, a strategy for resisting injustice and maintaining a basic (if sexually undifferentiated) sense of self-worth. This father-daughter connection, more or less effective in opposing one tyrannical patriarchy, proved most durable against the ravages of Stalinism. Her childhood remained for her that unassailable "spiritual homeland," a domestic paradise that provided her with a first sanctuary and a lifelong spiritual resource. Formed in this context, Chukovskaia learned to define her worldview in terms of an extended family structure and to heed a benevolent "unofficial" paternal authority over all. In comparison with the many other Russian writers who sought spiritual sustenance in their art, Chukovskaia derived perhaps surer support from the well-developed "religion" her father practiced; her artistic convictions, severely tested under Stalinism, were founded not only on personal need, but family loyalty and "religious" tradition.

On the debit side, however, Chukovskaia assumed definite limitations and hazards in her father's model. Abiding by his values and tastes, she never al-

Father and Daughter 43

lowed herself to posit her own difference as a reader and a critic. *To the Memory of Childhood* demonstrates why she obligingly replaced her gendered subject position with the adoring "generic" formulations of "he" and "we." As her father absorbed the mother, grandmother, and even the child into himself, Chukovskaia read his model as already heterogeneous, universal, and absolute, encompassing both sexes and all classes, and she could dismiss what lay outside of it. From him she adopted an evaluative framework that masked the influence of gender on writing and reading and that encouraged, with its insistence on the moral and political virtues of the artist, a puritanical and sometimes self-righteous critical approach. Far more hazardous, perhaps, was an inherited deprecation of her creative ability. Impressed by her father's general theories about literary development and his complex self-perception (his presumed lack of talent), Chukovskaia seemed conditioned to pursue a secondary role as a writer. If she was a bright, creative child, she inferred that she was no different from all other children cultivated by her father's methods; if her prodigiously gifted parent was a willing helpmate, then she could aspire no further. The everychild-creation could not exceed the father-creator; the father, it seems, both enabled and confined his daughter's writing life.[35] Yet, as I will consider in the next chapter, what is most intriguing in Chukovskaia's case is that, without questioning or defying her paternal inheritance, she eventually was compelled by circumstances to assert a distinctive authorship, to venture into different expressive modes and creative interactions. Her father may have been the Prospero of her childhood, but he could not divert the tragedy of her adult world. In spite of her sense of deference and to her own astonishment, the forces of history transfigured the dutiful, self-effacing daughter into an eloquent heroine.

3.
ALTERNATIVE SCRIPTS AND NOVEL THERAPIES

> Swallowing up whole blocks of the city physically and—spiritually—our conscious and unconscious thoughts, shouting its own carefully crafted lie from every newspaper page and radio-megaphone, the torture chamber demanded at the same time that we not utter its name in vain—even within four walls, one on one. . . . Surrounded by muteness, the torture chamber wanted to remain at once all-powerful and nonexistent; it did not want to permit any word to summon it from its omnipotent nonbeing.
>
> *Notes on Anna Akhmatova*[1]

Since its long-awaited publication in 1988, Soviet critics have read Chukovskaia's first novel *Sof'ia Petrovna* as history rather than fiction.[2] A reviewer for the journal *Novyi mir* (New world) argues its status as "document" and implies that its revision would amount to a distortion of the facts.[3] Another critic, accepting the novel as "authentic eye-witness testimony," even pronounces its writing a heroic act.[4] The assumed truth of *Sof'ia Petrovna* is crucial to its value: What is most extraordinary about the novel, the reviewers seem to agree, is that it is one of the few texts, perhaps the only text, that dares to "name the torture chamber" in its presence—to record and respond to the events of Stalinism where and when they occurred.[5]

Over the course of her long literary career, Lidiia Chukovskaia wrote two critically acclaimed novels, and by and large, both were composed during and focused on the Stalinist years.[6] She wrote *Sof'ia Petrovna* in an astonishingly short time, from November 1939 to February 1940. *Spusk pod vodu* (*Going Under*) required a longer genesis; begun in 1949, it was completed in 1957, because, as she recalls, the years after Stalin's death absorbed her with other pressing obligations.[7] Both works seem to issue a deeply emotional, self-consciously moral response to their context.[8] They were written secretly and hidden carefully until the conditions of the "thaws" permitted their partial circulation.[9] Both emerged and remained in a single variant. Without renouncing the fiction of either, Chukovskaia asserts that the eponymous protagonist of *Sof'ia Petrovna* was meant to stand for hundreds of actual victims she had witnessed; in the case of *Going Under*, she allows that the heroine's ordeal overlaps with her own experience.[10]

Given their horrific context, however, there remain important questions concerning the writing and reading of these novels. Reviewers can testify to the fact of Chukovskaia's heroism but are less able to explain its source and form. How could Chukovskaia defy the torture chamber with these singular texts? Why did she choose—in a striking departure from her father's practice—to manifest this defiance in narrative fiction? What place do these texts occupy in her life work? And, finally, what might they signify about the respective roles of women and men and the possibilities of moral resistance and artistic creation in Stalinist society?

Emulating Chukovskaia's self-analysis in *To the Memory of Childhood*, the few tentative interpretations assayed underscore her family background. At least in part, the *Novyi mir* reviewer traces her "freedom from fear" to "the spiritual atmosphere of a family inseparable from Russia's cultural intelligentsia" (249). The critic Efim Etkind expands on this claim, grounding the argument of heredity in historical environment: "Truly, K. Chukovskii 'was not empowered to pass his talent on' to L. K. Chukovskaia. Because she, the daughter, had a different talent, formed on the same foundation as that of her father, but in a different epoch."[11] He suggests that just as the father's talent was nurtured and shaped by the rich cultural environment of Russia in the early twentieth century, so the daughter's talent was forged to withstand the fantastic cruelty and tastelessness of its Stalinist surroundings. After a lengthy consideration of the father's accomplishments (this in the afterword to the *tamizdat* Russian edition of *To the Memory of Childhood*), Etkind produces a more austere portrait of the daughter. He envisions her as a kind of warrior persona—a pure, stern queen—whose causes are Memory (*Pamiat'*) and the Word (*Slovo*) and whose writing is "permeated with honor and courage" (281). Doubtlessly intending to pay homage to both, Etkind also conveys the impression that Chukovskaia's work was simplified by its mission, forced into an uncompromising defensive pattern. Coming of age in a peaceable world, he implies, the father could indulge in the luxury of art; the daughter had to streamline and commit all her resources to the war effort.

Etkind's analysis nicely summarizes a traditional approach, but our reading requires more nuanced attention to Chukovskaia's works. Certainly both father and daughter wrote in dialogue with their worlds. Certainly Kornei Chukovskii's oeuvre describes a more extensive and varied activity—in large consequence, I submit, of more favorable historical and *domestic* circumstances. Yet it is essential to recognize that the harsh environment of Chukovskaia's adulthood not only "forged" her defense, but enabled a different kind of work. Beset by the same terrible conditions, the father was compelled to retreat from subjective criticism to more formal literary scholarship (his major project in these years was a scholarly study of the poet Nekrasov), while the daughter was able to write novels and poetry and keep a journal of her meetings with a poet persecuted by the regime. This last comparison is offered not to argue Chukovskaia's greater heroism, but to move toward an adequate evaluation of her art and its relationship to its Stalinist context. The written evidence is undeniable: Chukovskaia worked out a different creative mode of responding to that context. As ironic as this may appear, she seemed to draw a kind of creative empowerment from her experience in the torture chamber.

Chukovskaia herself perceives her creative impulse as an overwhelming emotional imperative. Queried about the composing of *Sof'ia Petrovna*, she insists that "it was easier to write than not to write"; elsewhere she states that she could not *not write* the novel.[12] Particularly in the case of *Sof'ia Petrovna*, her creative writing was engendered in a period of terrible personal and national trauma. The purges had devastated Soviet society, her workplace was wholly dismantled, and her husband was arrested and sentenced to "ten years without right of correspondence" (what she later learned was a bureaucratic euphemism for execution). Indeed, both of her novels were connected to this last bereavement: *Sof'ia Petrovna* emerged in its painful wake and *Going Under* retold it. Creating *Sof'ia Petrovna* in the year after these events, Chukovskaia found relief—as she terms it, "salvation"—from a suffering she could not otherwise express and share (Latynina). If she had not written the novel, she admits that she might have "gone to pieces" (*razorvat'sia na chasti*).[13]

Her creative approach therefore personalizes her father's practice of writing therapy. At one point in *To the Memory of Childhood*, Chukovskaia recounts the deaths of her sister and two brothers and observes how her father seemed to displace sorrow over their loss with more intense work: "Work kept grief at bay, shielded him, helped him 'keep a tight grip on himself.' And further, it raised his resistance by requiring him to lift his spirits" (114). When Chukovskaia resorted to this therapy, however, she delved into a kind of writing which—from the somewhat detached vantage point of fiction—allowed her to explore her trauma and articulate her pain. Even the modes of narration she employed (as I will show in analyses of each novel) emphasize the full psychological experience of her characters—their conscious, semiconscious, subconscious, and sometimes pathological perceptions and feelings. For Chukovskaia, it would seem, writing became a way of understanding and accommodating her grief. At the same time, these fictions expressed moral action; she could not "not write" on account of the double impulses of emotional pain and moral obligation.

Through their genesis, focus, and form, then, *Sof'ia Petrovna* and *Going Under* work out Chukovskaia's personal, moral response to her times. They are set in her very present context; they are born and reflective of her particular (and, as it turns out, representative) pain; they consequently feature female protagonists and enact plots based on women's specific experience, and as such, they establish the female helper as a novelist in her own right. Because these novels ultimately seem to propose a moral stance (on negative and positive examples), they comprise an almost prescriptive complement to the documentary *Notes on Anna Akhmatova*. That is, they dictate Chukovskaia's own "alternative scripts" on female heroism and the domestic sphere (including the extension of the prison lines). The following analyses read *Sof'ia Petrovna* and *Going Under* as the careful creative designs of a highly conscientious female helper—as her reflections on and prescriptions for the roles of women and men in the Stalinist context and, particularly, their manipulation of the connections between written word, private life, and political resistance.

Sof'ia Petrovna

When *Sof'ia Petrovna* was first issued in English translation, it bore the title *The Deserted House*—the result of an editorial decision that explicitly linked the work with Akhmatova's great poetic cycle *Requiem* and, in particular, the phrase uttered by another bereaved mother: "that bright day and deserted house." The reference is important, but the substituted title, as Chukovskaia objects, "is an attempt to change the basic idea" of her novel.[14] *Sof'ia Petrovna*, like *Requiem*, depicts the ordeal of the mother during the Stalinist purges, yet attends, above all, to the continuous development of its title character—to Sof'ia Petrovna's entry into and engagement with Stalinist society. We undergo, with Sof'ia Petrovna herself, the full extent of her tragedy, especially because we are bound to her perspective. Chukovskaia relates Sof'ia's experience through what the critic Dorrit Cohn has termed *psycho-narration*—a third-person voice permeated and sometimes deliberately limited by the mindset of a given character.[15] In lieu of Akhmatova's quest in *Requiem* for an adequate verbal monument to all the victims, Chukovskaia tries here to convey the reality of the Terror by charting, in a gradual, persuasive and interior way, the particular course of one ordinary woman's life. What makes Sof'ia Petrovna's story so distinctive is the unexpected perversion of her success; from a plateau of integration and fulfillment she is plunged unawares into a nightmare of loss, disruption, and isolation.

In fact, the ingredients for success—in socialist realist or (initially) feminist terms—are tantalizingly displayed in the novel. In the character of Sof'ia Petrovna, Chukovskaia has obtained a woman "different" from herself, but representative of her society and times—a woman who, until the (natural) death of her husband, had been contented with the traditional roles of wife and mother and is then drawn into public life. Before the action of the novel begins, it is implied that Sof'ia Petrovna had little contact with the world beyond her home and family. Although the Soviet regime has already encroached on her domestic domain, carving up her comfortable apartment into smaller units, she has managed to preserve and maintain a corner of it. Her husband had been a successful doctor, her only child—a son named Kolia—is hard-working and self-reliant. Sof'ia Petrovna is educated, but by no means politically enlightened. In a wry twist, her one dream of employment de-politicizes a popular concept of Russian radical thought and fiction: She longs to own a dressmaking shop where "[i]n a large, light room pretty girls would sit bent over billowing lengths of silk and she would show them the fashions and engage in worldly conversation with elegant ladies when they came in for fittings (4)."[16] With what will prove to be characteristic myopia, Sof'ia Petrovna simply misses all the political implications of this setting (women's employment and financial autonomy, opportunities for radical education) through her attention to surface images, her judgment according to the restricted categories of a bourgeois femininity (good manners, attractive appearance, and smooth social intercourse).[17]

Identified as "typical" in her limitations, Sof'ia Petrovna is then launched, somewhat obliquely, on a course of self-realization and public fulfillment. Her move out of the home and into a profession is first motivated by notions of self-sacrifice and male achievement. Widowed, she must work to support her teenage boy, especially since her husband "would never have allowed his son to go without a higher education" (3). Finding employment as a typist in a Leningrad publishing house, Sof'ia Petrovna settles on a service position most often staffed by women and symbolizing her own concern with superficial appearance and external decorum.[18] Yet she benefits from her new job within her basic limitations. She learns to groom herself for her new authority; she is flattered, though not informed, by her exposure to the manuscripts of new literary works. In short order Sof'ia Petrovna finds herself recognized and advanced for her efficiency and dutifulness. She is placed in charge of the typing pool; she is chosen to address a political meeting on behalf of all nonparty employees; she is elected the official representative for her now communal apartment. By the time she is permitted her first vacation, she discovers that her orientation has been completely reversed: Rather than savor her return to the home, she longs to go back to work. As she absorbs Party speeches and press reports, Sof'ia Petrovna comes not only to accept her public fulfillment, but to identify and revere the power that "scripted" it:

> Sofia Petrovna now completely agreed with Kolya when he expounded to her on the necessity for women to do socially useful work. Yes, everything Kolya said, and everything that was written in the newspapers now seemed to her completely obvious, as if people had always written and talked that way. (14)

In this first section, the plot echoes the formulae and imperatives of socialist realist fiction as well as some of its famous nineteenth-century precedents.[19] The new Soviet state has facilitated the heroine's move from the domestic to the public domain. It reduces her bourgeois apartment to a single room, thereby devaluing this part of her life, and rewards her venture into the public world of work. In keeping with official policies on women's roles, it lays out the course and sets the limits of her liberation. An anonymous "they" (her beneficiary is rarely named) enlist Sof'ia Petrovna in various housekeeping and supervisory activities: She distributes typing jobs to her "young ladies"; collects union dues from the office; enforces regulations, and writes reports for her communal apartment. This faceless establishment—"the Party Organization and the Mestkom"—officially recognizes her contributions with a basket of flowers on International Women's Day, a Soviet holiday dedicated to (and so specifically marking) women as a group. Aware now of the state's benefactor role, Sof'ia Petrovna cherishes the gift as a token of her approved membership and displays it in her home near other such tokens—the collected works of Lenin and a little bust of Stalin (18).

Yet Chukovskaia's novel demonstrates how this "benevolent" establishment actually reinforces Sof'ia Petrovna's traditional middle-class hierarchy of gender roles and relations. For the most part, the men in her worlds exist as remote and/or idealized figures, beyond the range of her understanding and control. The high Party officials from Moscow who visit the publishing house are "stout men in foreign-made suits" (11). Her director, a young man viewed in his imposing office or graciously caring for his daughter at an office party, elicits her motherly adoration; far from being attracted to his position, she considers him a wonderful model for her son. In clear contrast, Sof'ia Petrovna presumes greater authority among the women at her workplace and in her communal apartment. Interestingly enough, in this context her regard for class distinction is most vehemently in evidence. She befriends and, in a sense, matronizes Natasha Frolenko, the best worker in the pool (and the daughter of a colonel), inviting her home and advising her on how to improve her appearance. While lamenting the fact that her neighbor, a policeman's wife, is "such a sloven" and is apparently responsible for her children's learning handicaps, Sof'ia Petrovna is "on good terms" with this kind, unassuming woman who lives in their former study and depends on Sof'ia Petrovna's advice. On the other hand, Sof'ia Petrovna dares to disapprove of the women who exhibit a lack of decorum—rude manners, coarse language, provocative dress. She regularly criticizes Erna Semionovna—a young woman she considers the worst worker among her typists—and, in an unconscious class judgment, links her with her former "fresh" housemaid. The wife and daughter of the accountant (the whole family resides in her former diningroom) shock her with their vulgar behavior, the more so because the wife comes "from the gentry" (15). Anna Grigorievna, the chairperson of the Mestkom and the one woman Sof'ia Petrovna might accept as senior, is rejected for her dirty nails, poor taste in clothes, and spoiled, unpleasant son. Now doubly trained to accept men as the bearers of power, Sof'ia Petrovna defines her own sphere as separate and supportive and, moreover, an arena where she exercises control as a law-abiding "mother," nurturing the good women who are modest, kind, hard-working, and obedient, and punishing the bad for their greed, rudeness, and insubordination.

Predictably, although Sof'ia Petrovna dreams up an appropriate fiancée for her son—an idealized postcard image (27)—she is fated never to find his female equal among the women she can judge. Natasha, the one woman she particularly endorses, is dismissed as too unattractive to be her Kolia's bride. A match may be impossible: In political and cultural terms Kolia represents the epitome of the official "son." He reincarnates the figure of the socialist realist hero seen, most unusually, through the apolitical (but no less idolizing) consciousness of his mother. His clean-cut, athletic, controlled image is made to order:

> Her son had become handsome, with his gray eyes and black brows, tall, and more confident, calm, and cheerful than Fyodor Ivanovich had been even in his best years. He had a sort of military way about him always, tidy and energetic. Sofia Petrovna would look at him with both tenderness and fear, glad and yet

afraid to be glad. What a good-looking young man, and healthy, too, he didn't drink or smoke, a good son and loyal Komsomol member. (19)

Given the "representative" realism of *Sof'ia Petrovna*, Kolia seems to project a documented instance of a socialist realist character. In his first extensive appearance in the novel, he qualifies himself with state-approved credentials and scripts, informing his mother of his new Komsomol membership, announcing his organization of a "comrades' court show-trial" (to condemn a fellow student's anti-Semitism), and reciting Maiakovskii, the Soviet poet laureate. Together with his friend Alik Finkelstein (a less impressive figure and a foil to Kolia) he studies hard to obtain his degree in mechanical engineering—one of the technical fields promoted by the industrializing Soviet state. When a call goes out for technical experts in Sverdlovsk, an industrial center in the Urals, he and Alik set off to prove their loyalty and enthusiasm, to become the shock workers endorsed in official Soviet fiction and the press.

Perceived through his mother, Kolia functions, in large part, as her metonymical connection to the state. He articulates and enacts its values and priorities. He explains for her the "justice" of the purges conducted after Kirov's murder; he keeps her informed about the international situation from a Soviet point of view. Before he leaves home, Kolia equips Sof'ia Petrovna with a radio—the state's ubiquitous mouthpiece. Writing to her every week from Sverdlovsk, he preempts his private life with a public record, reporting on the operation and achievements of his factory. When he sends her a present, it is—rather than the sewing machine she hopes it to be—the first cogwheel made by the "Fellows' cogwheel cutter" he developed, the product of his public labor, the quest object of a socialist realist plot (26). Bewildered but indulgent, Sof'ia Petrovna accords the cogwheel a place of honor in her home as yet another emblem of official approval.

Even when he is living at home, Kolia remains allied to the public sphere. Although Sof'ia Petrovna worries about providing him the space for his own life—particularly for a future wife—her son shows little need for or interest in this kind of privacy. Aside from his friendship with Alik, he conceals all other personal involvements and treats his home as an extended workshop, a place where he and Alik experiment with various engineering projects. He defers the whole question of a personal life by moving to Sverdlovsk. After his departure, Kolia's image coincidentally takes on a public dimension for his mother. At the movies Sof'ia Petrovna discovers that the state-approved film characters— "[t]he pilots with their white teeth, accomplishing great feats"—remind her of her son. With his invention of the cogwheel cutter, Kolia himself is transformed into a public icon of achievement and dedication and appears, to his mother's surprise and delight, as a model hero on the pages of *Pravda*.

On her part, although Sof'ia Petrovna learns to appreciate and absorb her son's state-prescribed worldview, she never undergoes a complete conversion. She still senses the limitations in his model and presumes in him an inadequacy which she, as mother, must fill. Kolia either hides or dismisses private needs and feelings; while he remains at home, Sof′ia Petrovna supplies those missing parts of domestic comfort and emotional support. When he goes away, she deems him incapable of caring for himself and spontaneously appeals to Alik—a Jewish boy who does not conform to the manly Stalinist prototype—to look after her otherwise heroic son. Frustrated by Kolia's official letters, she even writes the "mothering" Alik for news about their domestic circumstances. For the first time, on an intuitive level, Sof′ia Petrovna is dissatisfied with the inadequacy of official expression when it touches on the vital subject of her son.

The limitations of both characters—indeed, their neat division of conventionally masculine and feminine traits—explicitly demonstrate the inequality between the sexes that underlies most socialist realist plots. While seeming to liberate herself from assigned gender roles, Sof′ia Petrovna simply has exchanged one form of subordination for a new one that reapplies, but does not assign primary value to, her housekeeping and mothering skills. Kolia endorses a single pattern of political and pragmatic action for both sexes, excluding the very possibilities of a nonpublic space and a differentiated self. Neither character works out an independent set of social values or conceives of themselves outside of the imposed frameworks of tsarist patriarchy or Stalinist system. Yet, judged according to a socialist realist model, their situation still holds important potential. Kolia is the socialist realist hero "incarnate"; his mother, while hampered by the evil relics of her bourgeois past, has traveled far on the road to socialist enlightenment, purged of her former class privilege, employed as a worker, involved in political reeducation. In fact, in her son's absence, she becomes in her own way *more* absorbed in Soviet political culture by going to movies, listening to the radio, and talking with Natasha. For roughly the first third of the novel, Chukovskaia seems to be recording a socialist realist success story.

The perversion of this success, therefore, underscores the terrible deceit inherent in Stalinist society and the official literature that misrepresents it. The first alarm sounds during the grand illusion of the office party. Characteristically, Sof′ia Petrovna and Natasha have interpreted the event on their own terms—as a kind of celebration of the family—and they buy presents for all of the employees' children and bedeck the room with icons of Lenin as a child and Stalin as a benevolent paternal figure (30). There Sof′ia Petrovna is told of an arrest which is threatening by analogy: They have picked up Doctor Kiparisov, her husband's old colleague and Kolia's godfather. Yet, far from alerting her, this news and subsequent similar reports simply dupe her into the general mass hysteria. Having developed no other means of evaluation, she clings to the official interpretation reiterated in the papers and on the radio. Even the arrest of the director can be dismissed as the result of a personal rather than a professional indiscretion. She demonstrates the extent of her delusion when she chances on her counterpart, the wife of Doctor Kiparisov. Bound to her petty standards of decorum, Sof′ia Petrovna simply registers a physical change—Mrs. Kiparisova has "let herself go terribly"—and while she insists on the "misunderstanding" of the doctor's arrest, she is incapable of reading the signs of her friend's ordeal (36–37).

Sof'ia Petrovna is shaken, but no more enlightened, once her son is in danger. When Alik, having failed in caring for his charge, comes back to inform her of Kolia's arrest and to help her make the rounds of police and prison, she is still loath to relinquish her trust in the state. The latter half of the novel chronicles her pathetic struggle to cope with this monstrous rift between an official society—where official doctrine is articulated and enforced—and a world of unofficial experience and association. With her son's arrest, the boundary between public and domestic spheres is made irrelevant for Sof'ia Petrovna, and she is cast into an unofficial netherworld that she is ill equipped to navigate and use.

She enters this realm instinctively, making her way to the prison—the one reference point she already knows.

> She noticed a large crowd of women in the middle of the street. Some were leaning against the parapet of the embankment, others walked slowly along the sidewalk or on the pavement. Sofia Petrovna was surprised that they were all very warmly dressed, muffled in scarves over their coats, and almost all in felt boots and galoshes. They were stamping their feet and blowing on their hands. "They must have stood here a long time to be so cold," Sofia Petrovna reflected for lack of anything to do, "it's no longer freezing, the thaw has begun." All the women looked as though they'd been waiting for hours on end for a train at a waystation.
>
> Sofia Petrovna took a careful look at the building across from which a crowd of women was standing—an ordinary building without any sort of sign on it. What was it they were all waiting for? In the crowd there were ladies in elegant coats and also simple women. Again for lack of anything better to do, Sofia Petrovna walked once or twice through the crowd. One woman stood there holding an infant in her arms and another child, muffled crosswise in a scarf, by the hand. Near the wall of the building there was a man standing alone. All their faces looked a little green—maybe it was the half light of the morning that made them look that way? (47–48)

Like some kind of amateur ethnographer, Sof'ia Petrovna happens on a group that exists outside the customs of her time, place, and activity, and communicates only through cryptic questions and messages. Over the course of the next few weeks, Sof'ia Petrovna masters the customs, if not the meaning of this world: where to go; how to dress; what to ask of the prison or police officials; what information she can expect to obtain about her son's whereabouts and punishment. She learns to distinguish what she had missed in Mrs. Kiparisov's face; she can even detect among casual passersby which women are on their way to stand in the lines at the prison, the prosecutor's office, the secret police headquarters. In fact, Sof'ia Petrovna internalizes these women as her constant companions:

> She knew now, when she left home after a short sleep, that wherever she went—on the street, on the staircase, in the corridor, in the hall, on Chaikovsky Street, on the embankment, at the prosecutor's office—there would be women, women, women, old and young, in kerchiefs and hats, alone or with small children or babies—children crying from lack of sleep and quiet, frightened, laconic

women; and as in her childhood, when upon closing her eyes after an excursion to the woods she had seen nothing but berries, berries, berries, now when she closed her eyes, she saw faces, faces, faces. . . . (57)

Overwhelmingly female, sharing the same stigma and hardship of the lines for the sake of their imprisoned loved ones, this company could offer Sof'ia Petrovna a kind of support—at the very least as living proof of an ongoing political terror. Alik, who helps her keep vigil, certainly draws this conclusion, observing first that "[a]ll those mothers standing in line somehow look an awful lot like Sof'ia Petrovna" and then insisting, after he learns of Kolia's confession, that "a colossal plot" is afoot. Natasha, her other helper, falls into a despair of confusion and doubt, unable to debate the heresies Alik proposes, at a loss to explain Kolia's confession to the authorities. Yet Sof'ia Petrovna counters their protest and hesitation with an unswerving belief in official lies. She censures Alik for his rash behavior and even suspects her son of disobedience. Most vehemently, Sof'ia Petrovna refuses to approve and befriend the unofficial company she is forced to keep. Queuing up with hundreds of other victims, she judges them much as she criticized other women for their bad manners. Both groups, in her limited mind, are damned by their insubordination:

> No, Sofia Petrovna had been quite right to keep aloof from her neighbors in the lines. She was sorry for them, of course, as human beings, sorry especially for the children; but still an honest person had to remember that all these women were the wives and mothers of poisoners, spies and murderers. (60)

Because Sof'ia Petrovna has embraced official standards as her own, she eventually condemns herself, allowing the very characters she instinctively disliked—the vulgar, materialistic Erna Semionovna and the accountant's wife—to victimize her in the name of the state and for personal gains. She loses her job largely through the machinations of the unscrupulous Erna; she is accused of stealing and threatened with eviction by her co-tenant. When Alik is arrested and Natasha commits suicide, only the policeman's wife remains to offer Sof'ia Petrovna occasional consolation. She subsists in terrible isolation, "afraid of everyone and everything," including the newspapers which, for her, had once proclaimed the irrefutable truth. She responds by effacing herself both at work and at home, and she transforms her private refuge—her cherished, tidy room—into a messy storage place for goods to be sent to Kolia. Her circumstances combined with her limitations reduce Sof'ia Petrovna from worker, mother, and budding citizen to the most primitive kind of mother—a woman who lives only to get food and clothes to her suffering child.

The strain of living alone outside the bounds of official society finally breaks Sof'ia Petrovna; the ordeal distorts her thinking and perverts those few independent instincts she has displayed. Pushed to the limits of her endurance, hearing from Mrs. Kiparisova that some prisoners are being released, Sof'ia Petrovna readmits herself to society by appropriating the state's reality-making fictions. Seemingly unaware of what she is doing, she lies to her co-workers and neighbors about Kolia's pending release and feels renewed by their congratulations. In official favor once again, she can care for herself—improving her tea-and-bread diet, cleaning up her room. Sof'ia Petrovna then awaits written confirmation of her lie and restored public life from Kolia. Yet the letter she miraculously does receive exposes a very different reality and, more, a very differently speaking Kolia. Imprisoned and tortured, the socialist realist hero now dwells only on emotional ties and physical pain. He has been beaten to confess until he is deaf in one ear; he is anxious over the welfare of his loved ones; he begs Sof'ia Petrovna to make an emotional (not ideological) appeal to the authorities as his "old mother."

It is intriguing that at this critical juncture Sof'ia Petrovna seeks advice from another woman. For the first time she voluntarily links her fate with a co-sufferer in the lines. Unfortunately, she turns to her counterpart, Mrs. Kiparisova—a woman who has more experience with the penal system but no more capacity to resist its dehumanizing influence. In the two women's sporadic meetings since Kolia's arrest, Mrs. Kiparisova has served as ambiguous mentor, passing on rumors and advising a cautiousness bordering on paranoia. When Sof'ia Petrovna runs to her with Kolia's letter, she discovers the doctor's wife already in the next stage of persecution, seated on a trunk in an empty room, awaiting deportation. Thoroughly terrorized, Mrs. Kiparisova draws Sof'ia Petrovna into her bathroom (the last refuge in her terrorized home) and warns her not to write an appeal:

> "Don't write it!" whispered Kiparisova, bringing her huge eyes, ringed with yellow, close up to Sofia Petrovna's face. "Don't write one for your son's sake. They're not going to pat you on the back for an appeal like that. Neither you, nor your son. Do you really think you can write that the investigator beat him? You can't even think such a thing, let alone write it. They've forgotten to deport you, but if you write an appeal—they'll remember. And they'll send your son farther away, too. . . . And who brought this letter, anyway? And where are the witnesses? . . . And what proof is there? . . ." She looked around the bathroom with wild-looking eyes. "No, for God's sake, don't write anything." (108)

Like a more extreme version of Sof'ia Petrovna, Kiparisova yields only negative reinforcement. She confirms Sof'ia Petrovna in her yearning to be obedient, in her impulse to avoid a reality that reveals the surface of normal society to be a monstrous lie. In lieu of inspiring courage and lending support, her words corner Sof'ia Petrovna into further submission and self-censorship. Returning home to think, Sof'ia Petrovna does not think at all. The narration slips from her confused consciousness to thoughtless action:

> Sofia Petrovna took a box of matches out of a drawer. She struck a match and lit a corner of the letter. It burned, slowly turning to ash, coiling up into a tube. It curled completely and burned her fingers.
> Sofia Petrovna threw the flame on the floor and stamped on it. (109)

Sof'ia Petrovna concludes with this episode of terrible destruction. By burning her son's letter the protagonist psychologically and symbolically destroys herself. She is not strong enough to articulate and oppose the state's deception. More poignantly, she is not strong enough to be a protective mother under these horrific circumstances. Through her action she reveals that she can no longer preserve what she once naturally desired—the expression of private (and now incriminating) needs and feelings, her son's emergence as vulnerable human being. Out of terror and confusion, Sof'ia Petrovna turns away from the last, the most vital personal connection remaining to her and performs the complicit treachery encouraged by the regime.

In composing the story of Sof'ia Petrovna, Chukovskaia uses a woman as the most effective (and affective) measure of the devastation of Stalinist society. Echoing her own experience on a less sophisticated level, her female protagonist appropriates the role of the "little man" in nineteenth-century Russian literature, relating through her limited consciousness and mundane aspirations the most telling critique of political tyranny.[20] Just as Aleksandr Solzhenitsyn adopts the simple perspective of the peasant Ivan Denisovich to probe the full horror of the prison camp, so Chukovskaia reveals the nightmare of daily life *in* Soviet society through a simple and most representative character—one of the thousands of women who waited in the lines. Sof'ia Petrovna presents a strong case study because as an ordinary woman—someone trained and eager to serve within the bounds of a given system and to submit to authoritative male models—she demonstrates the incredible power (both attractive and destructive) of the Stalinist regime. Supported by the new order, she moves naturally from home to workplace; she is surprised and flattered by her easy professional success. As good wife, good mother, and good worker, she maintains for herself and imposes on others (most readily on women) absolute standards of obedience and loyal service. She absorbs Party doctrine without question—largely through the explanations and actions of her exemplary son.

Yet Sof'ia Petrovna does not (indeed, cannot) foresee the perils of her wholehearted commitment. While seeming to expand her horizons and link the separate compartments of her life in a single devotion, she in effect relinquishes almost all her roles and modest spheres of influence to Party control. Made official and promised approval, her life still does not acquire primary value in her society. Her contributions as helpmate are presumed, exploited, and encouraged, but always contained. Moreover, her concern for Kolia's private welfare (the one response that lies outside official interests) proves at first to be irrelevant and then is punished as criminal association. When, on the basis of her crime of motherhood, Sof'ia Petrovna is forced to endure the horrible metamorphosis of official sanction into total punishment and terror, she has left herself no grounds for resistance. Committed to believe and obey, she submits to and suffers from the self-serving manipulations of "bad" characters still enjoying official approval. Watching the destruction of the obedient and the "good," she nevertheless abhors and suspects any form of dissidence.

So doomed by the nature of her participation, Sof'ia Petrovna is driven to a fundamental denial of herself and others. Her fate is the more terrible because it is worked out within and against a newly forming potential—a world which, for all its bleakness, testifies to an unofficial reality and gathers the victims together in a random community. Because she subscribes to the official interpretation of her experience, Sof'ia Petrovna cannot locate her own place—a possible refuge and source of resistance—in the company of these women, whom she presumes to be the wives and mothers of the enemy. Renouncing their positive image and association, she is led to distrust her own unofficial response as a loving mother and an intuitive woman and, in the end, yields to the annihilating silence of the torture chamber.

Going Under

With the confused despair and final surrender of its heroine, *Sof'ia Petrovna* imprints Chukovskaia's darkest reading of Stalinist society. The novel charts the insidious progress of totalitarian control—what Chukovskaia depicts as a plundering of perception and expression. Privy to the semi-verbal workings of Sof'ia Petrovna's consciousness, we witness and understand her inevitable capitulation; she possesses no spiritual or cultural funds to prevent it. Mother love, her surest virtue, alone proves to be no match for this overwhelming perversion. Chukovskaia's second novel, however, composed over the long years of survival, proposes a kind of recovery from the final breakdown of *Sof'ia Petrovna*. For this purpose, Chukovskaia necessarily selected a different protagonist, one closer to herself in mentality and vocation and therefore endowed with a deep knowledge of and love for literature. Nina Sergeevna, the *speaking* heroine, is a woman of cultural means, and the novel *Going Under* at once posits and explores her healing potential.

Chukovskaia clearly equips her protagonist to be her own writer and analyst. Nina Sergeevna belongs to the Union of Soviet Writers, and while this membership does not guarantee her talent, it identifies her conscious professional commitment and connects her tangibly with the literary scene. This heroine is highly skilled in the manipulation of words. She has long since graduated from the simple service of Sof'ia Petrovna; at one time she was employed as a shorthand typist, but for the duration of the novel she works (officially) as a translator. More importantly, Nina Sergeevna insists on what she feels to be the honest use of words and relies on her own writing for emotional and spiritual sustenance. She writes herself here in self-conscious diary form, through a first-person mode that not only records, but meditates on, her present experience and exercises a novelist's sensitivity to character and imagery. In contrast to the diffuse range of a daily diary, her account is contained and propelled by her sense of urgent mission.[21] Nina Sergeevna, like Chukovskaia, has lost a husband in the purges, and she aims to penetrate the enigma of this bereavement—now over a decade old, but no less troubling—during her month at a writers' rest home. A widow writing about a widow writing about her loss, Chukovskaia seems to sug-

Alternative Scripts and Novel Therapies   57

gest *Going Under* as a metatext for her own practice. This connection also perhaps accounts for the more prescriptive and overtly moralizing tone of her second novel.

Nina Sergeevna, then, enters the scene as a professional woman with an established career. Her plot, in an interesting departure, removes her from both public and domestic spheres and locates her in a strange blend of hospital and workplace—a space where she can rest, recuperate, and work. For Nina Sergeevna this combination of comfort and freedom is essential:

> And here I am at home. From the lounge came the musical deep sound of a clock striking and immediately one could hear the measured assiduous pounding of an electric power-station. At long last I would be living alone in a room, for the first time since the war. As if I was in my own home in Leningrad. Sitting down at a desk which would not have to be turned into a diningroom table three times a day. Working in quiet. My thoughts and musings would not be run down, mutilated by somebody's words from the kitchen. . . . I rested the palm of my hand on the blue pipe of the radiator: it was hot. (6)[22]

Her room in the sanatorium affords her the refuge she might have enjoyed at home—a refuge, she implies, that has been chipped away by state design and family duty. Although she professes nothing but love and concern for her daughter Katya (her first act in her new room is to set out the "flags" of her ink-well and her daughter's photograph), here she enjoys a double respite from the daily grind of domestic relations in a communal apartment and the daily chores (if not the anxiety) of mothering. Here, too, she escapes from the demeaning bureaucracy of Moscow life into a world of solicitous people and "kindly pretence," where public exchange is still informed by courtesy and a concern for one's individual welfare. With its specially prepared meals, tidied rooms, medical treatments, and leisure activities, this world effectively mothers Nina Sergeevna, providing her—the traumatized victim—with the physical well-being necessary for her recovery.

Granted these special privileges, Nina Sergeevna is at pains to distinguish her enjoyment from what she early on identifies as crass hedonism. Her first thoughts, intended to commence her "meeting with [her]self," digress instead to the foil of Liudmila Pavlovna, the well-appointed matron of the sanatorium who is probably pleased to "work in such a smart place," but "bored to death" by its pure air and natural setting (6–7). Nina Sergeevna presumes that she alone can appreciate the depth of her new home's restorative power, the delights of house and forest. Reminiscent of Chukovskaia's own Kuokkala, the natural world surrounding the rest home entrances her with its sparkling silence and dancing birch "families" (family once again recurs as an important motif) and constitutes for her a special meeting place with texts and people. If the comforts of the rest home nurture her in a material way, then she receives from the forest the same sort of poetic nourishment Chukovskaia obtained from outings with her father. Her long walks in the woods culminate in spontaneous recitations. For Nina Sergeevna, as for Chukovskaia, poetry and nature are recorded as complementary phenomena:[23]

> Looking around, I saw that I was quite alone and I began to recite some poetry. I tried to fit the sounds to the birch-trees, to this treacherous snow.
> I tried out Pushkin, Pasternak, Nekrasov and Akhmatova. Yes, they were all from here. They all fitted in. "All Correct", as one would say in checking a telegram. . . . All the words grew from this soil, and drawing in a deep breath, stretched upwards to the sky like the birch-trees. (55)

To a remarkable degree, the sanatorium institutionalizes the place of Chukovskaia's idyllic childhood, echoing the perfect synthesis of parents, home, and Finnish landscape with the imperfect, but certainly beneficial, complex of medical staff, rest home, and surrounding woods.[24] Yet this place can only imitate that past: In contrast to the happy plot and setting of childhood in Chukovskaia's memoir, her novel represents the convalescence of a troubled adult—a woman constantly victimized and, above all, spiritually *disrupted* by the world outside. Nina Sergeevna suffers from the same social schizophrenia that undoes Sof'ia Petrovna, but she is made intelligent and brave enough to diagnose its cause and fortunate enough to find temporary relief. In this place she hopes to restore herself by shutting out a false public life and reviewing her past experience, a process she describes as "going under" as she descends into the semiconscious state of remembering and dreaming arrests, interrogations, and prison queues.

Nina Sergeevna sets the stage for this process with the record of her first nightmare. Here she names the central, compelling source of her pain—the loss of her husband, Alyosha. Experienced and recovered, this dream represents for her a subconscious attempt to penetrate the unknown, to realize "a horror without color or smell" (19). She approaches this horror obliquely, fearfully, through a patchwork of related memories, dreams, and commentary. The nightmare moves her beyond the enigma of interrogation and prison camp to an incriminating account of Alyosha's return:

> I am lying on the low soft bed. Black deep silence. My heart is pounding as if I had been performing under the circus big top, had missed the trapeze—and fallen into the net.
> Tonight I understood why I was guilty. I understood in my dream. I am alive. That was why. I am alive, I am still living after they have shoved Alyosha into the water with sticks. He had come back for a moment to reproach me. That was what I saw in my dream. (20)

Like Sof'ia Petrovna, Nina Sergeevna has been most affected by Stalinist repression through the loss of a loved one. Yet, as this narrated dream already shows, she is working out a positive, sanity-preserving response to her bereavement through the act of writing; "going under" entails both recollection and inscription. Her subsequent descents are planned, voluntary assays to *write across* the terrible chasm between surviving self and murdered husband,

Alternative Scripts and Novel Therapies

present existence and the netherworld, and these culminate in an all-important book:

> It will stand on the shelf with other books, it will be picked up, leafed through, put back in place. The dust will be wiped off, dust of the quiet of this place, of today, through which Alyosha's voice and Katya's tears return to me.
>
> The book was me, the sinking of my heart, my memory, which nobody can see, just as nobody can see, for instance, a migraine, a point of pain in my eye, yet it will become paper, binding, a new book on the market and—if I plumb the depths fearlessly—someone's new soul. Creating it, Alyosha's voice and Katya's tears will permeate this soul. (36)

Like so many other unofficial texts written in this period, her book is assigned a dangerous status and a transcendent mission. In the course of *Going Under* she *divines* her book in secret (like Chukovskaia, she intimates her creation as an involuntary act) and camouflages her writing with reported work on a translation project. She does not risk her work's distribution, although she employs the same imbedding device used by Bulgakov and Pasternak, including it as an "untitled" excerpt in the frame narrative (98–110). But Nina Sergeevna does declare her ultimate goal in writing it: "I want to find brothers—if not now, then in the future. All living things seek brotherhood and I seek it too. I am writing a book to find brothers, even if only there in the unknown distance" (38).

Chukovskaia's heroine, like Chukovskaia herself, simply conflates the masculine and the universal in evoking such a "brotherhood." It is somewhat ironic, therefore, that the text of her book mainly features female characters from her past—the undersociety of women in the prison lines. (Nina Sergeevna even contemplates entitling it "Daughter.") Her first-person chronicle of a "routine" morning, this text explores the possibility of articulating the women's experience and describes their first, fearful attempts to interact and share. At the outset her account emphasizes silence: The waiting women converse very little among themselves, and none of them, including Nina Sergeevna, can explain their presence to a curious onlooker. In fact, the longest passages of dialogue are attributed to the police commandant, who barks out the regulations and fends off timid questions with lies and flirtatious remarks. Nina Sergeevna depicts how the women are herded into a single line moving toward a door they enter one by one; once inside, they receive identical information from a disembodied bureaucrat who hides behind a high wooden shutter. Shunted through this assembly line, the women become a mass of identically silenced and dismissed victims.

Yet despite the silence, distrust, and forced conformity she records, Nina Sergeevna also indicates how she enters into a hesitant process of individuation and interaction. She notes the intermittent appearance of an old Jewess with a mustache who herself manages to speak to the commandant and then to her co-supplicants. And she especially distinguishes a young Finnish woman and her lovely, frail baby daughter:

> The little baby girl sneezed beneath the starched pale-blue cloud, her mother lifted the tulle and I caught a glimpse of a tiny delicate face, pink like her blanket, so delicate that a speck of ash which had settled on her cheek looked like a heavy, black stone. She was blessed with eyelashes which seemed to reach halfway down her cheeks. She had a teeny little face—and there in the blanket were tiny red heels, tiny little fingers with tiny toy nails and all her fragrant velvety little body.
> "Wrap her up quickly," I said. It was terrible to think that the frost might touch that little face. (100)

Nina Sergeevna vaguely marks the progress of mother and child through the line. Although she wonders at one point why the woman is holding the baby on outstretched arms, she cannot spare any further reflection until they are both released from the building into a little courtyard. Here an apparently normal world of family and society is instantly restored, with bundled children playing under the supervision of their nannies, and Nina Sergeevna gradually becomes conscious of a terrible change: Instead of cradling the baby in her lap, the mother has laid her daughter beside her on the frozen bench. For the first time Nina Sergeevna shifts her concern from missing husband to present companion and rushes over to help, but her efforts are too late. The baby had died several hours before, the mother had remained in line out of love for her husband, and Nina Sergeevna can only help her catch her tram home.

By the conclusion of her inset text, Nina Sergeevna has indeed portrayed herself in contact with one of her sisters. She proves able to express compassion and commit herself to help. Her involvement cannot alter the horror; the icon she recognized in the child is nevertheless destroyed. Yet in acting and then writing down that action, she establishes an important precedent and creates a powerful symbol. In contrast to a paralyzed Sof'ia Petrovna, she demonstrates the possibility (if not the immediate benefit) of interaction and support among these "suspect" woman. And she conveys the seemingly inexpressible emotional ordeal ("Alyosha's voice and Katya's tears") through a tragic tableau vivant enacted by women—a baby daughter's death, a woman's anguish over lost husband and dead baby, a female onlooker's compassionate grief for mother and child.

During the "descent" of her book, Nina Sergeevna does risk contact and ventures into some of the lives of her fellow victims. What she does not anticipate is the possibility of discovering "brothers" among her present company in the sanatorium. Unfortunately, her refuge, compared to Chukovskaia's Kuokkala, attracts a very different sort of visitor—approved members of an official union rather than a group of dedicated artists. She enters the sanatorium with the intent to isolate and immerse herself and, during her first days, shies away from any other association. Yet these official writers are an intruding, demanding presence at the dining-room tables, in the lounge and the bathing cubicles, even on the forest paths. And as Nina Sergeevna must meet and intuitively read these characters, she expresses certain conventional, moralizing patterns of classification and dismissal. All the other "artists" at the sanatorium happen to be men. They are the characters most likely to engage her in discussions about work, literary tastes, and literary politics. With a few important exceptions,

Nina Sergeevna hears them as parrots of official rhetoric and judgment. She illustrates their conformity by juxtaposing their "impromptu" opinions with radio and newspaper accounts. Although these men possess other faults, Nina Sergeevna judges them most harshly for their speech, which, like the Stalinist newspeak she openly condemns, rings false in its very "monotony, word order, syntax, tone and intonation" (96).

The women exemplify an altogether different Stalinist vice. They make up the staff of the rest home and the families—the wives and girlfriends—of the visiting writers; they either serve or accompany the "artists." In Nina Sergeevna's critical reading, they, too, devalue culture, but in a more physical way; she scorns them as the embodiment of vulgar materialism and sensual indulgence. The wry disdain she expresses for Liudmila Pavlovna—a fashionable woman "bored to death" by nature—characterizes most of her judgments. At first intrigued by a dark-eyed young woman in the dining room, Nina Sergeevna very soon concludes that she is too pretty to be a writer (21), and then is wholly disillusioned by her beauty when the woman begins to flirt with other guests. In her most self-righteous mode, Nina Sergeevna assumes an intellectual limitation, even a kind of spiritual inadequacy, in these well-dressed, attractive women—as if their concern for external appearance betrays an inner emptiness and, worse, acquiescence to a false, repugnant material standard.[25] Although she observes this kind of materialism among men as well, she locates its source in women—specifically in the figure of the *wife* who, in her judgment, can both incarnate and determine the value system of a household. She ponders this phenomenon in the case of the journalist, a man she admits that she may have misjudged until she meets his spouse:

> Since I had seen his face there on the bridge I had almost believed that the fur collar and the fancy knob had no special meaning and were not so directly connected with him. But now, seeing the wife's well-proportioned figure, the handbag slung over her shoulder and hearing her voice and laughter I thought "No, both the fur collar and the knob were not accidental. They had a meaning.". . .
> "But what a revealing thing one's wife is," I thought, as I walked behind her shapely hips and watched her happily spitting. The words "It's fun to do it with your mouth" appear to him to be wit; the carthorse strength and lightness of step—beauty; and that stupid laugh—candor. In her spitting he sees something spontaneous, childlike maybe, and intimacy with ordinary people. (56–57)

As in her search for "brothers," her dislike of the materialistic wife implies a rather male-centered worldview—one perhaps unreflectingly transmitted by her author. It is characteristic that Nina Sergeevna highlights only one villain from her domestic life "outside"—her neighbor, Elizaveta Nikolaevna, who evinces no good wifely qualities (she has no children and cannot "sew, mend, or bake") and lives to tyrannize and exploit others. A truly evil wife, this woman is mainly responsible for violating the refuge of Nina Sergeevna's home, spoiling her previous "descents," and forcing her to seek peace and privacy elsewhere.

Among this conventionalized assortment of lying "intellectual" men and grasping "physical" women, Nina Sergeevna conveniently figures as a shining anomaly. She is the only woman who is a writer; more, she is the only female character (aside from the doctor, a background figure) who demonstrates any sort of intellectual ability. According to her own criteria, her appearance confirms her capacity. She admits her shabbiness when she is first accosted by visitors in the forest: "Prosperous, well-dressed people! I immediately thought of my old coat, my unpermed and untinted hair" (11). She bears none of the trappings and expresses none of the desires of a materialistic wife. She refuses to indulge in the flirtatious atmosphere of the rest home; when confronted with the prospect of a love affair, she is wearied and even repelled. In effect, Nina Sergeevna "transcends" the embodied materialism that she ascribes to other women.

At the same time she is the only writer in the sanatorium who explicitly protests official lies and voices her own independent opinions. When the journalist, echoing a critical paragraph in the newspapers, complains that Pasternak is obscure, Nina Sergeevna, echoing Lidiia Chukovskaia, delivers an impassioned speech about the necessity of a poetic education and the unfathomable greatness of the poet. Of all her companions, she alone (and despite a friendly warning) objects when the critic Klokov endorses the state's new anti-Zionist campaign. Unable to restrain herself, she insists on the "blatancy of the lies" in print and the consequent innocence of all those who had been publicly accused. Although Nina Sergeevna realizes that such outbursts are useless and often dangerous, she has, in fact, performed a remarkable feat within her context: She has broken through the silence and paralysis that cripples her society and has made her private belief a public stance.

Refusing materialist entrapment on the one hand and intellectual sycophancy on the other, Nina Sergeevna might seem impossibly virtuous and unapproachable. Yet she finds that she exercises an attractive and synthesizing power; involuntarily, she develops into a new sort of heroine. While attempting to shun contact, she invites all manner of confidences and attachments—from surprising sources and, most often, in the forest she had hoped to preserve as her solitary refuge. Liudmila Pavlovna, who had provoked only her scorn and suspicion, suddenly gains her sympathy; Nina Sergeevna finds her weeping as she walks along a snowy path and there hears the matron's confession about her sister's second arrest and deportation. The same day, making polite conversation with another patient, she stumbles on his horrific life story as he tells her how the Germans immolated his wife and two of his three children during the war. In another instance, she is even called upon to sort out "poetic truth" when the Jewish poet Veksler asks her to compare his Yiddish poems with their Russian translations and she obliges, earning from him a deep respect for her editorial skill.

Meeting her by chance and encouraged by her sympathy, these characters serve to endorse Nina Sergeevna's special capacity as a listener and a seeker of hidden "truth." She is cast as a kind of caretaker of their most precious secrets, as someone to whom they can relate every aspect of their existence. Veksler repeatedly asks her to listen to and comment on his work. Still maintaining the pose of gracious matron, Liudmila Pavlovna depends on her to keep her secret and offer occasional advice. Nina Sergeevna alone seems equipped to preserve an essential integrity in both moral and cultural terms. She even functions as surrogate mother when she befriends Lyolka, a little girl who lives in the village nearby and is the sister of one of the maids at the rest home. Struck by the girl's sad situation (her father is missing, both her mother and sister work, and she must take care of her year-old brother), Nina Sergeevna tries to provide Lyolka with the kind of poetic education Chukovskaia records receiving from her father. She plays cultural parent to the girl, treating her to sweets and a book of fairy tales, silencing the newspeak of the blaring radio in their hut by reading aloud. In this sense, Nina Sergeevna begins to generalize the relationship she has preserved with her daughter Katya and shows how, as an educated writer and a mother who resists the state's manipulation, she might manage to save the souls of many such daughters.

For Nina Sergeevna all these unexpected contacts afford glimpses of potential "brotherhood"—an imperfect or as yet undeveloped communion. Yet she enters one relationship that promises immediate fulfillment. Another guest at the sanatorium, the writer Nikolai Bilibin, comes to exist for her as a human emissary from the world of the camps. She attracts him as well, and although she rejects his early romantic advances, she appreciates a kind of physical ambiguity in him—something "veiled" in his eyes and actor's voice. He continues to pursue her even after she has publicly compromised herself with her defense of Pasternak and, just when she predicts the next ploy in his flirtation, seduces her with a very different disclosure: He tells her of his camp experience. Nina Sergeevna quotes his stories at length, paying homage to the essential information he gives her. In return, she shares with him the precious secret of her husband.

After these first confessions, their relationship develops, in pattern and intensity, like a love affair. Overhearing Bilibin's flirtatious banter with other women, Nina Sergeevna feels secretly possessive of his "real" voice (46). Dismayed by his assumed pose with the other guests, she longs to be alone with him and listens avidly for his footsteps outside her room (61). When he does not appear, she even seeks him out and, because of her urge to talk with him, saves him from dying of a heart attack. Her passion, however, depends on the exchange of forbidden stories. In contrast to her random contacts with Veksler and Liudmila Pavlovna, she and Bilibin both throw themselves into the roles of witness and listener: "He could not have had many opportunities for talking about camp life because he spoke with the same insatiable voraciousness I felt listening to him" (68).

Indeed, it is the knowledge she receives from Bilibin that allows her to reconsider human intimacy. Telling her the very probable scenario of her husband's execution, Bilibin actually dispels her nightmares with his facts and makes her widowhood definite and bearable. Their conversations eventually preempt all her other writing and remembering and realign the spiritual configuration of her world. She actually permits contact with another human being to supercede her solitary communion with nature:

> The grove no longer lived for itself, its own secret life, at one with the snow, wind and clouds, but existed for us, existed to imprint our footsteps in the snow, existed to cover them over in a flurry of flakes; to fill them with water, for the wind to roll over our heads; to change the color of his eyes by the greyness or blueness of the sky; to preserve us from the whole world and not to hinder us as we listened to one another. (111)

The exacting Nina Sergeevna gradually comes to treat Bilibin as a full-fledged "brother," valuing his narrative, worrying about his health, and relying on him for emotional support. Yet in the end she discovers that Bilibin cannot maintain the comprehensive standards she has set for them both. She herself registers an early warning: "poetry kept us apart." As it turns out, Bilibin's deafness to poetry implies a greater insensitivity and incapacity. At first he misreads their relationship as a case of erotic love. It is revealing that Nina Sergeevna does not so much object to the notion of love as Bilibin's trite expression of it:

> ... But why and how had we suddenly started talking in such a stupid way: 'rival', 'successful rival', 'unsuccessful rival'. 'Rival' in what? How could we have degraded what we had experienced together by using those trite words? (120)

Yet her final break with Bilibin stems from his deliberate miswriting of his life. Nina Sergeevna is already contemplating him as an actual reader of her "book" and naturally consents to look at his manuscript, expecting to hear there his "real voice." Instead she reads the perversion of his camp experience into a standard socialist realist novel. Paraphrasing his text, she spells out its falsification of his camp stories—the reduction of real characters to stereotyped and officially approved ciphers, the addition of improbable hero and heroine and a ridiculous plot, the distortion of state persecution into a glorification of state productivity. Judged by her (and Chukovskaia's) practice, Bilibin has committed the most terrible sin: He has borne false witness in creating a work of art. Feeling a "shame so strong that time came to a stop," Nina Sergeevna pronounces her verdict to his face, dismissing him from her "brotherhood" as a coward and a liar.

The novel does not conclude with this betrayal; instead Nina Sergeevna is moved from self-righteous condemnation and willful seclusion to compassion—a pattern that informs the entire narrative. Within the "meeting place" of the forest, she now observes Bilibin from afar, feeling remorse as he struggles with his weak heart. Although she does not approach him, she relates her own extensive interior monologue of forgiveness and these words, even unuttered, represent an important emotional reconciliation: "I felt sorry for him, and I felt sorry for myself, and for everyone. 'Russia, my motherland,' I thought in someone else's words" (135). Without abandoning her goal, she begins to consider and accept its imperfect human realization — on a national scale. Rather than pass judgment and shun sinners, she entertains a hope for shared grief and shared renewal. During the train trip home from the sanatorium, she eavesdrops on her companions and suddenly imagines a collective "going under":

> The words "Russia, my motherland," came back to me. I surreptitiously began to scrutinize the other passengers.
> What sort of people were they? What went on inside? How could I glance within and make contact with them? . . . What did each of them see in their darkness when they closed their eyes to go to sleep? If only I could go under with them and see what they saw. That would really be a descent. Together with them. Getting into their memory. (138)

The novel closes at the moment of Nina Sergeevna's reentry into the normal world. The context for her return is beset with daunting obstacles: the train is met by Bilibin's wife, another decorous, well-dressed matron; the Moscow streets "look black" in comparison with her dazzling forest; at home she must face the odious Elizaveta Nikolaevna before Katya returns from school; Bilibin makes superficial small talk for their public parting. Nina Sergeevna is deposited once again in a venal, deceitful, abusive society. Yet, even confronted with these bleak impressions, her perception (and that of her reader) is enhanced now by a sense of duality. She is surfacing, in effect, from a first exploration of collective depths. While traveling to the sanatorium at the beginning of her narrative, she fiercely protected her solitude and excluded her companions; she comes home filled with the knowledge of their characters and, despite her disappointment, is now attuned to the double life that surely exists all around her.

Her reentry, in turn, coincides with her reader's reentry into the world outside the text. Intended (ultimately) for a Soviet audience, her diary-novel in its entirety proposes a first plan of action, demonstrates a new conscientious role model. In *Going Under*, a lone woman, temporarily freed from the duties of work and home, transcends the conventional limitations of the men and women around her to achieve a heroism that originates out of her unofficial widowhood and features an overwhelming sensitivity to and care for others and their hidden "truth." In spite of the threats and temptations that waylay the other characters, in lieu of spectacular feats and dramatic schemes, her heroism consists of writing and sharing the forbidden life stories she deems essential for her nation's spiritual and cultural renewal. Within her present situation she alone is qualified to perform such heroic acts, yet in the course of her journal she discovers how she might involve and help others in the same process. As she is lured out of her moral isolation into the roles of compassionate witness, intimate confidante, and surrogate parent, she begins to effect a potential cure for her society's schizophrenia. In this way Chukovskaia elaborates the female writing role first articulated in Akhmatova's *Requiem*; she develops both the creative and transformative potential of the female mourner and witness. Her heroine's experiment of "going under," then, concludes at the point of its most critical application.

Viewed in sequence, the fictional records of *Sof'ia Petrovna* and *Going Under* offer a continuous reading, from a female perspective, of gender roles and positions during the Stalinist period. In both, Chukovskaia portrays women as the characters who are left behind, burdened with a seemingly unbearable responsibility. Men, who dominate the ruling and intellectual elite, are shown to be far more absorbed in the public domain and removed from the demands of domestic life. At the same time, because of their high public profile, they are most immediately and harshly victimized by the regime, disappearing from the public eye into the unseen, "unreal" world of the prisons and labor camps. Although no longer relegated to the domestic sphere, women remain involved in both work and home; at work, they seldom are allowed or enabled to progress beyond a supportive role. Their lesser public status and greater domestic involvement shields them somewhat from the brunt of the purges but does not ensure them refuge since even their home life—their modest domestic privilege—comes under indirect Party control. When they are not arrested or deported for "criminal association" with their husbands and sons, Chukovskaia depicts women as compelled, by their own concern, to occupy the threshold of the prison world. In the somber public space of prison and police stations, they figure as the dispossessed, the unacknowledged, the inexplicable. They pursue their own victimization; they are driven to effect a link between "normal" society and the unreal world of the torture chamber. Chronicling women's experience of the threshold, both *Sof'ia Petrovna* and *Going Under* illustrate the overwhelming difficulties of this task. Even Nina Sergeevna, convinced of the state's villainy, cannot fully overcome the alienation and silence of the lines. To bridge the gap between the two worlds, she must retreat to a separate refuge where she is free from daily cares and more sheltered from the state's incessant physical and verbal siege.

While it is unclear *where* these women will find reliable sanctuary within their society, Chukovskaia does indicate *how* they can maintain these vital connections—if they dare. Both protagonists are trapped in a world which pronounces their personal feelings and allegiances criminal, which dismisses their perception and intuition as unreal. To keep faith with their loved ones (and preserve their own sanity), Sof'ia Petrovna and Nina Sergeevna must reject the official lie and believe in and articulate their private experience—an experience based, above all, on the state's persecution of their family. For both, their ability to write and read "private" recording texts ultimately predicts their own survival as compassionate, honorable human beings. Sof'ia Petrovna, overwhelmed by what she cannot (and will not) acknowledge, destroys possibly the last testimony of her beloved son. A conventional, culturally uneducated woman, she is left a paralyzed and muted object easily manipulated by the state. In contrast, Nina Sergeevna can overcome her victimization by "meeting," recording, and sharing it. Endowed with Chukovskaia's own training (and prejudices) as a "fortunate daughter," she resists the fate of becoming victim and accomplice by hesitantly putting that training to work, accepting her new acquaintances as potential members of her national spiritual family and healing their moral and psychological wounds by expressing and upholding the "truth." From different vantage points, then, both *Sof'ia Petrovna* and *Going Under* assert that for those left behind in the involuntary and primarily female position of caretaker and mourner, the only possible acts of heroism are, in a sense, communicative and re-creative. And these are works which, according to Chukovskaia's autobiographical and fictional examples, a poetically educated woman is bound and empowered to perform.

4.
NOTES ON ANNA AKHMATOVA

> I think that every religion arises out of the certainty that the dead have not left us. Is this belief in God? No, rather it is a belief in the miraculousness of human meetings, words, connections. And every history of a people begins with the resurrection of an image of the dead.
>
> *Notes on Anna Akhmatova*[1]

Just as Lidia Chukovskaia could not "not write" the novels of *Sof'ia Petrovna* and *Going Under*, so her keeping of *Notes on Anna Akhmatova* originated as an automatic, unreflecting impulse. Indeed, it would seem that her family training had groomed her most specifically for this task. In *To the Memory of Childhood* she recalls her father's explicit endorsement:

> A few decades later, when I was no longer seven, but thirty, I remember telling him that I was seeing Anna Akhmatova regularly (at one point he had introduced me to her briefly). His response was to demand anxiously:
> "I hope you understand that you ought to record every word she says?"
> I understood . . . (73)

The exchange marks a critical rite of passage in which the daughter depicts herself acknowledging and taking up her paternal legacy. Her father has raised her to pay proper homage to the artist; here she proves her ability to practice his "religion" on her own terms. With Anna Akhmatova—a woman eighteen years her senior and one of the great artists who visited her childhood home—Chukovskaia is almost inevitably (but, as it turns out, not finally) cast in her accomplished role as dutiful daughter.

Although Chukovskaia consciously did not adhere to any models in writing *Notes*, the form of her tribute reflects her father's influence as well.[2] Through his literary portraits of the great and his careful record of visits and associations with various artists (in particular, an album of drawings, inscriptions, and autographs entitled *Chukokkala*), Chukovskii manifested an awareness of history which his daughter clearly sensed and appropriated. Her *Notes*, as one reviewer remarks, "reveal[s] a mind of great sensitivity which is quick to apprehend the essence of place and moment."[3] Relating immediate impressions with a sense of their historic meaning, *Notes on Anna Akhmatova* can be characterized not only as an extension of Chukovskii's example, but as a new addition to the corpus of recorded cultural memoirs—a twentieth-century Russian counterpart to Johann Eckermann's journals of Goethe or James Boswell's *Life of Samuel Johnson*.[4]

In fact, this larger literary context better highlights the main features of her work. Chukovskaia, like Eckermann and Boswell, exhibits a devotion different in range, intensity, and significance from that of her father. Her *Notes*, conducted for almost three decades (1938–41, 1952–62) and dedicated mainly to a single artist, holds a more urgent, essential status in her creative self-perception and oeuvre. Her father wrote himself as the contemporary of many, a knowledgeable connoisseur of artistic personalities, yet Chukovskaia establishes herself as a memoirist of one great artist who seems to bear a singular resonance for her life and times.[5] Her subject proves to be utterly imposing: Chukovskaia simply replaces her ongoing diary with the record of *Notes* and construes these two very different modes of autobiographical writing—with their different positioning of the author's self—as the same project.[6] In the introduction to the first volume, she explains such drastic self-effacement as an inevitable consequence of her situation:

> Every day, every month my fragmented notes became less and less the reproduction of my own life, turning into episodes from the life of Anna Akhmatova. Within the spectral, fantastic, sad world surrounding me, she alone seemed real and not a dream, although at that time she was also writing about phantoms. She was indubitable, authentic among all those wavering uncertainties. Muffled in a spiritually deadened existence during those years, I seemed to myself ever less truly alive and my non-life (*nedozhizn'*) less deserving of description. . . . By 1940 I almost never kept notes about myself and was writing more and more frequently about Anna Andreevna. (I, 12)[7]

As Chukovskaia indicates, *Notes on Anna Akhmatova* was born of the same emotional crisis and moral imperative to record the truth that generated all her creative work during the Stalinist period. The person of Akhmatova proves to be as potent and necessary to her as her self-reflecting fictions. Written under the same perilous circumstances, *Notes* also performs a heroic feat, "a personal act of witness": that is, a laudatory inscription of the life of an officially slandered and persecuted artist.[8] In this case, however, the heroism is implicitly shared. By keeping such a journal, Chukovskaia exposed both herself and Akhmatova to considerable risk without the poet's permission. Yet she justifies this risk by inferring her duty, writing to carry out Akhmatova's mandate of naming and remembering the torture chamber (I, 10–11).

Her choice of Akhmatova as subject further links *Notes* with the "scripts" of her novels. Once again, Chukovskaia has elected to focus on a female protagonist in this horrific era, a woman who—in addition to being a great poet she cannot help but admire—has endured the same terrible experience of the prison lines. Chukovskaia's first entry, dated 10 November 1938, founds their relationship on that basis: "Yesterday I visited Anna Andreevna on business" (I, 14,15). As she explains in the added footnote, she went to Akhmatova for advice because she heard that the poet had persuaded the authorities to release her son, Lev Gumilev, and her second husband, Nikolai Punin, from prison; Chukovskaia hoped to work the same sort of miracle for her husband. Although Akhmatova's information could not prove useful (by this time Chukovskaia's husband had probably been executed), their meeting and Chukovskaia's record of it demonstrates that Akhmatova is as representative in her family tragedy as the characters of Sof'ia Petrovna and Nina Sergeevna. Akhmatova even refers openly to her threshold experience in this first entry, remarking that another woman in the lines began to cry when she heard the poet's name (I, 16). Chukovskaia has thus discovered in Akhmatova the living symbol, the realized ideal which her novels explore through fictional examples: a woman who suffers the unhinging persecution of the Stalinist regime and manages to expose and resist it through written testimony. Her *Notes*, therefore, results from this miraculous coincidence of predisposition, ability, and fate. Chukovskaia was not Akhmatova's closest friend, but—inspired by the poet's greatness and capable of transcribing her aphoristic speech—she was the one associate who could and did undertake such an extensive, monumental record.[9]

Accomplished in large part by her skill and devotion, Chukovskaia's text is also shaped by the poet's compelling presence and self-creative strategy. Indeed, the poet and her memoirist enter into a remarkable artistic collaboration, for just as Chukovskaia is sensitive to the significance of her subject, so her subject seems acutely aware of the impressions she creates. By the time Chukovskaia visited her "on business" in 1938, Akhmatova had already established herself as a major Russian poet and had evolved—through an interesting relationship with her readers and admirers—into a richly symbolic figure. Although she made her poetic debut in distinction from the then dominant Symbolist movement, her personal relationship with her work—both in and beyond the text—continued and revised the Symbolists' deliberate neo-Romantic conflation of their life and art. In her early verse, Akhmatova differed from the Symbolists chiefly in her precise, contained self-projection; rejecting a cosmic symbolic function for her poetic personae, she nevertheless informed them with certain autobiographical attitudes and details.[10] Yet with the ravages of Soviet history—the execution of her first husband, the poet Nikolai Gumilev, for counterrevolutionary activity in 1921, the multiple arrests and incarcerations of her son Lev Gumilev (1935, 1938, 1949) and third husband Nikolai Punin (1935, 1949), her defamation and censorship by the authorities as an "anachronistic, aristocratic poetess," and her state-induced poverty—Akhmatova's fate and poetic expression of that fate achieve a grandly symbolic significance in the perceptions of her friends and readers.[11] Along with Osip Mandelstam, Boris Pasternak, and Marina Tsvetaeva, Anna Akhmatova has come to be received as persecuted poet and human martyr, a great artist who lived, divined, and articulated the history of her nation. In choosing Akhmatova for her subject, therefore, Chukovskaia has tapped into a core narrative of her time and place.[12]

By almost all accounts, Akhmatova never lost sight of her significance and managed, subconsciously or voluntarily, a most remarkable synthesis of work and life. This synthesis took various forms, depending on the perceiver. The critic and essayist Lidiia Ginzburg, meeting the poet about ten years before the first entry of *Notes*, characterized her movement and intonations as ritualistic and theatrical and concluded, in a surprising equation, that Anna Andreevna resembled her "poetic method" rather than her created heroines.[13] More frequently, however, observers were struck by similarities in physical image and character type. Impressed by her queenly manners and majesty (Kornei Chukovskii, in fact, identified the latter as her most dominant feature), her visitors resorted to picturesque equivalents in their descriptions.[14] As one critic notes, they regularly compared her to religious figures—a mother superior, a novice, an anchorite (Rosslyn, 19–20).[15] From the very moment of her debut, Akhmatova's audience generally seemed obsessed with her image.[16] Her face, with its striking hook-nosed profile and deep-set eyes, and her tall slender figure as a young woman, often posed in pensive or mournful attitudes, generated a stunning array of Akhmatova artifacts and memorabilia, including portraits, photographs, sculptures, and other artwork.[17] Even with her enforced public effacement after 1921, her portrait continued to be painted, and devotees of her poetry privately assumed the task of collecting and preserving the bits and pieces of her outlawed image.[18]

The peculiar nature of the poet's reception invests Chukovskaia's *Notes* with a vitally important function. Akhmatova was one of the first Russian women to be acknowledged a great poet; she assumed the role of creator in a modernist age when many male poets, stylizing their own artistic personae, tended to encode and objectify women as icons of spiritual and/or demonic "otherness."[19] The power of these icons depended on their mystery and detachment—indeed, their silence. Akhmatova herself indicates this in a wry comment on Liubov' Blok, the wife of the Symbolist poet Aleksandr Blok and the flesh-and-blood model for the figure of "The Beautiful Lady" in his early work. Disgusted by Liubov's self-revealing memoirs, she snaps to an acquaintance: "There was only one thing she needed to do to remain the Beautiful Lady—be quiet!" (Il'ina, 112).[20] It is predictable, then, that Akhmatova—a striking female presence and a poet often equated with her female personae—was objectified early on; what is remarkable is how she managed to exploit this objectification artistically without strictly keeping silent.[21] As so many have testified, Akhmatova *cultivated* a consonance with her art, speaking as she wrote her poetry, punctuating her thoughts with meaningful silences.[22] But to exercise the power of her person, Akhmatova had to locate obliging mirrors and so control her pictorial and biographical reflections. It seems that she actively participated in her own image-making. Akhmatova "allowed" certain artists to paint her; for instance, when A. Liubimova, a young artist, begged to sketch her in 1944, Akhmatova informed her that she was the twenty-second painter to do her portrait and, during their sessions, occasionally advised the novice on pose and placement.[23] In much the same way, Akhmatova obliquely directed a written portrait. She, unlike the diminished Liubov' Blok, never managed to complete her autobiography.[24] Instead, she came to rely on others to help articulate her version of her life and generation. This dependency was especially apparent in her later years when, among an ever-growing coterie of admirers, she dispensed exceptional favor to

Amanda Haight, a young British doctoral student who could fulfill the poet's wish for a published, authorized biography.[25] Nevertheless, as one observer concludes, Akhmatova's desire for a truthful, accessible record of herself and her contemporaries worried her most of her life:

> She was not afraid that she would be forgotten, but that she would be slandered. She was afraid not only for herself, but for her friends and, above all, for the Acmeist poets Gumilev and Mandelstam, whose definitive literary fate she did not distinguish from her own.... Thus, throughout her life, from her early years on, she kept returning to detailed memories of events, relationships, and people—to all that which made up the character of the epoch as she saw it.... *Conscious of her own place in the epoch, she wanted others to talk about it and not she herself.* (Italics mine.)[26]

Akhmatova succeeded in persuading (most often indirectly) quite a few men and women to tell her story, to write down both their impressions of her and her impressions of others.[27] Although it is not clear if Akhmatova knew of Chukovskaia's project, the resulting text to a great extent reflects the female poet's oblique self-creative strategy.[28] Like Akhmatova's other scribes and portrait painters, Chukovskaia was responding to her extraordinary (and not infrequently staged) presence; recording this presence, she thus authorizes the poet's image and significance. Her *Notes*, moreover, offers perhaps the most comprehensive and affective authorization of the poet because of the extensive, important period it carefully documents (for the most part, the period of Akhmatova's greatest crises and most painful oblivion) and the complex relationship it portrays between the female poet and her skillful female helper.

Description

In fact, Chukovskaia's journal commences in 1938 at a point of terrible danger, high tension, and, as it turns out, great artistic potential in the poet's biography. Akhmatova, who (according to one astute witness) lived in "a pathos of renunciation," was ennobled by the stark deprivations of the Stalinist era.[29] The authorities, intending to diminish her in the public eye as an outmoded aristocratic lady-poet, achieved the opposite effect: They cast her literally as bereaved wife and mother.[30] Suffering the loss of both Sof'ia Petrovna and Nina Sergeevna, Akhmatova immediately identifies with and creates from her symbolically tragic position. As I noted above, the poems of her powerful cycle *Requiem* dismiss the capricious erotic personae of her earlier work and probe instead the psychological experience and various cultural resonances of grieving wife and mother. Chukovskaia, then, confirms this identification at a further and more authoritative remove. In the introduction to the first volume of *Notes*, she unveils this figure as Akhmatova's essential image:

> The fate of Akhmatova—something bigger than even her own personality—took

shape then before my eyes, fashioned from this famous and abandoned, strong and helpless woman—a statue of sorrow, orphanhood, pride, courage. I knew Akhmatova's early poems by heart since childhood, and her new verse, together with the movement of hands burning paper over an ashtray, together with a hook-nosed profile clearly etched in dark-blue shadow on the white wall of the transit prison, entered into my life with the same immutable ease as entered, long ago, the bridge, St. Isaac's, the Summer Garden, and the embankment. (I, 12)

Chukovskaia christens the entire project of *Notes* with this composite portrait of physical image and artistic text placed carefully against the signifying background of the prison. Her record aims to establish the poet as redemptive touchstone; throughout *Notes*, she re-contextualizes (and so revalues) the symbolic figure of Akhmatova, documenting her beauty as it is besieged by and then triumphs over her persecutors. Their first visit initiates this pattern. Prefacing her account with earlier enchanted recollections of the poet (Akhmatova at a poetry reading, Akhmatova strolling down a lovely pathway to the sea), Chukovskaia relates an unexpectedly grim approach as she rediscovers her subject in a shabby room of a communal apartment—beyond a foyer with torn wallpaper and a kitchen hung with wet laundry. She is admitted by a woman with soapy hands; laundress and laundry forecast the poet's lowly estate. Akhmatova's private room shows little improvement:

> The general look of the room is one of neglect, mess. By the stove is a chair without a leg, stripped, with springs sticking up out of it. The floor is not swept. The lovely things—a carved table, a mirror in a smooth bronze frame, folk paintings on the walls—do not beautify, but, on the contrary, emphasize the shabbiness even more.
> The one thing that is really lovely is the window onto the garden and a tree looking straight through the window. Black branches.
> And she herself, of course. (I, 16)

The interior is striking in its unintentional allegory: Random "lovely things"—including the poet herself—are strewn carelessly about a dirty, desolate space. Given their function and beauty, the artifacts within might all be totems of Akhmatova's life and work; the room can be read as her present situation under the regime. The lone tree in the window portends a more hopeful connection, the presence of nature still visible in her decimated private world.

Akhmatova's words, recorded verbatim by Chukovskaia, intensify this tragic first impression. The poet acknowledges her state of abandonment and resignation, wondering if she should bother to hang pictures on the walls, explaining her recent separation from Punin (she is still living in a room of their once shared apartment), claiming her serious, possibly terminal illness as the "one good thing" in her life. She explicitly compares her situation with the more dramatic fates of other Stalinist victims; she dares to announce (and Chukovskaia dares to record) that the poet Kniazev is dead and the critic Sviatopolk-Mirskii has gone begging. (Both men were arrested in 1937 and perished in labor camps.) By image and word Akhmatova is framed here as a tragic figure—a beautiful woman, a creative genius—who is outcast, persecuted, and despairing within the context of Stalinism. Chukovskaia's first entry maps the extent of her persecution, the violation of her body and private domain.[31]

Chukovskaia primarily contextualizes Akhmatova within their domestic spheres and modes of interaction. The poet is portrayed in her own poor room, Chukovskaia's apartment, or, once Chukovskaia has moved to Moscow, at the homes of other obliging friends. At home her presence is almost always juxtaposed with her shabby surroundings, which are sometimes worsened by the evident hostility of her neighbors (including Punin and his family), and sometimes ameliorated by friendly visitors (including, in the 1938–41 period, her companion Vladimir Garshin). In the second volume of *Notes*, she lives a nomadic existence, coping with the cramped quarters her Moscow hosts can spare her.[32] When Chukovskaia does depict Akhmatova in transit between these private residences, she reveals the poet at her weakest. Not only does Akhmatova go unrecognized among her people, but she proves almost incapable of functioning there on her own; as it turns out, she "is afraid of the streets" (I, 29) and depends on an escort to help her cross them.[33]

Over the course of *Notes*, then, Akhmatova emerges as a forceful presence, a real-life heroine, within the milder purgatory of domestic interiors and among the sustaining company of friends. Her actual battles, however, seem to be waged on the even smaller scale of her own person. These derive from a variety of specific causes—from poverty and poor physical and mental health—but, as Chukovskaia tends to diagnose them, they are all symptomatic of the poet's one overwhelming battle with Stalinism. Chukovskaia generally begins her visit-entries with a quick imprint of the poet's image, what amounts to a kind of report from the front. She pays scrupulous attention to Akhmatova's person, dress, and pose. Here she identifies the signs of attack—shabby clothes, recumbent posture (a frequent symptom of illness), poor coloring, an aged look, or, most interesting, an indistinctness of feature. An early entry, for example, contrasts Akhmatova's stately beauty with "an old coat, a faded, flattened hat, and coarse stockings" (I, 18); subsequent entries note her "yellowed, dry face" and her figure lying on the couch beneath a rough blanket (I, 27, 28, 44, 45). Through these regular reports, Chukovskaia documents the poet's daily, homely martyrdom.

At other points, she testifies to Akhmatova's voluntary triumph over her persecution. She cites the poet's claim that she can always "look as [she] wishes—like a beauty or a hag" (I, 39). As if in support, she subsequently witnesses Akhmatova's astonishing metamorphosis from "indistinctness" into an elegant, majestic figure (I, 121–26). She is alert to any efforts on Akhmatova's part to maintain her beauty, welcoming a new dress, a string of pearls, a touch of lipstick or rouge as if these were small victories, a partial restoration of her idol to rightful glory. And Chukovskaia marvels, over and over again, at the constancy of Akhmatova's icon, the relief of her features on the threatening, dehumanizing backgrounds of the prison lines (I, 40) or the dirty wall of a hospital room (II, 121). Thus, after a ten-year hiatus (to Chukovskaia, an inexplicable break in their relationship) she still discerns the former Akhmatova in the heavy, graying woman before her:

> It's a strange thing: listening to her speech, I recognized her again. Her former appearance. Not only the intonations or the angry turn of the shoulders, or words. I did not even notice at what instant her whole former familiar look came back to me. It was as if ten years had not elapsed and she, it turns out, had not changed at all. The hook nose, the stateliness, the bangs, the silence. (II, 2)

For Chukovskaia, this immutable image becomes fixed, in its fashion, as an historical landmark. Like other chroniclers of the poet, she indulges in pictorial comparisons, discovering Akhmatova's reflection in Russian portraits of legendary Russian women. For instance, as the poet expounds on Stalin's evil (this in the spring of 1956), she is said to resemble Repin's painting of Peter the Great's thwarted half-sister, Tsaritsa Sof'ia—an angry, indignant, imposing figure (II, 136). Donning a black kerchief, Akhmatova is instantly transformed into a humble pilgrim or, recreating Surikov's fiery portrait, the Old Believer Boiarina Morozova: "It was as if [her] vague bulkiness were no more and immediately form (that is, essence) shone through: race, Russianness" (II, 448). On the infrequent occasions when Chukovskaia persuades her to venture beyond the interior—to stroll along the streets of Leningrad or to make a day trip to the old Muscovite town of Zagorsk—she apprehends the poet's special affinity with her Russian surroundings, her almost physical bond to place and history. Remembering the trip to Zagorsk, Chukovskaia declares that Akhmatova herself "was better than all the architectural wonders" and remarks on her sure, solemn grace framed within one of the local churches (II, 17). Through these sorts of comparisons and settings, filtered through Chukovskaia's constant awe, Akhmatova's figure achieves a kind of "monumentality"; in contrast to her official public reputation during those years, the privately kept *Notes* asserts her status as national poet, even national emblem. Chukovskaia's method is perhaps most impassioned in her wartime entries, when the outside threat to the Soviet Union seems to materialize Akhmatova's deep connections with nation and people. Hearing of Akhmatova's evacuation from a besieged Leningrad to Central Asia, Chukovskaia automatically links poet and native landscape: "Akhmatova in Chistopol! That is just as inconceivable as the Admiralty Spire or the Arch of the General Staff in Chistopol!" (I, 210). When the poet is en route to Tashkent, Chukovskaia observes in her a mirror image of her suffering compatriots:

> At the stations, on the platforms, side by side, women, children, bundles. Eyes, eyes.... When Anna Andreevna looks at these children and women, her face begins in some way to resemble their faces. A peasant woman, a refugee.... Watching them, she falls silent. (I, 216)

In this way, Chukovskaia's description of the poet builds an intricate synthesis of private experience and public significance, frail humanity and enduring cultural value. By contextualizing her image in the everyday, Chukovskaia both validates Akhmatova's position as victim and proves her national status. Her testimony refutes the official representation of the poet's narrow upper-class orientation and any mistaking of Akhmatova's "privilege" as a writer. Akhmatova visibly, tangibly suffers the fate of many Stalinist victims and qualifies, in this sense, as a truly (and not officially) *representative* figure for her time. Yet Akhmatova, in Chukovskaia's awed account, is never cast as a mere everywoman; her image is informed and empowered by what Chukovskaia deems to be the transcendent qualities of her work and being. Her icon not only remains intact through persecution, ill health, and old age, but increasingly manifests a national essence, assumes a national importance. The *Notes*, then, registers the immense power of her symbolic duality—her position as both victimized woman and great Russian female poet. At the same time it is interesting that this "nationalization" of her image and role conveniently releases Akhmatova from the social and cultural confines of her gender. Rather than question assumptions about women's "second-rate" artistry, Chukovskaia projects Akhmatova as a magnificent anomaly, a female poet who achieves the position of national martyr and national bard and so transcends the demeaning reputation of being a "poet for women" or, worse, a "poetess."[34]

Transcription

The transcription of Akhmatova's words, as we have already seen, complements her description. Chukovskaia indicates repeatedly that for her the poet is inseparable from her voice and speech, and she receives the whole person of Akhmatova as living symbol and (almost) divine oracle. Writing down their dialogue, she tends to paraphrase or summarize her own comments, and to yield place of importance to the poet's quoted remarks. The topics of their conversations are most often set by Akhmatova; these range from reminiscences of her past (generally her early years as a poet) to a discussion of current events (mainly after Stalin's death). But most of all, the two women focus in some way on literature. Typically they begin from a present reference—a literary work they happen to be reading or a book they rediscover in their rooms. A volume of Pushkin lying on Chukovskaia's table, for example, elicits Akhmatova's spontaneous commentary on his short story, "The Queen of Spades"; their discussion of Pushkin's prose then leads them to Tolstoi and Akhmatova's irritated outburst on *Anna Karenina* (I, 22–23). Their first meeting after a ten-year absence is filled with the poet's "lectures" on Gogol', Tolstoi, and Dostoevskii (II, 3–5), and although Akhmatova promises not to repeat this performance, *Notes* continues to feature her comments and speeches on other writers and to underscore both women's preoccupation with the history, conduct, and meaning of literature.

In part, the emphasis on literature in *Notes* is pragmatically motivated. As Chukovskaia explains in her preface, their "literary conversations moved into the foreground" because she dared not transcribe their talk about the torture chamber—their naming of its architects and actions (I, 11). Yet this emphasis, unbalanced by a stated concern for families and friends, seems neither false nor simply compensatory.[35] After all, both women were writers by profession and vocation; as an editor and a critic, Chukovskaia was especially involved in a great many aspects of literary production. Moreover, on the evidence of *Notes* (and given our knowledge of Chukovskaia's training), literature afforded both women an unfailing source of emotional and spiritual sustenance. From Chukovskaia's perspective, their exchange of literary likes and dislikes served as the most effective way of getting acquainted, of appreciating the personality of another (particularly that of a great artist). In the early years, she refuses to debate with Akhmatova's provocative opinions because she is more interested in listening; she is delighted, in turn, when their literary tastes coincide (I, 25). To a somewhat less exuberant degree, Akhmatova finds the same use for literature, remarking at the end of one visit: "What a good talk we had today—heart-to-heart. And it is all literature and literature" (II, 25). Although Akhmatova is not as absolute as Chukovskaia in her demands on the person and work of the artist,[36] she does presume a certain ethical (if not explicitly stated) connection between the two and observes this connection in her reading and writing.[37] Thus, both women's engagement with literature is shown to be deeply rooted in their sense of morality and concern for the lives and values of others.[38]

Indeed, within the censored context of Stalinism, discussing and quoting literature becomes for them the one possible way of telling the truth and affirming certain fundamental cultural and moral values. Their conversations restore a crucial historical continuum on an intimate scale. Encouraged by her audience of one, Akhmatova is offering up secret treasure—those early decades of twentieth-century Russian culture severely censored under Stalin.[39] Juxtaposed with the Stalinist cultural establishment—which dictated a uniform evaluation of literature according to political criteria—the record of *Notes* assesses literature through the private dialogue of two women who subscribe to a modernist aesthetics joined with the ethics of the pre-revolutionary (and non-terrorist) Russian intelligentsia. While for them literature is surely bound to external reality and committed to preserving the truth, both Akhmatova and Chukovskaia insist on and cherish its aesthetic achievement, its success as art, as an equal value.

Instead of rendering their literary conversations a poor substitute, then, Chukovskaia's self-censorship actually shapes an appropriate reading of her text. Both volumes, edited and issued after Akhmatova's death, preserve a structure that demonstrates the double value of these conversations—as a revelation in themselves and (especially in the first volume) a cryptic response to an inexpressible reality.[40] The body of the text appears as it was kept; even with the relaxed censorship of the post-1953 entries, Chukovskaia saves certain information for appended footnotes and endnotes. Perhaps because of the harsh circumstances under which it was written, her principles of organization in the first volume are more clear-cut. She includes "only the most essential information" in the asterisked footnotes, adds a section on specific unnamed victims of the torture chamber—Akhmatova's son and her husband—and offers more copious background information in detailed endnotes. In comparison, the second volume seems less urgent and furtive, outfitted with more extensive footnotes and endnotes and omitting any separate biographical section.[41] Yet in both volumes the reader is, in a sense, signaled to read the text two or three times. In fact, the structure of the text not only mirrors the layers of existence and expression in which Akhmatova and Chukovskaia were forced to abide, but exposes the double texture of the work itself—the art of the journal and the scholarship of its presentation. Even without its explanatory apparatus, the journal can be savored as a marvelous re-creative literary achievement. The additional "notes" fulfill Chukovskaia's self-imposed obligations as historian and conscientious editor.

Above all, the transcription and presentation of these literary conversations highlight the most important story and central value in Chukovskaia's text: the making, receiving, and maintenance of Akhmatova's poetry. From their very first meeting, Chukovskaia emphasizes the power of these texts. Recounting her first journey home, she demonstrates just how much she has been moved by Akhmatova's recitation:

> I left her home late. I was walking in the dark, remembering verses. I had to remember them right away, from beginning to end, because already I could not be parted from them for an instant. In those places where my memory slipped, I put in my own words to preserve the rhythm—and in response somewhere in the depths of my memory these unsuitable words lured out her real ones. I remembered everything, word for word. But on the other hand, as I was washing up and undressing for bed, I could not remember one step of my walk home. How did I get through the Zanimatel'naia nauka building? How did I cross Nevskii?
> I was walking like a sleepwalker, led by verses instead of the moon, and the world did not exist. (I, 17)

Here, in lieu of the forest of *Going Under* or her sublime childhood synthesis of poetry, father, and nature, Chukovskaia finds herself displaced from a grim reality into the world of the text. Yet, as subsequent episodes show, her poetic journey comprises more catharsis than escape. Akhmatova's verses from the nightmare years of the 1930s and 1940s transport Chukovskaia with their art even as they express her pain. Many years later, when Chukovskaia asks the poet to recite these verses, she fears that she will burst out sobbing because once more she stands "face to face with all that [she] has lived through" (II, 77). She confesses the most telling instance of this effect in December 1939, when she finally learns that her husband has been executed. She records in the *Notes* the experience of those first dreadful days—her confusion, numbness, and physical pain; the futile efforts of her friends to console her; her visits with Akhmatova. On 14 December she responds to one of Akhmatova's summons and reveals her news only at the end of her visit; on 15 December Akhmatova herself visits Chukovskaia and there, at the grieving woman's request, recites her poetry and brings about a first powerful sensation of release: "And again out of this infusion of grief I felt such happiness that I did not have strength to bear it. I understand Boris Leonidovich [Pasternak]: if this exists, then one can die" (I, 59).

Chukovskaia's journal narrative thus bears witness to the incredible therapeutic power of Akhmatova's poetry. The structure of *Notes*, in turn, puts the poetry itself on display. Both volumes contain, in the first place after the journal, an appendix of "those [poems] without which it would be difficult to understand my notes." Having read through the story of its making, of its life and effect in context, we are enjoined to experience the art itself—to receive the key revelation of Chukovskaia's experience and historical moment. Chukovskaia's inclusion of the poetry might well have been an editorial (and of course personal) decision, a conscientious attempt to provide the reader with all the materials relevant to her text. But it is significant that this structuring of *Notes*, like that of *Going Under*, corresponds to the artistic and ontological strategies of *The Master and Margarita* and *Doctor Zhivago*. Here, too, the author elects to relate the story of the artist and his or her text and also reproduces that text in full, thereby ensuring its survival and suggesting its transcendent value.

Yet *Notes* delineates, entry by entry, an important difference in the story of the text's creation. In *The Master and Margarita* and *Doctor Zhivago*, the female helpers care for the person of the artist and prove incapable of saving the manuscript; the text survives only through a kind of miraculous intervention. Recording the daily intercourse between creator and helper, *Notes on Anna Akhmatova* focuses chiefly on the *present* life of these texts and chronicles the *human* maintenance of this life. Furthermore, Chukovskaia's text shows that this maintenance is, from beginning to end, a truly collective effort, a task performed by poet and helper alike.

Relationship

The different story of the text in *Notes*, therefore, stems in part from the worldly limitations of nonfiction (supernatural aid is precluded), but mainly from the different relationship that obtains between the two protagonists. I have already remarked on Chukovskaia's characteristic veneration for Akhmatova as a great poet and symbolic figure. In comparison with her subject, she readily demotes herself to "a nothing, a zero" (II, 468). Yet Chukovskaia admits and ministers to another incarnation of the poet. She regularly discerns in Akhmatova a "strange combination of helplessness and haughtiness" (*"strannaia smes' bespomoshchnosti i nadmennosti"*), a paradox that Vladimir Garshin, the poet's one-time companion, claimed as her distinguishing characteristic (II, 81). Persecuted by the regime, Akhmatova necessarily survives by depending on others; embracing a "pathos of renunciation," she at times seems to choose this dependency. In the early days of their acquaintance, Chukovskaia takes special note of her self-neglect. On their first stroll (and for several weeks thereafter), she discovers that Akhmatova is limping because of a broken heel (I, 21, 24). She remarks on the woman's torn, threadbare clothing (I, 30), and she learns that she needs to bring her food because the poet rarely cares to fend for herself (I, 27, 30). The final impressions of her 29 July 1939 entry are representative:

> Then everything followed the usual pattern: I escort her home, there are drunks on the street, at the intersection she grabs me by the sleeve and is afraid to take a step. The entryway and infernal darkness on the stairs.
> "I only eat now when Ol'ga Nikolaevna [Vysotskaia] feeds me," said Anna Andreevna. "She forces me somehow." (I, 34)

Chukovskaia soon learns to anticipate her helplessness and to accommodate Akhmatova's invariably urgent calls—buying her food, visiting her sickbed, listening to her frustrated accounts of tangling with the bureaucracy over money, housing, or publication. Even when she is overwhelmed with responsibilities and herself seriously ill, Chukovskaia does not hesitate to serve.[42] She rarely exhibits any irritation over Akhmatova's presumption and the consequent inconvenience for her own life and work; the poet's demands and crises are primary.[43] When Chukovskaia once admits Akhmatova's rude behavior, she does not complain on her own behalf (except for the unpleasant duty she has assumed in recording it), but faults the poet for sinning against her own image: "The great woman did not conduct herself in a great manner.... If you are Akhmatova, then be great every minute, in everything, everywhere" (II, 420). She interprets the break in their friendship (beginning in autumn 1942 and extending to the summer of 1952) in a similar way. When Akhmatova begins to insult her openly and forces her to retreat, Chukovskaia is most pained by her own absence of guilt; it is much harder for her to accept that Akhmatova believes in false rumors about her: "I was vitally concerned that I, not she, turn out to be the guilty one: after all, my complete faith in her absolute nobility was my best feature" (II, xvii).[44]

Given Chukovskaia's veneration for the poet (as artist and exemplar), their relationship might be classified as that of disciple and "master," yet in its exchange of demands and services, its display of emotional and even physical dependency, it also bears a strong familial resonance. It would be tempting to cast Akhmatova and Chukovskaia as mother and daughter; certainly Chukovskaia has proved herself in the latter role. But their parts are not so clearly drawn. In age and attitude, Chukovskaia might seem to play the poet's surrogate daughter, yet Akhmatova's often childlike helplessness (even before she has reached a childish old age), compels Chukovskaia and others to play mother as well—for example, to agonize over her welfare and to make sure that she is housed and fed.[45] Once Chukovskaia has moved to Moscow, she has the opportunity to observe this relationship from the outside: Akhmatova, visiting from Leningrad, is the frequent guest of the actress Nina Antonovna Ol'shanskaia, and she clearly thrives under her hostess's mothering care.[46]

Throughout their relationship Akhmatova reciprocates these maternal gestures.[47] I have already mentioned her "chance" visit to Chukovskaia the day after she learns of her widowhood. Akhmatova shows great solicitude for her admirer-friend (particularly during Chukovskaia's ordeal in the purges), and Chukovskaia, never one to ask outright for help, is moved by the poet's capacity to understand and console: "I still don't know: is she simply good by nature, or is it her noble mind, her highly developed aesthetic taste which forces her to do good deeds?" (I, 33) Akhmatova remembers Chukovskaia's birthday when she herself forgets it (II, xvi); she visits and cares for Chukovskaia when the latter is ill. Indeed, the poet announces her scorn for those who refuse sickbed duties, insisting that "if a person wants to help another, wants to strongly and unselfishly, then he can always manage" (I, 131). Akhmatova, in short, can do for others what she neglects to do for herself: She can nourish, nurse, comfort (I, 46). At certain points in the first volume she even appears in the role of surrogate mother to the two boys of her neighbor, Tania Smirnova. Compared with this uneducated and sometimes abusive woman, Akhmatova functions as a model parent, a realized Nina Sergeevna who buys sweets for the boys, reads to them, and attempts to intervene when their mother beats them. Impressed by her tenderness, Chukovskaia predictably casts Akhmatova as the epitome of motherhood, transforming her, as she holds the younger boy in her arms, into a statue of the Madonna (I, 150–51).

In contrast to the protagonists in *The Master and Margarita* and *Doctor Zhivago*, therefore, the poet and her disciple in *Notes* share the roles of helpless victim and facilitating helper; in familial terms they combine the responses of mother and daughter. However unconventional their upbringing and experience may have been, these two women are shown to rely on certain traditional female gestures in their relationship—acts of domestic service, expressions of maternal solicitude. In this sense, although Akhmatova at times reincarnates the helpless passivity of the Master and Zhivago, she manifests a consistent capacity for emotional and domestic support, for pragmatic good deeds. And Chukovskaia, despite her voluntary self-effacement, emerges as a powerful (if not artistically equal) partner, a helper whose mentality and behavior are reciprocated and specifically authorized by the creator herself.[48]

Their relationship achieves a greater equality, too, because it revises another traditional family bond—that of husband and wife. Akhmatova's and Chukovskaia's friendship was platonic; we find no repetition here of the love affairs in Bulgakov's and Pasternak's novels. Akhmatova entered other liaisons after her break with Punin, but for much of this period she lived alone and clearly depended on the ministrations of women to survive. While Chukovskaia most frequently characterizes the poet's dependency as childlike, Akhmatova, as transcribed, indicates that her helplessness may also be a subversive strategy, a voluntary rejection of the duties a good "wife" is supposed to perform. Reviewing her past marriage to Punin, she implies that it foundered because she could not accommodate that traditional role:

> "Nikolai Nikolaevich [Punin] has now found a new reason to be offended with me: why, when we lived together, did I not write, and now write a great deal? For six years I could not write. The whole situation oppressed me—more than any grief. Now I finally understand why: for Nikolai Nikolaevich the ideal wife was always Anna Evgen'ievna: she works, receives 400 rubles a month salary, and is an

excellent housekeeper. And he persistently laid me on that Procrustean bed, and I am neither a housekeeper nor a breadwinner. . . ." (I, 80)

For Akhmatova, it seems, the attempt to be Punin's "ideal wife" directly threatens her ability to write poetry. It is no accident that her conclusion echoes the attitude of Nina Sergeevna, Chukovskaia's alter ego in *Going Under*; both women assert the cultural devaluation, even the corruption, in the concept of the grasping wife. Akhmatova's sharp judgments reveal not only her traditional prejudice, but also her precarious hold as a "great" female poet. She can manipulate some traditional gender constructs to her advantage (the objectification of the female image, the behavior of the great lady), but there are other roles she must vehemently resist. She is fierce about the hazard of being or having a wife for artists in general. In the heat of reading about one writer's family life (Dostoevskii's), she even professes that she "always hated the wives of great people" (II, 284). Her generalization implies some astounding assumptions: that all great people are men and that their wives are all grasping and destructive.[49]

Akhmatova detects one specific instance of this danger close at hand—in the domestic situation of her fellow poet and survivor, Boris Pasternak. Despite their mutual admiration, the relationship between these two poets, from Akhmatova's perspective, is fraught with irritation and occasional injury. Pasternak periodically reveals a kind of dismissive ignorance of her work; he suffers little of the material hardship that burdens her existence; at his second wife's bidding, he sometimes avoids receiving her altogether. Chukovskaia, caught between two poetic idols, finds Akhmatova's irritation perhaps the bitterest pill to swallow.[50] Akhmatova may well have envied Pasternak's less troubled life, but her anger is fundamentally directed at his domestic arrangements—that is, at the "wives" to whom he had the weakness to submit. Even before he meets his mistress, Ol'ga Ivinskaia, Akhmatova uncovers a pattern of seduction and material entrapment in his marriage to Zinaida Nikolaevna Neigauz. Chukovskaia quotes the poet's long diatribe in her entry for 6 May 1940:

> He is perishing at home. . . . He is no longer writing his own verse because he is translating others'—nothing really destroys your own verse so much as translation. . . . But Boris Leonidovich's main misfortune is something else: his home. . . . Zina fools with cards all day, Lenichka (Pasternak's son) is neglected. . . . Everyone saw from the very beginning that she is rude and vulgar, but he did not see, he was blinded by love. Since there was decidedly nothing to adore, he adored the fact that she scrubs her own floors. . . . And can one really work in such a situation? Near such vulgarity? Poverty has never bothered anyone yet. Grief either. Rembrandt painted all of his best things in the last two years of his life after everyone had died: his wife, son, mother. No, grief does not interfere with work. But such a Zina can destroy everything. (I, 92–93)

Akhmatova's attack is defensive in aim. Inverting the practice of so many male modernist poets, she exposes the base (and to her unworthy) source of Pasternak's feminine ideal, deflating his characteristic celebration of a woman at her domestic chores. (From her evidence we see that Pasternak was enthralled by Zina's housekeeping long before he wrote tributes to Lara's laundering and ironing in *Zhivago*.) Although she criticizes the poet for his blindness and weakness (he allows the vulgar Zina to make a home for him), she locates the greatest evil in "such a Zina" who, as the epitome of the limited and limiting wife, commits the greatest sin of all: Her presence, her imposition of a materialistic value system on the household, inhibits the making of great art.

Akhmatova's prophecy certainly proved incorrect; Pasternak both suffered and benefited from the presence of his "wives" and, in any event, did not stop writing. But her protest on his behalf discloses an important clue to her own necessary creative environment. The presence of the "wife" naturally holds far more danger for Akhmatova than for Pasternak. As one of the few first-ranked female poets, she needed to distinguish herself from the "lesser" wives of her male artistic peers. Being or being like a wife (a role which in her mind requires, at best, a self-effacing devotion to one's husband and, at worst, an obsession with material welfare) would involve a reduction of her cultural value, a limitation of her artistic resources (her time and energy and focus), her creative death.[51] Therefore, Akhmatova offers the paradigm of the surviving Rembrandt as superior to that of Pasternak's conventional marriage. In lieu of a husband-wife relationship, she herself chooses to improvise a domestic life founded on her own bereavement and abandonment and supported by a circle of friends who are very often themselves bereaved wives and mothers and, at the same time, devoted to the supreme value of art. In effect, as we discover in the example of Chukovskaia, the poet allows other women to perform certain tasks for her that a wife might perform, yet they never fully assume (and are never diminished by) that role.

Condemning certain "wives," Akhmatova (with Chukovskaia's help) nevertheless asserts the general worth of women's response and behavior in a different sort of application. The cryptic testimony of *Notes* also shows women to be most involved in caring for the absent victims in Stalinist society. It is revealing that Chukovskaia explains this distinction in statistical terms—there are more men than women in prison and so more women in the lines—whereas Akhmatova, the self-professed hater of "great men's wives," implies female superiority: "'You know, over the last two years I have started to think badly of men. You have noticed that there are almost no men *there*. . . .'" (I, 23–24). As in the case of Pasternak, the poet boldly states deductions about gender roles and capacities which her helper reports but is reluctant to endorse.[52] Yet, whatever her interpretation of this phenomenon, Chukovskaia conscientiously records the fact of women's greater effort—particularly when Akhmatova must care for her imprisoned son Lev. With the striking exception of Kolia Davidenkov, Lev's friend and peer, the poet's helpers in this endeavor are women—Aleksandra Liubarskaia, Ol'ga Vysotskaia, Vera Anikieva, Chukovskaia herself. They assist her in locating and gathering clothes to send to Lev; they accompany her in the prison lines; they check up on her after her various ordeals. Here, for the first time in her oeuvre, Chukovskaia testifies to the development of an informal, clandestine, primarily female network of support. Her *Notes* documents its existence and conveys its utter importance. Akhmatova perhaps best expresses its value when, after one joint visit to the prison, she tells Chukovskaia: "'I do not thank you. There are no thanks for this'" (I, 39).

Throughout her *Notes*, Chukovskaia regularly reports on the functioning of this network—this banding together of a few individuals in order to withstand or, in some instances, to try to influence the machinations of government bureaucracy. Their causes range from obtaining prison or camp release for relatives and friends to locating jobs and apartments for those who have been politically stigmatized and dispossessed. Both poet and helper equally commit themselves to these actions; their commitment is not explained or analyzed, but represented as a given. In much the same way, but to a far more detailed extent, these women spontaneously form another benevolent, restorative network—as the voluntary caretakers of artistic texts. Focusing on this network, I now return to the central story of *Notes*, what comprises—in contrast to the fragmented, revelatory tales of the Master's novel and Zhivago's poems—a kind of biography of an unofficial work of art generated under Stalinist conditions.

Creative relationship

The creative relationship of Akhmatova and Chukovskaia emerges as a natural extension of their daily interaction. In fact, as we shall see, the two women foster the whole creative process—the birth and maintenance of Akhmatova's texts—as a kind of natural life, the creation of another being. The comparison of artistic creation with human birth has long been commonplace in literature, but the record of *Notes* extends and contextualizes this comparison in a unique way. Because the texts "born" in *Notes* are, in many cases, unofficial and unpublishable, they must somehow be "kept alive" privately. Even those poems which are nominally accepted for publication are often subject to officially sanctioned editorial abuse—to rearrangement, censorship, complete erasure. Rather than entrust the existence of the text to the public official-commercial enterprise of Soviet publishing, Akhmatova and Chukovskaia personally undertake its preservation in their homes or, in the rare case of a text that is to be published, they attempt to prepare (to fortify) it as much as possible before they relinquish it to the editorial bureaucracy. In their assumption and interpretation of this responsibility, these women maintain an almost constant involvement with the text in all its stages of development. And this involvement, painstakingly recorded in *Notes*, evokes their gender assignments, their social conditioning as female caretakers of the domestic domain. Without insisting on an absolute correspondence, I suggest that their engagement with Akhmatova's poetic texts resembles their respective relationships with human dependents, reflecting much the same immediate and pragmatic caretaking, emotional attachment, and long-term commitment. Even their collaboration reinforces this similarity, because, as I have just shown, Akhmatova's care for Lev often results from a collective effort.[53]

Indeed, their collaboration is fortunate since Chukovskaia, of the two, proves more attentive to detail. She is truly responsible for the "biography" and much of the caretaking of Akhmatova's work. During the 1938–1941 period, when Akhmatova is composing the poems of the *Requiem* cycle, Chukovskaia is frequently present from the near-inception of the text. (In one entry she notes how their silence together is broken by Akhmatova's whispering: "it seems that this was some line of verse" [I, 159].) Although Chukovskaia is thrilled and moved by each new poem, she observes no such exhilaration in the artist herself. In place of the romantically exalted poet, Chukovskaia most often depicts a woman made exhausted, even ill, by her creative effort. She presumes to connect the poet's human weakness with artistic sacrifice, understanding the cause of Akhmatova's "jaundice, dishevelment and insomnia" when she hears her recite a new work (I, 91). In contrast to the diagnosis of Vladimir Garshin, who treats his lover's symptoms as evidence of "neurasthenia," Chukovskaia transcribes Akhmatova's self-diagnosis—that although she cannot "walk or sleep or eat," she can and must write—and justifies the poet's sacrifice with her own interpretation:

> but one can ask: if every night a person performs the most necessary and most difficult task in the world and is afterwards naturally depressed and tormented—why must this condition be described as "unable to fight [her] neurasthenia"? (I, 67)

Discerning a "necessary and difficult task" and a "natural" physical reaction, Chukovskaia transforms Akhmatova's act of creating from neurotic symptom into a normal, positive physical process perhaps most akin (given its necessity, difficulty, and physical stress) to the birth of a child. She implies that she and Akhmatova are driven by the same sort of creative impulse—a sense of compelling emotional, moral, even physical obligation. In this way, both poet and disciple would seem to evince the same creative response to their context; with Akhmatova, however, Chukovskaia feels free to accentuate its nobility.

The art Akhmatova "necessarily" creates out of this period is not only painful to deliver but also terribly dangerous to maintain. If the naming of their context is construed as subversive by the authorities, then each poetic text—amply equipped to inform and affect—enters their world as a full-fledged act of treason, the daring exercise of what Chukovskaia terms "a rival power" (*"sopernichaiushchaia vlast'"*) (II, xi). Akhmatova and Chukovskaia are not foolhardy heroines; the enormous drama of *Notes* obtains in the tension between their admitted fear (mainly for the others who depend on them) and their courage to act. Chukovskaia respectfully conveys Akhmatova's fear, relating what others dismiss as her paranoid delusions. Feeling herself under surveillance during the Terror and long after Stalin's death, the poet periodically detects evidence of police searches among her things—a carefully placed hair taken from her notebook (I, 160) or torn books and missing texts (II, 349). She is wary of unknown callers; at one point she insists (in spite of the assurances of Chukovskaia and Lidiia Ginzburg) that a visiting poet must be an informer (I, 56). Akhmatova's accuracy is less important than the fact of her constant fear, her heightened sensitivity—shared with Chukovskaia—to their dangerous circumstances.

Acutely aware of this environment, then, Akhmatova and Chukovskaia observe special precautions from the very moment of the text's delivery. In some critical cases, they devise for it a different "life" which they support in a repeated ritual. Chukovskaia poignantly documents their labors in the preface to the first volume:

> Anna Andreevna, visiting me, read me verses from *Requiem* in a whisper, but at her own place in Fontannyi Dom she could not even bring herself to whisper; suddenly, in the middle of a conversation, she would fall silent and directing me to the ceiling and walls with her eyes, she took a piece of paper and pencil; then she loudly said something very mundane: "Would you like some tea?" or "You're very tan," then quickly scribbled over the paper and handed it to me. I would read the verses and, having memorized them, would return them silently to her. "Autumn came so early this year," Anna Andreevna would say loudly and, striking a match, she burned the paper over an ashtray.
> This was a ritual: hands, match, ashtray—a beautiful and mournful ritual. (I, 11–12)

Performed most often in the years of the Terror, this ritual radically alters the very concept of the text, reconstitutes the very act of creating. In her own case (and in the reflective fiction of *Going Under*), Chukovskaia allows for the possibility of a manuscript, a carefully concealed record. But with Akhmatova's work they must resort to even more secretive methods of safekeeping. The inscription of the text represents only the first stage—as a furtive act of silent communication. The text next undergoes the de-materialization I described in the first chapter and is reincarnated in oral form. The first volume of *Notes* conveys this painstaking subterfuge—marking the fact of Akhmatova's "recitations" and even the "cozy" crackling of the woodstove (I, 68) (with its implication of her burned texts), but naming the actual poems only in the uncensored footnotes and reproducing the texts themselves in the appendix.

Although, as we shall see, not all of Akhmatova's poems are preserved in this way, her most "subversive" texts were long sheltered in individual human memories. As late as May 1962, Akhmatova restricts herself to checking Chukovskaia's recitation while they sit on a secluded park bench; she cannot resolve to write her poems down. In these relatively benign years, Chukovskaia dares to refer openly to their ritual and even analyzes their fear of naming names and writing down all the facts, but she still cannot report the seven other people who have memorized the poems of *Requiem* (II, 411–414).[54] By this time their cautiousness has become an indelible habit; their memories, exercised so desperately in that savage period, simply cannot entrust to paper what was so crucial to conceal.[55]

Thus, for many years these texts have no separate physical existence, no definition as written artifacts. Recited and memorized, they cannot be classified strictly as oral poetry, because their creator and audience are conscious of their written form. Yet, in a sense, their "unwritten" existence grants them the sort of undifferentiated power Chukovskaia ascribed to poetry in early childhood; like the "unseen" poems of Nekrasov, these spoken texts regain the status of natural phenomenon. Moreover, existing in human memory, they are virtually incorporated into the psyche of their "readers." By reembodying the text, Chukovskaia enters into an intimate, immediate relationship with it; it functions as an essential resource in her conscious and subconscious thought—very much like a memorized prayer. And naturally enough, as Akhmatova and Chukovskaia become accustomed to performing this ritual, the resulting text seems more and more a collective creation, a work of art truly born of two "parents." Akhmatova marvels at their intuitive collaboration, exclaiming to Chukovskaia that "I have the impression that you know my poems by heart five minutes before I write them. Perhaps not ten minutes before, but certainly five minutes" (I, 77).

This documented ritual of "hands, match, ashtray" (what Chukovskaia, with her unerring sense of the historic, establishes as the frontispiece to *Notes*) wields special power because it evokes, in part, an archetypal female role drawn from classical antiquity—one which both Akhmatova and Osip Mandelstam figure in their own poetic response to the time. The classical image of women performing a mourning ritual in Greek and Roman societies resurfaces in both poets' verses. I have already identified the role of the "blessed wife" in Mandelstam's poetry; both Mandelstams, in turn, envisioned Akhmatova as a "mourner" (*"plakal'shchitsa"*), a woman who weeps for the fallen martyr and warrior.[56] Yet the "beautiful and mournful ritual" described in *Notes* at once evokes and revises this powerful image. As mourners, Akhmatova and Chukovskaia assume a culturally assigned female duty, but by transforming their own bodies into living "archives" of the text, they improvise for themselves a new productive role which is founded on their symbolic capacity as mothers. Together Akhmatova and Chukovskaia project a striking new archetype of women in positive opposition to their harsh context: In their example, women not only mourn the dead, but (in a necessary inversion of the birthing process) volunteer to bear the living for as long as necessary. The scene of "hands, match, ashtray" depicts them at once giving birth, destroying, mourning, and secretly re-conceiving.

This ritual represents the most dramatic and innovative aspect of Akhmatova's and Chukovskaia's creative relationship. For the most part, however, Chukovskaia's *Notes* testifies to a much more mundane, though no less important collaboration of writer and helper in which their roles tend to be differentiated according to the family patterns I have described above. In those instances where Akhmatova is actually requested to *write* or publish her work, she often succumbs to a kind of indifference or helplessness. In part this indifference stems from a distaste for compromise: She does not believe that her poetry will be published according to her wishes.[57] She also claims to be ashamed of her completed work. As she confesses to Chukovskaia, her *printed* verses seem to her indecent, as if she "had left [her] stockings or brassiere lying on the table" (I, 76). In any case, she appears to treat her work as an extension of herself, her artistic body or offspring; it is interesting, therefore, that she inevitably relinquishes the care of her accepted, publishable poetry to others.[58]

In her artistic dependency, Akhmatova discovers Chukovskaia to be the ideal helper-caretaker. Raised to revere the text, professionally trained to be an editor, Chukovskaia eagerly, conscientiously takes up the obligations which the poet avoids. In a sense, Chukovskaia is simply extending the practice of her *Notes*. As editor of Akhmatova's poetry, she is transcribing a more formal level of the poet's verbal art; moreover, she is performing a literary act which the poet seems both unwilling and *unable* to complete. Early in their relationship when Chukovskaia is laboring over Akhmatova's galleys for a proposed collection of verse, the poet makes an extraordinary confession:

> Anna Andreevna roamed around the room and, looking over my shoulder, marvelled again and again at the proof symbols. In vain I swore to her that this was as simple as could be and that I would teach her these symbols in an hour.
> "I not only cannot remember the symbols you insert so easily," she replied, "but I cannot even write down one of my poems because I do not understand how." (I, 146–147)

Frequently enlisted to transcribe and prepare her poems, Chukovskaia soon guesses that Akhmatova never does this work herself (I, 139). By offering her professional skills, Chukovskaia has already assumed the position of Akhmatova's intermediate unofficial editor, but in view of Akhmatova's incapacity, their collaboration becomes even more amorphous and essential.[59] As it turns out, the quality which makes Akhmatova's poetry so memorable and portable, enabling it to exist for decades in oral form, also seems to derive from her creative method. Although Akhmatova is influenced by specifically written poetry, she creates this "written" effect in her own verse orally. For her the line between recited and written verse seems indistinct; she even professes at one point that she "has dreamed all [her] life of writing without stanzas, without a break" (I, 27). Like an ethnographer recording oral songs and tales, Chukovskaia is charged with transferring these spoken verses correctly into another medium, with fixing Akhmatova's speech in an undistorted, permanent script. For the most part she must manage this delicate operation on her own; in one session with a helpless Akhmatova, she eventually asks the poet to recite her verse so that she can study and transcribe her intonation (I, 98). In place of the normal collaboration between writer and editor, their relationship evolves into that of artist and translator or, perhaps more accurately, oracle and recording priestess.[60]

Over the course of this collaboration, Akhmatova's dependency, Chukovskaia's ability, and their extenuating circumstances naturally result in a redistribution of creative control. Chukovskaia never presumes to take credit for Akhmatova's work, but in her roles as conscientious caretaker and "recorder" she assumes more and more responsibility for the correctness and even the artistic value of her "text-charges." When, for example, her memory yields up slightly different versions of the *Requiem* poems than those Akhmatova remembers, she notes, with uncharacteristic doubt, that she is not sure if she or Akhmatova has forgotten the original texts (II, 414). The *Requiem* cycle remains more or less uncontested; these texts do not undergo the trials of transcription and editing.

But the biography of Akhmatova's other major work—*Poèma bez geroia* (*Poem without a Hero*)—reflects the extreme intricacies of co-production. The creation of the *Poem* develops into an all-consuming project. Akhmatova labors longer over this text than any other, composing its first sections in 1940 and continuing to write and rewrite it almost up to her death in 1966. According it primary place in her oeuvre, she shows great anxiety over its interpretation. The richly allusive *Poem* is designed, in large part, to explore and connect her sensation of and position in different moments of Russian history; its misreading would constitute a disastrous misunderstanding of that history and her place in it.[61] Periodically dismayed by her readers' reactions, Akhmatova strives to guarantee her work safe passage into the future by "clarifying" certain sections and asking others to provide commentaries.[62]

Kept from 1952 to 1962, the second volume of *Notes* necessarily documents Akhmatova's preoccupation with the *Poem*. As one of the poet's chief helpers, Chukovskaia is constantly on call for its transcription and revision and is recruited as an important "listener." In fact, when Akhmatova includes an explanatory "Letter to NN" in the manuscript, Chukovskaia instinctively (and correctly) guesses that she is its addressee (II, 79–80). Throughout the complicated genesis of the *Poem* Chukovskaia ventures (and is encouraged by Akhmatova) to accept her involvement literally. In the process she demonstrates a greater, more powerful conception of her helping role. She takes an active part in the making of the *Poem*; she devotes more of her narrative to her own critical analysis of Akhmatova's text. The entry for 11 June 1955 chronicles a typical contribution. Chukovskaia recovers a stanza of the *Poem* which Akhmatova discarded in Tashkent, and Akhmatova instantly agrees to include it:

> "Up until this point I never remembered it, but now I remember and I remember that you liked it. Let's put it in right away. . . ."
> In an instant she had found a place for it. She entered the lines after the rendezvous in the Maltese Chapel. Judging from the rhymes, [these lines] had been right there. Only the introductory phrase was somehow different. (II, 92–93)

In this instance, Akhmatova accepts the piece her helper has kept so faithfully, but at other points she and a much more insistent Chukovskaia debate over the making and re-making of the *Poem*. Reading through Akhmatova's revisions (inserted after the poet has "tested" her work for clarity), Chukovskaia actually vents her objections in the *Notes* and even disobeys Akhmatova's orders to destroy earlier variants (II, 72). When Chukovskaia is convinced that Akhmatova's *art* is endangered, she doubts the oracle herself and dares to launch her defense on absolute terms:

> Leafing through the *Poem*, Anna Andreevna said, "I will take this piece out altogether, otherwise it will be misinterpreted."
> I looked over my shoulder: she was pointing at the Cameron Gallery.
> "What will you take out altogether?"

> " 'And now to go home, swiftly/Through the Cameron Gallery.' " I did not believe it.
> "You are going to throw out the Cameron Gallery?"
> "Yes."
> What madness! And she still scolds Boris Leonidovich [Pasternak] for correcting his early verses!
> "It would be better to throw out the whole *Poem*," I said, losing control. "This is my favorite place. The height of heights. Take out everything else, but leave this."
> "Ah, yes?" said Anna Andreevna. "And I thought that you loved the *Poem*. I was mistaken."
> I saw that she was not really angry and I dared to speak. Of course, I said, the entire *Poem* is a "classic of the twentieth century," as she herself recently characterized the poetry of Boris Leonidovich. But there are *especially inviolable lines* in it. (II, 76, italics mine)[63]

What is at issue here, of course, is a matter of different taste and interpretation, but Chukovskaia's sense of "inviolable lines" and her consequent "loss of control" are significant. As expressed, her objections stem not from a higher opinion of herself as critic, but from her seeming conception of a primordial perfect text. Compared with the poet's other work, the *Poem* becomes a most vulnerable "text-charge" at an earlier stage of its life; Chukovskaia is on hand for many of its multiple births and plays both midwife and nurse. It appears that her own critical commentary is included, therefore, in much the same way as her creative work was elicited. She writes not to display or impose herself, but in direct response to certain imperatives—in this case, Akhmatova's request (II, 312) and her own sense of duty before the "classic" *Poem*.[64]

Whatever her specific responses to the objections and suggestions of her helpers, Akhmatova clearly recognizes the *Poem* as a collective effort. Her "Letter to NN" formally acknowledges the enormous role of her readers—the misreadings and "sincere indignation" that inspire her to extensive revision of her work (II, 91–92). Although Akhmatova discards the "Letter" in subsequent versions, she pursues this collaboration throughout her writing. Indeed, when Chukovskaia claims that the introductory lines of the *Poem* were suggested by her friend Tamara Gabbe, a critic who analyzed Akhmatova for Akhmatova one night in 1940, the poet not only seems to admit this debt, but describes the entire genesis of the work in this light: " 'It is a strange thing,' she said. 'Very strange. I have always written my poetry myself. But with the *Poem* it is different. I have written the whole thing in chorus, with others, as if I had been prompted' " (II, 122).

To a remarkable extent, the making of the *Poem* reflects her evolved creative relationship with helpers like Chukovskaia. Akhmatova begins the work after she has become accustomed to entrusting her poetry and life story to the bodily safekeeping of friends. The *Poem* represents particularly precious cargo, because it combines within itself her art and her own reading of her history. In consequence, Akhmatova seeks to preserve it through the joint strategies she has developed as persecuted writer and female cultural object. On the one hand, she depends on her helpers for the material maintenance of the text, and on the other, she works closely with them—directing their reading, soliciting their comments, accepting their contributions—in order to articulate a clear image of her past and self in her work. Producing and distributing fragments of the long, complex *Poem* for twenty-five years and over vast distances (Leningrad, Moscow, Tashkent), Akhmatova relies physically and artistically on her friends to help her restore and fit these scattered pieces into a coherent, meaningful whole.[65] The story of its creation in *Notes* reveals, then, as never before, the ingenious improvisation of unofficial literary production under Stalinism. Expelled from the official literary establishment, deprived of a broad audience, Akhmatova uses her small circle of qualified helpers as a crucial (and ultimately effective) substitute for a missing artistic community and professional staff—as personally recruited editors, readers, publishers, and kindred creative spirits.

Chukovskaia's role in the production of *Poem without a Hero* definitely indicates her improved status as helper—her more assured, active contribution as editor and critic. It may also reflect her development as *creator*. Chukovskaia writes her two novels during the long course of her friendship with the poet; her surety about what constitutes great art was very likely deepened by her own literary venture. At the same time this experience enriched and expanded her relationship with Akhmatova, for Chukovskaia comes to interact with the poet not only as helper but as an artist in her own right. And just as Akhmatova relies on her helpers as the editors (and even critics) of her unpublishable work, so Chukovskaia enlists Akhmatova as a critical reader—perhaps the primary reader—of her novels.[66] Once more Akhmatova serves as touchstone for Chukovskaia's artistic and spiritual values, but this time in the capacity of creative mentor.

In the case of both novels, Chukovskaia avidly records Akhmatova's encounter with her texts, closely reading her idol's expressions and attitude and hanging on her comments. Their first session is permeated by the general atmosphere of the first volume: Chukovskaia does not burn her manuscript, but she dares not name *Sof'ia Petrovna* in her *Notes*, and she invites Akhmatova to her home (presumed to be the safer of the two apartments) in order to read her just completed novel aloud:[67]

> I read for a long time and the whole time I felt ashamed of my poor prose. To read it—to her! Why did I start this? But now there was nowhere to retreat, and I read.
> It seems to me that she listened to the first part with boredom.
> She listened to the second part attentively, not tearing herself away, and, as it seemed to me, with great agitation. In one spot, it seems to me, she even wiped away tears. But I was not sure about this, I read without looking up.
> It all lasted an eternity. A long story, as it turns out!
> When I finished, she said: "This is very good. Every word is true." (I, 69)

Related through her customary qualification and self-deprecation, the scene still yields a powerful endorsement of her work—in Akhmatova's immediate emotional reaction and (for Chukovskaia) her talismanic pronouncement of the "truth" of the manuscript.[68] This entry quietly adds a new level of exchange to their collaboration. Here Chukovskaia documents receiving from the revered person of the poet authoritative confirmation of her novel's achievement—its value as moving, truthful testimony. Without intending to elevate herself, Chukovskaia has let Akhmatova establish her as an important and talented writer.

The second reading takes place and is recorded in the relatively freer climate of 1958. In consequence, it emphasizes a more open working relationship between the writer and her mentor. Once again Chukovskaia's effort is approved, and she discreetly celebrates Akhmatova's "not not liking" of *Going Under* with "flags in her soul" (II, 239). Here Akhmatova's response to the manuscript consists of a business-like list of remarks, major and minor comments jumbled together. The inclusion of this list indicates that Chukovskaia can refer to her text more explicitly (although she only provides complete quotations from *Going Under* in her footnotes); it also suggests Chukovskaia's growing skills as a writer. Here, in keeping with the basic patterns of the second volume—the collective preoccupation with the *Poem*, the many entries devoted to textual exegesis and debate—Akhmatova herself plays exacting critic for the already established novelist. Although Chukovskaia does not presume equality with the poet, she is treated as a member of the same profession, a woman capable of creating as well as caretaking who is now ready for pragmatic advice from her mentor (II, 241–42).

Chukovskaia's creative achievement, however, does not alter her expressed self-image as helper in *Notes*. True to her father's precedent, she seems unable to admit her own importance as a writer. Yet in the end her modesty curiously backfires. Upon receipt of a copy of *Sof'ia Petrovna* in November 1962, Akhmatova tells her that she has performed a great "feat" ("*podvig*") in producing this work, that while "we" were engaged in the ritual of memorizing and burning verses, she "wrote under the axe," knowing the consequences (II, 454). Chukovskaia does not argue with the poet in person, but she elaborates an extensive rebuttal in the *Notes*, insisting that writing this novel was a "non-feat" ("*ne*podvig"), an act as necessary and unremarkable as "breathing or washing" (II, 455). She identifies another hero:

> Izia Glikin performed the feat, Isidor Moiseevich Glikin, who took my notebook for safekeeping when they began to drag people into the Big House in search of "documents about [19]37," and I decided to go to Moscow with Liusha and have my operation. To preserve [it]—now that was a feat. And at starvation point, with his last strength, to walk from one end of the city to the other in order to hand my notebook over to his sister—that also was a feat. (II, 455)[69]

Deflecting Akhmatova's praise, Chukovskaia intends self-effacement, but inadvertently celebrates her own main role as helper. To add to the irony, she has chosen a most effective display for this "greater" heroism. Set during the purges and the war, her story foregrounds the private act of a civilian who spends his last strength saving her manuscript, helped in this valiant effort by his sister.

Glikin's sacrifice is dramatic in the extreme, and his example inevitably ennobles Chukovskaia's own caretaking efforts. In fact, against all her intentions, this entry offers a double endorsement of her heroic roles: The oracle Akhmatova proclaims the "feat" of her creation and Chukovskaia, in typically oblique fashion, pays forceful tribute to her other "feat" in preserving Akhmatova's work.

Chukovskaia's formal recognition of the helper beautifully rounds out the pattern of her creative relationship with Akhmatova. As recorded in *Notes*, her contribution has always been a substantial one; she serves as scribe, editor, critic, and human archive for a poet who speaks her art and relinquishes it to the care of others. At times the poet-disciple relationship even approximates a kind of collective creation—of a poetry perceived and restored as common property, an intuitively shared articulation of their shared experience. Yet it is only when she has gained the vantagepoint of an unofficial artist that Chukovskaia can acknowledge (albeit obliquely) their complete interdependency, their essential collaboration as creator and helper. Aware of her own debts as a proscribed writer, she can at last glorify what she has been providing all along. Documenting her intricate, evolving, mutually supportive relationship with Akhmatova, Chukovskaia ultimately conveys a complete appreciation of the unofficial literary process, illuminating and valuing all the component functions—the creating, writing, editing, and preserving—that were rendered heroic by her punitive age.

Of all Chukovskaia's unofficial writings, *Notes on Anna Akhmatova* represents the most hopeful, inspiring response to the disruption of Stalinism. This journal delineates a kind of tested blueprint for the successful maintenance of unofficial literature and biography in a totalitarian society. Without the aid of the Devil or a powerful official patron, the female poet and her female disciple manage to preserve manuscripts which they themselves have burned. How, then, did they effect this real-life miracle? To be sure, Akhmatova and Chukovskaia were relatively fortunate. Escaping imprisonment, exile, and execution, they could utilize the shabby domestic refuge still left them. But given this tiny breathing space, they seem equipped to succeed in part because of their specific conditioning as women. The state brings them together by imprisoning their husband and son; they are overwhelmed by the same family tragedy and respond with the same fierce, altruistic spirit. Although they disdain the role of conventional wife (with their reading of its materialistic selfishness), Akhmatova and Chukovskaia both prove capable of and willing to provide for others—to nurse and comfort, nurture and protect. In fact, despite the admitted difference in their talents, Akhmatova and Chukovskaia never fully demarcate their respective functions and roles in the *Notes*. To varying degrees, each perceives and interacts with the other through their shared capacities as mothering friend and childlike charge, intelligent critic and creative artist. Together with other women, Akhmatova and Chukovskaia form a comprehensive, flexible, reciprocal network of support which sustains them physically, emotionally, and spiritually, and maintains their dependent creations.

Their success, too, stems from the lucky match of their specific characters.

Akhmatova finds in Chukovskaia perhaps the most obliging, most flattering mirror of all. The poet can depend on this deferential younger woman to be a model attendant at her unofficial court. Diligent, devoted, possessed of a sure instinct for what is artistically effective and historically important, Chukovskaia erects a great verbal monument to Akhmatova's work and person—a monument which both preserves the poet's enigmatic power as symbol and cultural object and proves her credentials (her specific suffering and unlimited artistry) as national bard. For Chukovskaia, on the other hand, Akhmatova serves as ideal subject and mentor. Chukovskaia imbibed certain traditionally female notions of service and self-worth from her father, but she seems to achieve her full potential in her relationship with and related service for Akhmatova. For the first time she is engaging with a female subject who reflects and endorses almost all of her experiences, impulses, and felt obligations—her painful widowhood, domestic cares, and maternal solicitude. Moreover, as evidenced in the combined record of *Sof'ia Petrovna*, *Going Under*, and the *Notes*, Chukovskaia's experience of the purges forces her to modify her father's creative model, to work out her trauma through a more self-reflective kind of writing. Within her configuration of real and re-created female characters (including herself), Akhmatova exists as the realization of her self-styled ideal—a bereaved, victimized woman who holds fast to her private moral and cultural values, ministers to others, and bears miraculous creative witness. As it turns out, Chukovskaia happens to inscribe her most important role—in a sense, her passage from dutiful daughter to more powerful sister—as the chronicler and literary partner of her idol.

Finally and most paradoxically, the creative success of these two women—the remarkable works they produced "under the axe"—also derives from their horrific context. It is impossible to predict how Akhmatova and Chukovskaia might have developed as artists without this terrible experience; it is absolutely certain that neither woman desired it. But, most clearly in Chukovskaia's case, this experience enables them to grow creatively—in part because it renders their fate tragic and powerfully symbolic and also because it reorders their very perception of the creative act. For both women recording their forbidden experiences, be it in poetry or fiction or biography, becomes a means of psychological survival. To different extents they are psychologically liberated by these conditions: Their writing of the personal is thereby purified from a self-indulgent, self-exposing project into a mission that their sense of obligation before the persecuted and the dead drives and frees them to complete. And Chukovskaia, compelled to be of service, resorts to artistic creation and re-creation as imperative moral action. In *Sof'ia Petrovna*, *Going Under*, and *Notes on Anna Akhmatova*, she fathoms this course thoroughly, reflectively, artistically. By the onset of various political "thaws" in the 1950s and early 1960s, she has virtually written herself to the flash point of public dissidence, of fighting openly for human rights and artistic truth. Yet it is through these first works of creative heroism, I contend, that Chukovskaia wins her most profound victories of salvation and renewal, forever preserving the human lives, works, and meetings her government would obliterate and so truly commencing "the resurrection of an image of the dead."

Nadezhda Mandelstam

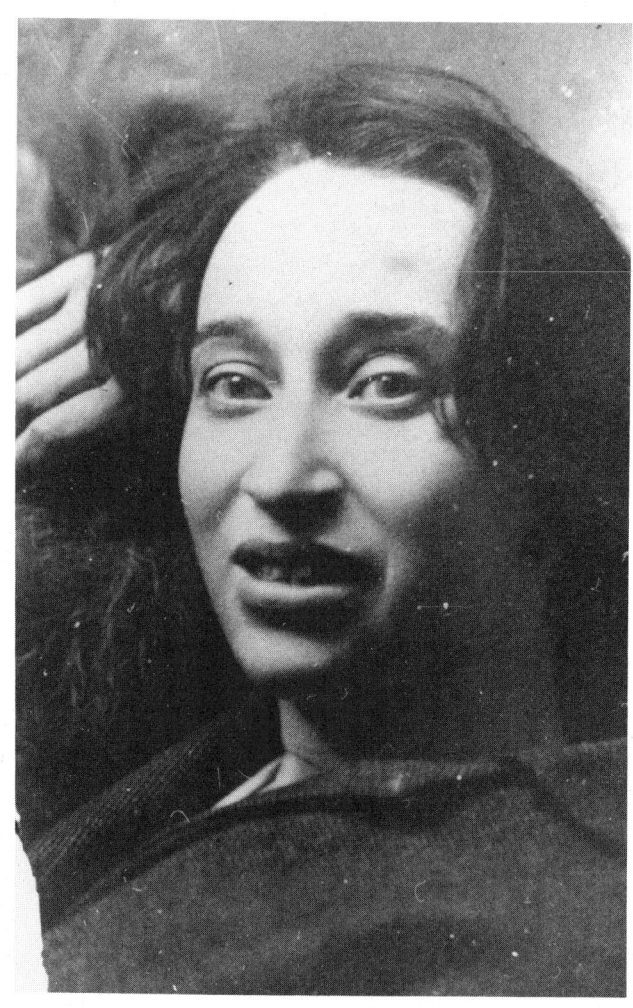

Nadezhda Mandelstam

5.
HUSBAND AND WIFE

> Surely it is rare to find such a marriage, such understanding, such spiritual kinship. Nadezhda Iakovlevna was equal to her husband in intelligence, education, and her enormous spiritual strength. I never heard her complain, I never saw her irritated or depressed. She was always even-tempered, outwardly calm. Without a doubt she was Osip Emil'evich's moral support. Their life depended on her. His difficult, tragic fate became hers. She took this cross on herself as if there was no other way.
>
> Natasha Shtempel'[1]

> With her long hooked nose, large mouth, and jutting teeth, bow-legged Nadia was a celebrity in that club of worldly people. How did she manage this? With her glib tongue? Of course. With the self-assuredness of a girl who tosses out the paradoxes she has picked up from smart people? Undoubtedly. With the daredevil tricks of a mischief-maker (*ozornitsa*) who knows how to drink and not get drunk? That, too. But when her loud shameless laughter died down, the tender watercolors of her face became more noticeable: soft ashen hair, bright blue eyes (slanted, don't forget) with bird-like pupils, rosy delicate skin, prominent white forehead.
>
> Emma Gershtein[2]

In her late sixties, commencing her second volume of memoirs, Nadezhda Iakovlevna Mandelstam finally permitted herself reflections on the very possibility of selfhood and autobiography. She announces that she excluded herself from the first volume because she "still did not exist" (II, 11);[3] the lost "you" of her husband—her authorizing subject—morally prevented any autobiographical focus, any assertion of the "shameful" word "I" (II, 4). It is only after she has fulfilled her "main task" of preserving Mandelstam's poetry and telling his life story that she is able to recover her "self." And even at this point of recovery, when she insists that she will "write about [herself] alone," her narrative projects an extraordinarily diffuse focus, ranging over a vast array of topics, episodes, and characters (all the "scraps of experience" stored up during her life).

The "autobiographical" writing of Nadezhda Mandelstam thus suggests a basic resemblance to the "childhood memoir" of Lidiia Chukovskaia. Both women appear to establish their identity through important relationships—particularly a loving, serving, sanctioning relationship with a male artist. In the person of father or husband they connect with a synthesis of social and spiritual authority—an exemplary man in a patriarchal society and a creator of art (for both, a supreme value). The circumstances of their attachment, however, are significantly different and foster different self-conceptions. Chukovskaia was sheltered and raised by her powerful father; her childhood laid an emotional, cultural, and spiritual foundation that sustains her throughout her difficult adulthood. She gratefully accepts that she has been "created" since childhood, and she lives according to that design. Mandelstam, on the other hand, is set adrift in the chaos of civil war and a fumbling new order and chances on a spiritual guide—a husband-teacher—who, by her own account, transforms and "saves" her. According to this scenario, she defines the formative period of her life as her twenty-year relationship with her husband and even consents to be "the work of his own hands" (II, 181–82, 217–18).

On the surface, therefore, Nadezhda Mandelstam's self-effacement seems more drastic, dictated by what she interprets as the exigencies of her political context. In her effort to foreground her husband's moral resistance to the destructive Soviet state, she explicitly devalues whole periods in her development. Her childhood amounts to no more than "a preparatory stage" (II, 181); she disparages her youth as a "stampede" when she served the new government as a member of a left-wing artists' collective (II, 13). In place of these ordinary phases, she tends to evoke the dramatic, allusive plot her husband enacted with her: that of a spoiled, silly young girl—a "Europa"—whom her husband abducts, tames, and trains to share his tragic destiny as "Leah," the faithful Jewish wife.[4] In effect, she imposes this ready, man-made plot on doubly uncharted territory—on the life of a woman spent in unconceivable conditions.[5] Yet even though she seems to endorse this plot, Nadezhda Mandelstam gradually reveals a far more capacious, ambiguous, and boisterous self-image, which in spite of her retrospective criticism of "the silly girl," she seems to relish and even indulge. Over the course of two volumes of memoirs and sketches for a third, with public recognition of her own writing achievement (however self-deprecated), she actually discloses what *she* brought to this formative relationship and demonstrates how this marriage, while dedicated to her husband's artistic genius, was a true collaboration of talent and temperament that sustained both partners, preserved *his* poetry, and engendered *her* distinctive authorship.

Family life

To appreciate her development both within and outside her relationship with Mandelstam, I propose to reconstruct the narrative of Nadezhda Mandelstam's premarital life—to compile and reorder the information she sporadically revealed and, wherever possible, corroborate these data with the testimony of her friends and associates.[6] I do so not to discount her own projection of self and autobiography, but to analyze what I consider to be the productive paradox in her self-conception and to begin the long-neglected task of mapping her biography as a writer. It seems most appropriate to proceed from the end of her oeuvre, for there she allows herself the most direct exposure. Her evidence is casually offered: In her last years Nadezhda Mandelstam recalled childhood and family in three diffuse fragments—"Father," "Family," "Girls and a Boy."[7] Written under the double constraints of poor health and a persistent self-disregard, restlessly shifting in focus and time sequence (from childhood to revolution to Stalinist era), these fragments nevertheless intimate the specific importance of her girlhood. Nadezhda Mandelstam offers no systematic analysis of her early years—her religious training, schooling, routine family life. Unlike Chukovskaia, she delineates no coherent pattern of family worship. Yet we can recover certain facts and features from her desultory comments: that she was the youngest of four children born to Vera Iakovlevna and Iakov Arkad'evich Khazin—the baby of the family and the object of her brothers' merciless teasing; that her family was materially comfortable, able to travel in Europe and inclined to eat too well; that her household was not religious but observed Orthodox fasts out of respect for their devout cook; that, after a series of English governesses, she eventually attended a girls' gymnasium with a "male" (i.e., implicitly more difficult) curriculum that required impressive subjects like Latin.

While her sketches stylistically reflect her irreverence for certain autobiographical conventions, they mainly register the constant interference of political context. Nadezhda Mandelstam's venture back into childhood is precarious, dramatized by attendant memories of its destruction. In paying tribute to their pious cook, for example, she laments that the poor woman's savings "were eaten up" by the revolution (80). A review of household goods concludes in their necessary sale or confiscation; Nadezhda Mandelstam drily notes that "[i]n the revolution we lived on tablecloths, not jewels" (82). Recollections of family members are shadowed in much the same way. Describing a family portrait that features everyone but the as-yet-unborn Nadezhda, she is suddenly prompted to relate "the terrible life" of her two oldest siblings: Her sister died virtually alone and impoverished in the dark days of the Stalinist purges, and her eldest brother, Aleksandr, disappeared while serving in the White Army during the civil war. Although she spent roughly her first sixteen years in the more or less stable world of the Kiev middle class, Nadezhda Mandelstam, it seems, is inevitably drawn to the time when her comfortable life was shattered. She filters the habits and appurtenances of her middle-class life through the purifying, sharp-eyed lens of loss; she itemizes individual objects and episodes as if they were the few remaining artifacts of an extinct culture, a destroyed paradise. In her narrative, militant outside forces (most often Soviet) lay constant siege to this childhood world—stealing the family's money and furniture, carrying off her brothers, and threatening them all (a Jewish family converted to Christianity) with pogroms.

Indeed, the political world and public life early on impressed her as undesirable and dangerous. In her sketch "Girls and a Boy" she recalls an unexpected holiday when her whole school was ordered out to greet the visiting family of Tsar Nicholas II. She claims to be moved by the sight of these royal children—"the very handsome boy and four sad girls"—and she eventually ponders their tragic murder, but she first detects in their situation another, more insidious hazard:

> I suddenly understood that I was much happier than these unfortunate girls: after all I could run around with the dogs on the street, make friends with the boys, not learn my lessons, make mischief, go to bed late, read all kinds of junk and fight—with my brothers and anybody else. . . . I and my governesses had a very simple arrangement: we'd leave the house together, purposefully, and then go our separate ways—they to their rendezvous and I to my boys—I didn't make friends with girls—you can only really fight with boys! But these poor princesses were bound in everything: they were polite, affectionate, friendly, attentive. . . . They couldn't even fight. . . . Poor girls! (90–91)

By juxtaposing herself with the tsar's daughters—prisoners of decorum and eventual victims of political intrigue—Nadezhda realizes her own private advantage. She discovers real freedom and pleasure in informal play, an unscrutinized existence. She depicts herself conniving her life free from the restrictions of class and gender, escaping the supervision of parents and teachers, taking to the plebeian streets, and behaving as lady-like etiquette would never permit.

In their focus and content, Nadezhda Mandelstam's childhood recollections gradually describe an idiosyncratic set of values derived from family practice and her own temperament and dismissive of certain institutions and conventions in her society. To a large extent, these values involved a kind of inner freedom coupled with tolerance and solicitude for others.[8] We learn, for instance, that her mother had a special theory for their upbringing: "you had to spoil children silly—otherwise they wouldn't survive this unbearable life, and in order to discourage capriciousness, you had to anticipate every wish so that your children could think up nothing more . . ." (87). Her father, "lacking [her] mother's imagination," was "simply an obedient and meek parent . . . whose voice had no commanding tones" (88–89). It was this indulgent father, a confirmed atheist, who taught Nadezhda to respect the Christian scriptures. Tolerance informed her parents' class attitudes as well; for example, they accepted Daria, their cook, as "a friend and family member" and respectfully addressed her by her name and patronymic (80).

Nadezhda Mandelstam also conveys the value her family placed on material well-being. In particular, it seems her parents could not deny themselves good food. She points out her father's weakness for *pirogi* and sturgeon; he would risk missing his train in his quest for good fish at the station buffets. She recalls the delicious meals her family enjoyed and specifically commends Daria on her amazing culinary talent (80).[9] In contrast to the unmentioned household operations in *To the Memory of Childhood*, this sort of domestic art is clearly prized in her narrative. When, in turn, such comforts are no longer attainable, Nadezhda Mandelstam reveals another family trait: the pragmatic ability to adapt and survive. I have already noted the tablecloths her family "lived on" through the revolution. With the same matter-of-factness, Nadezhda reports that all of her father's pants were made over into skirts for her sister-in-law during the postwar years of shortages. Although she does not dwell on her parents' Jewish heritage, her digression about the remarkable endurance of the Jews seems to redound to her family's credit, for she has just recalled them repelling one wave of *pogromshchiki* after another in the civil war (82–83).

Compared with Chukovskaia's re-created family "religion," Nadezhda Mandelstam's set of values is far more diverse, unorthodox, irreverent, indulgent, and even materially oriented. She appreciates the abilities of father, mother, and cook; at the same time she enjoys and celebrates her own autonomy. Yet the two women's recollections bear one interesting resemblance. Nadezhda does not overlook her mother, but she, too, offers little evidence of any girlish upbringing and, instead, devotes an entire sketch to the memory of her father. It may be that she remembers a more sharply defined rather than more important relationship with her male parent. Her father, Iakov Khazin, died in the early 1930s; her mother Vera survived until World War II and reappears in both volumes of the memoirs as a resilient partner, aiding her daughter through the trials of arrest and exile. Mother and daughter form an implicitly seamless network of support, and Vera Khazina—a "mite" ("*kroshka*" [79])—never attains the distinctive stature of her husband.[10] Nadezhda Mandelstam's description of Iakov Khazin, on the other hand, recalls the impressive portrait of Kornei Chukovskii:

> I was standing by the window and suddenly saw father crossing the street. Tall, straight, he walked with a heavy step. He always wore suits of the same cut and made by the same tailor. He had a fleshy face, a wide bulbous nose, an enormous forehead, and small hazel eyes. . . . He walked without hurrying, heavily, and he was enormously tall. All of a sudden I saw clearly that he was a *barin* ("gentleman"). (79)

Her father is framed in the world outside, yet another benevolent (albeit ponderous) giant. Although Nadezhda does not name him as the measure of her world, she dignifies him with the label "barin"—her own defiant reappropriation of a derogatory Soviet term. Just as Chukovskaia proudly relates her father's ascent from the *meshchanstvo* into the realms of the culturally great, so Nadezhda Mandelstam attributes her father's "nobility" (clearly uninherited, since he was a Jew) to his intelligence and education. Her father is entitled as her intellectual mentor, her link with an urbane cultured world. We learn almost nothing of her mother's profession, despite the fact that Vera Khazina was one of the first group of Russian women to train successfully as medical doctors.[11] Nadezhda remembers that after her father completed a degree in mathematics, he finished law school in a mere two or three months and staggered his professors with his brilliance (81). It was her father who moved them from provincial Saratov to the cultural center of Kiev in a successful search for a job. Interestingly enough, her father also presented her with a model of informal, yet serious scholarship. She reports that in his leisure time he read Greek tragedies in the original; he quietly encouraged his daughter to buy good books and read important authors (85).

Aside from being a self-made "barin," Iakov Khazin impressed and influenced his daughter with other appropriable qualities. As I noted above, Nadezhda remarks on her parents' loving indulgence of their offspring; her father, with his insistence on costly English nannies who "respect children," seems the most extravagant example. She does not describe their daily routine—presumably her father works outside the home—but she chooses to highlight his involvement and affection. A remembered photograph fixes this image: "he squats down for the children returning from their walk, with his arms flung wide open so he can embrace them all at once" (88). In sharp contrast to his domestic tenderness, however, Iakov Khazin was easily and vehemently provoked by public lawlessness. His daughter claims that when the soldiers and "officers with university pins" tried to carry out a pogrom of their household, her father "drove them out with such choice swear words that they retreated" (82). He attempted, in vain, to sue the Cheka (then the Soviet secret police) for evicting them from their apartment. His daughter relates his characteristic response, when he applied to work as a defense attorney under the new regime:

> They asked him if he knew Soviet law. He replied that he learned Roman law in two weeks, "but two hours would be enough for me to learn yours." . . . They didn't accept him as a public defender, and thank God. If they had accepted him, he would have perished right away—he would have snapped out the naked truth (*pravda-matka*) and that would have been the end of it. (83)

Iakov Khazin, like Kornei Chukovskii, presents his daughter with a potent synthesis of intellectual and family-oriented values steeled by a public moral stance. Yet in contrast to Chukovskii's controlled and chaste model, Khazin also condones a lively impudence, an irresistible urge to tell the whole truth and counter indecent action with indecent language. In this regard, the two sets of memoirs offer a coincidental and intriguing point of comparison. Early in *To the Memory of Childhood* Chukovskaia remembers the frightening game she played with her father when she asks him to sit her on top of the cupboard. After she has gotten properly terrified, she begs—using the right "magic words"—to be taken down. Their game is formalized and instructive; father and daughter act out their roles of benefactor and petitioner. In the sketch entitled "Family," Nadezhda Mandelstam describes an extraordinarily similar scene, but in her case she ends up atop a wardrobe because her mean older brothers have abandoned her there. In place of Chukovskaia's harmonious, orderly family ties—with father-commander and children-followers—she implies a family free-for-all. Far from being protective, her brothers used their little sister "as a soccer ball" to be kicked back and forth. And she was by no means the passive victim or the dutiful little girl, but a "little foolish creature . . . who went around snorting and acting up" (89). Her giant father rescues her from her perch on the wardrobe, but the father-daughter relationship is not played out as savior and victim. When the man who swore his household to safety cannot raise his voice against his sons, his little foolish daughter takes up her own defense:

> and I howled and learned how to swear: "Idiots, blockheads!." . . . I've had great success with this all my long life. Father said, "Why do they hurt the little one?" and comforted me as best he could. . . . And I kissed him and said, "You tell them, those blockheads." (89)

In this episode, Nadezhda depicts herself acquiring a crucial role—one both suggested by her father's public conduct and encouraged by his indulgence, but taken to greater extremes. Saved by her gentle father, she complements him with her verbal scrappiness; she acts the part of the unabashed belligerent, the profane truth-teller. This scene may well mark her debut in a lifelong role.

Pieced together from these diffuse laconic sketches, Nadezhda Mandelstam's childhood experience, like that of Chukovskaia, seemed to privilege family practice over institutional sanction and, in particular, a paternal model of belief and action. While her family was clearly patriarchal in its authoritative structure, Nadezhda gained, within its confines, a wide-ranging set of values and an important, albeit relative autonomy. She learned to appreciate material comfort, domestic art, and a pragmatic will to endure in equal proportion to the products of high culture. Parental indulgence allowed her to ignore the pressures of school and the rules of proper "feminine" decorum and explore her own appetites. Indeed, her father endorsed and elicited her unorthodox fighting spirit. As a child, therefore, Nadezhda Khazina was exempted from the strictures of a larger patriarchal system by the milder, more indulgent and differentiated authority of her family.

Unfortunately, Nadezhda Mandelstam offers no specific account of her adolescence, when she reaches sexual maturity and makes the important transition from family life to participation in the wider world. Born in 1899, she comes of age during the First World War and ensuing Russian revolutions. Once the barely adult Nadezhda does appear in her work (in *Hope Abandoned*), what we mainly learn is that she is changed for the worse:

> I am not proud of my early youth. The image that comes back to me is of a great herd of cattle stampeding over a field of ripe corn and trampling it underfoot in vast swaths. In those days I ran around as one of a small herd of painters. (II, 13)

Her account distorts her accomplishment, degrading her experience as bestial and denying her capacity for independent thought and action. Yet during her "stampeding" youth, Nadezhda was working in the studio of Aleksandra Ekster, one of the most renowned theatrical artists of the Russian avant garde.[12] Although she will subsequently relegate herself to the status of "dabbler" (218), her connection with this teacher is impressive and her experience with the "herd," even as she judges it here, conveys some of the heady excitement she must have felt at the time. In particular, she describes the curtain call she shared with her friend Vitia and the stage decorator for their part in the famous 1919 presentation of Lope de Vega's *Fuenteovejuna* in Kiev. She also itemizes the artists' "hectic round of pleasure" spent painting, frequenting night clubs, buying "mountains of pastries," and charging about the streets after curfew. For a brief time after the October revolution, Nadezhda's irreverent, free-spirited tendencies gained official sanction, and she made no distinction between her private and public life.[13]

It is intriguing, however, that her one flirtation with worldly success incurs such strong condemnation in retrospect. On the one hand, her response is marked by a sort of ascetic pride: She disdains her foolishness in joining the establishment and in accepting the world's opinion of her. On the other, she dismisses her own talent as a creator, for she represents herself as an undifferentiated member of a falsely self-important collective of artists, a group that unwittingly serves its new "masters." Her self-criticism and iconoclasm combine to cast her as a deluded sinner, a young woman who must renounce her prideful claims of importance in order to save her immortal soul. And these notions of excess and conversion strike a resonant chord because they partially evoke her relationship with her father. He was the one who quietly, effectively rebuked her when she ridiculed the Christian scriptures; her escape from the "herd" is facilitated by similar paternal mentors. The first such instruction takes place in Ekster's studio: Nadezhda has the weakness to laugh at a cruel verse about killing tsarist officers and Il'ia Ehrenburg, already disaffected by the bloody carnival, is on hand to scold her:

> He gave me such a talking-to that I still respect him for it, and I am proud that, silly as I was at the time, I had the sense to listen to him and remember his words forever afterward. This happened before my meeting with M., so that he did not have to cure me of the head-hunting mentality. . . . (I, 107)

Sporadically noted, the pattern is nonetheless important. Her father, it seems, prepared the way for Ehrenburg, and Ehrenburg prepared the way for Osip Mandelstam. Nadezhda Mandelstam's life story is not so much created as formalized by her husband's imposed plot of "Europa-Leah." Reviewed from the beginning, her "wildness" is no early expendable stage, but a permanent condition periodically tempered and redirected by an older, seemingly wiser male authority.

In their carnival surroundings, then, Osip Mandelstam happened on a ready listener in Nadezhda Khazina. They met in a nightclub and entered into a casual liaison, but the effect of their union was instantly significant. The collective singled out Mandelstam as an undesirable influence: "Our sudden friendship annoyed everybody for some reason" (II, 16). Their apprehension of Osip's difference, however, only sanctioned her choice. With the great benefit of hindsight, she remembers appreciating his prescience and wisdom: "in the Kiev of 1919, Mandelstam was perhaps the only person I knew who pondered the meaning of events" (20). His improvidence was distinct from the frivolity of the herd; his attitude, she realized, implied "a serene acceptance of life" (21). Arguing his singularity, she also indicates that she was "different" enough to heed it, for the established poet and the apprentice painter already shared the qualities of "light-headedness and a sense of doom." Among her thoughtless companions, Nadezhda alone seemed predisposed to absorb Osip's unusual reflections, to be entranced by the cautious glimpses he granted her of his inner world.[14]

Osip's difference and Nadezhda's attraction—the chemistry that "saves" the course of her life—are perhaps best illustrated in a later episode from *Hope Abandoned*. Nadezhda Mandelstam relates another "theatrical" event from their first days together in Kiev—Mandelstam's public reading of his verse. The event was staged in the same theatre that presented *Fuenteovejuna*; Mandelstam, in effect, was venturing into her terrain. Yet, despite her professed pleasure in the visual and technical aspects of the stage, Nadezhda Mandelstam here interprets this context as a kind of synecdoche of state-enforced art. At that time, she explains, the audience was in the process of being re-programmed to applaud official propaganda and hiss any suspect notions. Plays aimed for the "crude effects" of *Fuenteovejuna*, and poets, emulating the exhibitionist Futurists, trained "to become stage performers or variety artists" (II, 308). As a set painter, she clearly contributed to this stylized, manipulated interaction; she was behind the scenes, creating and maintaining the very conditions of delusion. But when Mandelstam read his poetry, he was "alarmingly untheatrical, completely out of place on the broad stage across which he sauntered alone, as though walking down the street" (II, 309) His nonperformance both worried and awed her. Independent in his values and behavior, Mandelstam resisted the pressure to perform and revealed himself as a "true" poet, an artist who, according to her analysis of his convictions, stood utterly opposed to the actor. It was precisely this image of the nonperforming, nonconforming Mandelstam that recurred to Nadezhda during their year-and-a-half separation.

Yet as powerful as Mandelstam's influence is remembered to be, Nadezhda's decision to go with him may have reflected a need to escape more than anything else. The very foundation for a career, a home, or any kind of coherent life was swept away in civil war Kiev. When Osip abruptly left for the Crimea, Nadezhda had plans to join him but could not move "with all the bloodshed in the streets" (II, 21). By the time he returned for her, her family had been evicted twice from their home. A novelist could not have staged their union more symbolically: On the backdrop of an emptied apartment, in counterpoint to a vulgar chorus of female criminals who have been commandeered to clean the place, Mandelstam reads his poetry to his beloved and announces that he will take her away (II, 22). The young woman (she is twenty-one) thus leaves her ruined family and invaded home for the makeshift refuge of life with an artist. As Nadezhda Mandelstam interprets it, their casual relationship was renewed and truly forged by luck, a strange coincidence of temperament, and extenuating, dramatic circumstances.

The marriage relationship

I have attempted to review Nadezhda Mandelstam's autobiography *without* Mandelstam up to the period she deems formative in her life, the period that functions as the centripetal core of almost all her writing. She herself designates three further stages in her relationship with her husband, with each stage advancing them toward a more complete union. The first phase encompasses their life in the early twenties, when the poet stubbornly secluded his wife from social contact and trained her to appreciate poetry. The second phase takes shape in the aftermath of Osip's affair with another woman, Olga Vaksel; Nadezhda threatened to leave, he struggled to keep her, and their relationship was mended and renewed. The "third and final stage" is prompted by "his journey to Armenia and return to writing verse" (263); despite their physical persecution, they were happy with each other and the poetry Mandelstam could now produce. Each stage presumes Mandelstam's larger importance; his creative success is a key factor in their good relations. Each stage also depends on the determining role he plays in their marriage. Nadezhda Mandelstam may have rebelled against his control, but she was inevitably the one who responded, adapted, and made compensation.

But why did Nadezhda Mandelstam submit? She is painfully frank about her degradation—at least in the early phase of their relationship. She admits that she then "felt like a horse in the hands of a trainer," "a compliant and easy charge" (II, 260).[15] In subsequent years her husband's domineering role softened somewhat: He was frightened into behaving "much more like a protector and friend than as an overseer and trainer." Nevertheless, Nadezhda Mandelstam lived with the hard fact that she was important, loved, and kept in large part because Mandelstam had invested so deeply in her "creation." She accepted this unflattering truth and stayed with him, but as she herself seems to sense, love cannot adequately explain her attachment. To understand her "submission," therefore, I offer the following analysis of their relationship—its distribution and revision of various gender roles and plots, its obvious costs and subtle benefits—as it is revealed in Nadezhda Mandelstam's writing.

As in her account of childhood, political context is depicted as the most overwhelming influence. In her narrative, the Soviet regime fundamentally, inexorably shapes their relationship; the "sense of doom" that Nadezhda shared with Osip was only confirmed over the years. Unlike so many other witnesses to Soviet history, she views the first postrevolutionary decades as a steady downward slide into totalitarian control. Mandelstam's harassment began in the 1920s, as did the movement toward a conformist society. Nadezhda Mandelstam experiences and reports this oft-named "liberal" decade as a time of desperate confusion, uncertain work, and grinding poverty. The 1930s then ushered in true political terror, and Mandelstam—arrested, exiled, and arrested once again—was virtually sentenced to death. Facing such horrific physical and psychological conditions, husband and wife were both compelled and inspired to remain together. They joined in a single unit of support as their only means of physical and moral survival. Of the two, Nadezhda Mandelstam seemed to have the better chance to escape by divorcing Osip and recanting her association. But she chose, again and again, the noble, tragic role of sharing his life and persecution, working for him and even begging with him as they staved off his inevitable doom.

Along with pain and suffering, then, the Stalinist context also imposed an unforeseen benefit. It redefined both the terms and nature of their relationship. In his reading of Nadezhda Mandelstam's work, Charles Isenberg has astutely observed that the Stalinist terror allayed her other great terror—that of a conventional marriage.[16] Just as it disrupted careers and lives, so the regime, in their case, undermined the possibility of a "bourgeois family romance." Isenberg draws a fascinating parallel between the Mandelstams' marriage and the relationship of Jean-Paul Sartre and Simone de Beauvoir. For both couples, he asserts

> [I]t is the writings of the female partner that create the relationship as a literary phenomenon, and both the Russian and the Frenchwoman represent their primary relationships as a critique of, and counter-example to, the ideology of marriage in its Stalinist-bourgeois and French-bourgeois forms. And both women portray couples that are morally exemplary in their determination to live their values. (195)

Isenberg tends to trace Nadezhda Mandelstam's critique to her fear of being abandoned (197–98). Certainly she herself "is quite prepared to admit" that, given a normal life, Osip might have left her for another woman (II, 264); after all, she dates the second, improved phase of their relationship from her husband's break with just such a dangerous rival. But, as we might suppose from her childhood sketches, her critique also reflects her longstanding aversion to middle-class convention and institutionalized practice. Mandelstam attracted a confirmed iconoclast and free spirit with the prospect of a "counter-marriage"—what seemed to be an adult version of her family refuge.

As she was deprived (conveniently) of the possibility of a Stalinist-bourgeois marriage, Isenberg argues that Nadezhda Mandelstam embraced other "womanly" roles—roles, I would add, that have ready sanction in a patriarchal society and evoke the man-made characters of Lara and Margarita. First and foremost, Nadezhda Mandelstam takes advantage of the script her husband has written for her, recognizing the gender assignments he developed in *Tristia*:

> M. had a peculiar way of dividing the world into "men" and "wives." The "men" bore all responsibility for worldly matters, while the "wives" are mourners, fortune-tellers, and gatherers of "the light ashes that remain." Only he never allowed me to tell fortunes, and it upset me to be barred as a "wife" in this respect. Once, finding me with a fortune-teller, he chased her away and said: "Why do you need a fortune-teller? You know everything as it is." Lord, what did I know then, if even now I know nothing? . . . (II, 61)

Her self-deprecating comments aside (and these also may indicate a discomfort with her "idealization"), Nadezhda Mandelstam is certainly empowered by this mandate. The poet divined for her a conserving, interpreting, passive role based on his own recodifying of European culture, truly christening her a "blessed wife." Like Chukovskaia and Akhmatova, Nadezhda Mandelstam finds her work and identity are made potent through the invocation of this composite image of woman as mourner and seer. Although the Soviet authorities prevented her from gathering up his ashes, she commemorated her husband as best she could, and she was largely heeded and commended (and Mandelstam's poetry hailed as prophetic) because she enacted his vision.

By assuming this role, moreover, Nadezhda Mandelstam is included in another sanctioning and signifying tradition of Russian women who deliberately share their loved ones' persecution. In her voluntary and extreme devotion, she recalls the wives of the seventeenth-century schismatic Avvakum and the nineteenth-century Decembrists.[17] In fact, it is Akhmatova—that emblematic authority on bereavement and self-renunciation—who pronounces her a Decembrist wife.[18] The association entails authorship as well: Through the autobiographical writings of female political activists and martyrs, she achieves both a ready public image and an approved public voice.[19] Following in the footsteps of Princess Natal'ia Dolgorukaia (1714–71)—the first self-sacrificing, testifying wife—Nadezhda Mandelstam appropriates one traditional role of a *writing* Russian woman.[20]

While their marriage-made-comartyrdom transformed Nadezhda Mandelstam into beloved wife, noble archetype, and sanctioned female writer, it also enabled her a very different mode of being and (eventually) writing. Fortunately, her husband's authoritative example, tempered by their hard life, accommodated and fostered certain extant features of her character. On the most urgent level, he elicited the sturdy pragmatist in Nadezhda. In this connection their marriage projects an interesting variation on the caretaking relationships I have outlined thus far. Unlike the fictional models of the Master and Doctor Zhivago, Osip Mandelstam intended from the very outset to both supervise and support his wife. He acted as the protector of a vulnerable, helpless girl: "In his eyes I was always the younger one who had to be soothed, protected and, if need be, taken in hand to stop me from doing silly things" (II, 127).[21] He wished her to cultivate a "dignified wifely charm," while he retained his primary position as nurturing, providing husband. Yet, as their living conditions worsened, his health flagged, and his persecution became more apparent, Osip was compelled to rely on the domestic and *professional* ministrations of his wife. I will analyze Nadezhda Mandelstam's function as his literary secretary in the following chapter; this service, it seems, was something Mandelstam always presumed, demanded, and received. But what he did not anticipate was *her* role as provider. Having abandoned her modest career as an artist for a more absorbing life with Osip, Nadezhda suddenly found herself forced to improvise a livelihood. Under such extenuating circumstances, she became, by her own admission, "the breadwinner" in their household (II, 125), taking on the translating and editing jobs Mandelstam could or would not perform.[22] Thus, their relationship partly, but involuntarily reenacts the plot of weak male artist and provident female helpmate and at the same time resembles the interdependency of Akhmatova and Chukovskaia in which the roles of caretaker and charge are shared over time.

It is remarkable, too, that Nadezhda Mandelstam, a decided *non*feminist, comes to identify her caretaking ability as a female strength. She has intimated it as a family trait in her sketches of childhood; in *Hope against Hope* she conveys it more specifically as maternal legacy. After Mandelstam's first arrest, when she and Akhmatova were struggling to cope, it was her mother, just arrived from Kiev, who immediately sized up the situation and put the household in order (I, 21). When the couple was sent into exile, Vera Khazina gave them all her money and tried to keep their Moscow apartment until their return. Although her presence is intermittent in her daughter's narrative, we know from letters and other testimony that she regularly substituted as Mandelstam's caretaker when her daughter went off on necessary errands.[23] Paying brief tribute to her mother's resourcefulness, lauding the similar industry and solicitude of other women (e.g., the "wives" who visit them after Mandelstam's first arrest, the saintly figures of Anna Akhmatova and Vasilisa Shklovskaia), Nadezhda Mandelstam eventually draws this bold conclusion in *Hope Abandoned*:

> When the hard times came it became clear that the women who had affected the part of lady or little bird were the main organizers of daily life and, indeed, were the builders and mainstay of the family . . . the women were always stronger than the men, as everybody sees well enough today. (II, 105)

Yet as powerful as she became in providing for her husband, Nadezhda Mandelstam was never fully developed or objectified as a "typical" Soviet wife—that is, that materialistic amalgam of housekeeper and breadwinner condemned by Akhmatova. While he eventually had to live in dependence on Nadezhda, Osip neither desired nor encouraged her to become "the high-powered, protective" spouse his friends urged him to secure (II, 141). By running off with her husband, Nadezhda Mandelstam had renounced, in effect, all goals of worldly accomplishment, any track of the upwardly mobile. Just as she forsook her own career, so she rejected the vicarious career of ambitious wife. Unlike the writers' wives equally disdained by Akhmatova and Chukovskaia, she demanded none of the rewards given the successful and approved—the nice apartment, good salary, special goods and privileges. She still longed for the domestic wellbeing of her childhood years, but this longing is made distinct from the materialism of the "wives." Nadezhda Mandelstam's hankering for certain comforts and luxuries is linked with a general enjoyment of life rather than a desire for status: "We were not at all ascetics by nature and neither of us had a tendency toward self-denial. It simply turned out that we had to renounce everything because they demanded too high a price for an increase in one's rations" (II,236). She and her poet-husband appeared to live according to the same worldview—

one that combined a free aesthetic sensitivity with ethical concern and earthly pleasure.²⁴ And as their relationship matured and Mandelstam had to yield more responsibility to his "foolish" younger wife, the two of them achieved a kind of balance of non-status, an equal level of childlike helplessness and "light-headedness." Nadezhda Mandelstam offers a most apt description of their state in her last letter to her husband:

> Osia, what joy it was living together like children—all our squabbles and arguments, the games we played, and our love. . . . Like two blind puppies we were nuzzling each other and feeling good together. (II, 620)

In this way, their difficult marriage did not transform the playful child—the "little foolish creature"—into an official writer's materialistic wife. Although Nadezhda Mandelstam evinced a greater capacity for pragmatic action, she acted out of necessity, not ambition; her mild materialism, in turn, was shared with and endorsed by her husband. By maintaining her childhood values and temperament, she thus voluntarily resisted the role of wife in a Stalinist-bourgeois marriage. Her mentality and self-image were not so much made by Mandelstam as intersecting, at crucial junctures, with his authoritative model. Furthermore, Nadezhda Mandelstam indicates that she was able to progress from being the "kitten" or "puppy" kept in tow by her husband to a partnership in which husband and wife alternated the roles of parent and child and, in their happiest moments, managed to live as children (or puppies) together. In the process she reconstructs Mandelstam as a kind of husband/brother—a "man-who-would-understand"—who proffers an empathetic "alternative to patriarchal power and dominance," the more so since their partnership is never imbalanced by children.²⁵

Nadezhda Mandelstam avoided yet another occupational hazard: In contrast to the lovers and wives of other male poets, she was never scripted and silenced as an icon of female beauty. With characteristic acumen, she hones in on this essential difference between Mandelstam and the arch-Symbolist, Aleksandr Blok:

> In his personal life M. was the complete opposite of Blok. I would even say that he was by nature anti-Blok, since the highest aspect of love was not, for him, service to the "Beautiful Lady," but something quite different which he summed up in the word "my you." His anti-Blok nature was also reflected in his choice of a wife—not a "beautiful lady," not in fact even a "lady" at all, but a mere slip of a girl, someone belonging to a lower order of womanhood with whom everything was simple, funny, and frivolous, but with whom he gradually attained to relations of such supreme closeness that he could say: "I feel free with you." (II, 245)

Mandelstam did fix his wife with various images and plots, but he mainly conceived of her as an extension of himself, not a female Other or an embodiment of the Eternal Feminine.²⁶ Nadezhda Mandelstam was never idolized as a beauty; although she was sexually attractive, she refused to mystify her appeal

Husband and Wife 111

in the fashion of the Symbolists, and she rejected the rituals and mannerisms of a great "beauty" like Anna Akhmatova.[27] In fact, despite her deep affection for the female poet, she criticizes Akhmatova's constant posing as a leftover habit from the early twentieth-century cult of "beauties"—women who groomed themselves and were worshiped as the belles of Petersburg high society. I will explore this important friction between Akhmatova and Nadezhda Mandelstam in detail in the chapter on *Hope Abandoned*. What is essential for my analysis here is the fact that Nadezhda Mandelstam uses these "beauties" as another defining antipode for her own image and conduct. In place of artful games, high melodrama, and worship of the "Beautiful Lady," she states her preference for sexual frankness, casual liaisons, and the easy company of the "girl friend." In this regard, she is for once proud of the "destruction" wrought by her contemporaries:

> My generation, which destroyed the institution of marriage (something I still regard as an achievement), did not recognize vows of fidelity. We were ready at any moment to break off a marriage (regarded anyway only as a protracted love affair) and get a divorce—or rather separate, because in fact there was no real marriage to begin with. It is amazing that such markedly casual relationships often resulted in lasting unions which were very much more stable than the respectable marriages, founded on lies and pretense, of earlier generations. (II, 136)

As a "girl friend," she argues, she was far more beneficial to Mandelstam: She was a lighthearted companion who renounced all rights and demanded no care (II, 139). And it is highly significant that Nadezhda Mandelstam ventures to claim this attitude—with its emphasis on honesty and disregard for convention—as possibly her one creative contribution to their relationship: "Although he influenced me greatly and molded me in his own image, I also affected him in certain ways with my impatience and readiness to pack up and leave at any moment" (II, 137).[28]

Thus, by playing out the role of "girl friend," Nadezhda Mandelstam escaped the venality of the materialistic wife and the objectification of the beauty. At the same time, her "happy-go-lucky" role, in part anticipated by Mandelstam's cooption of her as his "you," harbored a more aggressive power. Since she alone had undergone his intensive, intimate training—had allowed him in part to remold her into an extension of himself—she received both the right and duty to speak in his name. She was the one who could and should tend to his archive (as we shall see, this also entailed her service as living archive); more, she was the one authorized spokesperson for his views. However, her self-styled role as "girl friend" and the attitude it implies unmistakably shaped and extended her fulfillment of these tasks. As the unlovely, irreverent, impatient girl friend, Nadezhda Mandelstam evinced a constant impulse to "unmask" and reassess people and events in plainspeaking and even provocative terms.[29] The companion and confidante of great poets, she dared to write and elucidate what they said in confidence or uttered enigmatically; she functioned, in a sense, as their prosaic uncensored alter-ego, the truth-telling fool in their discreet royal court. With Mandelstam in particular, this role accrued from beloved precedent. Here she seemed to resume the stance she first learned with her father: Mandelstam's idiosyncratic authority not only exempted her from the more inhibiting patriarchal conventions of her society, but finally inspired her to take the part of unabashed defender, to be provoked into speaking the "whole truth."

In these subtly indicated ways Nadezhda Mandelstam formulated a complex self-conception and authorship over the continuum of childhood and marriage. Contrary to her statements in both volumes of memoirs, her childhood afforded her an essential preparation for her adult life. It was during this happy time that she established the basic life patterns and values later canonized through her relationship with Mandelstam. Within the refuge of her family, she enjoyed a tolerant atmosphere and an unconventional autonomy; she learned to appreciate a wide array of arts and pleasures. In her relations with her father, she seemed to discover the makings of two productive roles—that of the wild girl brought to reason and the wild girl unleashed as sharp-tongued fighter. Reviewing the formative period of her childhood, I would amend her extreme conclusion: Although Nadezhda Mandelstam confesses that she is "the work of [her husband's] own hands," she actually co-authored her life text with her husband, negotiating an important tension between obedience and wildness, altruism and a complex self-indulgence.

Her "submission" to Mandelstam, then, comprised an intriguing combination of self-renunciation and self-assertion. Giving up her independence as an artist and a professional, she acquired through him an articulation of a worldview similar to her own and a most compelling and enabling mission. Nadezhda Mandelstam's iconoclasm and *joie de vivre* came already embodied and approved in the poet. Her selfless mission to preserve him and his work granted her a powerful public image and, most surprisingly, a speaking part she would never have otherwise assumed. Moreover, in the course of serving and then preserving her husband, Nadezhda Mandelstam gradually recognized her own distinctive strengths and position. She discovered her greater ability to cope and endure, an ability she even identifies as female. She proved her own empowering singularity as a woman; resisting material entrapment and objectification (as well as the docility her husband demanded), she maintained an unusual freedom of action and expression. And by pursuing her own creative variant of the role of girl friend and confidante, she developed into a powerful, distinctive writer who displayed great storytelling and rhetorical skills, a liberating irreverence toward convention, and an almost self-indulgent passion for telling "the whole truth."

Yet, however productive her relationship with Mandelstam proved to be, it is important to note that Nadezhda Mandelstam could become an author only after she was widowed.[30] Their relationship created the impetus and essential source for her writing, but she could not presume to write until her husband's authoritative voice and person—for her, the greatest values of their marriage—were absent. Nevertheless, as I will discuss over the next two chapters, once

Nadezhda Mandelstam began to write, the process of self-realization gained incredible momentum. In *Hope against Hope* and then *Hope Abandoned*, she progressed to grander thematic vistas and bolder, more idiosyncratic assertions of her authority. In effect, while ostensibly tending to Mandelstam, she dared to advance from a re-creative to a critical and creative voice—an extraordinarily powerful voice which, I contend, still influences our general understanding of Stalinist history. Confronting the audacity of her final work, we can recall that her complex character and creative approach were founded in childhood and abetted by her loving, demanding, but unsuspecting husband.

6.
HOPE AGAINST HOPE

While Nadezhda Mandelstam's first volume of memoirs, *Hope against Hope*, was still circulating as a *samizdat* manuscript in the 1960s, the famous poet and editor Aleksandr Tvardovskii deftly summarized its merits:

> I read [the book] in "one gulp" for there's no other way to read it. It is written as if it was being related one night to a good friend before whom there is nothing to hide or prove. . . . But at the same time it is written with exceptional strength and talent and, judging it from a literary point of view, with a special sense of the necessary in its exposition, for despite its length nothing seems superfluous. Even the peculiar repetitions, flashbacks, flash forwards, digressions or distractions—it all appears to be natural and justified. (10)[1]

That her book was being so widely read, that a powerful literary figure like Tvardovskii had considered and approved it—these formal indicators of success came unexpectedly to Nadezhda Mandelstam. When she commenced *Hope against Hope*, she did not set out to become a famous writer.[2] Instead (as Tvardovskii astutely sensed) she simply had been ready and able to share her story with "good friends." After Stalin's death in 1953 and the de-Stalinizing Twentieth Party Congress in 1956, she finally wrote out Mandelstam's poems and lobbied for an official commission to rehabilitate her husband's biography and work. In the meantime, she did not hesitate to take his rehabilitation into her own, more reliable hands. In *Hope against Hope* she restores the obliterated life of her husband; she testifies to invalidate what she perceives as the "false" memoirs of others—particularly those of Russian émigrés in the West.[3] It seems that she intended *Hope against Hope* to set the record incontrovertibly straight.

From another perspective, the writing of *Hope against Hope* marked and facilitated a significant change in Nadezhda Mandelstam's self-perception. Indeed, this text formally inaugurated the so-called "third period" in her life:

> The third period was from the end of the 50s when I regained the right to speak my name, to say who I was and what I thought. Almost at once two parts of my life—the first and the third—came together, crushing the second one in the middle and flattening it like a pancake—made not of flour, of course, but something nasty. My life became a single whole again, particularly after I had written my first book describing what had happened to us. In the period of waiting, when I didn't live, but only hid and lay low, I had two aims: to preserve the poetry and to

leave something in the nature of a letter telling of our fate. The first book is in fact such a letter, which I managed to write in a rather detailed way. (II, 183)

Composing the first book, Nadezhda Mandelstam assumed not only the possibility of writing but the meaningful coherence and reception of her life. Intent on restoring Mandelstam's biography, she happened in the process to discern the broad outline of her own. Moreover, she could now presume an audience who believed and valued her testimony; her concept of self once again developed in contiguity and community. Just as her "I" was confirmed and sanctioned by her husband, so her first-person authorial voice seemed to emerge through the encouragement of like-minded friends.

The declaration quoted above also indicates, by negation, an important unnamed factor in the writing and impact of *Hope against Hope*. As in her representation of childhood, we are led to dismiss entire decades of her life; she only values the periods when Mandelstam is a present influence either in person or expressible memory. The second "flattened" period is a nightmarish blank. Nadezhda Mandelstam spent twenty years—from Osip's second arrest in 1938 to the "thaws" of the late 1950s—in lonely, humiliating, unofficial exile, fleeing the attention of the authorities as she wandered from one provincial hole to another, earning her diploma and eking out a poor living as a teacher of English.[4] The combined conditions of bereavement, hardship, and terrible political repression irrevocably embittered her notions of a career and independence; she became a professional woman only out of dire necessity. Yet this terrible, devalued period must have been formative as well—in fact, as much a prerequisite for her writing as the relaxed circumstances of her third and final stage. While Nadezhda Mandelstam found an encouraging environment for her work in the 1950s and 1960s, she had prepared for it, in effect, over her twenty years of solitary wandering, remembering, studying, observing, and reflecting. Involuntarily, she gained important experience of the professional world and proved successful in securing its credentials, even completing a dissertation in her chosen field of linguistics.[5] She grew accustomed to being and thinking and (to a much more limited extent) speaking on her own. She accumulated data along the way that was crucial for her analysis. And at the same time, through her constant vigil over Mandelstam's poetry, she absorbed and appropriated its style and substance. Joseph Brodskii makes this eloquent point in his obituary for Nadezhda Mandelstam:

> Gradually the lines of those poets became her mentality, became her identity. They supplied her not only with the plane of regard or angle of vision; more importantly, they became her linguistic norm. So when she set out to write her books, she was bound to gauge—by that time unwittingly, instinctively—her sentences against theirs. The clarity and remorselessness of her pages, while reflecting the character of her mind, are also inevitable stylistic consequences of the poetry that had shaped that mind. In both content and style, her books are but a postscript to the supreme vision of language which poetry essentially is and which became her flesh through learning her husband's lines by heart. (151)[6]

In sum, during this period Nadezhda Mandelstam underwent a second, more arduous apprenticeship and, surviving it, she attained a whole vision of her experience and the self-assurance and seasoned language to bear witness.

Created from these various experiences and impulses, *Hope against Hope* tumbles out into a shape quite distinct from the conscientious *Notes on Anna Akhmatova*. Although both texts propose a similar goal—an authentic record of the poet under Stalinism—they ultimately project a different voice and focus and intimate, beyond these signals, different assumptions about the role and privilege of the author. Most fundamentally, Chukovskaia and Mandelstam contrast in their approach to the act of writing. Chukovskaia adhered to a professional standard set in large part by her father. She was adept and careful in the handling of texts, the citation of sources, the writing of commentary. She consciously figured herself as the scrupulous, deferential assistant; hence her text offers a model record—with extensive quotations, careful eyewitness reports, and painstaking documentation. Mandelstam never embraced writing as a profession or a vocation, despite her education according to a "male curriculum" and her later studies as a linguist. From what we know of her creative process, she worked unencumbered by self-consciousness, or, for that matter, pretentiousness. Varvara Shklovskaia and her husband Nikolai Panchenko witnessed the birth of her first book and can recall her casual mode of composition as she sat tailor-fashion on her bed and typed out her manuscript nonstop.[7] She sought no help in her creation; she distributed her manuscript to friends to test for interest, not to solicit criticism.[8] It would seem that her approach to writing was as unconventional and informal as her childhood behavior or (closer to the mark) her marital life. Nadezhda Mandelstam was no conscientious biographer-critic, but simply "competent to tell what she knew."[9]

Her text, therefore, unfolds as a continuous *relation*. Her editors since have added footnotes to explain certain references, but Nadezhda Mandelstam, writing outside of the restrictions of censorship and scholarship, does not utilize the layered structure of *Notes on Anna Akhmatova*. She appends no final display of her husband's poetry; she has performed this critical duty elsewhere. Instead, she produces a marvelous, energetic, all-encompassing narrative—a peculiar blend of memoir, analysis, and adventure story. Endeavoring to define her work, her readers have compared *Hope against Hope* with such varied models as the *Illiad*, *Tristram Shandy*, and Herzen's *My Past and Thoughts*.[10]

Rather than be enticed by these analogies, however, I find it more useful to pursue its comparison with *Notes on Anna Akhmatova*—especially with the clear strategies of representation in the latter work. In Mandelstam's *Hope against Hope* there are many observations on the poet's personal conduct, views, and creative process that reinforce the reading of artist and art in the *Notes*. Nadezhda Mandelstam's distinction can be best discerned, perhaps, by analyzing how this shared core of information is related and positioned in her text. As Charles Isenberg has remarked, her relationship with and observation of her husband—especially over the last, most dramatic years of his life—serve as an enabling foundation for her entire narrative:

If we think of chronology as the neutral principle of narrative structure in a memoir, the main figure of narration in Nadezhda Mandelstam's first volume is disclosed as a particularizing synecdoche: a slice of roughly five years condenses the drama of half a century. Everything outside this culminating phase of Mandelstam's life, which coincides with the Great Terror, becomes in effect a flashback or a flash forward.[11]

It is this phase of the poet's life, evoked sequentially but not contiguously in her text, which outfits Nadezhda Iakovlevna with a double authority as author and (this more apparently in the second volume) judge. This condensed life story embodies a most important value: that is, a life related to be lived in consonance with the free, joyous, culture-saturated properties of Mandelstam's art, a witnessed union of art and life bravely pursued under the disruptive conditions of Stalinism. It was of urgent importance that Nadezhda Mandelstam deliver this model of the courageous poet; his paradigm seemed so essential and desirable that she may have bent the facts somewhat to support it.[12] Indeed, it fell to her, the surviving witness and spokesperson, "to align the facts of the poet's life with the mythologies of his writings" so as to fulfill Mandelstam's own prophecies and establish his authority.[13]

Life story

In content, this life story maintains clear parallels with Akhmatova's portrait in *Notes*. Nadezhda Mandelstam's description of her husband's genius reiterates many of the features that Chukovskaia identified in the female poet—the utter absorption in an uncensored (and particularly European) world culture (255–56); a joining of aesthetic sensitivity with moral decency and "social concern" (262); a distaste for state-endowed privilege and an innate sympathy for the common people (150, 265).[14] In most ways, despite the striking differences in their art, she allows Mandelstam and Akhmatova like virtues and arrays them in the same approved community. The notion of Acmeism is thereby transformed from a somewhat haphazard grouping of young poets into a worldview shared and enacted over a lifetime by two great artists, an approach to life and art that integrated the ethical and the aesthetic, the mundane and the spiritual. Both Acmeists offered perhaps the most inspiring model to their chroniclers precisely because they endorsed this sort of consonance. As re-created, their lives fulfilled their art.

On the other hand, because they contrasted in terms of persona and physical presence, this fulfillment is expressed in each case through different textual strategies. Whereas Akhmatova could be viewed and recorded as a living monument, Mandelstam was better narrated a life story that realized his own mythological self-prophecies. This mandate to create "a canonical image of the poet" befitting his work consequently developed Nadezhda Mandelstam as narrator; like an author of religious philosophy or even didactic fiction, she wrote to delineate a coherent lesson, a meaningful plot. Furthermore, given her intimate relationship with Mandelstam, she could adopt an informal, flexible approach to her subject. As much as she loved her husband and respected his "gift," she never confined herself to the awed reportage of Chukovskaia. From the very outset, she assumed the bolder tasks of synthesizing, interpreting, and *retelling* her material.

Therefore, while the person and voice of the poet are present in *Hope against Hope*, the categories of description and transcription—scrupulously observed in the *Notes*—are here subsumed by a flow of subjective recollection and analysis. And this diffuse portrait derives as much from its object as its beholder. In contrast to his close friend Akhmatova, Mandelstam was said to project a much more elusive physical presence. Clarence Brown devotes several pages of his biography to the debate over the poet's appearance; witnesses disagree as to his size, good looks, and physical power.[15] For her part, Nadezhda Mandelstam handily decides this issue in *Hope against Hope*, rejecting as caricature his frequent portrayal as "a puny, delicate Jewish type" and declaring her husband to be of medium height and "much more robust" build (306). While her description is revealing (it reinforces her characterization of Mandelstam as a "real man" and life-loving poet), its brevity tells us even more. Mandelstam never functions as a visual icon in her text. Instead, his power emanates from his manner and voice, his most characteristic states of unaffected joy or poetic possession.[16] To be sure, Nadezhda Mandelstam, like Chukovskaia, does testify to the physical toll the regime takes of the poet (especially after his first arrest and incarceration), but her account never formalizes his appearance as a component of his greatness.

Her record of Mandelstam's voice differs for other reasons. She is not capable of transcription:

> I well remember M.'s voice and the way he read, but it was inimitable and lives on only in my ears. If people could hear his voice, they would understand what he called "interpretative reading" or "conducting." Phonetic notation could only give a crude rendering of his pauses, of where he raised or lowered his voice. His treatment of vowel quantity and the timbre of his voice could not be indicated. But what memory could ever preserve all the inflections of a voice that fell silent a quarter of a century ago? Yet something of his voice is preserved in the very structure of his verse, and now, when the years of silence are coming to an end, thousands of youngsters have caught the intonation of M.'s poetry and involuntarily reproduce it when they recite him. (276–77)

Her account occasionally quotes her husband—a repeated motto or, more often, a pungent comment that introduces or highlights an important theme. Nadezhda Mandelstam does not demonstrate the stenographic facility of Chukovskaia; it is a difficult enough task to take down her husband's dictation of his work.[17] But more to the point, she deems this sort of record superfluous. As she indicates in the quote above, his voice is truly reincarnated in his written work; in some mysterious way, even its oral idiosyncracies can be sensed in the texts.

Unlike Akhmatova—who, according to Nadezhda Mandelstam, is best expressed in her poetry and *conversation* (not written prose)—Mandelstam is only "fully revealed" in his writing.[18] She notes his "reserve" in speaking about what becomes manifest in his poetry (66); elsewhere she claims that "the key to his behavior [is] to be found in his verse and prose" (252). In *Hope against Hope*, Mandelstam is reincarnated through the powerful sound and sense of her *rereading*.

Her poet, then, must be monumentalized in a different way. If he is to be received as he writes himself—according to the "mythologies" and kenotic topoi of "the last Helleno-Christian poet"—Nadezhda Mandelstam must bear confirming witness to his tragic and redemptive life. Gregory Freidin brilliantly analyzes the opening paragraph of *Hope against Hope* with this strategy in mind, showing how her account is framed by Mandelstam's gesture of defiance (exposing Aleksei Tolstoi as a false prophet) and intimations of his eventual Passion and martyrdom.[19] After this first dramatic forecast, Nadezhda Mandelstam periodically signals her husband's prescience and sense of mission. She portrays him greeting the secret police with equanimity during his first arrest, for, like the figure of Christ, he already knows that they have "come for him" (5). Aside from a period of confused silence in the 1920s (what amounts to a requisite temptation), the poet is credited with foreseeing the failure of the revolution's promised millenium and the certainty of his own doom. He lives in accord with his "poetic rightness," conscious of the subversive power the regime fears in his poetry (170), convinced of his "right to make himself heard" (196). Wielding this verbal power, he nonetheless abhors and avoids any manifestation of political will. He flees meetings with government luminaries like Trotskii and the foreign minister Chicherin (104) and is wary of the state's patronage through official writers' organizations (153). In Nadezhda Mandelstam's text, her husband longs for no earthly kingdom. His fate and role are always that of a charismatic poet—a diviner of dreams, a compelling voice of the spirit. Even the final tales she gathers of his death reflect this calling: In one account he appears as "the Poet" (388), and in another he is remembered reciting verse to a group of respectful criminals (393).

Along with this plot of spiritual mission and knowing sacrifice, Nadezhda Mandelstam reifies another important element of Mandelstam's mythologies: his position as outcast. Just as Akhmatova's nature is seen to embrace both haughtiness and childlikeness, so Mandelstam is said to contain the paradox of self-assured poet and upstart intellectual or *raznochinets*.[20] And just as Akhmatova's childlikeness protects her from a conventional lifestyle and poetic silence, so the role of *raznochinets* in Mandelstam's case serves as an antidote to the conformity and complacency lurking in the poet's high estate, a means of breaking free from a muzzling establishment. Nadezhda Mandelstam highlights the most dramatic psychological effect of this assumed role, charting Mandelstam's progress from *The Egyptian Stamp* to *Fourth Prose* in which he clearly "extend[s] his hand to the upstart intellectual" and so exorcises his own self-doubt and begins once again to write poetry (176).[21]

Throughout this first book, Nadezhda Mandelstam assays a virtually seamless life-work synthesis of the poet, testifying to his self-prophesied power and basing her conclusions (like any conscientious disciple) on the explicit evidence of his texts. In contrast to Chukovskaia's description and transcription of the artist, she produces a kind of narrative exegesis of Mandelstam's joined person-persona. And in a more audacious move, she ventures beyond the texts of her husband—his revealing poetry and explanatory prose—to narrate bolder, more sweeping scenarios of his prominence. This she manages by working out and authorizing her own critical perspective, what she designs as the definitive view of her husband.

Her evaluation of her husband's place in Soviet society and culture counters any sort of official framework or hierarchy. In a characteristically unsystematic way, Nadezhda Mandelstam situates him through a rambling series of comparisons and contiguities, an ongoing scrutiny of other persons' lives and their interactions with her husband. As might be expected, she tends to focus more keenly on his peers in the Soviet cultural establishment. These are the people with whom she and Osip are in most regular contact, who most directly aid or abuse them and reflect, to different degrees, the state's influence over their behavior and art. Although Nadezhda Mandelstam clearly favors those who resist that influence, it is interesting that, unlike more orthodox critics in the Soviet Union or the Russian emigration, she refuses to draw an absolute line of judgment between the elect and the fallen. Her portrayal is invariably tempered by human factors—a single act of kindness (or malice) shown, her husband's display of interest or approval.[22] Therefore she remembers Demian Bednyi, a devoted writer of the new order, as an ineffectual rather than soulless figure—a man who refused to intercede after Mandelstam's arrest but was distraught by the "execution of Russian poetry" and later disgraced on account of his passion for books.[23] Leopold Averbakh, one of the interim architects of the new Soviet literature and "a very typical product of the first decade after the Revolution," is by no means approved, but his absolute judgments are considered an interesting artifact because Mandelstam was "fascinated by the workings of Averbakh's mind" (165). Even when the poet Nikolai Tikhonov provokes his own separate chapter, he is not simply vilified but explored as a sometimes charming and usually doctrinaire literary bureaucrat. Nadezhda Mandelstam notes that her husband initially "fell under his spell" and admits, after itemizing his misdeeds, that "[i]t is difficult to dismiss entirely the 'young Kolia,' the youth with the expansive gestures, as we had once known him" (234).

Within this complex human network of ideological ambiguities, varying talents, and personal ties, one element, however, remains constant: Mandelstam is fixed at its center, an uncompromised, but altogether human artist. Nadezhda Mandelstam re-positions him both diachronically and synchronically—through her revision of Russian literary history and her intuition of contemporary poetic genius. I have already mentioned her revaluation of the 1920s in Soviet literature; her views on the whole span of its history presume to topple similar sacred cows. She firmly rejects two established interpretative progressions—the party-directed history of the Soviet establishment and the émigré vaunting of the Silver Age and its martyred antecedents. Instead, citing her husband, she asserts a strong connection between the Symbolists and the Bolsheviks and argues that both groups manifest the same instinctive dislike of the Acmeists:

> They [the Acmeists] brought something with them that provoked blind fury in both literary camps. Viacheslav Ivanov and his entourage as well as the Gorky circle met them with hostility. . . . For this reason the war against them was one of annihilation and was waged much more fiercely than against other poets. O.M. always said that the Bolsheviks preserved only those who were passed on to them by the Symbolists. There was no such favor shown the Acmeists. And in Soviet times the Lef group and the remnants of the Symbolists all levelled a fundamental blow against the surviving Acmeists—Akhmatova and Mandelstam. (154)

As Nadezhda Mandelstam randomly surveys the scene, the Acmeists emerge as distinctive martyrs, vehemently ostracized by all the other groups which have insinuated themselves into the establishment. She generally does not fault the most talented artists in these opposing factions (especially when they have been in some way approved by her husband); poets like Blok, Belyi, and Maiakovskii are by and large depicted sympathetically, despite their weakness for propagandizing and proselytizing. Instead she accuses the power-invested villains—writers such as Briusov, Brik, and Gor'kii who undertake the management of literature. She records Briusov's petty insults against her husband (154); Brik's stigmatizing of Mandelstam and Akhmatova as "internal émigrés" (172); and Gor'kii's underlying hostility to "spineless intellectuals" (evidenced, in Mandelstam's case, when he refused to issue the poet a pair of trousers during the civil war [117]).

Moreover, in comparison with the common historical opposition of Futurism to Symbolism, Nadezhda Mandelstam's analysis emphasizes her husband's fundamental revolt against his Symbolist predecessors and, predictably, implies the superiority of his Acmeist worldview. Mandelstam, she remarks, answers Blok's pessimism about the oncoming demise of civilization and humanistic culture with the "conviction that culture, like grace, is bestowed by a process of continuity" (249). Through a similar strategy she inserts an extensive, approving description of her husband's views by juxtaposing him with the philosopher Nikolai Berdiaev; because she admires the latter's work, "the contrast between Berdiaev and M. applies only to those features of Berdiaev which he shared with the Symbolists" (268). Against Berdiaev's "Symbolist" notions of a dreary life, unearthly beauty, and elitist license, Mandelstam is said to espouse a love of earthly things, a joy in "the pleasure and play" of life, a respect for communal morality (and even the oft-maligned middle class), and a bond ("natural for any poet") with the street (263–68). In Nadezhda Mandelstam's re-creation, it is Mandelstam the Acmeist—not the Symbolists or the Futurists—who poses the greatest threat to the literary establishment because he refuses to disown the power of the ordinary, the value of the earthly, and the poet as poet rather than a "fisher of men."[24]

In his wife's schema, then, Mandelstam assumes the moral high ground in the progression of twentieth-century Russian literature. Disregarding the official sequence of revolutionary and then socialist realism, scorning the nostalgic approval of a glorious Silver Age and liberal 1920s, Nadezhda Mandelstam promotes the Acmeists (i.e., the "real" Acmeists like Mandelstam, Akhmatova, and Gumilev) as major poets and—far more—as bearers of an essential antidote to the moral disease infecting almost all other artists in her era. As she portrays them, their subversive power is sensed and feared and persecuted throughout their existence.

While the Acmeists are the only *group* which merits this high placement, they are not the only artists lauded in *Hope against Hope*. Nadezhda Mandelstam devises another measure of her husband's greatness by linking him with other major poet-martyr contemporaries—specifically Akhmatova, Pasternak, and (to a somewhat lesser extent) Tsvetaeva. As we have seen, the creative and personal paths of Mandelstam and Akhmatova most nearly coincide in her narrative. Apart from a very brief period when Mandelstam mistakenly renounced his ties to her and all Acmeists (174), the two poets remained bound by their early experience, similar worldview, and mutual respect and affection. As Nadezhda Mandelstam recalls, it seems that Akhmatova was with them in their neediest times. Her presence—as true friend, kindred poet, and a "Cassandra" who divines her age—both proves their intense bond and graces Mandelstam's "non-status" with spiritual dignity, the sanction of a noble co-sufferer. Thus Nadezhda Mandelstam depicts Akhmatova as sharing the trappings of martyrdom and solemnly commemorating their visits with poetry; Akhmatova recites her poem about her Voronezh visit once they have come to Moscow (217) and her poem about Leningrad "as a transit station to exile" during their very last meeting (318). To a certain extent, Akhmatova serves in *Hope against Hope* as she functioned in *Notes*—as an iconic figure who embodies others' unnamed suffering. The female poet is remembered for visual and dramatic effect: " 'Poetry is power,' [Mandelstam] once said to Akhmatova in Voronezh, and she bowed her head on its slender neck" (170). She is recorded for her wise, pithy comments and her eloquent gestures. It is Akhmatova who transforms a simple egg into a poignant symbol of wisdom and consolation (and redemption?) the night of Mandelstam's arrest: "Suddenly Anna Andreevna said that O.M. should eat something before he left and she held out the egg to him. He agreed, sat down at the table, put some salt on it and ate it" (9).

Marina Tsvetaeva, on the other hand, is invoked more tangentially. Nadezhda Mandelstam will explore and appreciate her character in greater detail in *Hope Abandoned*; here she simply presumes Tsvetaeva's value as a poet and uses her as another worthy point of comparison for her husband. Tsvetaeva, she notes, is also denied publication as an unofficial great. She, more than other poets, resembles Mandelstam in her renunciation of any worldly birthright and a "seat by the columns" under the new regime (151, 154). By mentioning Tsvetaeva so casually and reflexively as she discusses Mandelstam, Nadezhda Mandelstam suggests an automatic, absolute link among "true poets"—a genius which, whatever its individual idiosyncracies, is recognizable, incontrovertible, and bonding.

Pasternak manifests that same common property, but as in *Notes on Anna Akhmatova*, his more fortunate life poses certain problems of association. The Mandelstams, unlike Akhmatova, are not bothered by the interference of Pasternak's wife (in fact, Nadezhda Mandelstam declares she is glad that they never visit him at home), but the differences between the two poets are so palpable that she chooses to compare them in a chapter entitled "Antipody" ("The Antipodes"). The term is used to contrast and correspond:

> In certain respects O.M. and Pasternak were antipodes, but antipodes are located at opposite ends of a single space. They can be connected by a line. They do have common features and qualities. They co-exist. Neither of them could ever have been the antipode of, let's say, Fedin, Olshanin, or Blagoi. (149)

This figure therefore allows for Pasternak's difference within the established constellation and casually excludes other, lesser writers from the high circle of "the poets." What fundamentally distinguishes the two artists is not talent but Pasternak's presumption of material privilege and professional status, his desire to be included in and outfitted by the literary establishment. In one sample anecdote, Pasternak drives Mandelstam into a fury when he suggests that an apartment is necessary for the writing of poetry; the episode shows Mandelstam to moral advantage, for his anger reflects his aversion to corruption (the price the artist must pay for such apartments) and his sensitivity to a "whole nation . . . utterly deprived of basic needs" (150). Although Nadezhda Mandelstam is careful to imply rather than state her husband's superiority, her representation of Pasternak very much reinscribes his slightly ambiguous portrait in *Notes*. In matters of domestic arrangement and professional conduct, Pasternak serves as something of a mild foil to these other poets. During the actual years of Stalin's rule, he conformed too much and suffered too little to achieve the tragic magnitude of Mandelstam and Akhmatova.

The Mandelstam-Pasternak relationship is curiously complicated by Stalin's infamous phone call to Pasternak—a dictator's query to one poet about the worth (and danger) of another.[25] For although Pasternak was treated as an approved member of the establishment (Stalin himself was interested to know why he was upset about Mandelstam's arrest), he dared to express his concern and managed this treacherous conversation very well—certainly to Mandelstam's satisfaction (148). Yet even admitting all these ambiguities in Pasternak's character and conduct, Nadezhda Mandelstam ultimately "purifies" his connection with her husband by invoking his final tragedy—the scandal of *Doctor Zhivago*. It is this ordeal which enables her to assert their similarity in fate as well as talent:

> For both, destiny was hatched from their spiritual natures, like a butterfly from a chrysalis. Both turned out to be doomed by the literary establishment, but Pas-

ternak for a time sought points of contact with it, while Mandelstam always shied away. Seeking a stable life, especially in a material sense, Pasternak knew that the path to it lay through membership in the establishment. He never left it or shunned it. After all, Doctor Zhivago is a poet as well as a doctor; Boris Leonidovich didn't break with the establishment, but Zhivago did—and then only when his author saw that the rift was inevitable. (151)

Mandelstam, Akhmatova, Pasternak, Tsvetaeva—these figures emerge in *Hope against Hope* as a consort of "true poets" somehow set apart from the conforming, pampered, spiritually numbed literary establishment under Stalin. Over time and space, through revised literary history and validating company, Nadezhda Mandelstam thus confirms her husband as a great poet and an exceptional hero. Indeed, elevated by the various strategies of her narrative, Mandelstam functions as a virtual prototype for the artist martyred in Stalinist times. And as an artist who is shown to link creative work with social concern and moral integrity, he is positioned to project spiritual and ethical primacy as well. In *Hope against Hope* Nadezhda Mandelstam effectively relates her corroborated version of Mandelstam's life as a tragic, instructive, and realized legend. She conveys his model of being and judging as exemplary and generative.

History

With her husband ensconced as the central value and most qualified seer of their context, Nadezhda Mandelstam obtains the license to generalize from his example. Her life with Mandelstam serves as a core from which her narrative fans out in time, space, experience, analysis, and authority. Her husband once refashioned his autobiography into a recovery of "cultural memory"; now Nadezhda Mandelstam follows suit, elaborating history from biography.[26] Her narrative describes a constant movement between the particular and the general, the anecdotal and the categorical. Writing out her "letter" at last, she avails herself of its flexible, multifunctioned structure.

Her leap from biography to history is easiest and surest when she generalizes about the literary process, for here she operates on utterly familiar ground. In comparison with Chukovskaia's careful observations and intimations, Nadezhda Mandelstam issues bold summaries and what would appear to be irrefutable information:

> I first understood how poetry is made in 1930. . . . In Voronezh I got a particularly clear impression of it. Our life together in a rented room, that is, in a kennel or a lair or a sleeping bag (however you choose to describe it), nose to nose, without outside witnesses, hopelessly uprooted and restricted—this meant that I could observe closely all the details of his "sweet-voiced labor." (180)

For the reader her conclusions must seem ironclad, based as they are on such hard-won empirical evidence. The authority of her statements is wrested—stark clause after stark clause—from her extreme vantagepoint ("nose to nose" in "a kennel or a lair"). Oddly privileged by this bare existence, Nadezhda Mandelstam can account for the sequential stages of her husband's composing: his restlessness, the moving of his lips, the ebb and flow of anxiety at certain points of "writing." Although she does not claim the same absolute sequence for other poets (she has the opportunity to observe a much more restrained Akhmatova at work), she nevertheless states certain generalizations about the whole process. As she does so, her transition from particular to general goes unmarked, effected by a subtle shifting of pronouns; a reliance on citation and paraphrase; an introduction of conceptual nouns, impersonal constructions, and rhetorical questions:

> In these verses O.M. speaks about the sound of "remembering" lips. But is it only a flutist's lips that know beforehand what they have to say? The process of composing verse is somewhat like recalling something that has never been said before. What is the search for "the lost word" ("I have forgotten the word I wished to say, like a blind swallow it will return to the abode of shadows") but an attempt to recall what does not yet exist? This is the concentration with which we seek the forgotten thing that then suddenly flashes in the mind. In the first stage the lips move soundlessly, then they begin to whisper and "suddenly an extended arch resounds in my mumblings." An inner music has resolved into units of meaning. The recollection is developed like an image on a photographic plate. (187)

The link between her generalized description and Mandelstam's own practice is almost seamless, especially given the interweave of poetic quotations. But it seems that her statements, however derived, are put forward as basic truth. This intent is more clearly manifest when Nadezhda Mandelstam judges other poets by her husband's example. Later in this same chapter (entitled *"Topot i shopot"* ["Rumbling and whispering"] after the sounds of Mandelstam's poetry-making) she asserts that during the creative process the inner voice takes complete possession of the poet and that is why

> I do not believe Maiakovskii when he said that he stepped on the throat of his own song. How was he able to do this? From my own unusual experience—experience witnessing poetic creation—I would say that you cannot put a bridle or a muzzle on a poem and you cannot step on its throat. It is one of the most exalted manifestations of a human being, the bearer of world harmony. (188)

Nadezhda Mandelstam repeatedly insinuates her husband's poetic worldview and practice as fundamental. Thoroughly trained on his example, she concludes for all that poetry-making is a process of listening and recovering; that the poet, "the bearer of world harmony," speaks with (not for) all people and is compelled by the urge to serve them. Moreover, much as she draws Mandelstam as the prototype for all poets, so she extrapolates the role of helper from her own experience. To be sure, she does not figure herself as gifted or important, nor does she indicate that her service is as extensive as that of Chukovskaia. She may transcribe her husband's verse, but that is due to his laziness, not his incapacity (181). Rather, subscribing to her family's values, Nadezhda Mandelstam presents herself as a clever, practical-minded helper whose strategies are rattled off in the chapter *"Arkhiv i golos"* ("Archive and Voice"). Here she relates how she learned to save manuscripts in the homely, domestic refuge of trunks and cushions: "Generally I stuffed [manuscripts] in every cubbyhole, but some copies I handed to other people for safekeeping. During the search of our apartment in 1934 we saw where they looked, and our poems were already sewn into cushions and hidden in saucepans and shoes" (271). She remarks on the preservation and "disappearance" of specific manuscripts, naming both saviors and thieves.[27] Her account reveals, but does not vaunt, her ingenuity and perseverance; rather, it pays careful tribute to the others (her brother, Natasha Shtempel') who helped her in this lifelong enterprise. When she discusses her role as "living" archive, she is quick to emphasize both her limitations and typicality:

> One way or another, I might make it to the end with few losses, although the end is not yet in sight. I have had to give up only one method of preserving [Mandelstam's] work because of my age: until 1956 I could remember everything by heart—both prose and verse. . . . In order not to forget anything I had to repeat a little to myself each day and I did this while I still believed I had a good while to live. Now it's late. . . . And in conclusion I will tell a story about someone else.
>
> This woman is still alive and so I won't give out her name. In 1937 there were daily newspaper attacks on her husband, a very high official. He sat at home waiting to be arrested and not daring to go out because his house was surrounded by police agents. At night he wrote a long letter to the Central Committee which his wife memorized in pieces. They shot him and she spent twenty years in labor camps and prisons. When she returned, she wrote out the letter and took it to its addressee, where I hope it has not disappeared forever. . . . How many of us are there spending sleepless nights repeating the words of our dead husbands? (276)

It is intriguing that when she touches on her own vital part in the literary process, Nadezhda Mandelstam most closely resembles Chukovskaia. She underplays her extraordinary work, viewing it in terms of necessity and physical capability. The ellipsis following the phrase "Now it's late" seems to convey both regret and resignation. When she next addresses the reader, she defers to the noble sacrifice of another woman.[28] It is only after she has established this woman's story as reference that she allows herself to ponder the contribution of all faithful wives, diffusing herself in the pronoun "we."

In *Hope against Hope*, then, Nadezhda Mandelstam retells much the same blueprint of the unofficial literary process as was solemnly delineated in *Notes on Anna Akhmatova*. That her conclusions should bear out many of Chukovskaia's observations reflects not only the likeness of their subjects but certain shared cultural beliefs and political circumstances.[29] On the evidence of their texts, both women were included in and awed by the process of poetic creation. Both were convinced of the Russian poet's spiritual mission. Both cherished and acted on these beliefs through years of terror and deprivation. And both construed their task as the preservation of poet and poetry. Again, their difference mainly lies in their fulfillment of that mission, their development of authority and authorship. Nadezhda Mandelstam observes no hierarchical boundaries between journal record and critical essay, the voice of the witness and the omniscient, judging stance adopted by the historian or critic. She does not relegate her bolder suppositions to footnotes or divert them into the mouths of fictional characters or compile them in an article. In her text, she lays idiosyncratic claim to a variety of authoritative narrative roles—most particularly, the role of "historian."

In fact, Nadezhda Mandelstam appears unabashed and undaunted as she ventures into the less familiar territory of social and political analysis. My reading of her function as "historian" therefore begins with an examination of her narrative voice and its strategies and assumptions. Judged by professional standards, her approach seems almost defiantly naive. Throughout the text—whether she speaks as "I" or the more authoritative "we"—Nadezhda Mandelstam projects an absolute connection between her writing voice and real-life person. Countless writers and theorists of autobiography have labored to underscore the implicit tension between persona and person in this genre, but she seems to ignore it altogether.[30] She rarely reflects on the problematic nature of her enterprise—the possibilities and distortions involved in transforming life into text. She claims no artistry and seems utterly confident of her written authenticity. According to her close associates, Nadezhda Mandelstam showed remarkably little concern over her text *qua* text. After *Hope against Hope* was published, she worried about factual errors and would correct these by hand in her friends' copies of her book, but she never implied that her text was a sacrosanct work of literature.[31]

Her subjectivity is made explicit in her style and very method of analysis. Although she periodically resorts to a more impersonal narration (as I have already shown in her discussion of poetry), Nadezhda Mandelstam embraces, above all, a first-person stance. This stance, implied as both physical and psychological, is crucial to the reception of her work. The landscape of *Hope against Hope* may not be as circumscribed as the chamber world of *Notes*, but her account almost always emanates from the vantagepoint of personal experience (whether it be hers or acquired secondhand). Nadezhda Mandelstam speaks from within Stalinist society—an observer at risk—and her narrative, even at a twenty-year remove from the worst horrors, cannot help but reflect the fear and guilt of her ordeal. In fact, by her own admission these conditions are so pervasive as to jeopardize her reliability; recognizing that the survivors of Stalinism have been left "unbalanced" in some way, she questions their (and her) value as witnesses (88).[32] For all her authorizing strategies, Nadezhda Mandelstam writes in full disclosure of her materially grounded, humanly limited perspective.

Yet while this approach would seem to undermine her authority, it also intensifies her influence. As I mentioned at the beginning of the chapter, Nadezhda Mandelstam writes *for* a specific audience—an audience in a literal sense because they were present listeners. While she seemed aware that *Hope against Hope* might one day be circulated beyond the Soviet Union, she was most intent on a new generation of Soviet readers who never knew the Terror and were then avid for the revival of poetry in general and Mandelstam in particular.[33] At the time of writing *Hope against Hope*, Nadezhda Mandelstam did not yet have her own apartment, but she had already been sought out by young devotees of her husband's work; that is, she had already renewed the habit, long repressed, of openly sharing information and opinions with others. One such seeker, Mikhail Polivanov, made a special pilgrimage to see the "poet's widow" in Tarusa in January 1962 and discovered that "[i]t was easy to become friends with her. She was straightforward, frank, sharp-tongued, and simple. She taught her interlocutors both freedom of thought and freedom of expression."[34]

Her memoirs seem, at least in part, to evolve from these new opportunities for communication. (As we shall see, *Hope Abandoned* is particularly encouraged by this experience.) Although it would be difficult—given the absence of an oral record—to pinpoint the similarities between text and conversation, witnesses have remarked on a general thematic resemblance between the two. Nadezhda Mandelstam conveyed much the same information to her readers and listeners. In some instances it even seems that she used her text, once written, as a script for spoken monologues.[35] She does not cultivate a markedly oral style in her writing—with emotive punctuation and frequent interjections—but she intimates some of the features of this exchange: anticipation of a present audience, peremptory shifts in theme, her self-aware performance as collector and teller of instructive tales. Her account is packed with personal and overheard anecdotes. Her relation describes a flow of unrestrained recollection and reflection—an in-process analysis—rather than a studious attempt to reorder and *rewrite* her life and thoughts in a conventional, methodical form.

The emplotment of *Hope against Hope* also demonstrates her idiosyncratic means of engaging and informing her readers. Although her text is broadly organized in sequence with the last years of Mandelstam's life, it specifically proceeds by association, pausing at times for outright digressions, cohering in its repetition of certain themes and imagery.[36] Upon the inexorably unfolding tragedy of her husband's persecution and death Nadezhda Mandelstam spins a capacious and thoroughly engrossing narrative out of some eighty short chapters. Varying in length from two to fifteen pages, these chapters are named to capture the reader's attention; their titles most often consist of catch phrases—either summary descriptions or quotations—that alert and predispose us to the following content. Titles like "Confiscation," "Leaving for Exile," "The Leap," and "Journey to Voronezh" herald adventures and disasters undergone; others—like "Theory and Practice," "Profession and Sickness," "The Change of Values," and "The Social Structure"—signal an analytical, even pseudo-sociological approach. Still others comprise ironic references to famous literary works or political slogans—for example, "A May Night," "Morning Thoughts," "Who Is to Blame," "Our Literature," "The First of May." In citing such titles, Nadezhda Mandelstam subverts their fixed resonance and exposes the contrast between the traditions and conventions they evoke and what she personally experiences or values. In overall effect, then, this composite structure seems to project a blend of fictional tale and reference work. The quickly changing chapters and wry titles recall the pace and self-aware, intermittently ironic narration of a novel (perhaps most evocative of a first-person detective or adventure story), whereas the book's analytical titles and encyclopedic scope suggest its use as a personalized digest of information about the Stalinist period.

Yet even given these subjective features of her narration and inquiry, I would argue for the utility of reading Nadezhda Mandelstam as a historian. First of all, this approach invokes more recent investigations into history-as-text, theories which argue that the writing of history has always entailed the author's subjective (albeit concealed) designation, selection, ordering, and interpretation of the "facts." Despite the historian's presumptions of "objectivity" and the accurate reconstruction of a recoverable past, some critics have maintained that history is as liable to be plotted, "troped," and subjectively fabricated as any form of imaginative writing.[37] Analyzed this way, *Hope against Hope* might be categorized as a kind of amateur metahistory which reveals this ever-present subjective impulse at work. In her text, one could posit, Nadezhda Mandelstam boldly includes us in the normally secret passage from experience and personal reflection to the statement and interpretation of the "facts."

More specifically, her "history" highlights the conditions of its genesis. Nadezhda Mandelstam writes a mere decade after Stalin's death and several years after his influence has been only partly condemned by the state. Understandably, she is not dispassionate in reviewing her horrific past. Her inquiry is explicitly unprofessional and limited in scope; her anti-Stalinist bias is strong; her designation of historical "facts" depends almost solely on personal experience. She has virtually no access to documents that affirm or describe her "unofficial" existence. Yet her problems of bias and access—danger signals to most historians—have been standard, until recently, for all professional Soviet scholars writing on this period. Even after the Twentieth and Twenty-Second Party Congresses, the distinguished Soviet historian Roy Medvedev found it necessary to resort to unpublished "documents, memoirs and eyewitness accounts" in order to write his copious study *Let History Judge*. As he explains, these sources were essential "because many of Stalin's illegal orders and actions were not recorded in any documents during his lifetime."[38] Aleksandr Solzhenitsyn, a non-historian who, like Nadezhda Mandelstam, was driven to report on one aspect of "unofficial" Soviet life, relied on masses of personal testimony in *The Gulag Archipelago*:

> This book could never have been created by one person alone. In addition to what I myself was able to take away from the Archipelago—on the skin of my back, and with my eyes and ears—material for this book was given me in reports, memoirs, and letters by 227 witnesses, whose names were to have been listed here....
>
> From among them I would like to single out in particular those who worked hard to help me obtain supporting bibliographical material from books to be found in contemporary libraries or from books long since removed from libraries and destroyed; great persistence was often required to find even one copy which

had been preserved. Even more would I like to pay tribute to those who helped me keep this manuscript concealed in difficult periods and then to have it copied. (xi)[39]

Because of the Soviet government's longstanding practice of repressing negative information and statistics, it was difficult for Soviet and non-Soviet historians alike to feel confident of their primary sources or to attempt to approximate the types and extent of various government activities under Stalin. In the pre-*glasnost'* editions of *The Great Terror*, his seminal book on the purges of the 1930s, the British historian Robert Conquest appends an extensive explanation to his bibliography, laying out the problems of data-gathering and research outside the Soviet Union.[40] Non-Soviet historians may have obtained further circumstantial evidence—for example, written accounts by non-Soviet visitors or counterintelligence reports or internal documents confiscated under the Nazi occupation—but when they undertook a description of Stalinist society and its adjunct labor camp and prison system, they, too, had to depend on the eyewitness testimony of its victims. Their work, based on such evidence and so oriented against the official representation of Soviet life, has often manifested an anti-Stalinist (and sometimes anti-Marxist or antisocialist) bias. This tendency to bond historical inquiry with ideological and moral judgment (a tendency of both dissident Soviet and Western historians) may seem an appropriate response to the atrocities of Stalinism. It has also been encouraged by the pressures and opportunities of the cold war long waged by the Soviet Union and the United States.

On this background, Nadezhda Mandelstam's sources seem no more suspect and her bias no more vehement than that of some professional historians. She offers her readers the closest available approximation of the facts—that is, information derived from personal observation and experience. In comparison with many of her professional colleagues, she is at least honest in declaring her bias. Moreover, Nadezhda Mandelstam seems peculiarly qualified to produce this sort of informal history because, ironically speaking, she was in the right place at the right time. She was not only an observer within the system but also an outcast forced to live in its margins and made aware of its underworld of security forces, prisons, and camps. Like Chukovskaia and Akhmatova, she was never fully admitted into this underworld and was compelled to study it, in large part, because it victimized her husband. Yet, as she writes her experience, Nadezhda Mandelstam differs from these other women in the scope and depth and keen interest of her analysis. She, for one, is ambitiously curious about the workings of this other world.

Her nomadic existence, then, was particularly advantageous—at least for the purposes of her history. Like Chukovskaia in *Notes*, she must present an interior view, but she was placed in many different kinds of settings.[41] Outside of the predictable urban centers of Moscow and Leningrad, she lived (with and without Mandelstam) in the smaller towns of Cherdyn, Voronezh, and Kalinin; the resorts at Sukhumi and Samatikha; and more distant places like Ulianovsk and Tashkent. Nadezhda Mandelstam observed a variety of working environments as well. Beyond the world of writing and publishing highlighted in Chukovskaia's texts, she experienced a provincial hospital in Cherdyn, a diverse set of educational establishments (a teacher's training college in Ulianovsk, the university at Tashkent), and even a textile factory in Strunino. Her private view, however, emanated from a position of near-homelessness; to survive, she had to forego any sort of "burrow" liable to detection (38, 50). So effaced and unencumbered, Nadezhda Mandelstam managed to survive as a witness to great poets and terrible events, to observe and analyze from within and below.[42] On account of her position, she could perform many of those eavesdropping and spying roles that the critic Mikhail Bakhtin has deemed essential to the depiction of private life in the novel. Those roles usually are enacted by marginal or criminal figures—rogues, prostitutes, procurers, and spying servants; within the Stalinist framework, Nadezhda Mandelstam qualifies as a new version of the same—the fugitive wife of a state "criminal" and an uninhibited teller of tales.[43]

Perhaps most importantly, Nadezhda Mandelstam was temperamentally suited to exploit this privilege. Her disdain for convention, her openness to new experience, her avidity for telling the "whole truth"—all these character traits contributed to her successful development as a cultural critic or, in Isenberg's words, "an acute field anthropologist" (205). Even her "wildness" came into play. At one point in the text she explicitly connects her ability to write with the breakdown of her "self-control and discipline" (287), her refusal to abide by the official code of silence and polite submission. Here she can fulfill her intuited role as Mandelstam's fighting partner; in fact, she specifically echoes his example, for he never observed these "rules of Soviet etiquette" (286). His values of poetry, simplicity, and compassion fix the goals she prescribes for her society, but it is her writing—her vehement and "undisciplined" commentary—which effectively persuades her people to heed him and review their own misconduct.

In keeping with her character and training (both marital and circumstantial), Nadezhda Mandelstam develops her own methods for writing and authorizing her version of Stalinist history. She is, first and foremost, a consummate storyteller—sensitive to resonant details of personality and scene, skillful in manipulating different points of view and pacing her narrative.[44] In the first paragraph of her book, she creates a fine suspense by adopting Akhmatova's viewpoint (the poet is contemplating her visit to a desperate Mandelstam) and highlighting the "brilliant, irritable," doomsaying figure of Nikolai Punin. She then flashes forward to the ironic twist in Akhmatova's fate; despite her lover's predictions, the poet is never arrested but is "always seeing others off on their last journey"—including Punin and implying Mandelstam (3). A colorful cast, portentous scene, and all-knowing narrator combine to convey the sweep of historical fiction, or the realism of a nineteenth-century novelist observing her society and projecting a talkative, omniscient authority.

In many other instances Nadezhda Mandelstam redirects her storytelling into social and political analysis. A sample passage from the first chapter neatly illustrates this technique. Describing how the secret police conduct Mandelstam's arrest, she abruptly pauses for more general reflection:

> In the language of the secret police this was called a "night operation." As I learned later on they all firmly believed that they were liable to meet with resistance on any given night or in any given apartment. To keep their spirits up they regaled each other with romantic legends about the dangers of night raids. I myself once heard the daughter of an important Chekist, one who had come to prominence in 1937, telling a story about how Babel', resisting arrest, had seriously wounded one of "ours." For her these stories were bound up in anxiety for her kind, indulgent father when he went out on "night work." He was so fond of children and animals that at home he always had the cat on his knees and he taught his daughter never to admit that she had done anything wrong and always to say "no." This homebody with a cat could never forgive the people he interrogated for admitting everything they were accused of. "Why did they do it?" the daughter repeated after her father. "Think of the trouble they made for themselves and for us!" And "us" meant all those who came at night with warrants, interrogated and passed sentence on the accused, and whiled away their spare time telling stories of the risks they ran. And these tales remind me of the tiny hole in the skull of Babel', a cautious, clever man with a high forehead, who probably never once in his life held a pistol in his hands. (5–6)

Here we find anecdote and irony put to work as analytical devices. Rather than dwell on her experience as victim, Nadezhda Mandelstam opens up a double perspective in her text by exploring the viewpoint of the police. She manages this through the story of an insider, a sympathetic member of the police "family." As she relates the daughter's tale, the categories of "us" and "them" completely shift referents and the concept of normality is revealed as unbearably sinister. In a surprising inversion, Nadezhda Mandelstam figures the secret police—the agents of the underworld—as conventional, cliché-ridden, and even bourgeois in their habits. She cites their euphemistic language, discloses their trite romantic mentality, and finally implies their terrible embrace of normalcy and atrocity.

Although irony serves her well in her judgment of the police, Nadezhda Mandelstam also chooses to introduce her own contrasting measure of value—the chilling concrete image of "the tiny hole in the skull" of the executed writer, Isaac Babel'. She deflates the legends of the police with the clinical "fact" of Babel's death; their false romanticism is utterly damned by her naturalistic evidence. Here and elsewhere her authority accrues with her ability to name what appear to be basic human values and sins and sufferings—to apply the "ordinary" earthly morality espoused by her and her husband.

Throughout her memoirs, Nadezhda Mandelstam will propose many similar investigations into the mentality and methods of her tormentors—indeed, of the whole police state apparatus. In *Hope against Hope* this analysis contextualizes the story of Mandelstam's particular persecution: his first arrest, the different stages of interrogation and then exile, his second arrest and disappearance. So in the second chapter, entitled *"Vyemka"* ("Confiscation"), she reflects further on the general procedure of arrests and searches. As in the passage cited above, her investigation here tends to rely on chance informants from within the system (in this chapter she identifies a writer who "in the thirties held a modest post in the secret police") and highlights the human conventions and limitations of the agents (6–9). Nadezhda Mandelstam comments on the (perhaps prescribed) ritual of offering hard candy to the victims—a gesture first witnessed on that fateful May night and later performed by her writer informant. She remarks on the agents' varying degrees of expertise—their clumsiness in conducting the search, their deliberate and sometimes obtuse perusal of Mandelstam's poetry. Her anecdotal account is punctuated, in turn, with concluding, historicizing statements. Reflecting on the nature of the search, she contrasts it, on the one hand, with a search from the post-1937 "period" and, on the other, with operations in the early days of the Soviet state: "The procedure was worked out to the last detail and it was quite different from the hectic manner in which it was done in the first days of the Revolution and during the Civil War" (8).

In general, Nadezhda Mandelstam demonstrates great skill in exploiting the analytical style of a historian. She marshals vocabulary, tone, and syntax in order to voice her analysis as definitive. Typologies, hierarchies, rhetorical questions and exclamations, clear designations of cause and effect—all of these features outfit her narrative as an authoritative text and project it above the modest testimony of a personal memoir. For example, in the ninth chapter entitled *"Teoriia i praktika"* ("Theory and Practice"), she maps out the vast spy network functioning in her society. She elaborates an extensive typology of informers based on the categories that she and Mandelstam devised, itemizing and labeling "the young men of military bearing," the "admirers" (colleagues or neighbors who are fellow writers), the "adjutants" ("young devotees of literature"), and the "real lovers of evil" (35–36). She speaks extensively and surely about how this network operates and asserts some sweeping conclusions:

> All of this took place on a massive scale and affected even those who were not specifically followed. Every family was always going over its circle of acquaintances, trying to determine who were the provocateurs, the informers, and the traitors. After 1937 people stopped meeting with each other altogether. And with this the secret police were well on the way to achieving their goals. Apart from gathering a constant flow of information, they aimed to weaken the bonds between people, to create an alienated society, and they had drawn large numbers of people into their circle, calling them in from time to time, harrassing them and swearing them to secrecy by means of signed statements. And all these crowds of the "summoned" lived in eternal fear of being found out and were therefore just as interested as regular members of the police in the stability of the existing order and the inviolability of the archives where their names were on file. (34–35)

The passage is loaded with superlatives, designations of the multitudes involved and the total extent of their involvement. "Every family was always" reviewing suspect contacts; "crowds of the 'summoned' " lived in "eternal fear." Thematically and stylistically, Nadezhda Mandelstam conveys a sense of purposeful inexorable mobilization—listing first the goals, then the methods, and finally the "success" of the secret police; stating an absolute link of cause and effect ("and with this" "and were therefore"); building proofs out of connective clauses and repeated verbal structures. In its cumulative effect, her narration in this passage overwhelms us with its declarative language and onrushing sequence. She provides no documentation for her "definitive" statements, but as a narrator she has done everything in her power to make us take her at her word.

In tandem with her analysis of official procedures and practice, Nadezhda Mandelstam writes her own intellectual history, assuredly explaining the intelligentsia's involvement with the new Soviet regime. This history evinces the same revisionist, totalizing, and concretizing features I have identified elsewhere in her text. In the chapter entitled *"Kapituliatsiia"* ("Capitulation"), she mentions in passing her own principles of historiography: "People's memories are such that they remember not actual events but only vague stories or legends about them. To extract the facts, one must shatter the myths, but this can only be done if one first defines the circles in which they have been created" (168). More often than not, her deflation and re-contextualization of such myths invoke a prefatory sequence of "capitulations," an account of how these "circles" come to collaborate, voluntarily or involuntarily, with the regime. Like her revised interpretation of Soviet literature, her history of the intelligentsia dismisses the "golden age" of the 1920s and instead posits the intellectuals' progressive collusion with and subordination to the state. As in the passage cited above, she emphasizes the enormous scope of this response, describing the "mass surrender" of the intellectuals and the "powerful chorus that drowned out all other voices." And she does not hesitate to name names and relate specific episodes connected with this capitulation; although she counts the Shklovskiis as friends, she even cites Shklovskii's novel *Zoo* as prime evidence of the Soviet intellectual's grateful submission to authority (166).

Yet, despite these sweeping generalizations and specific accusations, despite her role-playing as self-styled historian, Nadezhda Mandelstam claims neither objectivity nor immunity for herself; she does not convey the impression that her authorship somehow transcends or is detached from her material experience. Rather, the issues of reliability and documentation are dwarfed in her text by considerations of complicity and responsibility. However impersonal her constructions or condemnatory her tone, Nadezhda Mandelstam always implies herself (and many of her potential readers) as culpable. Throughout *Hope against Hope* she insists, with disturbing honesty, that everyone is at once a victim and an accomplice of the Stalinist state. Here she begins a process she will elaborate fully in *Hope Abandoned*. Beyond exposing and explaining a repressed world, she writes her version of history as a kind of self-analysis and, if possible, self-corrective.[45] In lieu of careful documentation and an "objective" account, she produces a text that is explicitly, imperfectly human in its claims, appeal, and address. Her intent seems ultimately moral rather than historiographical. She writes not purely to inform, but to exhort her readers to repent and reform themselves according to the human model of Mandelstam and (to a much lesser degree) her own example.

Given this intent, Nadezhda Mandelstam's "history" can do no better than to compile and analyze a mosaic of life stories, tales that document and engage and offer a human's-eye view. If her primary concern is to restore the unofficial human values repressed in her age, then she succeeds by asserting her subjectivity and recording the evidence—both positive and negative—of other human lives. In general, her "evidence" entails a swift desultory imprint of an individual's physical image, psychological makeup, characteristic gestures, and (always) accompanying biographical anecdotes. These portraits range from Mandelstam's approved (although never idolized) fellow poets to marginal figures like Demian Bednyi to the most politically compromised—characters like Tania, "the non-Party Bolshevik," who looked the part of the " 'progressive' schoolmarm," "remained true to the style of the sixties and worshiped Belinskii and Dobroliubov," and bartered away the clothes of her stepdaughter Tatka (Mandelstam's niece) the day before Tatka's death (308–12).[46] So densely populated with character sketches, her text even appears to reverse her husband's dire prediction of the "end of the novel" and human biography. In the early 1920s Mandelstam had concluded:

> It is clear that when we entered the epoch of powerful social movements and organized mass actions, both the stock value of the individual in history and the power and influence of the novel declined, for the generally accepted role of the individual in history serves as a kind of monometer indicating the pressure of the social atmosphere. The measure of the novel is human biography or a system of biographies. . . . The future development of the novel will be no less than the history of the atomization of biography as a form of personal existence. What is more, we shall witness the catastrophic collapse of biography.[47]

Hope against Hope undertakes to restore the value and influence of biography—in a necessarily fragmentary, transitional form. Nadezhda Mandelstam does testify to de-individuating "social movements and mass actions," yet she begins to salvage at least partial biographies from otherwise silenced or masked lives. This process begins with and centers on her husband and finally encompasses a vast array of different women and men. Nadezhda Mandelstam pieces her way toward the coherence of a realist novel and the totality of history with her own haphazard "system of biographies." It is as if she enters the house of history through the back door, by way of the kitchen where the residents are least inhibited and most apt to confide and gossip. And throughout she imposes herself as the synthesizing, interpreting narrator of these gathered stories, an old woman who refuses to suppress and even dares to generalize from her own complex individuality and experience.

The conclusion of *Hope against Hope* strongly asserts this method. The final chapters—*"Data smerti"* ("The Date of Death") and *"Eshche odin rasskaz"* ("One Final Account")—amass all the stories Nadezhda Mandelstam has heard concerning her husband's last days.[48] She suspects any official documentation and focuses instead on the possible and dubious accounts by "emissaries from the 'other world' " of the prison and labor camp system. She cites a wide range of stories—from the confused memories of her first emissary, Kazarnovskii, to the clearly falsified and malicious rumors disseminated by a certain Tiufakov. "The Date of Death" then ends on what would seem to be a concluding statement: "This is all that I know about the last days, illness and death of Mandelstam" (391). Yet it is intriguing, especially for our analysis of Nadezhda Mandelstam as a storyteller-biographer, that she saves one last tale for a separate and final chapter. She recapitulates this "final account" (by a physicist called L.) in full detail, paying attention not only to remembered facts about Mandelstam but to the physical and emotional state of the witness. (The original narrator, it would seem, had told his tale well.) Thus presented, this "final account" offers the most coherent and affective story of Mandelstam's last days. Its inclusion at the end accentuates the storytelling texture and primacy of "told data" for all of *Hope against Hope*. Nadezhda Mandelstam concludes both the life story of Mandelstam and her first attempt at a history of her time with this approximate, human, and artistic document.

To her credit as an amateur historian, however, she appends a final paragraph that admits her imperfect authority:

> There is nowhere I can make inquiries and no one will tell me anything about this. Who is likely to search through those terrible archives for the sake of Mandelstam, when they won't even publish a volume of his work? . . . Those who perished are lucky if they have been posthumously rehabilitated, or if, at any rate, their cases have been discontinued for lack of evidence. Even rehabilitation takes place on two levels in our country and Mandelstam has received second-class status. . . . Therefore I can only gather this meager evidence and speculate about the date of his death. And I keep repeating to myself: the sooner he died, the better. There is nothing worse than a slow death. I hate to think that at the moment when my mind was set at rest on being told in the post office that he was dead, he may actually have been still alive and on his way to Kolyma. The date of death has not been established. And I am helpless to do anything more to establish it. (396–97)

So *Hope against Hope* closes on a last story and a confession. It is as if we had worked our way, along with our determined narrator, to the absolute limit of her power. After such a magnificent display of memory, perception, analysis, and narration, Nadezhda Mandelstam chooses, in the end, to remind us of her human frailty—her real position in her all-too-real context. Her book has been no more and at the same time no less than a personal articulation of an unspeakable past.

In assessing the achievement of Nadezhda Mandelstam's *Hope against Hope*, her reviewers have been most assured in positing its worth as literary and biographical criticism. As George Steiner asserts in his *New Yorker* review: "It is a safe proposition that *Hope Against Hope* would be a classic even if only those fragments dealing with Mandelstam's habits of composition had survived."[49] Nadezhda Mandelstam has written an account which Mandelstam scholars are virtually forced to consider indispensable. Whatever their opinion of her skills as a critic or her bias as a biographer, they cannot afford to ignore her informed eyewitness testimony. So Charles Isenberg acknowledges her work as "the enabling condition, the virtual horizon, of Osip Mandelstam's" and points out its omnipresence in Mandelstam criticism (193). Mikhail Polivanov offers unadulterated praise from the Russian side, valuing her memoirs as "priceless commentary" to her husband's work.[50] In specific consequence, I would argue that *Hope against Hope* certainly matches the achievement of *Notes on Anna Akhmatova*. It does not repeat the daily record Chukovskaia dares to maintain, but it effectively depicts the "invisible" life of a proscribed poet and testifies to the successful making and conserving of unofficial art under Stalin. These two women writers seem compelled to perform the same important kind of service and provide the same vital documentation.

But Nadezhda Mandelstam's text "serves" more ambitiously, presumptuously. Chukovskaia described and transcribed Akhmatova as a monument, but Nadezhda Mandelstam synthesizes an even grander position for her husband. He is represented as a great poet, great man, and great martyr; he is established and used as an artistic, moral, and spiritual guide for his age. Nadezhda Mandelstam may pay ample respect to other writers in her text, but it is Mandelstam's views and practice which comprise the core reference for her analysis. In *Hope against Hope*, therefore, Mandelstam's life story emerges as most relevant to, revealing of, and instructive for his time; his biography irresistibly culminates in her history. And despite its idiosyncracies, Nadezhda Mandelstam's achievement as a historian has not gone unremarked, although her reviewers circle around this classification of her work. Irving Howe, for example, declares *Hope against Hope* "one of the greatest *portrayals* that has ever been written of how people actually lived under Stalinism" (italics mine).[51] Others have praised its broad scope, valuing its "thickly detailed, moment-by-moment account of what 'ordinary' life was like for a marked man during the crucial years of 1934."[52] Professional historians, in turn, have accorded it importance as a primary source. Echoing her practice, they appropriate her compiled stories as their own "data."[53]

These varying responses all testify to Nadezhda Mandelstam's enormous talent. Compared with the many memoirs and histories written about this period, *Hope against Hope* is remarkable in its trenchant combination of literary and historiographical effects. Through well-told tales and powerful rhetoric Nadezhda Mandelstam has managed to convince many of her accuracy and authority. Rather than contain her text in the categories of memoir or history, however, I would posit, along with critic Richard Pevear, that *Hope against Hope* is best characterized as a "work of art," for it not only analyzes but magnificently *relates* her experience of Stalinism.[54] Instead of an objective account of facts and events, we read in *Hope against Hope* the riveting real-life stories, human confessions, and categorical generalizations of a narrator who is explicitly subjective, involved, informed, opinionated, and unorthodox—a narrator peculiarly qualified to speak by virtue of her position and mentality. As the wife and then widow of a persecuted writer—a female nonperson—she is made familiar with both domestic and professional, official and unofficial spheres; she is exposed to and, in an ironic sense, privileged with an unmasked view of much of her society. And as the "wild girl" and Mandelstam's initiated "girlfriend," Nadezhda Mandelstam excels as a boldly observant, "undisciplined" teller of tales and dispenser of opinions. Grounded in her experience and charged with her distinctive genius, Nadezhda Mandelstam's *Hope against Hope* thus begins her retelling of Stalinist history as re-created biography and collective catharsis.

7.
HOPE ABANDONED

In the mid-1960s Nadezhda Iakovlevna would relate episodes from her *Second Book* as if she were honing them in conversation. And everything that later evoked protest—her bias, her hurtful injustice, her probably unfounded accusations against her best friends—all this seemed much milder in conversation. I still do not believe that her devoted friend Nikolai Ivanovich Khardzhiev could have destroyed the rough drafts and variants of Mandelstam's poetry so that his editing would be consistent. Nevertheless everything that took place *around* that edition (rather, non-edition) of Mandelstam, that pitiful booklet issued only in 1973 in which [Mandelstam] is slandered in the foreword and his poetry cropped to the point of unrecognizability—all this sparked her burning indignation and became a "point of insanity." It's not surprising that under these circumstances her friends forgave her a great deal.

I always found masses of people at her place. Acquaintances or quickly made good friends. The Shklovskiis were there most often, but there were many, many others. She made friends with two remarkable priests: Father Aleksandr Men' and Father Sergei Zheludkov. At her place I met Shalamov, Dombrovskii, Amusin, Lev Gumilev, the Meletinskiis, and the famous Moscow doctor Gel'shtein. But one shouldn't imagine that only eminent persons gathered there. On the contrary, there were many young people and "girls" who helped her out.

Mikhail Polivanov[1]

That evening was our first look at N.M.'s real "salon." A dozen or so people arrived and soon there was no place to sit. People wandered back and forth from bedroom to kitchen, and the bottles of wine and vodka we brought soon disappeared. Raisa Orlova later recalled N.M.'s evenings of this time, saying they attracted the best minds, most talented artists, writers, theologians, priests and philosophers.

Carl Proffer[2]

If someone had asked me to choose between a very interesting film, a very interesting play, some extraordinary rendezvous, or a visit to Nadezhda Iakovlevna, I would have chosen Nadezhda Iakovlevna without hesitating.

Liudmila Sergeeva[3]

By the mid-1960s Nadezhda Mandelstam had emerged from shelterless oblivion to a position of unofficial prominence. *Hope against Hope*—circulated underground and soon to be published abroad—had revealed her powers as a writer and gained her an appreciative audience. Just as important, she was at last permitted a real home in Moscow—a kitchen, bedroom, and bathroom in one of the big apartment buildings on Bol'shaia Cheremushkinskaia street. Through the informal network of *samizdat* and the modest space of her new apartment, Nadezhda Mandelstam improvised her own special forum on the margins of Soviet society. Her tiny home was converted into a makeshift center of unofficial culture, an accessible unpretentious "salon."

In practical terms, her home afforded her the most stable venue for her works. Somewhat like Chukovskii's villa in Kuokkala, it existed as an essential base of operations—a homely alternative to the academy and official cultural establishment. For although the publication of Mandelstam's work was underway in the 1960s and bits and pieces of his oeuvre were surfacing in the official journals, he had yet to be "rehabilitated" as a subject of research. The American scholar Carl Proffer notes the effective restrictions of the 1960s and 1970s; in those decades "a young person who wanted to study Mandelstam (or Akhmatova or Gumilev or Acmeism in general) could not do so in a university, officially" (26). Conversations with Nadezhda Mandelstam constituted the best professional training for any would-be Mandelstam scholars during this period. She vigorously developed this instruction on her own, providing introductions for those few verses that were being published, writing out textual commentaries for at least one Mandelstam scholar (Irina Mikhailovna Semenko), and, in general, dispensing all the information she could about Mandelstam and his work.[4] Her efforts increased as she grew frustrated with the slow, inadequate progress of the official commission approved to rehabilitate Mandelstam. She had entrusted her husband's work to the "experts," and their efforts clearly disappointed and even infuriated her. In the meantime, both Soviet and foreign scholars were seeking out *her* expertise. For them she proved to be no sentimental widow but a keen interlocutor who could appreciate and comment on her husband's art. Although she held very definite opinions about textual interpretation and disagreed with those who "counted syllables" or reduced Mandelstam to erudite references, she encouraged and helped many scholars.[5]

Beyond her role as curator, Nadezhda Mandelstam's bold performance in *Hope against Hope* truly established her home as a "salon." People came to her apartment not only to study Mandelstam but also to hear her uncensored stories and incisive analysis of Stalinism, to ask her opinion about everything from poetry to ongoing political events, and to meet other people who quietly shared the views she dared to articulate.[6] Her presence was key, for she embodied a tangible connection with an uncensored past and encouraged a free and easy atmosphere. Here at last she could resume being the Nadezhda Mandelstam formed in childhood and developed through her marriage to Osip Emil'evich. After decades of isolation and silence, she could thoroughly indulge her need for company.[7] Moreover, she fostered a society according to her own tastes — one conducted without regard for status or decorum and peopled by both important personages and "girls."[8] For hostess and guests these gatherings had a healing effect; in the words of one visitor, her humble kitchen "became a refuge for free thought and spiritual candor."[9]

In old age Nadezhda Mandelstam had recovered much of the life she enjoyed in her self-defined "first period" — that is, in the period when she demonstrated no need to write. Mandelstam's poems were safe, her accompanying "letter" was published, and her own apartment was filled with friends and well-wishers. Why, then, did she embark on *Hope Abandoned*? Some of her friends speculate that she had not written herself out in *Hope against Hope* and needed the wider scope of a second volume.[10] She had produced the first text as quickly as possible, trimming her memories for the sake of speed (she did not know how long she had to live) and her chosen focus on Mandelstam. *Hope against Hope* then brought her fame and community; some of her less provocative writings, in turn, had been printed in the official press. It would seem, therefore, that Nadezhda Mandelstam had gotten into the *habit* of writing. She still did not conceive of herself as a writer, but her writing had become ingrained as a regular practice as well as an extension of her social role. Like so many diarists and memoirists — and particularly "unprofessional" female practitioners of these forms — Nadezhda Mandelstam may well have found writing to be a therapeutic routine, yet another form of domestic art.[11] In any event, she tried to keep writing for as long as she was able. We know of *Hope Abandoned* and the sketches for an additional volume; her friends remember her various plans for a complete *Third Book*.[12]

Hope Abandoned was also specifically and poignantly motivated. Once again she began to write out of bereavement: Anna Akhmatova died in March 1966, and Nadezhda Mandelstam very quickly composed a memoir of her friend — a text that stands as the first variant of *Hope Abandoned*. According to P. Nerler, who managed to obtain a copy of this text and has published a portion of it in the journal *Literaturnaia ucheba* (Literary studies), Nadezhda Mandelstam completed the memoir by March 1967 and read it aloud to several friends.[13] She never published or circulated the work and even destroyed her own copies of it. But it is intriguing that Akhmatova's death served as a lasting stimulus for writing. In one sense, her passing signaled the loss and enabled the assessment of an important community for Nadezhda Mandelstam. In her memoirs, Mandelstam, Akhmatova, and she form an uneven triangle of close friends and like believers; Akhmatova's death invested Nadezhda Mandelstam with the duty to speak for all three. While both the first and final variants of *Hope Abandoned* carry out this duty idiosyncratically, Nadezhda Mandelstam also composed an altogether separate text—entitled *Mozart i Salieri (Mozart and Salieri)*—which compares and analyzes the creative process for Akhmatova and Mandelstam. Here she most explicitly fulfills her obligation as the witness to two great poets.

Yet, aside from imposing certain duties, Akhmatova's death also effected a kind of liberation in her old friend. Nadezhda Mandelstam was more intimate and unceremonious with the female poet than admirers like Chukovskaia, but she was well aware of how Akhmatova wanted herself written by others. With Akhmatova gone, she was freed from what she perceived as the restrictions of their friendship and could venture a more frank portrait of the poet. She could speak the entire truth—not only about Akhmatova but derived from all the information Akhmatova had confided in her. On yet another level, her reflection on Akhmatova eventually freed her to reflect on herself. Just as Akhmatova inspired and encouraged Chukovskaia's creativity, so she helped stimulate Nadezhda Mandelstam to autobiography and bolder notions of authorship. In each case, the female poet functioned as a particular mirror, mentor, and creative catalyst for her female associates.

These texts, then, emerge in progressive reaction to Akhmatova's death—the first variant of her second volume of memoirs, *Mozart and Salieri*, and the extant volume of *Hope Abandoned*. Although they differ in tone and scope, they share a special focus on Akhmatova. Read in close juxtaposition, they trace how the figure of Akhmatova helps to shape Nadezhda Mandelstam's self-conception, for over the course of these texts she explores a self sustained by an empowering "we" and particularly distinguished by a complex "she." In the following analyses I investigate the provocative, productive relationship that existed between these two women and highlight, along with her revelations about the unofficial literary process, Nadezhda Mandelstam's related development as autobiographical subject and ever bolder author-narrator. To trace the continuous genesis of *Hope Abandoned*, I read these works out of chronological sequence, turning first to *Mozart and Salieri*.

Mozart and Salieri

Mozart and Salieri, the interim piece, is perhaps the least provocative of the three, for it compiles Nadezhda Mandelstam's lifelong observations on the literary process. These observations are bound to an uncompromising credo: They insist on a kind of genetic tie between the person of the artist and his or her work, and emphasize both the spiritual and mundane aspects of human creativity. Nadezhda Mandelstam's requirements interestingly coincide with the "emphatically human" portraits of the artist displayed in the unofficial works of Bulgakov and Pasternak. It is crucial for her that the literary work never be too far removed from its author—that is, from the human voice, personality, limitations, capacities, and material context of the artist. She establishes this credo from the very beginning, when she discusses Mandelstam's attitude toward literary critics: He dismisses Marxists and formalists alike and prefers instead those who serve "as readers and 'interlocutors' with the poet" (10).[14] Figuring herself in these favored roles, Nadezhda Mandelstam then heeds what the poets say, write, and show about the creative process. Quoting her "sources" and observing them at close hand, she affirms the bond between artistic creation and the person of the creator:

> It is the searching spirit of a man which prays for revelation or, rather, for a moment of divine inspiration—after all, the source of art and all kinds of knowledge lies precisely in this. Each true discovery always reflects the inner state of the spirit of one who searched and found, thus leaving an indelible personal imprint on everything that is created or intuited by man. It is just this presence of a personal and spiritual foundation which distinguishes the original from the innumerable surrogates with which the huge, multi-voiced market of art and science is inundated. (26)

She explores this argument for every artistic or scientific "act of cognition." But she maintains especially that in poetry "each word is a self-confession, each completed work is part of an autobiography" (30). Returning to one of the topics of *Hope against Hope*, Nadezhda Mandelstam undertakes a kind of physiological analysis of this act, noting the poet's inherently receptive "wondering" state, describing—insofar as she has watched it happen—the very experience of the creative impulse. She defines the state of "prelyrical anxiety" preceding an important creative development (38); she traces the birth of the poem to the poet's "secret hearing" and records the examples of Akhmatova, Mandelstam, and Pasternak in action:

> Akhmatova regulated these states better than Mandelstam; she attempted to hide them so that she could escape, pretending she was sick. Mandelstam would become estranged even with people present; and once he began to listen to himself attentively, he would suddenly cease hearing what they were saying to him. His passion for walking and strolls—necessarily solitary—answered his need to be simultaneously among people (the passers-by), and alone. Pasternak, who was also a sociable person, who loved to charm and fascinate people, would suddenly become alienated from people, change the whole tone of the conversation, become abrupt and curt. These reversals would seem inexplicable if one did not know the secret necessity of a poet to be tête-à-tête with himself. (56)

As much as Nadezhda Mandelstam asserts the inner spiritual impulse of creation, she does not construe the creative process as a wholly spiritual movement. In fact, by listening to her two chief poets, she devises a more elastic dual model—one that derives from their analyses of Pushkin, the acme of Russian poets, and connects the figures of Mozart and Salieri (the subjects of one of Pushkin's *Little Tragedies*). Through these various layers of interpretation, Mozart is reduced to a metaphor for the intuitive, spiritual aspect of creation and Salieri for the elements of craft and control. Once again, Mandelstam serves as her ultimate guide, for, in contrast to Akhmatova's equation of Pushkin with Salieri, he sees both principles at work in every "true" poet. For him (and therefore Nadezhda Mandelstam) the poet must contain both mystic and craftsperson, must demonstrate both spiritual receptivity and careful industry. In addition, Nadezhda Mandelstam outlines two concomitant phases of the creative process—the inner impulse and the exercise of control (89–91). Developing this model, she is clearly recreating the Acmeist conception of the poet, yet at the same time she is extrapolating her own markedly personalized critical approach. According to both Acmeist poets and their reader, the artist must not be divested of his or her humanity in any way—either by theoretical dissociation or Romantic inflation.[15] Nadezhda Mandelstam points out the deep respect Mandelstam, Akhmatova, and Pasternak all hold for people with "real" professions, and she even likens Mandelstam and Akhmatova to "laborers" and expresses her own attendant desire to be "a cobbler's wife" (73–74).

In *Mozart and Salieri*, therefore, Nadezhda Mandelstam eschews the role of professional critic to be human interlocutor, witness, and reader. She serves in this capacity for two (and sometimes even three) poets; the voices and examples of Mandelstam and Akhmatova doubly validate her findings and increase her authority. She bases her openly subjective criticism on thoughtful testimony and clear admiration for her poets and their art. Yet even here, when she seems best behaved, Nadezhda Mandelstam sometimes manifests a certain impatience (if not irreverence) in her treatment of Akhmatova. In large part, after all, it is Akhmatova's mistaken reading of Mozart and Salieri which prompts her "corrective" essay (14–17). More generally, she is dismayed that the female poet cannot achieve Mandelstam's full consonance of life and art. Unlike her fellow Acmeist, Akhmatova cannot express her "true voice" in essays and instead muffles her opinions in the only surviving prose form of her age—the "pseudoacademic article." What Nadezhda Mandelstam misses in her essays is her "polemical fury" in real conversation:

> Akhmatova rattled off arguments like bullets and an enormous amount of preliminary work was necessary to turn a way of thinking and speech such as hers into a prose text. After all, it was not easy to force paper to maintain and transmit to the readers the furious raging of Akhmatova's intonation and thought. This demanded a new form and it simply would not be confined to the standard sort of academic article; and after all, it was into these very letters that Akhmatova was trying to squeeze herself. If she had listened to herself and not been afraid of preserving her voice in a written prose text, we would have been struck by the novelty, force and unexpectedness of this new prose; but work of this kind demands quiet and refusal of any pretense to being in the academic tradition, with its notorious propriety. (12)

In an altogether familiar move, Nadezhda Mandelstam spurns the academy and its propriety in her demand to "hear" the real Akhmatova (and, perhaps, an affirming echo of her own forceful style). Even more boldly, she intimates her own potential in articulating her friend. Akhmatova freely voices her opinions around everybody except Mandelstam; in his case, she exploits his wife as her uncensored mouthpiece:

> She had no doubts whatsoever that I would immediately blurt out all her secrets, not only those of her Pushkin criticism, to Mandelstam, even if I had promised a thousand times never to tell anyone. . . . And, furthermore, I knew that this was just what she needed, and I very conscientiously served as the means of transmission. (14)

Enhancing her role as witness for Akhmatova and Mandelstam, Nadezhda Mandelstam represents herself as a willing conduit for Akhmatova's "fury" and wit, a storyteller who appreciates the conversational art of the female poet and presumes to pass it along. Unintimidated by her husband and unconstrained by the weight of a poetic reputation, she can be audacious as friend and like artist on Akhmatova's behalf.[16]

First variant

Nadezhda Mandelstam develops this "mouthpiece" role further in her variants of *Hope Abandoned*. Even the first version, written in the year following Akhmatova's death, conveys quite a few startling revelations about the poet. Her memoir also proves self-revelatory; from the outset Nadezhda Mandelstam recognizes Akhmatova as correspondent:

> Thinking about Anna Andreevna, I keep returning for some reason to my own life—something which never occurred to me when I was writing about O.M. His fate was such that it swept away everything personal and intimate—everything now evoked by thoughts of our dear friend—Aniuta, Annushka, Anush, Anna Andreevna. (142)[17]

In contrast to Mandelstam, Akhmatova appears to trigger an especially distinguishing autobiographical response in Nadezhda Mandelstam; her example evokes feelings of deep solidarity (note the degrees of diminutives) as well as an interesting sense of difference. Commenting on their relationship in *Hope against Hope*, Charles Isenberg infers "anxiety" and "discomfort" in Nadezhda Mandelstam's reaction to Akhmatova; he attributes these feelings to her status as nonpoet and mere wife.[18] It seems to me, however, that by the writing of *Hope Abandoned* Nadezhda Mandelstam's critical response and consequent self-reflection have more to do with Akhmatova's real-life role-playing than with any emotional or professional rivalry. A widowed female survivor of the purges, Akhmatova shares with her many of the same physical, social, psychological, and moral coordinates. To a certain extent, their friendship resembles the relationship depicted in Chukovskaia's *Notes*; compared with the figure of husband or father, Akhmatova more fully echoes and endorses her experience, evoking the "personal and intimate" details of their daily life with and without Mandelstam. Yet, in contrast to Chukovskaia's circumspection, memories of Akhmatova lead Nadezhda Mandelstam to and beyond self-reflection to speculate about the characteristic features of *women*. In both versions of *Hope Abandoned*, her relationship with Akhmatova truly stimulates her to identify and consider assigned and assumed gender roles in her reading of the age.

Through her specific analysis of Akhmatova in this first variant, Nadezhda Mandelstam describes two basic patterns of interpreting herself and her sex. On the one hand, she ventures a positive evaluation from her similarities with the poet. The entire text begins with Akhmatova's loving inscription on one of Nadezhda Mandelstam's books: "To my friend Nadia, so that she remembers once more what happened to us." Inscription and quotation form a gesture of solidarity; what follows is the keynote of their shared ordeal. Once again Nadezhda Mandelstam dwells on the conditions of their overwhelming context—the fear that served as an "organizing principle" and its accompanying "feeling of shame and complete helplessness" (134). Yet under these conditions (which she and Akhmatova fully appreciate), they have somehow managed to survive and function; they have not succumbed to the "pitiful surrender" of cowardice. Of course, Nadezhda Mandelstam feels freer to recognize Akhmatova's courage. She cites the verses Akhmatova dared to write about their experience, and she notes that the poet was always the first to visit friends after their homes had been searched by the secret police. Her reflections on Akhmatova's strength presently result in a portrait of another brave woman (Ekaterina Livshits) and a digression about the general stamina of women in this context:

> Women came out of the ordeal less broken than men, they had fewer psychoses, they did not give in so easily, although they were also tormented by hunger, sleeplessness, and beatings. They even endured imprisonment with greater steadfastness than men. (135)

Her conclusions powerfully enlarge on Akhmatova's own statement (quoted, but protested by Chukovskaia) that more women than men undertake the ordeal of the prison lines. Although her observations move beyond the realm of their experience (neither she nor Akhmatova "know" the camps), she draws support from the testimony of Varlam Shalamov, a camp survivor and writer, who tells her that he can only remember women attempting to visit their spouses in the camps at Kolyma (135).

Yet Nadezhda Mandelstam does not pursue a simple opposition of strong selfless women versus weak selfish men. The next turn of the text presents Akhmatova's and her joint hypothesis on the nature of bravery; once more, she conveys the impression of two women closeted together, articulating a personalized, shared resistance to official persecution and thereby coming to grips with it. As was the case with husband and wife in *Hope against Hope*, it is almost impossible (and, I think, beside the point) to determine where the poet leaves off and her interlocutor begins. Out of these reflections Nadezhda Mandelstam elaborates an intriguing schema of good and evil. She associates those who believe in a cult of force and personal advancement with a kind of "he-man" strength which may flourish in combat but evaporates in the everyday conditions of a peacetime terror. Such falsely strong people use a force-affirming poetry to support their cynical views. Against them she juxtaposes the seemingly weak men who "together with women somehow struggle along, upholding the belief that a person could be regenerated, could repent and begin a new life" (135). This group seems to coincide with what she subsequently characterizes as an opposition—those who counter force with a "rightness" based on certain eternal moral and cultural values expressed in a different kind of poetry (135–36, 138). Boldly reorienting the male-centered visions of Bulgakov, Pasternak, and her husband, Nadezhda Mandelstam defines her own spiritual-cultural opposition to Stalinism along gender lines; implying the involvement of Mandelstam, Akhmatova, and herself, she claims that only these "weak" men and women (she does not specify what kind of women) can resist the destruction and corruption of a force-loving, stereotypically masculine Stalinism.[19]

This positive reading of women from shared experience resonates throughout the text. In fact, when Nadezhda Mandelstam comes to ponder the fundamentally poor, nomadic, solitary lives that she and Akhmatova have led, she elevates them both through her husband's iconic image of the "blessed wives." Wife and female friend, she implies, have realized Mandelstam's vision: "Nevertheless, we held our ground and did all we could. . . . We will remember the unwritten verses, we will gather them, we will not forget them" (149).

The material for Akhmatova's "monumentalization" is therefore glimpsed in this text, but it never quite coheres, mainly because Nadezhda Mandelstam disapproves of its conventional design. She is inspired by her friend's bravery, nobility, and strength, but she seems irked by what she deems to be other aspects of Akhmatova's womanhood.[20] Although Akhmatova develops natural, unaffected relationships with a chosen few (including the Mandelstams), Nadezhda Mandelstam observes her general tendency toward self-regard and studied posing. She notes Akhmatova's desire to see herself reflected in her associates, her secret anxiety about how people evaluate her looks (142, 149).[21] Already perceiving Akhmatova's strategies of "objectification," Nadezhda Mandelstam connects the poet's anxiety over her biography with her deliberate cultivation of a ladylike image: "with one part of her soul, she wanted a canonical portrait without the absurdities and foolishness that are inevitable in any person's life, especially a poet's. A beautiful, reserved, intelligent lady, and in addition a marvelous poet—that's what Anna Akhmatova thought up for herself" (146).

In Akhmatova, then, Nadezhda Mandelstam locates another kind of mask—one that is gender-specific and not politically motivated, but still dangerous and silencing. And Akhmatova's in-life mask clearly interferes with their friendship. Nadezhda Mandelstam comments that the poet did not like to go visiting with her in later years because in her presence she could not play the great lady and be the center of attention. Critical of this facade, Nadezhda Mandelstam prefers to celebrate the Akhmatova who quite often breaks through it—the woman she approves as a "hooligan and mischief-maker" (*"khuliganka i ozornitsa"*). The poet may have desired to become a lady with "one part of her soul," but she "did not very much like or appreciate a deferential, enraptured reception" and preferred a lack of ceremony, even a kind of "rudeness" ("*grubovatost*") "among her own people"—that is, with friends like Nadezhda Mandelstam (144). She volunteers this uncanonical portrait of the poet: "Under the light facade of a lady—sometimes genuinely amiable, but more often a little silly—dwelled this hooligan ("*bezobranitsa*") who always had a fire under her" (146).

Her preference is revealing: Nadezhda Mandelstam values in Akhmatova those qualities and behavior that seem to correspond to her own character. The need to discredit her friend's ladylike posture is therefore all the more urgent. According to her representation, the person of Akhmatova not only shares and helps explain her harsh experience but serves to affirm her forthright manner and free spirit. In this first memoir attempt Nadezhda Mandelstam explores a number of tactics to instate the *ozornitsa* Akhmatova and undercut the "lady"—dissecting and historicizing the "made" image of the poet, reveling in her plain-speaking intimacy with Akhmatova, and even "admitting" her own lack of conventionally feminine traits.[22]

Thus, when Nadezhda Mandelstam trains her writing on the subject of a great woman, she draws out issues of gender role definition and evaluation that lay submerged or undeveloped in her first volume of memoirs. The self-reflecting figure of Akhmatova proves to be a complex catalyst, a partner in loving devotion and a spur to critical definition. Reflecting on her long alliance with the poet, Nadezhda Mandelstam posits the greater endurance of women as a whole and theorizes an effective opposition to Stalinism waged by women and "weak" men. At the same time, through her observations of the "lady" Akhmatova, she recognizes the dangers and restrictions involved in conforming to a culturally assigned and accepted womanhood. In her desultory analysis, being a woman may guarantee a greater strength, but it also threatens a possible repression of her individual character. For Nadezhda Mandelstam, Akhmatova must remain problematic—a female authority who combines great strength and a free spirit with vestiges of a troubling conventionality.

Hope Abandoned

The portrait of Akhmatova which Nadezhda Mandelstam offers in the first variant is by no means unambiguous; here she has already violated the canonical vision of Chukovskaia's *Notes*. Yet it seems that she did not feel she had gone far enough—in a number of critical directions. She re-incorporated many sections of this variant into *Hope Abandoned*, but she scrapped the text itself as a finished composition. It may have been that she wanted to write entirely free of Akhmatova's authority or, more specifically, the worshipful accounts the poet cultivated among her followers.[23] In his introduction to the Soviet edition of *Hope Abandoned*, Mikhail Polivanov proposes a more complex reading of that interaction between poet and memoirist. He notes Akhmatova's clever method of indoctrinating her listeners to put down her version of literary history as their own; he is convinced that she imparted a great deal of this history to Nadezhda Mandelstam when they lived together in Tashkent during the war. What Akhmatova may not have foreseen is *how* Nadezhda Mandelstam would choose to retell her stories. I have shown how Nadezhda Mandelstam embarked on a self-styled mission to "liberate" Akhmatova in *Mozart and Salieri* and the first variant; Polivanov declares her mission accomplished in *Hope Abandoned*, arguing that the text presents a more extensive critical analysis of the poet along with a frank relation of the poet's own vehement opinions about her age.[24]

It seems, therefore, that the specific catalyst of Akhmatova and the supportive environment of her salon enabled Nadezhda Mandelstam to write and then rewrite her second volume of memoirs. And her aim to liberate Akhmatova appeared to catalyze an ever grander quest to liberate both self and society.[25] She destroyed the first variant in 1967; she commenced a new version in 1969 and completed it by 1971.[26] By this point her writing had burgeoned into a kind of compendium of everything she felt she had to relate and reveal about her age. To a greater and more varied degree than *Hope against Hope*, this text encompasses both anecdote and analysis, literary and cultural criticism (including quite extensive textological commentaries), and even philosophical digressions. Its structure overwhelms the episodic sequence and broad chronology of the first volume, billowing out into larger sections with separate titles and (more or less) organizing themes—"Digression," "Poetry and People," "Major Forms," "The Prodigal Son." In content and form this book most flamboyantly expresses the author's forceful will, personalized vantage, and narrative flair; as one observer concludes, Nadezhda Mandelstam composes this text entirely "through herself" (*"cherez sebia"*).[27] Polivanov perhaps best captures its effect when he describes it as "table talk," for the term conveys its capricious progress and its author's insistent, loquacious presence.[28]

"We" and "I"

Written "through herself," this book is also necessarily about herself, an emphasis announced by the "I" of the first chapter title. As I have already remarked, *Hope Abandoned* launches a full-fledged recovery of Nadezhda Mandelstam's self after it had been "crushed" under Stalin. In her first chapter, she specifically analyzes this oppression, itemizing different responses to a politically enforced loss of identity. Some people, she concludes, either renounced all values and pursued a course of "blatant individualism with its extremes of egocentrism and self-assertiveness." Others sank into a torpor of self-effacement and, in a few fortunate cases like her own, were sustained, if not fulfilled, by their need to serve a "you" (5–7).[29]

Yet what is the nature of her restored "I"? Does it define itself through separation or relationship, distinction or similarity? Does it evince any of the egotistic, "blatantly individualistic" traits of those who sought only to serve themselves? Nadezhda Mandelstam never explicitly addresses these questions, but over the expanse of the second volume she enacts an "I" which seems neither autonomous nor subordinate, which, in effect, replays the patterns of her childhood and marital life, maintaining a constant tension between commitment to an organic (not enforced) community and assertion of individual (not egotistical) difference. That is, in the terms of her text, she manifests a fluid sense of self which, on the one hand, connects with a special "we" endorsing certain spiritual and moral values and, on the other, unleashes a powerful "I" free to criticize and unmask and exercise what she now perceives as the power of the individual.

Moreover, because her reconstitution of herself as subject is by now inextricably linked with her writerly development (she has written herself to the point of self-recovery), this model of selfhood is variously played out in the authorial roles—self-styled literary critic and historian—that Nadezhda Mandelstam resumes from her first volume of memoirs. In her performance as literary critic, she most provocatively extends the reach of her "I." Nadezhda Mandelstam still founds her authority on the "we" of her marriage or, intermittently, the trio of Mandelstam, Akhmatova, and herself.[30] Her commentary still depends, in the main, on personal experience and concrete observation. Yet she is far more insistent in proving her superior "unprofessional" knowledge. In keeping with her stance in *Mozart and Salieri*, she refuses the formal designation of literary scholar, but here she sometimes contests the members of this profession on their own terms.[31] It would seem that she alone can assemble her husband's texts in their proper sequence since "[a]ll M.'s books, except the first two editions of *Stone*, were put together in [her] presence" (390); certainly no editor has proved capable of this task (57). Nadezhda Mandelstam proposes, in turn, her own textological analyses of the poems. She names addressees and referents with utter assurance, not hesitating to identify herself in some unflattering poetic address (246) and even detecting other subjects of Mandelstam's love poems (245–48).

Her textual analyses are equally forthright—often interspersed with more general commentary and fortified by her firsthand knowledge of the creator and his conditions. This passage from her exegesis of "Verse on an Unknown Soldier" is characteristic:

> I believe Mandelstam sensed the approach not merely of one war but of a whole series of them. The lines "Do you hear, night, stepmother of the stars' gypsy camp, what comes now and later?" clearly mark two future stages—"now," that is, soon, imminently, and "later"—after some interval of time, when people will have to fight "for air to live on," for a gulp of air, for the mere possibility of breathing. . . . The foreboding about a future lack of air may well have been provoked by his own shortness of breath—it could often be heard in his verse. "I am I, reality is reality" is a line that could have been uttered only by a man who has trouble breathing. From this line we can diagnose his illness—cardiac asthma. (I am pleased to see that this has been noted by a distant friend.) But in "Verse on an Unknown Soldier" this foreboding of a lack of air is dictated not by his own condition but by fear of the future, designated in the word "later." (486)

Her analysis does not imitate conventional scholarship. The presence of a demonstrably subjective first-person voice, the ellipses and asides, the self-assured link of the creative act with the physical state of the creator all mark this as her distinctive privileged reading. Yet by assuming many of the familiar duties of textual scholars (ordering and dating manuscripts, identifying referents, explaining imagery and theme) Nadezhda Mandelstam seems to be challenging their authority point by point and imposing herself—the reader-interlocutor and, now, textual expert—as perhaps the most informed source on her husband's work.

Building on this impression, Nadezhda Mandelstam wages a particularly vindictive campaign against other would-be caretakers of Mandelstam. The case of Sergei Rudakov had already surfaced in *Hope against Hope*; she refers to it here as a proven villainy. Rudakov, a poet and scholar also exiled to Voronezh in the 1930s, vied to become Mandelstam's authorized biographer and critic. He labored to put the poet's archive in order and convinced Nadezhda Mandelstam to give him "original copies of all of Mandelstam's most important work" (*Hope against Hope*, 273). After he perished in the war, his widow either lost or sold these texts, and Nadezhda Mandelstam construed the whole affair as a planned theft. With her version of these events, she effectively disqualifies a highly qualified contender for the role of Mandelstam authority.[32] It is out of the same sense of betrayed trust that Nadezhda Mandelstam launches a new and more consequential attack in *Hope Abandoned*—this time against Nikolai Khardzhiev, her long-time friend and editor of the then-pending Soviet publication of Mandelstam's work. She does not charge him with theft but accuses him of tampering with Mandelstam's texts. She, the mere widow, had been forced to give him all the manuscripts for editing:

> He did nevertheless return the bulk of the manuscripts to me, keeping a few items for his "collection" and destroying materials on which he wished to change the date or replace with some other text not considered the final one by Mandelstam—as in the case of "January 10." He even explained to me that a poet is often not the best judge of what is good and what is bad, and that it would also be necessary to "tidy up the archive" by removing the drafts of variants he rejected "so that it would always remain as I have made it. . . ." (396)

Nadezhda Mandelstam tempers her accusation somewhat by admitting Khardzhiev's "grave physical and psychological disabilities." Yet her charge remains damning, particularly if we consider her own critical practice. She had devoted most of her life and work to carrying out what she perceived to be Mandelstam's intentions; Khardzhiev, the "professional editor and critic," presumed that he knew better than the creator himself.

Naming these traitors, Nadezhda Mandelstam would seem to figure herself as her husband's true champion. At one point she draws the battle lines very clearly, remembering the pile of texts Mandelstam would bring her after a night's work and commenting bitterly that some of these survived "despite all the depredations of the security organs, the Rudakov couple, and Khardzhiev"

(536). Yet it is curious (and characteristic) that in asserting her personal authority, Nadezhda Mandelstam sentimentalizes neither her own image nor her relationship with Mandelstam. Her "I" is portrayed in unvarnished form. Just when it would seem to be most advantageous to paint scenes of domestic harmony — a co-creative partnership like that of Akhmatova and Chukovskaia — Nadezhda Mandelstam flaunts domestic squabbles, the tug-of-war between a demanding poet and his undocile wife-secretary. She describes, for example, their "holiday" at the Crimean resort of Gaspra, during which Mandelstam composes *The Noise of Time*:

> He dictated it in pieces, roughly a chapter at a time. Before each session he often went out walking alone — for an hour or even two. He returned tense and bad-tempered and ordered me to sharpen my pencil and start work at once. The first few phrases he dictated quickly, as though he remembered them by heart, and I could scarcely keep up with him. Later the pace slowed down, but I often got confused by the long sentences. He just failed to understand why I couldn't get them down at one go, but at the same time I found that he sometimes left out one or even several words, as if he were sure that I would hear them without his having to utter them. "Can't you hear that it doesn't hang together without that?" he would reproach me. I snapped back: "Do you think that I sit in your head and read your thoughts? . . . Fool, fool, fool!" He got angry at the word "fool" and called me an idiot in return. I shrieked with rage and he justified himself by saying that idiot is a beautiful ancient Greek word. So I was an ancient Greek fool into the bargain. . . .
>
> When a certain number of pages had piled up, he asked me to read them out loud, "only without any expression." . . . He wanted me to read like a ten-year-old schoolgirl — before the teacher has taught her to raise and lower her voice and put "feeling" into it. He checked every phrase by listening to it — what he really needed was a dictaphone and not a wife-secretary, but he couldn't demand from a dictaphone the understanding he wanted from me. If he didn't like something in the dictation, he wondered how I could have written down such junk without a murmur, but if I rebelled and didn't want to write something down, he said: "Sh! Don't interfere. . . . You don't understand anything, so keep quiet." (195–96)

Telling this story of the creative process, Nadezhda Mandelstam volunteers an astonishingly frank and entertaining account of the poet-helper relationship — one that adroitly narrates their human limitations. In her unpious characterization the noble poet is demoted to an abusive perfectionist, his loving wife made a beleaguered, resentful sidekick. Further on in this passage, she even entertains what might seem to be a demeaning connection between herself and their one-time cook, who, according to Mandelstam, knows as much if not more than his wife about poetry. Nadezhda Mandelstam partially accepts this judgment — perhaps because it fits with her family code of values; an excellent cook is an artist in her own right and may well deserve the superior ranking.

This kind of record substantiates Nadezhda Mandelstam's greater self-assurance as author and autobiographical subject. More than ever before she seems willing to disclose painful truths and issues of difference, assuming that such a disclosure will not threaten the existence of the "we" and undermine her own authority. She is bolder and surer in asserting her "I," in setting forth her own opinions—however partisan or "foolish" they may sound. As critic, she ventures far beyond the touchstone of her husband's work. Two larger sections in the text—"Poetry and People" and "Major Forms"—formally denote the breadth of her inquiry, which ranges from analyses of other individual texts (e.g., Akhmatova's unsalvaged play *Prologue* [350–64]) to criticism of general trends (the tendency toward "gigantomania" in the arts [343–46]).

Her review of these works and trends is no longer being conducted to prove Mandelstam's insight and authority. Instead it judges all others by his and, interestingly enough, *her* already established standards. Throughout the text her basic approach is to prescribe the writing and reading of literature as individual human acts that must engage the whole person of writer and reader. As in *Mozart and Salieri*, Nadezhda Mandelstam finds fault with the artists who cannot maintain the intense bond between life and work that she learned from Mandelstam. Moreover, she is intent on unmasking those writers and critics who would assume a grander, superhuman position—particularly with the sanction of the official establishment. Again, her attack is not confined to the usual political villains. So the Symbolist poet Viacheslav Ivanov is criticized for his "exaggerated view of the artist" and his dangerous function as lawgiver and myth-maker. He is even held responsible for abetting the various evils of nationalism, social regimentation, and condoned barbarism (402–407). Elsewhere Nadezhda Mandelstam blanketly condemns the "cultmaking" she finds typical of her age. She cites, in example, Il'ia Ehrenburg and Kornei Chukovskii for whitewashing Gor'kii's conduct; the poet Maximilian Voloshin for his pose as recluse; and (as if providing a foil for herself) the case of a wife who idolizes her cowardly, undistinguished husband (88–89).[33]

It is especially intriguing that she indicts Samuil Marshak (and, by implication, Lidiia Chukovskaia) as a representative "cultmaker." Tried in her court, Marshak is found guilty of pretense, deceit, and political collaboration:

> Not to get bored with the purely preventive aspect of their work, editors liked to think of themselves as connoisseurs of style, guardians of the language, and inspirers of new literary forms. One of the first to fancy himself in such a role was Marshak. In his hoarsely rhapsodic voice he explained to his authors (he had authors, not writers) how they were to write, developing and embellishing their subject matter, becoming accomplished stylists. . . . He wanted to make a writer out of anybody who wanted to write and had any kind of life experience. An engineer, a sailor, a hunter, a meteorologist—all possess experience and that is the very stuff of literature if it's related in a good style. To this end he created a special staff of junior editors, gradually promoting them to senior status, who polished, filed, and honed every sentence, every word and turn of phrase, until all manuscripts were reduced to the same presentably average level. The thought that they were creating literature with their own hands fairly made their heads spin, and no

editor who worked under Marshak will ever forget the heroic days when he made works of art out of nothing, converting what would otherwise have been mere propaganda pieces into smooth-flowing tales. . . .

Marshak was very much a man of his times in his determination to sweeten the pill of writing under orders, to create the illusion of literary life when it had been destroyed, and to smooth over all the rough edges. (411–12)

This passage highlights a most vivid contrast of style and approach. Chukovskaia faithfully serves in the ranks of Marshak's junior staff, embraces her fatherly mentor's belief in the creative potential of the editor, and, as we have seen, pays reverent tribute to his decorous pedagogic practice. Nadezhda Mandelstam recapitulates this practice irreverently and sarcastically, thereby "unmasking" Marshak and his "smoothing" manner, declaring the myth of his (and his editors') co-creativity, and even intimating his collusion with the authorities. Her sardonic demystifying approach sharply reverses Chukovskaia's tendency to celebrate and monumentalize.

Nadezhda Mandelstam also resumes her attack on what is, in her eyes, a depersonalizing academy. True to her pattern, her criticism focuses more on talented, unorthodox critics than Party hacks; in the chapter entitled *"Literaturoveden'e"* ("Literary Scholarship") she criticizes the esteemed Formalist Iurii Tynianov and his idea of the literary persona. In her analysis, Tynianov actually formulates her hated principle of the mask as a neutral literary device—an intermediary voice for the poet that can be changed at will and often in accord with the development of new literary trends. Nadezhda Mandelstam implies that this theory is incorrect (she says that Mandelstam's example refutes it) and declares that it betrays a more profound spiritual crisis:

At the heart of [this theory] lay the deep certainty that nobody has lasting convictions or beliefs, or is really capable of sticking to them and deepening them as he grows to maturity. This was the conclusion Tynianov drew from the life he saw around him. Such a theory could arise only at a time when the personality was disintegrating, when it was incomparably easier to note the flaws and seams in a person's life history than to believe in the possibility that he might maintain an unbroken unity of outlook throughout his career. Tynianov compares literary biography with a broken curve, a line that "is broken and dictated by the literary events of the times." The breaks in the line, according to Tynianov, correspond to shifts of literary allegiance, the transitions from one school to another. He saw such breaks in the literary biographies which were taking shape before his eyes, but his explanations did not address the real cause. I do not know whether he ever admitted even to himself that both he and his friends changed direction only out of the most primitive instinct of self-preservation. (328)

Nadezhda Mandelstam holds Tynianov and the other Formalists to account for their abandonment of the whole person of the artist, their attention to surface "style and techniques" rather than to the artist's "view of the world." Leveling the same sort of political charge that she suggested in Marshak's case, she insists that for the artist a persona serves as camouflage in a dangerous environment; in keeping with *her* worldview, she reduces it to a craven political strategy.[34]

As we have just seen, Nadezhda Mandelstam's critique of cultural legislators like Ivanov, Marshak, and Tynianov almost invariably entails sharp artistic, moral, and political judgments. But in Tynianov's case she ventures further in expressing the "naked truth." Although she deems him "one of the best and most pure" of her contemporaries, she does not refrain from depicting her last meeting with him, when he is already afflicted with a terrible deforming illness. Her portrait is as frank as her previous account of her squabbles with Mandelstam. She notes Tynianov's "wizened, shrunken" body, his legs "as thin as matchsticks," his helplessness and sorry dependency on a "real witch" of a wife (327). In consequence, Tynianov is indelibly etched as a pitiable figure "done to death . . . by his own wife and a wasting disease." Here we confront a perfect example of Nadezhda Mandelstam telling all that *she* knows, refusing to break the chain of associative memory for the sake of polite relations and a discreet memoir and, as we shall see, provoking the outrage of her subjects and their associates.[35] In such instances, her plainspeaking "I" resorts to what Joseph Brodskii has dubbed her "photographic" method — her instant imprint of the "naked truth."[36] In lieu of an airbrushed portrait, she exposes just what she thought she saw in all its unflattering (and very often arresting) detail.

Thus Nadezhda Mandelstam very broadly construes and applies her role as literary critic. Still bound to a validating "we," her "I" is audacious, quarrelsome, and sometimes venomous: she projects herself in the text as privileged reader-interlocutor, exclusive textologist, jealous caretaker, uncensored witness, and forthright judge. When she passes from literary matters to broader social criticism, she demonstrates many of the same postures and traits. Yet as she develops the role of social critic her notions of "we" and "I" are harmonized somewhat by the dynamic I first located in *Hope against Hope*. Nadezhda Mandelstam writes to testify and reform: To the latter end, "we" and "I" are used to illustrate the important considerations of complicity and responsibility. As in the previous volume, her first-person stance underscores her inclusion in the system, her shared and individual guilt for surviving within its structures and allowing its terror. At the same time, Nadezhda Mandelstam develops a saving dichotomy of "us" versus "them" in *Hope Abandoned*. Without presuming to deny or transcend her flawed humanity, she suggests a potential model of redemption for her compatriots.

To do this, Nadezhda Mandelstam manipulates an ever more imposing stylistic authority. She expands on the techniques of *Hope against Hope*, adopting a new mode of address in sections like her *"Otstuplenie v storonu"* ("Digression"). Here, as it were, she implies her role as a kind of informal philosopher. Quoting such powerful figures as Fiodor Dostoevskii and the philosopher Sergei Bulgakov, she establishes herself as an interlocutor with great thinkers as well as great poets. And by announcing her "Digression," she invokes the tradition of great author/authorities like Gogol', Dostoevskii, and Tolstoi, interrupting her narrative out of the urgent need to philosophize before her readers.

As social critic-cum-philosopher, Nadezhda Mandelstam then iterates an analysis of Stalinist society that privileges a tiny, besieged community of "we" and advocates the exercise of responsible (i.e., other-oriented) freedom. This program is outlined in the very titles of her chapters—" 'We'," "The Three," "The Five," "Our Alliance," " 'Pernicious Freedom'," "Freedom and License." It is shaped, in large part, by Nadezhda Mandelstam's reflections on Mandelstam and the Acmeists. In the company of Akhmatova and Gumilev (and, to a lesser extent, the poets Vladimir Narbut and Mikhail Zenkevich) Mandelstam discovered a "we" which helped "to mold his personality" and sustain him the rest of his life (25). This "we" contrasts positively with all the haphazard self-interested groups that emerge in the following decades. As Nadezhda Mandelstam figures them, these poets renounce "the cult of the poet and the principle that 'all is permitted' to the man who 'dares' " (45). At the end of the chapter " 'We'," she generalizes their achievement: "A real 'we' is unshakable, indubitable, and enduring. It cannot be broken up, pulled apart, or destroyed. It will remain untouched and whole even when the people included in this pronoun are lying in their graves" (29).

Once again Nadezhda Mandelstam projects the artist as a general role model. Over the course of *Hope Abandoned* the "we" of the Acmeists is reincarnated in various groups of individuals who resist the corruption and regimentation of Stalinism. Drawn from the top down, her scenario describes a small claque of evil leaders manipulating a vast rank and file (522–23); within this "organized mass" only "a few lone figures" are able to hold fast to their own unofficial values (122):

> The fateful years were the twenties, when people not only became convinced of their helplessness, but even exalted it and deemed any intellectual, moral or spiritual resistance old-fashioned, ridiculous, and absurd. It became a sign of backwardness—one could not hold out against the inevitable: the historical process was predetermined, as was the state of society. Every member of society was a mere particle, a chip, a drop among countless drops which made up a collective consciousness. In the twentieth century this collective consciousness was discovered, filled with something like crystals which are insensitive to good and evil, organized into the form of human beings, and instructed to swim with the current in the wake of a victorious leader. (164)

Only "a few lone figures," moreover, manage to withstand (at least temporarily) the seduction of "pernicious freedom" or license. Nadezhda Mandelstam launches an extensive investigation of this problem in her "Digression." It is significant (and predictable) that she refers here to Akhmatova and Mandelstam (her partners and "true poets") as well as authorities like Dostoevskii and Sergei Bulgakov. She credits Akhmatova with alerting her to the difference between license and freedom (273), and she concludes that her life with Mandelstam effectively prevented her own seduction. License, Nadezhda Mandelstam explains, is essentially a destructive, individualistic, exclusionary principle which "results from freely indulging one's desires" (276). It is manifest in "the deification of the People and nationalism"; it permeates all levels of the Stalinist state. In contrast, freedom is creative, inclusive, "based on a moral law" and pledged to the concept of a harmonious (not homogeneous) community.[37] Most important, her notion of freedom (like that of Dostoevskii) is bound to certain Christian beliefs—a basic humility and a sense of one's own sinfulness, the struggle to achieve "the image of God" in one's daily life (266, 282). We shall see that Nadezhda Mandelstam's model of redemption incorporates elements of her own Russian Orthodox faith.[38] But it is characteristic that while she invokes religion here, she emphasizes, above all, the presence and influence of such beliefs in the poet. The poets she admires (in these chapters Khlebnikov, Akhmatova, and Mandelstam) can only attempt to uphold this freedom, yet she implies that they are the lesser heirs to the saints (278–79). In her analysis, the poet substitutes for the spiritual leader: "This is the way of the great poet: as he goes through life his experiences temper him, deepening his thought and emotion. He shares the sins of the world, but he is capable of remorse" (266). Elsewhere she states the succession more positively: "the labor of the poet is a gift of freedom, bringing illumination, even if not deliverance from sin" (274).[39]

Poets are implied as leaders, but they are not the only "free" people Nadezhda Mandelstam names. In *Hope Abandoned* she continues the practice of recovering sample virtuous and corrupted biographies. Chapters like *"Nazidatel'naia istoriia"* ("A Cautionary Tale") and *"Polnaia otstavka"* ("Complete Retirement") relate the fascinating, sobering cases of the "fallen" who were co-opted into the network of surveillance and denunciation. Here she illustrates the insidious process of transforming often decent human beings into mere "chips."[40] But scattered among these case studies are tales of a few who managed to "survive with honor." One such survivor is the woman N.N. who refused to name "accomplices" in order to save herself from torture; I will consider her example more closely in another connection. Nadezhda Mandelstam also devotes an entire chapter to the "good person" of a cobbler, whom she meets during her wartime evacuation in Tashkent. The two somehow come to divulge their secret sorrows (he had been imprisoned for "sabotage"), and he befriends her, watching out for her welfare, inviting her to his home at Christmas and Easter (he and his wife keep the Orthodox holy days), and providing her with the invaluable gift of sturdy shoes. Nadezhda Mandelstam recognizes this man as a "rare bird" who sustained "her faith in people" and gave living proof that "human qualities are not yet totally extinguished" (601). In a sense, it is as if the person of the cobbler incarnates Acmeist values, for he joins the talent of the craftsman with innate virtue.

With this philosophized, demonstrated model of the responsibly free and the irresponsibly self-indulgent, Nadezhda Mandelstam has progressed from historical observation to moral schema, from the social to the ethical and even spiritual realm. What, then, has become of the "I" in this model and in her grander narrative stance? Far from being subsumed by the collective, the "I" in this "we" is still possessed of its own power. In fact, Nadezhda Mandelstam assumes this potential in every individual. Even when she describes the generation of a "collective consciousness" she remarks: "In some mysterious way, even the most ordinary of human wood chips . . . has the power to affect the direction of the current" (164). She argues, too, that each individual contains the elements of freedom and license, along with the potential for doing good and evil (282). And although Nadezhda Mandelstam is inclined toward pessimistic conclusions, weighing the inertia and immense capacity of the system against a few resisting souls, she continues to value and assert the power of the "I" up to the very end. In the penultimate chapter—"Gody molchaniia" ("The Years of Silence")—she foresees more pain and destruction, but she cannot gainsay her own potential:

> The most astonishing thing is that there are still a few people pottering about who try to make their voices heard, as it were, through an immense volume of water, from the bottom of the ocean. Among them I count myself, although I know what superhuman efforts are needed just to preserve a handful of manuscripts. Yet I could not have departed this life without telling something about the blithe spirit who lived with me and never let me lose heart; about poetry and people; about the living and the dead; and about the *stopiatnitsas* (women forced to live one hundred and five kilometers outside of Moscow), although they are still carefully hiding their past. (607–608)

She well understands that she may have no listeners, yet she cannot abandon her singlehanded mission: "But I say there can be no limit: one must keep talking about these things until every injustice and every tear are made known, until the reasons for what happened and still happens become clear" (608). This declaration, perhaps more than any other, accounts for her vehement, repetitive, voluminous book. It also intimates the enormous potential of her "I" to effect a kind of spiritual renewal.[41]

It would seem, therefore, that Nadezhda Mandelstam mutes any tension between "we" and "I" in her function as moralist. In keeping with her almost Dostoevskian views on "freedom," her conception of this relationship—the self in the community—seems to derive from the Russian Orthodox principle of *sobornost'* or spiritual fellowship, especially since she explicitly invokes *sobornost'* as an antipode to the state-made collective. The collective, she argues, is "a mechanical association" enforced by "fear, bewilderment, and the need for a ration card" (407). It demands subordination and promotes license and egotistic self-interest because it preaches a vague "responsibility of all for all" (407). *Sobornost'*, on the other hand, constitutes a "brotherhood" of people who "see themselves as children of the same Father"; its members value the free personality and assume individual responsibility for the good of all. In *sobornost'*—as in Nadezhda Mandelstam's model—the "we" and the "I" uphold the same values and coexist in harmony.

"She" and "I"

As I noted above, this harmonious religious model of the self emerges more as an ideal in her text—an ideal in which difference is not an issue, for it is not stigmatized. In fact, (aside from its male terminology) her model suggests a happy blending of gender constructs: With its combined emphases on individual rights and valued relationships, it moves toward a synthesis of certain posited male and female patterns of development.[42] Nonetheless, in her present context Nadezhda Mandelstam must cope with the stigmatized, restricted difference of being a woman; she must figure the relationship between "we" and "I" for herself in the problematic terms of "she." It is most remarkable, then, that she successfully applies this model of communal allegiance and individual freedom in defining and empowering herself as a woman. The pattern of solidarity and distinction that I traced in the first variant is expanded in *Hope Abandoned*, as Nadezhda Mandelstam enters and authorizes what might be best described as concentric circles of difference—first as a victimized woman in Stalinist society and then as a "free" woman among these women.

This pattern is intimated in the very first paragraph of the text. Reflecting on the "new task" of *Hope Abandoned*, she indicates her shared and unique female identity. She belongs among "the untold numbers of women roaming the country: mute, frightened creatures with and without children, diligent and timid servants constantly trying to improve their qualifications so as not to lose their jobs" (3). She only differs in that she possesses "a sealed bottle with a message," which she will cast upon the waves before she dies. Nadezhda Mandelstam typically understates her distinction; at the outset it seems more important that she foreground her connection with other women. She is frank in her portrayal, but she does not *overlook* her co-sufferers in the lines and involuntary exile.

Her occasional assessments of women as a group are generally sympathetic and often positive.[43] She ennobles the fate of these "mute, frightened creatures" when she casts them as "millions of would-be Antigones" who are cruelly denied the rite of burying their dead fathers, brothers, and husbands (144). I have already cited her observation that women prove stronger than men in hard times (105). At other points Nadezhda Mandelstam comments on women's great adaptability—that once deprived of their husbands they are always able to find work (293), or that, even as girls, they cope better with adversity than "their tender male counterparts" (527). In fact, as Nadezhda Mandelstam ponders the traits of the two great female poets, Akhmatova and Tsvetaeva, she hazards the extreme conclusion that "strength is probably a female quality" (*"zhenskoe svoistvo"*) (444).[44]

Her narrative is also illuminated with numerous sympathetic portraits and biographies of women. For example, she relates at length the tale of a violinist's widow, a woman who has lost two husbands to Stalinist persecution and now lives in fear and anxiety over the future of her son (169–73). She specifically names other inspiring figures. Natasha Shtempel', the addressee of Mandelstam's last poem, is commemorated as "a woman of rare spiritual grace" (230). Frida Vigdorova, the woman responsible for transcribing Joseph Brodskii's infamous trial, is portrayed as "a gray-haired girl with large earnest eyes [who] believed in truth and visited the officials in order to explain to these crafty cynics that one shouldn't play out courtroom farces" (377). She recalls how the female household of Galina Meck (mother and daughter) train her to survive after Mandelstam's death (610–11). Galina, the grandniece of Tchaikovskii, has spent decades in prison and knows to keep Nadezhda Mandelstam "awake" and on the move; her mother, whose husband had been shot, forces her to get into the therapeutic habit of reading. In all these instances, Nadezhda Mandelstam is cherishing the specific experience, capacities, and value of women under Stalinist circumstances. Their examples serve to reflect and authorize her own experience as representative. Bereaved, harrassed, impoverished, effaced, these like women are shown to survive and care for both the living and the dead.

She manipulates other portraits, however, to outline her distinctive character. Once again, Akhmatova furnishes a most productive juxtaposition, although Nadezhda Mandelstam will invoke other important figures for purposes of comparison and "liberation." In Akhmatova's case, she embellishes on her charges from the first variant, faulting the poet for self-regard in her behavior and work. It is in *Hope Abandoned* that she exposes the cult of the Petersburg "beauties," condemning Akhmatova's inclusion in this cult as well as her related preoccupation with "doubles"—that is, her tendency to look at people "as one looks into a mirror, seeking her own likeness and seeing her 'double' in everybody" (437). Indeed, according to Mandelstam, the poet perceives many of these "beauties" as her doubles, and she reveres one of them in particular—Olga Glebova-Sudeikina—as "the embodiment of all feminine qualities" (437, 456).[45] Censuring this "feminine" concern for appearances, Nadezhda Mandelstam probes its more insidious manifestations.[46] She is perhaps the first to speak of Akhmatova's oblique control over her own personal cult: "In her last years, Akhmatova 'put on her phonograph record' for each visitor, that is, she told him the history of Acmeism and her own life so that he would forever remember it and repeat it in her correct version" (454).[47]

Nadezhda Mandelstam sights and censures the same tendencies in Akhmatova's final masterpiece, *Poem without a Hero*. Her specific grievance has to do with Akhmatova's confusing dedication. The poet had first intended it for Mandelstam but then readdressed it to both Mandelstam and Vsevolod Kniazev, a poet who committed suicide before the revolution; she thereby implies these two figures as "doubles" for the sake of her self-indulgent "literary game" (433–37). Nadezhda Mandelstam deeply resents this implication because it equates Mandelstam's truly brave "free" death with suicide—"the greatest act of license" (436). She dislikes the *Poem* for other reasons as well. She may approve the judgment it seems to pass on the Silver Age (a licentious carnival staged by a self-styled elite), but she is repelled by its coy Symbolist echoes—"the cult of beauties, the evasiveness, the triple bottom, the 'mirror writing,' and even the musical allusions and many of the adornments" (442). In Nadezhda Mandelstam's reading, Akhmatova has reincarnated her posturing in her art.

As she pokes through these various facades, she is still clearly intent on recovering a "free" Akhmatova. She relishes those moments when the poet "let[s] herself go and [speaks] in her most earthy manner about the 'beautiful ladies' of

Hope Abandoned 161

the Symbolists" (438). She categorically distinguishes between the "great" and the "put-on" Akhmatova:

> As a friend, Akhmatova was beyond compare, and there was real greatness in her, but when she was surrounded by the women she referred to as "beauties," she gave in to their flattery and began to play the lady. In her very last years she began to lament that Mandelstam had written too few love poems—in effect she reproached me for this. I understood: the "beauties" valued only love lyrics and didn't give a damn about Mandelstam. There was not much room left for love in our terrible life. My Akhmatova was a fierce and wild female friend who stood by Mandelstam with unshakable loyalty, his ally against the savage world in which we spent out lives, a stern and merciless abbess prepared to go to the stake for her faith. All her "ladylike" manners were borrowed. If they came out in her verse (as, of course, they often did) it was only in the weakest of her poems and I yield these to her "beauties." I will keep her other side of self-renunciation and wrath. (247)

Once again, Nadezhda Mandelstam lays claim to a kind of self-reflective figure in Akhmatova—the loyal friend, the angry champion, the self-renouncing and yet wild woman. She even attempts—in her haphazard, associative way—to trace Akhmatova's "real" character from her family life. (Her assay at biography here is much bolder than her autobiographical sketches.) She presumes that Akhmatova inherits her domestic helplessness from her mother, her stern character from her judgmental (and apparently misogynist) father. But whatever her inheritance, it is "obvious" that Akhmatova "did not get on well" with anyone in her family. True to her role as mouthpiece, Nadezhda Mandelstam betrays the poet's secret: "She once confided to me in Tashkent that as a girl she had been very difficult—irritable, capricious, impatient, stopping at nothing in her rush to live" (443). This lack of restraint, which Nadezhda Mandelstam asserts as her basic character, resurfaces again in the poet's old age. Although we might expect Nadezhda Mandelstam to disapprove of this willfulness, she seems to enjoy it as a natural revolt from Akhmatova's "borrowed" ladylike pose. When she declares that she cannot conceive of the later "tempestuous, unsettled" Akhmatova as a salon hostess, she seems, above all, relieved: "I fear that Nedobrovo would have ruled over [her salon] and would have taught her not to make that angry gesture of putting her hand down on her knee. . . . Who could ever imitate that gesture?" (455).

Compiling evidence from Akhmatova's family life, friendships, and art, Nadezhda Mandelstam can only puzzle over the poet's self-imprisonment:

> Hordes of women and battalions of men of widely different generations can speak of her immortal gift for friendship, of her love of mischief (*ozorstvo*) which never deserted her even in old age, of the way in which, sitting at the table with vodka and *zakuski*, she could be so funny that people "fell off their chairs" from laughing. Why did she want to be the kind of great lady (if such exist) before whom people go down on their knees, when she was such a marvelous and madcap woman, poet, and friend? (455–56)

From the perspective of her less inhibited friend, Akhmatova thus enacts the dangers of subscribing to a limiting, socially constructed cult of femininity. Playing the "great lady," she conceals and falsifies her "real" self through decorum and pretense and an artful silence. At the same time, she retains the qualities of a "free" woman—one who is both altruistic and life-loving, morally steadfast and mischievous.

In this version of *Hope Abandoned*, however, Akhmatova is only one of several distinguishing female figures. Another great female artist, Marina Tsvetaeva, emerges as an altogether different model. Nadezhda Mandelstam's relationship with this poet is more limited and obstructed for a number of reasons— Tsvetaeva's utter scorn for all poets' wives; Nadezhda Mandelstam's odd assertion that Akhmatova must be the "best" female poet; but, above all, Tsvetaeva's indifference to the poetry of Mandelstam (460). Yet Nadezhda Mandelstam admires Tsvetaeva's great talent and her turbulent, natural, generous character (246, 462). Tsvetaeva contrasts completely with Akhmatova because "she could never have reined herself in" (462). She is able "to experience every emotion to the utmost"; she abides by no rules of ladylike decorum in her art and life. Nadezhda Mandelstam even maintains that she is glad Mandelstam fell in love with Tsvetaeva before they got involved, for the female poet "prepared" him to appreciate the character of his wife:

> I am sure that my relationship with Mandelstam would not have been formed so easily and simply if he had not previously encountered the wild and fierce Marina. She released in him a love of life and the capacity for spontaneous and unstinting love which so impressed me at the very beginning. I did not realize at first that I owed this to her and I am sorry I was not able to become friends with her. (467)

Tsvetaeva would seem in no need of liberation for she constantly manifests the "wildness" and generosity Nadezhda Mandelstam prizes. But the poet incarnates another vice—a willfulness that generates insensitivity to others or, to apply Nadezhda Mandelstam's basic theorem, an indifference born of license. Again, Tsvetaeva's model distinguishes her own character on a grander scale:

> This was a fashion of the time—a peculiar form of petty self-indulgence based on the principle "I do as I please." . . . It was cultivated in the pre-revolutionary years and took on absurd forms among less talented female representatives of the twenties. These women showed no emotional depth, but only a great ability to snub anyone who seemed "of little interest" at any given moment. The kind of feeling which erupted from the Tsvetaeva sisters (particularly the elder one) with almost elemental force took on the appearance of mere bad manners in other Moscow women of the twenties—I refer, of course, only to such of them as were connected with the arts. (I might well have been the same myself if it had not been for M., who would not tolerate such antics in anyone: you had to choose between him and indulgence in these stylish modern tricks). (463)

Given the two imposing poet models of Akhmatova and Tsvetaeva, it is significant that Nadezhda Mandelstam advances one more female figure as a means to self-definition. I return here to the story of N.N., the woman who managed to survive her camp sentence "with honor." The initials N.N. refer to Natasha Stoliarova, Il'ia Ehrenburg's secretary and Nadezhda Mandelstam's close friend in her later years. For the author, N.N. represents the ideal sort of hero—one of those who display the best side of themselves "naturally, without any pose or high-sounding words" (570). This distinction qualifies her as one of the women and "weak" men who prove truly strong in the face of adversity. Nadezhda Mandelstam posits that the system specifically targeted N.N. for her "open and independent character" (571); like Mandelstam, she is condemned by her inherently free nature. Viewing an early photograph of her friend, Nadezhda Mandelstam categorizes her face as that of a religious sectarian or a young female "seeker of truth"—a face that is "tragic and doomed . . . as though the future had already cast its shadow before" (576).

Her appearance notwithstanding, N.N. is "a true child of her times" and therefore subscribes to no religious beliefs or eternal spiritual values (a fact that sorely perplexes her chronicler).[48] Yet N.N. evinces a constant goodness and an inner freedom. Although she had been denounced by a self-serving acquaintance, she refuses to follow suit and never confronts her informer after she has been released. Her virture emanates naturally; she does good because she wants to, not out of fear or dutiful obedience. At the same time N.N. lives life at a giddy, voracious pace, with no time to spare for writing memoirs. To a great extent, N.N. embodies the kind of woman Nadezhda Mandelstam might have become without the exceptional tempering of Mandelstam—a vital, intelligent woman who disregards convention and professional ambition and is swept up in the excitement of living.[49]

Certainly N.N. proves to be as strong in spirit as Mandelstam and, for his wife, a particularly potent catalyst. Her example effects a far-reaching "conversion":

> I remembered a conversation with N.N. as we were walking along Herzen Street away from the Conservatory. It took place at the end of the fifties. She said that she was going to live as she pleased and not worry about "them" anymore. She would not try to adapt to their demands. . . . At that time only a few managed to free themselves from the general hypnosis, but this woman had such strength that contact with her released the inner strength of people deadened [by fear]. As she spoke, I realized she was trying to make good all the years wasted in the camps and miserable exile, when even she did not dare raise her head. Involuntarily, listening to her, I came to the conclusion that I must do the same myself, that is, make up for all the years of silence and passivity. I suddenly felt liberated. I don't quite know why, but it happened right there on Herzen Street, after this conversation with N.N. (577)

Here Nadezhda Mandelstam is liberated by a woman most like herself. Although she casts her liberation in more or less political terms, it also inevitably extends to her creative endeavors—to her very assumption of authorship. If the conversation with N.N. inspires her to break free of the years of silence and passivity, then it may well facilitate the articulation of her books. Despite her great admiration for the female poets, Nadezhda Mandelstam seems to locate the most accessible, applicable model for her own solitary life and active "nonpoetic" stance in the unassuming example of N.N. She has discovered at last an unflawed prototype of a "free" woman among women.

In the penultimate chapter of *Hope Abandoned*, Nadezhda Mandelstam then summarizes her relationship with other women, clarifying her position and potential. Once again she invokes her female co-sufferers, but now she fully understands their limitations: "Millions of women walked the streets and crossed bridges or stood in lines in exactly the same way, seeing and observing nothing. They did not comprise a 'we', but were simply grains of sand not sucked up by the great vacuum cleaner (614)." Here Nadezhda Mandelstam ventures to analyze the dilemma experienced by Chukovskaia's characters. The women in the lines can only exist as a bewildered, random community created by force and largely incapacitated by fear. Nadezhda Mandelstam empathizes with them and derives a certain sense of solidarity from observing their efforts to survive and cope. But in the final analysis they offer no defining "we"; their public silence and obedience preclude her own individual difference. She has had to liberate her capacity to speak and act through the inspiring (although often problematic) examples of exceptional women—the carefully humanized portraits of great female artists and the new icon of the prosaic, natural heroine. And in this chapter Nadezhda Mandelstam completes her rite of passage, marking how she overcomes (consciously and subconsciously) the obstacles that enslave other women "in her position"—the brutalizing desire for vengeance and the paralyzing fear. What emerges from these successive phases of liberation is "a crazy old woman [who] fears nothing and despises force"—a woman whose testimony may have at least the minimal effect of impressing the security forces assigned to destroy it (618).

Thus, in *Hope Abandoned* Nadezhda Mandelstam's recovered self describes, on several levels and to conditional degrees, a constant fluctuation between community and the free personality, a sanctioning or at least sympathetic "we" and a broadly empowered, complexly different "I." The principle of *sobornost'* or spiritual fellowship informs her moral vision and proves to be a capacious ideal, accommodating both women and men in its union. Under the conditions of a non-ideal world, however, Nadezhda Mandelstam sees fit to assert her "I" and exercise her idiosyncratic difference. She depicts herself resisting the regimented collectives of Stalinism, the dehumanizing ways of the Soviet academy, and (to her) the sanctimonious practice of various would-be legislators of Russian culture. Her frank portraits and vehement tone—even her "improper" language—seem deployed to collapse the multilayered facade of Stalinist society. As part of this extraordinary self-recovery, Nadezhda Mandelstam also conducts a liberating, self-validating critique of certain traditional gender constructs and assigned behaviors. Observing, analyzing, and writing as she does, she breaks the rules of political, cultural, and specifically "feminine" decorum.

Hope Abandoned

She is no longer silent and passive; she countenances no poses or masks for herself or her contemporaries. In consequence, her assertive, articulate, uninhibited "I" overwhelms both the script for the "blessed wife" and the restrained, tasteful speaking role of the female mourner and witness. Nadezhda Mandelstam has extracted a prodigious, distinctive sense of self and authorship from her extraordinary works.

Yet at the same time she continues to name and cherish her beloved "we"—in whatever incarnation. It seems absolutely appropriate that *Hope Abandoned* closes with the letter Nadezhda Mandelstam wrote to her husband after his arrest and before she learned of his death. This text is written and then rewritten to maintain their bond. In fact, it is the only sample of her writing (from an earlier period of non-writing) which she sees fit to display. Her letter is desperately focused on their relationship—addressed to the "you" of Mandelstam, fraught with anxiety for him, bolstered with assertions of their happiness together. And in its final paragraph Nadezhda Mandelstam conveys a last, resonant self-portrait:

> I do not know where you are. Or whether or not you will hear me. Or if you know that I love you. I did not manage to tell you how much I love you. I cannot tell you even now. I speak only to you, only to you. . . . You are with me always and I who was so wild and angry and never learned how to weep—now I weep and weep and weep.
> It's me, Nadia. Where are you? Goodbye. Nadia. (621)

Her wild "I" is last shown to be tempered by her overriding love and concern for the "you." The whole of *Hope Abandoned* concludes with this fundamental declaration of commitment, the voluntary dedication of one free spirit to another.

Contrary to Nadezhda Mandelstam's gloomy prediction, *Hope Abandoned* reached a wide audience, but its impact was much more ambiguous than she may have foreseen. Far from inspiring liberation in others, her recovery and assertion of self alienated many acquaintances and even good friends. Those specifically named and criticized were predictably upset; within the confines of her text, Nadezhda Mandelstam's "settling of accounts" must be one-sided and, to many, simply unfair. In his analysis of this reaction, Carl Proffer reckons that Nadezhda Mandelstam violated an implicit literary and social contract in *Hope Abandoned*:

> Russian literary people are not used to this—they usually prefer the hagiographic approach to the past and writers' biographies. Anyone who has tried to write a biography of a Soviet writer runs into this when he reaches primary sources such as friends, colleagues, and widows. There is little of the rough and tumble of Western memoirs and diaries; a Russian Anais Nin would cause cramps; Harry Truman's bluntness and language would be totally unacceptable. Everything is recorded on a very elevated intellectual plane. Art is mentally capital-

ized, sex does not exist. And unpleasant historical events are glossed over or not mentioned. (*The Widows of Russia*, 34–35)

In both content and form Nadezhda Mandelstam's text transgresses many of the implicit conventions of Russian and Soviet memoir writing—the whitewashed portraits, the decorous language, the proscription on the very intimate and unpleasant, the author's circumspection and self-effacement. Its misreading is perhaps inevitable. After all, the predominant mandate for Russian literature throughout the nineteenth and twentieth centuries has been to inculcate high moral values with little or no ambiguity; this moral mission engendered the very cult of the writer that Nadezhda Mandelstam seeks to reform and humanize. It comes as no surprise, therefore, that Chukovskaia, one of the most gifted and sincere supporters of this cult, reportedly lamented *Hope Abandoned* as "our misfortune."[50] Yet the various Russian critiques of this text often expose a kind of negative of Nadezhda Mandelstam's achievement. For example, the critic Emma Gershtein, one of Nadezhda Mandelstam's named "victims" and a close friend of Akhmatova, senses certain distinctive features (if not the underlying moral agenda) of the text:

> The most unpleasant thing about her work is her frank manner of settling personal accounts, playing on the political biases of her unsophisticated readers. They are unanimous in saying that she has depicted the epoch in her books with remarkable veracity. Defamation, slander, demagogy—isn't that the epoch? She has not only represented the epoch, but embodied her own utter lack of scruples.[51]

Judging her by the claims of her "unsophisticated readers," Gershtein reduces her complex, personalized, openly biased narrative to a statement of "untruth"—to quasi-Stalinist "defamation, slander, and demagogy." Her reaction is symptomatic: If Nadezhda Mandelstam is going to write her opinions, then she is striving for the same kind of transcendent legislating authority assumed by a steady succession of Russian author/thinkers. Since there is no exact precedent for Nadezhda Mandelstam's work, Gershtein opts to read her text as presumptuous and "defamatory," not as subjective criticism or narrative performance.

On the other end of the critical spectrum, the writer Veniamin Kaverin refuses to read Nadezhda Mandelstam as an author altogether. He relegates her text to the realm of "anti-literature" and dismisses her as the unworthy wife—or, more nastily, "shadow"—of Mandelstam, a nonentity who has no right to judge genuine artists and scholars. He formulated his attack in a "public" letter which was circulated in *samizdat* and published in the West. Commenting on this response, Proffer argues that Kaverin's letter reflects a startling (and endemic) intolerance for the individual's rights to judge and express opinions publicly (36). Yet it also testifies to the original, provocative power of Nadezhda Mandelstam's work. In a kind of inverted listing of its dominant features, Kaverin faults her text for its irreverent judgment, self-assertion, meandering form, inclusion of hearsay, and improper language:

> *Hope Abandoned* was dictated not by injured pride, but by a sick self-rapture based on the fact that you were the wife of a great poet. It is not so strange that this self-rapture is accompanied by a vulgar familiarity of which you even seem to be proud.[52]

Expressing his outrage point by point, Kaverin serves as an excellent barometer of a conventional sensibility that includes both ideologically orthodox and far more liberal writers and critics. Nadezhda Mandelstam has disrupted even traditional lines of opposition in her function as *provocateur* and truth-teller; she has dared to unmask the "liberals' idols of the past" (Proffer, 38). Kaverin is particularly incensed by her attack on Tynianov and, missing the whole of her portrait for its frank details, he simply declares that she lacks the "literary education" to understand the critic.[53]

Throughout his diatribe Kaverin depicts Nadezhda Mandelstam as a presumptuous, malicious, ignorant, and vulgar individual who profanes the sanctum of Russian literature. Yet this impression actually implies her artistic, if not moral, success. Kaverin neither accepts her version of the truth nor understands her call to reform, but he recognizes and responds to her highly personal authorship. Nadezhda Mandelstam has succeeded in transferring her living presence to her text; writing herself, she has made her idiosyncratic influence large and permanent in her society. This is all an individual can do, she claims, and at the same time this is a great deal indeed. *Hope Abandoned* concludes in her expressed belief that the individual who "keep[s] talking about these things" may be the single means to reform Soviet society; each person's uncensored memories are "the only thing that can give immunity" to a people who succumb, generation after generation, to a diseased system based on force, retribution, and material gain (617). Nadezhda Mandelstam may find few Russian readers who will forgive her one-sided frankness and appreciate the idiosyncracy of her approach, but in *Hope Abandoned* she has completely fulfilled her moral obligation according to her own uncompromising terms.[54]

In *Hope Abandoned*, then, Nadezhda Mandelstam writes to empower and liberate herself in all her various interactions and capacities. She asserts her abilities—in a defiantly subjective way—as critic, textologist, caretaker, historian, and moralist-philosopher. In addition, she links her development as author-narrator-subject with an ongoing consideration of her own distinctive identity and power as a woman. The result is extraordinary: We witness one of the rare moments in the history of Russian literature when a woman ventures into the male preserve of writing social, political, and moral commentary about the Russian people and, in so doing, does not efface her gendered difference. It is significant that Nadezhda Mandelstam feels she has the right and duty to dispense this sort of commentary, that her particular experience equips her with a valuable and necessary perspective. It is equally important that she does not affect the generic self-conception and the transcendent narrative stance of many of her male predecessors and peers. Although she is perfectly willing to manipulate different rhetorical styles to persuade her reader, she does not suppress the features of her "free personality" to achieve a more respectable, authoritative, de-personalized persona. It is imperative for her to relate and assess her age according to what she has termed a "human" scale. And while this scale does not derive exclusively from women's experience, she implies that it is best observed by the women and "weak" men who manage to resist the brutality of Stalinism. Nadezhda Mandelstam seeks to uphold this scale herself by speaking from her own experience in her own limited-yet-powerful, distinctive-yet-representative voice.

Hope Abandoned thus performs a remarkable and enduring feat. Commencing her work as biographical tribute, Nadezhda Mandelstam quickly reconceives it as a sort of expansive, applied autobiography—a frankly subjective recollection and judgment of the entire Stalinist epoch. As such, her text does merit inclusion in the strong Russian tradition of moralizing dissident historiography—from the seventeenth-century writings of Archpriest Avvakum through the memoirs of Aleksandr Herzen up to the essays and documentary prose of Aleksandr Solzhenitsyn. Yet Nadezhda Mandelstam's text stands as a unique contribution, for it was produced by a woman who neither intended nor was entitled to be a writer or a revolutionary or a moral legislator. Instead, her work emanates from her conception of herself as an irreverent girl friend, a free personality, an uncensored mouthpiece for the truth, and a crazy old woman; it benefits from the speaking and writing privileges she has garnered through childhood, marriage, widowhood, and a more comfortable old age. Moreover, it incarnates her personal presence and influence—her biased vision, lively narration, and importunate address. Through the writing of *Hope Abandoned*, as it were, Nadezhda Mandelstam potentially admits the entire world into her kitchen and talks them free of the fear, complacency, and self-censorship that would doom them to repeat her past. It is as if *Hope Abandoned* replays her sharp talk and freewheeling "salon" for everyone and always.

The Post-Stalin Legacy

8.
THE WIDOWS' MIGHT

> And finally, can one compare the power of Russian literary widows to the power of the official literary establishment—from the Central Committee through the Union of Writers down to the printing factories? . . . I would argue that Nadezhda Mandelstam was an extremely powerful woman, and that along with her the literary widows of Russia have had a strong and lasting effect on the history of Russian literature. Although in the short run the immense resources of the Soviet establishment enable it to set up and maintain its own territory, in the long run this huge puffball of pseudoliterature will disappear and the true literature will occupy its normal place.
>
> Carl Proffer, *The Widows of Russia* (63)

Carl Proffer was perhaps the most far-seeing in his praise, but certainly the majority of Chukovskaia's and Mandelstam's readers laud them for services rendered—to their husbands and friends, to the cause of Russian literature. This is the legacy they themselves would likely endorse; as I have shown, the narratives of both foreground their devotional mission, most often diffusing autobiographical revelations within an other-oriented text. Yet in accord with my own readings of their work, I want finally to review this legacy from a more specific (and heretofore invisible) angle, to consider what Lidiia Chukovskaia and Nadezhda Mandelstam bequeath to other Russian *women*. Their miraculous achievement as caretakers has been amply celebrated. Especially now that the disintegration of the Soviet state permits me to historicize their legacy, I propose to explore the models they identify for both women writers and women activists in the post-Stalin era.

Read in juxtaposition and at either side of the empowering figure of Akhmatova, Chukovskaia and Mandelstam could be said to exemplify two productive paradigms for Russian women writers. The two by no means exhaust the possibilities, but they encompass an important opposition in their self-representation and approach. In her nonfiction, Chukovskaia most exactly and eloquently fulfills the duties of the "literary widow," establishing herself as a model conservator and gatekeeper of Russian culture. With her unshaken set of moral values, her deference before art and artist, her scrupulous regard for careful reporting, and her observance of certain rules of social and cultural decorum (e.g., silence on matters of sexuality, profanity, or irreverent curiosity), Chukovskaia composes exemplars of perhaps the most popular tradition of unofficial Soviet memoirs—a tradition roughly correspondent to Proffer's category of "hagiography." Whether they be written about political figures or cultural figures-made-political victims, these memoirs express—in the best cases—the moral rectitude, painstaking lucidity, and sincere reverence manifest in Chukovskaia's *Notes* or *To the Memory of Childhood*. Moreover, while they are very often produced by women, they tend to uphold (at least explicitly) male-centered constructions of Russian culture and political action and to accept the variously confining roles and second-rate value culturally ascribed to Russian women. (Even *Notes on Anna Akhmatova*, which reflects a female poet so admirably, does so by ennobling Akhmatova's conservative self-construction as a "great lady" and by elevating her above her former reputation as a poet "for women.") In a sense, Chukovskaia's fiction restates many of the same traits and assumptions, for her novels illustrate how two widows, each strictly abiding by her own notion of moral behavior (and her own traditional views on women and men), ought or ought not to respond to the injustice and silence of the torture chamber. Yet while Chukovskaia never overtly challenges the culturally and paternally sanctioned model of a "poetically educated" woman (an enlightened female *intelligent*), she realizes, in both fiction and memoirs, the *creative* potential of a "literary widow" and demonstrates how this female persona (Nina in *Going Under*, Chukovskaia herself in *Notes*) might serve as a general prototype for heroic action and national redemption.

While executing the same duties, Nadezhda Mandelstam early on signals a different interpretation of her role. In the course of her varied performance as storyteller, truth-teller, "wild girl," and "crazy old woman," she gradually discerns her difference as a woman among women and dissects the gender constructs assigned by both state and society. She resists casting herself as the poet's dutiful wife and secretary; she violates the taboos on the intimate and the profane; she unmasks the artifice and distortion of various "beautiful ladies"; she refuses to canonize Akhmatova as a cultural object and instead celebrates her as an unreconstructed *ozornitsa*. Perhaps most strikingly, Nadezhda Mandelstam ventures her own explicit conception of the new "heroism" refracted in the artistic texts of Bulgakov, Pasternak, and her husband. In contrast to the warrior ethos of Stalinist culture, she ascribes real strength and power to women and "weak" men—not only to Christ-like male artists and their female helpmates but also to outspoken female artists like Akhmatova, Tsvetaeva, and (implicitly) herself. In this fashion Nadezhda Mandelstam incarnates a fascinating paradox: Although she begins writing in the roles of conservator and gatekeeper (and in fact consistently upholds many of the values maintained by Chukovskaia), she develops into a revisionist cultural critic who begins to acknowledge and explore gender differences. Rebelling against assigned social and cultural behaviors, voicing a liberating audacity, Nadezhda Mandelstam furthers a relatively infrequent, but nonetheless significant, pattern in Russian women's writing. She is one of the few women writers who transgress the behavioral boundaries for a female *intelligent* and assay a nontraditional critique and revaluation of their culture and society. She is preceded, for example, by another poet's wife, Liubov' Blok (the unsilent "Beautiful Lady" scorned by Akhmatova), who had offered a similarly transgressive self-portrait in her memoirs.[1] But certainly the most flamboyant representative of this tendency to date is the poet Marina Tsvetaeva, who practiced "contrariness" as a fundamental creative strategy and boldly manipulated and revalued the constructs of "literary femininity" and "literary masculinity."[2] It is no coincidence, I think, that Nadezhda Mandelstam discovers vital points of similarity between the "wild and fierce" Tsvetaeva and herself.

Therefore, although neither Chukovskaia nor Mandelstam intentionally position their work in any tradition of Russian women's writing, their texts reflect and elaborate certain recurring patterns of approach and authorship. It would seem that their different models remain productive if we examine the proliferation of Russian women writers in the post-Stalin era. Chukovskaia's modest, dutiful narrative stance regularly informs the autobiographical writings of other dissident women; her male-centered conception of Russian culture is seconded by many Soviet women writers, who "have undoubtedly internalized the consequences of being a small minority in the male-dominated Soviet literary establishment."[3] Nadezhda Mandelstam's revisionist and transgressive approach has had a fainter, more scattered resonance, but the fictional experiments of writers like Liudmila Petrushevskaia, Valeriia Narbikova, and Iuliia Voznesenskaia indicate that a growing number of artists are exploring unsanctioned female roles and perspectives (the heroine as social misfit and fantasist) and taboo topics (female sexuality). Now that the works of both Chukovskaia and Mandelstam have been published officially, it will be intriguing to chart their further reception and influence, to observe how they are analyzed and categorized and appropriated and, in tandem, how their texts are perceived to shape or "exceed" the notion of women's writing in the changing canon of Russian literature.[4]

Of more immediate influence, however, was their special status on the post-Stalin cultural scene, a celebrity that in part reflected the sociopolitical conditions of that era. According to sociologist Vladimir Shlapentokh, after Stalin's death there ensued a process of "privatization" or "destatization" (14) in which the state gradually lost authority "over all strata of the population" (153), and the Soviet people shifted their interest "from the state to their primary groups (family, friends, and lovers) and to semilegal and illegal civil society as well as to illegal activity inside the public sector" (13).[5] In this period the easing of state control and state terror guaranteed the domestic privilege that had been exercised so cautiously in Stalin's time; the family "became the leading institution in privatization" (164), and citizens learned to rely on family and friends and friends of friends for everything from political and spiritual development to material support. The domestic sphere was now actively developed as an arena for oppositional activities. It furnished the workplace for *samizdat*, what one historian describes as "the backbone of the Soviet human rights movement" and the means of establishing "the connecting links essential for organizational work."[6] It also housed a flourishing unofficial society in informal salons and *kompanii*— that is, groups of "regular guests who . . . were looking for opportunities to dance to jazz, drink vodka, and talk until dawn."[7] The human rights activist Liudmila Alekseeva (a one-time frequenter of the *kompanii*) itemizes their wide-ranging functions:

> *Kompanii* evolved their own forms of literature, journalism, music, and humor. They performed the functions of publishing houses, speaker bureaus, salons, billboards, confession booths, concert halls, libraries, museums, counseling groups, sewing circles, knitting clubs, chambers of commerce, bars, clubs, restaurants, coffeehouses, dating bureaus, and seminars in literature, history, philosophy, linguistics, economics, genetics, physics, music, and art.[8]

In their writings and lifestyle, Lidiia Chukovskaia and Nadezhda Mandelstam clearly utilized and helped create the new capacities of this sphere. Both contributed in characteristic, sometimes overlapping ways to the development of unofficial Soviet society. Both, of course, were involved in the forum of *samizdat*, as writers and readers. Both participated, to varying degrees, in these private gatherings and networks. I evoked Nadezhda Mandelstam's salon in the preceding chapter; according to the accounts of her visitors, her gatherings fulfilled many of the functions listed by Alekseeva. Chukovskaia was linked to various circles of friends and identified as an important member of the entire dissident network.[9] She also hosted special literary gatherings and managed, along with her daughter Elena, to maintain an unofficial museum dedicated to Chukovskii and housed in his old Peredelkino dacha.[10] In contrast, however, to Mandelstam's informal socializing, Chukovskaia's involvement quite often surfaced in public acts of association—in testimonials and letters of protest or intercession.[11] Within the still necessarily discreet forums of *samizdat* and dissident society, she dared to assume the role of public spokesperson, defending—in her own name—everyone from famous writers like Siniavskii and Solzhenitsyn to a young woman in Odessa charged with distributing *samizdat*.[12]

In fact, the lives and texts of Chukovskaia and Mandelstam comprise an extraordinarily complete and useful guide to the works of other female dissidents. The roles they informally assumed and articulated were developed more systematically by succeeding women; their improvised strategies were elaborated into more extensive, formalized networks of communication and support. The practice of *samizdat* became so sophisticated and widespread that by April 1968 the *Chronicle of Current Events* (*Khronika tekushchikh sobytii*)—a journal testifying to human rights violations in the U.S.S.R.—commenced "publication" under the editorship of Natal'ia Gorbanevskaia.[13] A professional editor, Gorbanevskaia seemed to extend Chukovskaia's model, applying her expertise to the production and maintenance of unofficial writing and, more specifically, to a project that involved the careful ongoing documentation of state repression. According to the fragmentary record of dissident memoirs and official arrests, quite a few women participated in the production and distribution of *samizdat*. In one such anecdotal account, Alekseeva describes how she managed to earn substantial income (she had already been dismissed from her editorial position) by typing up *samizdat* books for some of her "better-paid friends."[14] (One of the books she "published" was Nadezhda Mandelstam's first volume of memoirs.)

Women also figured prominently in the establishment and operation of support services for political prisoners and their families. The necessarily informal networks described by Chukovskaia and Mandelstam were supplemented by more widespread associations with highly visible organizers. For example, the writer and journalist Frida Vigdorova served as "executive secretary" for a "benevolent society of good deeds" and gained a reputation as "one of the first public figures of a new type"; in her unflagging attempts to defend and provide material aid for political victims, Vigdorova's action "exceeded the boundaries of the smaller world of relatives, friends, acquaintances, and assumed a social significance."[15] With the development (and repression) of dissident society, other charities formed, predictably enough, around the wives of political prisoners — particularly Mariia Rozanova and Larisa Bogoraz, the respective wives of the imprisoned writers Andrei Siniavskii and Iulii Daniel'. No longer terrorized into the fugitive existence of Nadezhda Mandelstam, these writers' wives consciously acted as public contacts for offers of aid and consultation with both *samizdat* and the foreign press; their redistribution of donated money and goods to other prisoners resulted in the creation of an unofficial "Red Cross" (1968), which was eventually systematized under the supervision of Liudmila Alekseeva. The operation of this "Red Cross" resembled the parcel-sending expedition described in *Notes on Anna Akhmatova* — only on a much broader, more coordinated scale. Its volunteers assembled and sent off packages, smuggled money inside book covers, maintained a penpal network, and even purchased homes for those sentenced to internal exile.[16]

Reiterating and formalizing the examples of Lidiia Chukovskaia and Nadezhda Mandelstam, women like Vigdorova, Gorbanevskaia, Alekseeva, and Bogoraz helped to shape a new sort of Russian underground which did not rekindle the conspiratorial terrorism of late nineteenth-century groups, but, at least within the human rights movement, upheld nonviolent methods, voluntary and individual participation, and an egalitarian structure based on ties of trusted friendship and resistant to any sort of flamboyant heroism. It would seem that the human rights movement incarnated just what writers like Chukovskaia and Mandelstam had proposed — a most effective opposition or "we" which would undo the warrior ethos, strict hierarchy, enforced collectivity, and violent control of Stalinism. Alekseeva likens this movement to the "moral oppositions" of the early Christians in the Roman Empire, the populists in Russia, the followers of Gandhi in India and of Martin Luther King, Jr. in the United States.[17] It also bore a particular resemblance to the Argentinian "Mothers of the Plaza de Mayo" who banded together in the 1970s to demand information about their "disappeared" children. Indeed, these "mothers" expressly correspond to the Soviet women standing in the Stalinist prison lines, with the impressive difference that the Argentinian women dared to organize protest demonstrations in public spaces and in the press.[18]

Fundamental in creating and sustaining the Soviet human rights movement, women also acquired special power and opportunities through their service. In contrast to the Soviet political establishment, work in the opposition frequently entailed loss of employment and material benefits and promised no compensatory status of underground "leader." Both women and men felt called to take up this work, but women more specifically benefited from its egalitarian and altruistic principles. Not only did women emerge in the movement as prominent writers, editors, "administrators," and lawyers (Sofia Kallistratova and Dina Kaminskaia were reported to be the "leading practitioners" of "dissident law"), but they made the crucial transition from clandestine helper to unofficial public figure.[19] Chukovskaia serves as one important example; others include the signatories of public human rights petitions (e.g., Tat'iana Velikanova and Tat'iana Khodorovich); still others carried this role to the "extreme" of conducting peaceful public demonstrations against government injustice. In perhaps the most renowned demonstration, Larisa Bogoraz, Natal'ia Gorbanevskaia, and five other dissidents publicly protested the Soviet invasion of Czechoslovakia in 1968.[20] This public display, complete with Gorbanevskaia's new baby lying in its carriage, marked just how far women had ventured since the Stalinist terror. In fact, it projected a kind of contrasting tableau to the threshold scene from *Going Under*: The helpless, isolated, bereaved mothers and wives in the prison lines are here replaced by women who join with men in active protest and mutual support and include (but do not have to sacrifice) a new baby in their act of "moral opposition." For at least one small segment of the population, the potential of Chukovskaia's Nina Sergeevna had been realized.[21]

Like Chukovskaia and Mandelstam, the women involved in the various dissident movements rarely set themselves apart from men; only a few explicitly feminist groups surfaced in the late 1970s and early 1980s and were promptly repressed by the KGB.[22] And for all the supposed egalitarianism of the human rights movement, it remains unclear how the workload was specifically divided between the sexes—for example, who did most of the writing and who did most of the typing in *samizdat*, who was largely responsible for assembling and mailing packages to political prisoners. Yet, while recognizing these qualifications, I find that perhaps the most revolutionary aspect of the legacy of Chukovskaia and Mandelstam recurred in the lives and works of many female dissidents for they, too, experienced and commemorated liberating, empowering relationships with other women. I have traced the course and impact of these relationships at length in the texts of Chukovskaia and Mandelstam. Both writers conceived of certain ideals on the basis of the remarkable women they knew and loved (Anna Akhmatova, Natasha Stoliarova); first and foremost, these exemplary women showed them how to cope with and overcome their victimization by the state. Yet their relationships also educed a more fundamental lesson of self-definition and self-respect. In their women friends and mentors, Chukovskaia and Mandelstam located specifically female creative and heroic models to be valued and emulated.

The texts of other dissident women present variants of the same important pattern. To name just a few examples: in her *Memoirs* Raisa Orlova (1917–89) devotes a chapter to Frida Vigdorova in which she highlights an entire series of formative, sustaining female relationships. She herself regards Vigdorova as "the kind of person by whom everything was measured" (284); among the other subjects of her memoirs, only Andrei Sakharov receives a like accolade. She testifies to the special friendship between Chukovskaia and Vigdorova, whose death Chukovskaia mourns as the collapse of her "main support" (283).[23] Yet Orlova most clearly establishes Vigdorova as a female role model when she focuses on family relationships. To her, Vigdorova appears "to be a remarkable mother; that is, a mother who was seeking, making mistakes, and suffering. She was an enlightener in everything, including her relationship with her daughters" (275). Orlova then emphasizes the fruits of this enlightenment in her portrait of the daughters: "During the period of her serious illness, I saw her devoted daughters, daughters who were friends at her bedside, daughters who were stern, frequently jealous and protective of their mother" (276).[24]

Irina Ratushinskaia (1955-), in turn, writes from the perspective of such a "daughter" (or perhaps "granddaughter"). A dissident poet who was sentenced to seven years' hard labor in 1983, Ratushinskaia was incarcerated with other female political prisoners in the "Small Zone" of a Mordovian labor camp. Her narrative of this time, *Grey Is the Color of Hope*, therefore offers a uniquely focused account; she, like many other women memoirists of the camps, describes a sex-segregated world of political and common prisoners, but she mainly attends to the high-minded intellectuals and dissidents of the "Small Zone." Her text serves at once to document injustices committed (this in keeping with the legalistic methods of the human rights movement) and to commemorate the inspiring examples of her zone-mates—women like Tat'iana Velikanova, Tat'iana Osipova, and Natal'ia Lazareva (incidentally, one of the editors of the feminist journal *Mariia*). She discovers a ready community of dissident women, and she chronicles how its members organize and share their work load and domestic chores; how they maintain an atmosphere of tolerance and caring support; and how they try to conduct their lives in accordance with their deeply held (and sometimes rather narrowly defined) moral convictions.[25] Ratushinskaia identifies one particular mentor in Tat'iana Velikanova—"the closest friend, the wisest counselor and an example of that incredible patience toward the failings of others that should be a hallmark of life in the camps."[26] But Ratushinskaia's approach reflects a sense of established precedent, transmitted instinct. A child of the post-Stalin era, she grew up on *samizdat* (she knows the prison routines from reading Solzhenitsyn), and she quickly perceives that she is "amongst my own kind" in the camp:

> I absorbed these basic tenets of Zone life as my due heritage, and they suited me

down to the ground. In fact, I had observed these norms even earlier, in the frightening solitude of the KGB investigation prison, partly through instinct and partly through common sense. (42)

Situated chronologically between Orlova and Ratushinskaia, Liudmila Alekseeva (1927-) relates the most straightforward example of transformative friendship. In her memoirs she recalls that her girlhood heroine had been Zoia Kosmodemianskaia, a wartime incarnation of the official warrior type. According to the newpaper accounts of 1942, Zoia was a nineteen-year-old partisan who set fire to a stable filled with "German horses" and consequently was tortured and hanged, although not before she could deliver an inspiring speech to her villagers.[27] Zoia's story, as it turned out, was modeled after the story of Tat'iana Solomakha, a martyr of the civil war. Alekseeva tests herself to follow in Zoia's footsteps, and later, as a Party educator, even develops lectures to reinvigorate the Zoia legend. (In an interesting twist, Alekseeva actually meets Zoia's mother, who has come to recite her daughter's canonized story in a dispassionate, "automatized" way.)[28] But as Alekseeva begins to acknowledge her difference from others (largely, it seems, in a political sense), she replaces Zoia's model with that of her close friend, Larisa Bogoraz; that is, she abandons the physical derring-do of the socialist realist warrior-martyr for the "calm fearlessness" and "natural sense of justice" her friend displayed during the trial of Siniavskii and Daniel'.[29] This shift, moreover, enables Alekseeva to activate her own kind of heroism. She recounts the whole progression as she realized it during an "interview" with the KGB:

> I was alone among the enemy. I knew that I stood to lose everything I had accomplished in my forty years. It was a Zoya situation, except I no longer wanted to be like Zoya. Now I had another role model: Larisa Bogoraz. I thought of her cool self-control at the KGB interrogation in the case of Daniel and Sinyavsky. A few months earlier, before signing the petitions, I would have fallen short of my new role model. But I had made my choices, and now it was just a matter of following through, even if that meant becoming a seamstress at the Bolshevichka sewing factory.
> As I listened to my own answers, I realized that I was not playing Larisa. I was being myself. It wasn't Larisa, it was I who was delighting in the opportunity to tell them that I would not wag my tail in their presence, that from now on I would not defer to them to tell me what's right, that from now on my soul would be my own and that nothing they could do would hurt me.[30]

Orlova and Vigdorova, Ratushinskaia and her celebrated zone-mates, Alekseeva and Bogoraz—these documented bonds between other women activists advanced the pattern that was sensed and mapped so perceptively by Lidiia Chukovskaia and Nadezhda Mandelstam. Their relationships expanded on the variously written and cast scripts of a quiet, everyday, comprehensive heroism encompassing the written word, private conduct, and public act. At the same time these female friendships poised them on the brink of further transformation, suggested to them the primary values of women's works and capacities. I have argued that this kind of revaluation is an implicit part of the legacy of Lidiia Chukovskaia and especially Nadezhda Mandelstam, a potential they disclose but do not champion. It was explored further by other dissident women, although it was rarely taken up as its own deserving campaign. Now it remains to be seen how this part of their legacy will be reinvested under the conditions of a radically different post-Soviet state. What roles and powers will Russian women be able to retain or adapt now that the state is undergoing a chaotic transition to capitalism, the public sphere has grown more blatantly materialistic and opportunistic, and the domestic sphere is overwhelmed by problems of consumption? How will those women once involved in unofficial culture and politics navigate the hazardous passage from a clear-cut official/dissident opposition to a confusing market economy that no longer respects intangibles like high culture, moral resistance and, for that matter, women's equal rights?[31] After the first euphoria of *glasnost'*, it was as if an age of innocent valor had passed; the present situation simply disregards Chukovskaia's and Mandelstam's visions of a "brotherhood" ensuring freedom of the personality and freedom of the word.[32] It also augurs an old/new economic devaluation of women, evidenced by the sharp increase in female prostitution and unemployment. I cannot predict how the legatees of Chukovskaia and Mandelstam will respond to these more gender-specific threats to their value and freedom—if they will be attracted to various feminist programs or choose to maintain the "brotherhood" of old. Yet in the current climate there are also unprecedented opportunities for the activation of an altogether new, more textured "we" comprised of Russians and non-Russians, women in the system and well-wishing scholars and outside observers. This book is already a product of and for that community. At this transitional moment in Russian history and particularly Russian women's history, I think it crucial that our newly joined "we" at last pay informed tribute to the *sisterhood* inscribed and enacted by Chukovskaia, Mandelstam, and others, and that all of us keep record of their ingenious, activist, personalized, and visionary works for future adaptation and use.

NOTES

Introduction

1. Anna Akhmatova, the introduction to "Requiem" in *Requiem and Poem without a Hero*, translated by D. M. Thomas (London: Paul Elek, 1976), 23.

2. In her introduction to *Autobiographical Statements in Twentieth-Century Russian Literature* (Princeton: Princeton University Press, 1990), Jane Gary Harris provides a good description of this trend, but does not link such writings with any political agenda (18–22).

3. Marietta Chudakova identifies this phenomenon in her article "Vzglianut' v litso," included in the anthology *Vzgliad. Kritika. Polemika. Publikatsiia*, compiled by A. Latynina and S. Lesnevskii (Moscow: Sovetskii pisatel', 1988): "After all, the means by which a society would normally appropriate its literary heritage had been destroyed: publishing and republishing books, bibliographic directories and archive descriptions, the manuscripts themselves . . . studies of the life and work of the writer, . . . anthologies of memoirs. But a holy place does not remain empty—readers and admirers began to create home-made collected works. . . . Everybody had to become the biographer, bibliographer and, as it were, publisher of their beloved poet and writer" (400).

4. I am indebted to Carl Proffer's book *The Widows of Russia and Other Writings* (Ann Arbor: Ardis, 1987), in which he relates the portraits of five such widows and recognizes their extraordinary contribution to Russian culture.

5. In her pioneering work, *Terrible Perfection: Women and Russian Literature* (Bloomington: Indiana University Press, 1987), Barbara Heldt forcefully argues for a tradition of Russian women's autobiography; analyzing a series of texts from the eighteenth through the twentieth centuries, she finds that the autobiographical form "freed women writers to say something which proceeded from the female self and which elaborated its own self-creativity" (9).

6. Both Marilyn Frye's *The Politics of Reality: Essays in Feminist Theory* (Trumansburg, NY: The Crossing Press, 1983) and Dorothy E. Smith's *The Everyday World as Problematic: A Feminist Sociology* (Boston: Northeastern University Press, 1987) argue, in different ways, for the development of a more effective, foregrounded evaluation of the everyday, "behind the scenes" contributions made by women in their assigned/assumed capacities as facilitators in the family, society, industry, the arts, etc. I am grateful to my colleague, Stephanie Jed, for bringing these studies to my attention.

7. Gayle Greene and Coppelia Kahn, "Feminist scholarship and the social construction of woman," in *Making a Difference: Feminist Literary Criticism*, edited by Gayle Green and Coppelia Kahn (London: Routledge, 1985), 20–21. Greene and Kahn argue for a "more inclusive notion of history" that focuses on women as well as men and admits the complexity of women's response—both their service to and subversion of a dominant culture.

1. Women's Works in Stalin's Time

1. Moshe Lewin, "Society, State, and Ideology during the First Five-Year Plan," in *Cultural Revolution in Russia, 1928–1931*, edited by Sheila Fitzpatrick (Bloomington: Indiana University Press, 1978), 41.

2. See, for example, Roy A. Medvedev, *Let History Judge: The Origins and Consequences of Stalinism*, revised and expanded edition, edited and translated by George Shriver (New York: Columbia University Press, 1989), 25–210; Robert C. Tucker, *Stalin*

in Power: The Revolution from Above, 1928–1941 (New York: W. W. Norton, 1990), 44–90; Isaac Deutscher, *Stalin: A Political Biography*, 2d ed. (New York: Oxford University Press, 1966), 228–344; Adam B. Ulam, *Stalin: The Man and His Era* (New York: The Viking Press, 1973), 234–356; Robert V. Daniels, "The Struggle with the Right Opposition," in *The Stalin Revolution: Foundations of Soviet Totalitarianism*, 2d ed., edited and with an introduction by Robert V. Daniels (Lexington, MA: D. C. Heath, 1972), 22–39.

 3. I base these figures on Robert Conquest's updated version of his classic *The Great Terror: A Reassessment* (New York: Oxford University Press, 1990), 486. These numbers, he asserts, are now being cited in Russian publications, including new high-school textbooks.

 4. For an extensive description of Stalin's vaunted expertise, see chapter 20 of Tucker's *Stalin in Power*.

 5. Medvedev, "The Social Basis of Stalinism," *Let History Judge*, revised and expanded edition, 618. See this entire section "Again on the Stalin Cult," 617–23.

 6. Ulam, *Stalin*, 461–62.

 7. Boris Grois, "Stalinizm kak esteticheskii fenomen," *Sintaksis*, 17 (1987): 98–110. For a fuller explication of this intriguing thesis, see Grois's *The Total Art of Stalinism: Avant-Garde, Aesthetic Dictatorship, and Beyond*, translated by Charles Rougle (Princeton: Princeton University Press, 1992).

 8. Abram Tertz, "Literaturnyi protsess v Rossii," *Kontinent*, 1 (1974): 160–62, cited from the English translation by Michael Glenny (in the English-language version of *Kontinent*) with my revisions (92–93).

 9. For his further comments on Stalin as artist, see Siniavskii/Tertz's article "Stalin—geroi i khudozhnik stalinskoi epokhi," *Sintaksis*, 19 (1987) and his book-length study *Soviet Civilization: A Cultural History*, translated by Joanne Turnbull with the assistance of Nikolai Formozov (New York: Little, Brown, 1990,) especially 93–113.

 10. Michel Foucault, "What Is an Author?" reprinted in *Textual Strategies: Perspectives in Post-Structuralist Criticism*, edited and with an introduction by Josue Harari (Ithaca, NY: Cornell University Press, 1979), 148.

 11. For one account of this consolidation, see Edward J. Brown, "The Mobilization of Culture," in *The Stalin Revolution*, 128–37. Brown also mentions "the incentive of higher pay" instituted to reward writers who contributed most directly to "socialist construction" (134–35). In her account of these changes, Katerina Clark recognizes certain advantages in this consolidation—that, although the Union of Soviet Writers "would guarantee a high degree of ideological conformity," it also was intended to end faction fighting between literary groups and include renowned writers who had been under attack by RAPP, the immediate predecessor to the Union. See her article "Little Heroes and Big Deeds: Literature Responds to the First Five-Year Plan," in *Cultural Revolution in Russia*, 189–206.

 12. In her groundbreaking work on the socialist realist novel, Katerina Clark has identified the recurring formulae of theme, character, and plot in this genre, although she is also careful to remark on its variations and productivity. I will be referring to her work more closely in my discussion of socialist realist tropes. *The Soviet Novel: History as Ritual*, 2d ed. (Chicago: University of Chicago, 1985), 3–24.

 13. Miklos Haraszti describes a milder form of this writer-state contract in socialist Hungary in *The Velvet Prison: Artists under State Socialism*, foreword by George Konrad, translated by Katalin and Stephen Landesmann with the help of Steve Wasserman (New York: Basic Books, 1987).

 14. Siniavskii/Tertz delivers the most pungent analysis of this state in "The Literary Process": "The Russian author has assumed the nightmarish status of an underground writer, that is to say, from the state's point of view he has chosen a life of crime, for which strict penalties and deterrents are laid down. Literature has become a forbidden, risky, and thus all the more fascinating activity" (Russian-language edition 143–44; English-

language edition 77). His article also pays tribute to Osip Mandelstam, the artist who perhaps first recognized his "criminality" under Stalin. In *Fourth Prose* (which Siniavskii/Tertz quotes for his epigraph) Mandelstam concludes that his work "is considered mischief, lawlessness, mere accident." Osip Mandelstam, *The Complete Critical Prose and Letters*, edited by Jane Gary Harris, translated by Jane Gary Harris and Constance Link (Ann Arbor: Ardis, 1979), 324.

15. Marietta Chudakova, "Arkhivy v sovremennoi kul'ture," *Nashe nasledie*, 3 (1988): 141–47.

16. There was, however, an interesting aberration in the history of Stalinist archives: the operation of the State Literary Museum by Vladimir Bonch-Bruevich. Bonch-Bruevich very aggressively collected literary archives in the 1930s and in the first half of the decade even tried to intervene with the secret police in order to save both workers and promised materials. A detailed history of his activity is provided in S. V. Shumikhin's dissertation, *Istoriia Gosudarstvennogo Literaturnogo Muzeia (1931–1941 gg.)*, Moscow, 1988 (written for the Istoriko-arkhivnyi institut). I am grateful to Mr. Shumikhin for the opportunity to read this history.

17. As I will discuss in later chapters, many of these methods are specifically documented in the works of Lidiia Chukovskaia and Nadezhda Mandelstam. In the beginning of "The Literary Process," Abram Tertz also cites the story of writer Anatolii Kuznetsov, who seals his forbidden manuscripts in preserving jars and buries them in the garden (144, Russian edition; 77–78, English edition).

18. In this way the religious character of the author-state contract was more than matched by a similarly religious fervor in unofficial literary relations; both owed a great deal to the nineteenth-century cult of the writer.

19. Nancy Armstrong, *Desire and Domestic Fiction: A Political History of the Novel* (New York: Oxford University Press, 1987); Gillian Brown, *Domestic Individualism: Imagining a Self in Nineteenth-Century America* (Berkeley: University of California Press, 1990); Anita Levy, *Other Women: The Writing of Race, Class, and Gender, 1832–1898* (Princeton: Princeton University Press, 1991). For an illuminating reassessment of the constructs of private and public spheres in American history, see Linda K. Kerber, "Separate Spheres, Female Worlds, Woman's Place: The Rhetoric of Women's History," *The Journal of American History*, 75 (June 1988): 9–39. I am grateful to my colleague, Nicole Tonkovich, for referring me to this work.

20. See Richard Stites, *Revolutionary Dreams: Utopian Vision and Experimental Life in the Russian Revolution* (New York: Oxford University Press, 1989). In his other excellent study, *The Women's Liberation Movement in Russia: Feminism, Nihilism, and Bolshevism, 1860–1930* (Princeton: Princeton University Press, 1978), Richard Stites notes the domestic programs of both Lenin and the famous Bolshevik woman activist, Aleksandra Kollontai. Kollontai advocated collectivizing both workplace and home (355–56), whereas Lenin specifically attacked the waste and pernicious effect of individual housekeeping (378–79). See also Mary Buckley, *Women and Ideology in the Soviet Union* (New York: Harvester Wheatsheaf, 1989), 45–47. For an informative synopsis of the various architectural experiments undertaken to redesign the Soviet home, see chapter 2 of Selim O. Khan-Magomedov's *Pioneers of Soviet Architecture: The Search for New Solutions in the 1920s and 1930s*, translated by Alexander Lieven and edited by Catherine Cooke (New York: Rizzoli, 1983), 341–98.

21. Buckley, *Women and Ideology*, 136.

22. Noting the *Kirche, Kuche, and Kinder* triad of these fascist dictatorships, Xenia Gasiorowska remarks that the Soviet government glossed over the latter two elements and transposed the first to correspond to the Party. *Women in Soviet Fiction, 1917–1964* (Madison: University of Wisconsin Press, 1968), 53–54. For an important account of the complex role of women in Nazi Germany, see Claudia Koonz's *Mothers in the Fatherland: Women, the Family, and Nazi Politics* (New York: St. Martin's Press, 1987); on women in fascist Italy, see Lesley Caldwell, "Reproducers of the Nation: Women and the

Family in Fascist Policy," in *Rethinking Italian Fascism: Capitalism, Populism and Culture*, edited by David Forgacs (London: Lawrence and Wishart, 1986), 110–41 and especially Victoria de Grazia's *How Fascism Ruled Women: Italy, 1922–1945* (Berkeley, University of California Press, 1992).

23. For a summation of this "composite ideal female" of worker, citizen, wife, mother, see Barbara Evans Clements, "Later Developments: Trends in Soviet Women's History 1930 to the Present," in *Russia's Women: Accommodation, Resistance, Transformation*, edited by Barbara Evans Clements, Barbara Alpern Engel, and Christine D. Worobec (Berkeley: University of California Press, 1991), 262–78. See also Gail Lapidus, *Women in Soviet Society: Equality, Development, and Social Change* (Berkeley: University of California Press, 1978), 103. What obtained was a composite icon of Soviet womanhood in which "the new image of feminine virtue incorporated wifely and maternal duties in addition to a contribution to the building of socialism" (Lapidus, 115). One "glaring exception" to this trend, however, was the government's praise for "wives of Stakhanovites (shockworkers)"—women who kept house and urged their husbands to greater feats of productivity. Cf. Buckley, 115–17. Historian Sheila Fitzpatrick also notes how leisured middle-class women were encouraged by some official publications to give first priority to husband and family. See her essay, " 'Middle Class Values' and Soviet Life in the 1930s," in *Soviet Society and Culture: Essays in Honor of Vera S. Dunham*, edited by Terry L. Thompson and Richard Sheldon (Boulder: Westview Press, 1988), 33.

24. Writing about women in official literature, Gasiorowska observes: "Women are never wreckers or saboteurs or murderers; they are not expelled from the party or sent to labor camps or even found guilty of ideological deviations. A woman's wrongdoings are possible only within the domain of morals and manners within the specific Soviet way of life. Conversely, however intelligent, educated, or dedicated a Soviet heroine may be, she does not rise above the invisible ceiling assigned to a woman's career" (*Women in Soviet Fiction*, 209–10). On women's secondary position in the Soviet Union, see, for example, Buckley, 117–18; also Lynne Attwood, *The New Soviet Man and Woman: Sex-Role Socialization in the USSR* (Bloomington: Indiana University Press, 1990), 117–18.

25. To a modified extent, I agree with Tat'iana Tolstaia's historical observation that Soviet women could escape to a "loophole of 'domestic life' " inaccessible to men, whereas men were "regularly punished, persecuted, imprisoned, and humiliated" because they "could not withdraw from the role of public citizen as easily as women." "Notes from Underground (review of Francine du Plessix Gray's *Soviet Women: Walking the Tightrope*)," *The New York Review of Books*, 31 May 1990, 3–7. But I question her consequent generalizations on behalf of all Soviet women—e.g., that Soviet women dream above all "to not have to work" and always prefer power over their families to "some kind of intangible political power over abstract people who don't want to submit."

26. Stites, *Women's Liberation in Russia*, 29–63.

27. For an informed history of their participation, see Barbara Alpern Engel's *Mothers and Daughters: Women of the Intelligentsia in Nineteenth-Century Russia* (Cambridge: Cambridge University Press, 1983).

28. *Mothers and Daughters*, 3.

29. *Mothers and Daughters*, 154–55.

30. Heldt, *Terrible Perfection*, 5, 12–24.

31. For the summary of her important argument, see *Mothers and Daughters*, 199–203.

32. Lapidus notes this behavior as well as Stalin's evident contempt for what he deemed to be the ignorance and conservatism of women (*Women in Soviet Society*, 76–77). Siniavskii/Tertz comments on Stalin's "passion for military style, titles, and trappings" (*Soviet Civilization*, 81).

33. I preface the term *masculinity* with qualifiers like "conventional" or "stereotyped" so as not to settle into an artificial binary opposition of masculine and feminine. Biologists, psychologists, and social scientists have been discovering that the concepts of mas-

culinity and femininity are actually "fuzzy sets" of attributes and behaviors which cannot be invariably applied, even though we still seem able to distinguish generally between the two. For a stimulating series of essays on these twinned concepts, see *Masculinity/Femininity: Basic Perspectives*, The Kinsey Institute Series, vol. 1, edited by June Machover Reinisch, Leonard A. Rosenblum, and Stephanie A. Sanders (Oxford: Oxford University Press, 1987).

34. See Elizabeth Waters's very interesting article, "The Female Form in Soviet Political Iconography, 1917–1932," in *Russia's Women*, edited by Clements, Engel, and Worobec, 225–42. She concludes that "[t]he male figure remained the universal—the symbol of the proletariat, revolution, and the victory of socialism. The female form, once allegory was abandoned, played only a supportive role, standing for women or the peasantry, subordinate social groups. Woman was the Other, or rather Others, since her personality was split: as working woman, she could aspire to political consciousness and public profile; as mother, she was the child of nature, the outsider, forever distanced from social action" (242). In her study of earlier representations of women (specifically workers and peasants), Victoria E. Bonnell also concludes that the female figure was rendered secondary or adjunct. "The Representation of Women in Early Soviet Political Art," *The Russian Review*, 50 (1991): 267–88.

35. Clark, *The Soviet Novel*, 73. The author observes that "the formulaic biography of Stalin"—the portrait of a resolute, tireless, steely commander—"functioned as a sort of example of examples for the life of the true Bolshevik leader."

36. *The Soviet Novel*, 114. Clark marks the shift from a horizontal fraternalist configuration to a vertical father-son allegiance after the completion of the first five-year plan (117–18).

37. *The Soviet Novel*, 120.
38. *The Soviet Novel*, 182–85.
39. Gasiorowska, *Women in Soviet Fiction*, 152.
40. *Women in Soviet Fiction*, 152.
41. *Women in Soviet Fiction*, 209.

42. Gasiorowska notes that scenes of sex and childbirth were rendered discreetly, if not puritanically (58). Housekeeping was depicted as product rather than process; the novels of the 1930s presented housework as efficiently and invisibly completed (54).

43. Clark chronicles these postwar changes. *The Soviet Novel*, 191–209.

44. Vera Panova (1905–73) deserves special consideration as one of the most evident practitioners of this new focus. Clearly an establishment writer, she nonetheless helped to revise the sensibility of socialist realist fiction and usher in the cultural thaw. In this regard, it is intriguing to note Edward Brown's essentialist assessment of Panova's gendered contribution. Asserting her "woman's angle of vision" and "pervasive femininity," he concludes: "The novelist Panova is a sensitive person, whose interests are those of a woman, and whose comments on life have feminine gentleness and tact. She is a Party writer, but one with sentiment. She wears the 'leather jacket,' but hers has, one could say, yellow ribbons on it. Her work is important because she introduced and insisted upon some of the most important themes of the immediate post-Stalin thaw. Her chief themes are those that traditionally have had special interest for women: love, the need for human tenderness and consideration, the reality of private emotion, the family, the education of children, their special character, their psychology, and their education" (196). *Russian Literature since the Revolution*, revised and enlarged edition (Cambridge, MA: Harvard University Press, 1982), 194–96.

45. Charles Isenberg, *Substantial Proofs of Being: Osip Mandelstam's Literary Prose* (Columbus, OH: Slavica, 1987), 31. Isenberg notes: "For the rest of his career, his work will grapple with the threat of being cut off from its wellsprings."

46. Jane Gary Harris coins this role in her essay "Autobiography and History: Osip Mandelstam's *Noise of Time*," included in *Autobiographical Statements in Twentieth-Century Russian Literature*, 113; an earlier version of this essay appears as the fourth

chapter in her monograph, *Osip Mandelstam* (Boston: Twayne, 1988). In his pioneering book, *Mandelstam* (Cambridge: Cambridge University Press, 1973), Clarence Brown elaborates on the poet's combining of high and low references: "The epic, heroic world of Homer and the tragedies is practically never to be found without a leaven of the domestic, the low, the thoroughly Russian. . . . His classicism is in a sense thoroughly unclassical, for the lofty, objective, and impersonal mode is always imbued with the naturalism and the homelessness of the New Testament . . . Petersburg itself was celebrated in his vision of it not only as the classical city of its buildings and avenues, but also as the 'Dutch' city of Peter, a city of handicrafts and commerce, belonging not to the imported architects alone, but also to native carpenters" (254–55).

47. Quoted from the English translation of "On the Nature of the Word" included in Osip Mandelstam, *The Complete Prose and Letters*, translated by Jane Gary Harris and Constance Link, 127–28.

48. Harris, *Mandelstam*, 65.

49. Isenberg posits that "Journey to Armenia" constitutes a "return to the vision embodied in his works before the years of artistic crisis [the latter half of the 1920s]." *Substantial Proofs of Being*, 167.

50. See the endnotes for Mandelstam, *The Complete Prose and Letters*, 669.

51. Svetlana Boym offers very stimulating and perceptive commentary on Mandelstam's gender constructs in her book, *Death in Quotation Marks: Cultural Myths of the Modern Poet* (Cambridge, MA: Harvard University Press, 1991), and a separate essay, "Dialogue as 'Lyrical Hermaphroditism': Mandel'shtam's Challenge to Bakhtin," *Slavic Review*, 50, no. 1 (1991): 118–26.

52. See, for example, *"Sumerki svobody"* and the title poem *"Tristia."*

53. These are the concluding lines of *"Sumerki svobody"* as translated by Clarence Brown (269).

54. Gregory Freidin, *A Coat of Many Colors: Osip Mandelstam and His Mythologies of Self-Presentation* (Berkeley: University of California Press, 1987).

55. Mandelstam makes this statement in the essay "Francois Villon" (1910).

56. It is interesting to note that in his poetic cycle *"Stikhi o neizvestnom soldate,"* the figure of Mandelstam the poet serves to distinguish and redeem all the unknown fallen soldiers from anonymity and oblivion. In *Mandelstam: The Later Poetry* (Cambridge: Cambridge University Press, 1976), Jennifer Baines comments that in his later work Mandelstam began to perceive soldiers as victims of the tyrants they served (138–39).

57. See, for example, Alan Richardson's discussion of how pre-Romantic and Romantic male poets "colonize[d] the conventionally feminine domain of sensibility" in order to achieve a male-dominated androgyny: "When androgyny functions as another manifestation of the male poet's urge to absorb feminine characteristics, his (or his protagonist's) female counterpart stands to risk obliteration" (19). "Romanticism and the Colonization of the Feminine," in *Romanticism and Feminism*, edited by Anne K. Mellor (Bloomington: Indiana University Press, 1988), 13–25.

58. Quoted from *"V Peterburge my soidemsia snova."*

59. Married women assume the duty of mourning in traditional Russian society, as Natalie K. Moyle points out in "Mermaids (*Rusalki*) and Russian Beliefs about Women," *New Studies in Russian Language and Literature*, edited by Anna Lisa Crone and Catherine V. Chvany (Columbus, OH: Slavica, 1987), 221–38. "[Married women], having experienced death in a rite that occurred at the very center of their lives, were treated as liminal beings. They were supposed to conduct ritual activity, especially rites which called for contact with the other world. . . . Having gone through a death-like transition themselves at marriage, it was women who lamented the deceased" (230–31).

60. Quoted from Brown translation, 271.

61. For Shtempel's account of her friendship with the Mandelstams, see her series of articles entitled "Mandel'shtam v Voronezhe" in *Novyi mir*, 10 (1987): 207–34; *Pod"em*, 5 (1989): 194–229; *Pod"em*, 6 (1989): 179–213.

62. Taken from the translation by Jane Gary Harris, *Osip Mandelstam*, 145, with my revisions based on the Russian original in Mandelstam's *Voronezhskie tetradi*, edited and with an introduction by Viktoriia Shveitser (Ann Arbor: Ardis, 1980), 110.

63. Pasternak received tangible proof of this fact. While he was writing *Zhivago*, the authorities pressured him to abandon his novel by arresting his mistress, Olga Ivinskaia, and sending her to a labor camp. For Ivinskaia's own account of her persecution, see her memoir *V plenu vremeni: gody s Borisom Pasternakom* (Paris: Fayard, 1978); English translation appears as *A Captive of Time*, translated by Max Hayward (New York: Doubleday, 1978).

64. For the creative biography of these works, see Marietta Chudakova, "Tvorcheskaia istoriia M. Bulgakova *Master i Margarita*," *Voprosy literatury*, 1 (1976): 218–53, and Lazar Fleishman, *Boris Pasternak: The Poet and His Politics* (Cambridge, MA: Harvard University Press, 1990), 253, 258–59, 273. Fleishman remarks that although Pasternak knew he would be unable to publish his work, he was quite open in sharing it with friends.

65. Quoted from the translation by Max Hayward and Manya Harari, 1958 (New York: Ballantine, 1986), with my occasional revisions based on the Russian edition issued by Société d'Edition et d'Impression Mondiale, 1959.

66. Quoted from Mirra Ginzburg's translation of *The Master and Margarita*, 1967 (New York: Grove Press, 1978).

67. J. A. E. Curtis, *Bulgakov's Last Decade: The Writer as Hero* (Cambridge: Cambridge University Press, 1987), 185.

68. As Andrei Siniavskii observes in his introduction to Pasternak's work, the poet interpreted Hamlet as "a drama of duty and self-renunciation." An English translation of Siniavskii's essay appears in *Boris Pasternak: Modern Judgements*, edited by Donald Davie and Angela Livingstone, with verse translations by Donald Davie (Nashville: Aurora, 1970), 154–219. See also Michel Aucouturier's essay "The Legend of the Poet and the Image of the Actor in the Short Stories of Pasternak," reprinted in the same volume (220–30); Aucouturier reads the "Hamlet" poem as "a parable of the destiny of Yuri Zhivago, which unites in one image the actor playing his role to the end, the character of Shakespeare (who embodies for Pasternak the drama of the great destiny, the heroic mission, the destiny entrusted into the 'hands of man') and the figure of Christ, faithful to his divine mission to the point of sacrifice" (228).

69. Ronald Hingley, *Pasternak: A Biography* (New York: Alfred A. Knopf, 1983), 206. In his study, *Bulgakov i Pasternak kak romanisty: Analiz romanov "Master i Margarita" i "Doktor Zhivago"* (Ann Arbor: Hermitage, 1984), Mikhail Kreps concludes: "The pathos and meaning of life for Zhivago is a repetition of Christ's work—the giving of himself, his talent, and his creation to people, a way of life based on giving and dispensation, not taking and hoarding" (42–43).

70. Fleishman offers this analysis of Pasternak's opposition to Stalinism: "The facts of Pasternak's life force us to conclude that the only *practical* escape from the situation that had been developing since 1946 was Christianity. The decision the poet made was conscious and free, but, then again, he had no real alternative. In his sharp turn to the Gospels and to the rituals of the Orthodox church we can see Pasternak's eternal proclivity to opposition or, to put it better, to legal opposition" (262).

71. Heldt, 146.

72. Heldt perceptively criticizes Lara as a "terribly perfect" symbol of domestic femininity (146).

73. I refer here to Abram Tertz's wry synopsis of one of the main plots of nineteenth-century Russian realism. Cf. *The Trial Begins and On Socialist Realism*, translated by George Denis, with an introduction by Czeslaw Milosz (Berkeley: University of California Press, 1960), 185–88.

74. In his *Between Two Worlds: A Critical Introduction to "The Master and Margarita"* (Oxford: The Clarendon Press, 1987), Andrew Barratt points out, however, the ex-

ceptionally chaste nature of their "illicit love"—its lack of sexuality and devotion mainly to "the furtherance of art" (266).

75. Barratt emphatically refutes any parallel between Margarita and Faust, suggesting instead that she resembles another Goethean heroine—the figure of Helen of Troy in *Faust*, who possesses a "'feminine'" courage "born of selflessness, love and mercy" (276).

76. Cf. Northrop Frye, *Anatomy of Criticism: Four Essays* (Princeton: Princeton University Press, 1957), 193.

77. James L. Brain, "An Anthropological Perspective on the Witchcraze," in *The Politics of Gender in Early Modern Europe*, edited by Jean R. Brink, Allison P. Coudert, and Maryanne C. Horowitz, *Volume 12, Sixteenth Century Essays & Studies* (Kirksville, MO: Sixteenth Century Journal, 1989), 14.

78. These citations are taken from the translation of *Requiem* by D. M. Thomas (London: Paul Elek, 1976).

79. Evgeniia Ginzburg, *Krutoi marshrut*, volumes one and two, with a foreword by Vasilii Aksenov (New York: Possev, 1985). English translation: *Journey into the Whirlwind*, translated by Paul Stevenson and Max Hayward, 1st ed. (New York: Harcourt, Brace and World, 1967) and *Within the Whirlwind*, translated by Ian Boland, with an introduction by Heinrich Boll, 1st ed. (New York: Harcourt Brace Jovanovich, 1981). Mariia Ioffe, *Odna noch': Povest' o pravde* (New York: Izdatel'stvo "Khronika," 1978). For a wide sampling of women's prison and camp memoirs, see the anthology *Do dnes' tiagoteet*, compiled by Semen Samuilovich Vilenskii (Moscow: Sovetskii pisatel', 1989).

80. Elena Bulgakova, *Dnevnik Eleny Bulgakovoi* (Moscow: Izdatel'stvo "Knizhnaia palata," 1990) and Olga Ivinskaia, *V plenu vremeni: gody s Borisom Pasternakom*.

2. Father and Daughter

1. See her account of this experience in her collection of essays, *V laboratorii redaktora* (In the editor's workshop), 2d ed. (Moscow: "Iskusstvo," 1963).

2. For a systematic summarization of the contents of Chukovskaia's works, see *Lydia Korneevna Chukovskaya: A Tribute by Bella Hirshon* (Melbourne: University of Melbourne, 1987).

3. See this passage in the "Afterword" of *To the Memory of Childhood*, translated by Eliza Kellogg Klose (Evanston, IL: Northwestern University Press, 1988): "But there was one more thing I had to do: write my reminiscences of him. After all, there aren't many people still alive who remember him as a young man. He'd four children. I am the sole survivor. I remember our childhood and his young years. It was up to me to write. I set to work on my reminiscences. I conceived of them in three parts, but felt I must write first of all about the time almost no one else could recall: Kornei Chukovskii's life in Finland, in Kuokkala (now the village of Repino), between 1912 and 1917" (146).

4. Susan Stanford Friedman argues this distinction most extensively. Citing the psychological findings of theorists like Rowbotham and Chodorow, she posits that the feminine personality is fundamentally defined in relationships—either with another individual or a group. See her "Women's Autobiographical Selves: Theory and Practice," in *the Private Self: Theory and Practice of Women's Autobiographical Writings*, edited by Shari Benstock (Chapel Hill: University of North Carolina Press, 1988), 34–62. In her *A Poetics of Women's Autobiography* (Bloomington: Indiana University Press, 1987), Sidonie Smith asserts that woman's " 'natural' story shapes itself not around the public, heroic life but around the fluid, circumstantial, contingent responsiveness to others that, according to patriarchal ideology, characterizes the life of woman but not autobiography" (50). See also Estelle Jelinek's historical generalizations in *The Tradition of Women's Autobiography: From Antiquity to the Present* (Boston: Twayne, 1986), 44.

5. Sofia Kovalevskaia, *A Russian Childhood*, translated and introduced by Beatrice

Stillman (New York: Springer-Verlag, 1978); Marina Tsvetaeva's autobiographical essays are included in *A Captive Spirit: Selected Prose*, edited and translated by J. Marin King (Ann Arbor: Ardis, 1980); Nadezhda Durova, *The Cavalry Maiden: Journals of a Russian Officer in the Napoleonic Wars*, translation, introduction, and notes by Mary Fleming Zirin (Bloomington: Indiana University Press, 1989).

6. Lidiia had two brothers and one sister; her younger brother, Boba, perished in action in World War II and her sister Mura, thirteen years her junior, died of tuberculosis at the age of eleven. It is interesting that both Lidiia and her older brother Nikolai chose to pursue literary careers. Nikolai Korneevich Chukovskii (1904–65) made his reputation as a writer of short stories and novels (*Iaroslavl'*, *Baltiiskoe nebo*) and a translator of authors ranging from Jack London to Sandor Petofi.

7. Lydia Chukovskaya, *To the Memory of Childhood*, translated by Eliza Kellogg Klose (Evanston, IL: Northwestern University Press, 1988), 142. All subsequent quotations refer to this text.

8. "Incidentally, although he had not yet written children's books, he was already composing whimsical children's rhymes, just for domestic consumption, easily, on the spur of the moment" (2).

9. It is also essential to remember that Chukovskaia wrote *To the Memory of Childhood* after the death of her father and, in part, with the knowledge that her work would be harshly censored. See her "Afterword" in the English translation of *To the Memory of Childhood*, 143–49.

10. Analyzing mother-child relationships in the Russian noble family, Jessica Tovrov identifies the strong pedagogical role a mother was expected to play in her son's early years and throughout her daughter's pre-marriage life. "Mother-Child Relationships among the Russian Nobility," in *The Family in Imperial Russia: New Lines of Historical Research*, edited by David L. Ransel (Urbana: University of Illinois Press, 1978), 15–43. For a discussion of how this role was officially implemented, see Carol S. Nash, "Educating New Mothers: Women and the Enlightenment in Russia," *History of Education Quarterly* (Fall 1981): 301–16. In *Mothers and Daughters: Women of the Intelligentsia in Nineteenth-Century Russia*, Engel asserts that in the memoirs of women in the intelligentsia the mother most often appears as the most positive, beloved parent (13).

11. In her tribute to Chukovskaia, Hirshon cites a letter from T. Litvinova that confirms this dim portrait. Litvinova only became acquainted with Mariia Borisovna when the latter was old and sick, and at that time "it was difficult to discern the features of her personality" (1).

12. Wendy Martyna suggests the psychological implications of this sort of language use in her article "Psychology of the Generic Masculine," in *Women and Language in Literature and Society*, edited by Sally McConnell-Ginet, Ruth Borker, and Nelly Furman (New York: Praeger, 1980), 69–78.

13. In the anthology *Balancing Acts: Contemporary Stories by Russian Women* (Bloomington: Indiana University Press, 1989), Helena Goscilo opens her introduction with a provocative statement attributed to Chukovskaia: "What does 'women's literature' mean? You can have a women's sauna, but literature?" (xiii).

14. Chukovskaia presents her institutional education as irrelevant—i.e., a matter of indifference to her father (19). In her most extensive description of her formal schooling, she tells of how Kornei Ivanovich withdrew her and her brother from the gymnasium after she saw the director beating a boy (50–51).

15. Reflecting on the question of her father's love for children, Chukovskaia answers with a simple character description: "The child in him never died" (128).

16. See this characteristic passage in Chukovskii's book on children's literary development—*From Two to Five*, revised edition, translated and edited by Miriam Morton, with a foreword by Frances Clarke Sayers (Berkeley: University of California Press, 1968): "In almost every kindergarten and every child center, in every school, I met promising children who, under different circumstances, could be developed into good

writers; but their giftedness withered in the nonliterary environment in which they found themselves" (73).

17. See the fourth chapter of Engel's *Mothers and Daughters* for a discussion of this phenomenon. She offers a preliminary sketch as well in "Mothers and Daughters: Family Patterns and the Female Intelligentsia," in *The Family in Imperial Russia*, 44–59.

18. Lidiia reports that when her grandfather finally visits them in an attempt at reconciliation, her father throws him out (125).

19. As Chukovskaia comments: "Of all our close relatives the only one we knew well and loved was Papa's mother, Ekaterina Osipovna" (123).

20. In an interesting contrast, Chukovskaia reports that when she visited her grandmother, Ekaterina Osipovna seemed unperturbed by her situation (she had never married) and insisted that Kornei's father was " 'a very, very good man' " (126).

21. In this connection, too, Chukovskii recalls the example of many radical young women who re-applied the values of their religious mothers—most often, their moral purity and extreme dedication—to revolutionary work. Engel, *Mothers and Daughters*, 4–5, 107–108.

22. In illustration, Chukovskaia recalls an almost allegorical scene: she forgets to remove her glove when shaking hands with the famous artist Repin, and her father is enraged by her thoughtlessness. Although she admits he was unjust, she expresses her belated gratitude "[f]or that instructive anger with which he exploded when he thought I did not show enough respect for the hand held out to me by art!" (77).

23. For an elaboration of this argument and its consequences for male and female modes of expression, see the first chapter "Representation, Reproduction and Women's Place in Language," in Margaret Homans' *Bearing the Word: Language and Female Experience in Nineteenth-Century Women's Writing* (Chicago: University of Chicago Press, 1986), 1–39. Homans summarizes that for men the symbolic order—language and figurative representation—is acquired when the natural bond to the mother must be repressed; language and literature come to function as substitutes for the loss of the mother and the natural world she embodies and extends. Women, on the other hand, communicate both within and outside this symbolic order because they need not renounce that earliest bond. Their memory of a presymbolic "language" may be conveyed as a preference for the literal or an emphasis on the aural-emotional quality of words.

24. Chukovskaia's experience would seem to testify to the success of her father's pedagogical approach with its concern for cultivating an enduring love of poetry. See especially chapter 3 of the English-language abridged version of Chukovskii's *From Two to Five*, 61–88. Here he observes children's innate appreciation for and production of poetry—first as impromptu oral games associated with movement, new impressions, etc., and then, after a brief chaotic period of transition, as emulation and appropriation of existing texts.

25. See her own interpretation of the meaning of style in her professional "textbook" *V laboratorii redaktora* (In the editor's workshop): "Yes, the style of the work, its form reflects everything—the honesty or falsehood of the writer; the passion or apathy of his temperament; the degree to which he is absorbed in the idea which informs his book; the depth of his understanding of his subject; his love, his hate and his indifference" (109).

26. Also note Chukovskii's criticism of the Formalists. His daughter quotes from his letter to Gor'kii, where he claims that these critics "insist upon formal method, demand that numbers, weights and measures be applied to literary work, but they stop there; I think it's necessary to go further, that on the basis of the formal study of the material, it's necessary to reconstruct what used to be called the soul of the poet. . . . Criticism ought to be universal, scholarly discoveries ought to lead to emotion. Critical analysis ought to culminate in synthesis: while the critic analyzes, he's a scholar, but when he turns to synthesis, he's an artist, creating an artistic image of a man from small and accidentally observed details" (134).

27. See, for example, chapters 14 and 16 of her text.

28. Stites provides an extensive report on the state of women during this period (1881–1917). *Women's Liberation in Russia*, 157–90.

29. Chukovskaia tells of Bronshtein's fate in one of the appendixes to the first volume of *Zapiski ob Anne Akhmatovoi*. In the relatively liberal period of the 1960s, she manages a brief commemoration of her husband's work in *V laboratorii redaktora* (In the editor's workshop) (293); she later writes an extensive memoir that focuses on their life together, but remains—of her own volition—unpublished. Chukovskaia's first husband, Tsezar Volpe, (by whom she had her daughter Elena), was also involved with literature, emerging as a prominent critic and editor in the 1920s.

30. Lidiia Chukovskaia, *Dekabrist Nikolai Bestuzhev: Issledovatel' Buriatii* (Decembrist Nikolai Bestuzhev: Explorer of Buriatiia) (Moscow: Geografgiz, 1950), 15.

31. Lidiia Chukovskaia, *Dekabristy: Issledovateli Sibiri* (The Decembrists: Explorers of Siberia) (Moscow: Geografgiz, 1951) 109.

32. Lidiia Chukovskaia, *"Byloe i Dumy" Gertsena* (Herzen's "My Past and Thoughts") (Moscow: Khudozhestvennaia Literatura, 1966), 143–44.

33. See her collection of *samizdat* essays, *Otkrytoe slovo* (The open word) (New York: "Khronika," 1976). Chukovskaia's stewardship included maintaining her father's Peredelkino dacha as a museum dedicated to his life and work.

34. Within the special dynamics of this father-daughter relationship, then, the daughter deeply submerges the "anxiety of authorship" that Sandra M. Gilbert and Susan Gubar identify in the case of many women writers who anticipate a battle with their male precursors. See Gilbert and Gubar's *The Madwoman in the Attic: The Woman Writer and the Nineteenth-Century Literary Imagination* (New Haven: Yale University Press, 1979), 48–49. Chukovskaia's "anxiety of authorship" is far too blasphemous to recognize; a break with her empowering, sanctifying father would not mean a bid for greater professional and creative independence, but an expulsion from paradise, a betrayal of the most valued moral cause.

35. Compare Chukovskaia's creative development, for example, with that of her contemporary, the poet Marina Tsvetaeva. In her autobiographical sketch, "Mother and Music," Tsvetaeva portrays her mother as yet another overwhelming, highly talented parent; in this case, however, the daughter demonstrates how she formed herself as a poet in opposition to her mother's extreme efforts to raise her as a musician. Afraid of being subsumed by her mother, Tsvetaeva chooses the alternative of contrary self-creation. Chukovskaia, for whatever reason—gender distinction, a likeness in interest and ability— senses no such threat in her relationship with her father and instead develops a talent which is profoundly conservative.

3. Alternative Scripts and Novel Therapies

1. Lidiia Chukovskaia, *Zapiski ob Anne Akhmatovoi* (*Notes on Anna Akhmatova*), T. I, 1938–41, 2d ed. (Paris: YMCA Press, 1984), 11.

2. Written in 1939–40, *Sof'ia Petrovna* was first slated for publication in the early 1960s during the political "thaw." When this contract was rescinded, Chukovskaia successfully sued the publisher for her full honorarium. For an account of this curious history, see her *Protsess iskliucheniia* (Process of expulsion) (Paris: YMCA Press, 1979). The novel was finally published in the Soviet Union, in both serial and book form, in 1988.

3. M. Korallov, "Nado zhit' dolgo," *Novyi mir*, 11 (1988): 248–50.

4. Alla Latynina, "Pisat'-èto bylo spasenie: Vstrecha s Lidiei Chukovskoi," *Moskovskie Novosti*, 17 (12 April 1988): 7.

5. Cf. Latynina, also Natalia Ivanova's "Khranit' vechno," *Iunost'*, 7 (1988): 86–90. Chukovskaia herself, characteristically modest about her artistic achievement, still claims this distinction. See her "Afterword" in the translation of *Sof'ia Petrovna* by Aline Worth

(revised and amended by Eliza Kellogg Klose) (Evanston, IL: Northwestern University Press, 1988), 111: "To this day (1974), I know of no volume of prose about 1937 written in *this* country and at *that* time."

6. Early in her career, Chukovskaia did produce other fiction (mainly under the pseudonym A. Uglov), but, to date, only *Sof'ia Petrovna* and *Going Under (Spusk pod vodu)* are remarked on in Russian literary histories. It is notable that Chukovskaia also wrote poetry all through this period, and her verses reflect on related themes of loss and bereavement. See her collection, *Po ètu storonu smerti: iz dnevnika 1936–1976* (Paris: YMCA Press, 1978).

7. Chukovskaia told me this and other valuable information during my meeting with her on 25 September 1989 in her Moscow apartment.

8. Hirshon maintains that both novels grew out of Chukovskaia's diary entries and "retained many features of her diary narrative" (157).

9. In Latynina's interview, Chukovskaia reports that after she had finished *Sof'ia Petrovna*, she actually read it aloud to a gathering of nine people.

10. Again, information related during our September 1989 meeting.

11. Efim Etkind, "Father and daughter" ("Otets i doch' "), the afterword to the Russian-language edition of *To the Memory of Childhood* (New York: Chalidze Publications, 1983), 273.

12. The first quote is cited in Latynina; the second refers to a passage in a letter I received from Chukovskaia dated 7 July 1989.

13. From my September 1989 meeting with Chukovskaia.

14. See "Afterword" to *Sofia Petrovna*, 119. For other textual changes made in this first *tamizdat* version of *Sof'ia Petrovna*, see Hirshon, 109–10.

15. For Dorrit Cohn's discussion and demonstration of all the variants of this narrative mode, see her *Transparent Minds: Narrative Modes for Presenting Consciousness in Fiction* (Princeton: Princeton University Press, 1978), 21–57.

16. All subsequent quotations refer to the English-language edition of *Sof'ia Petrovna* by Aline Worth with revisions and amendments by Eliza Kellogg Klose (Evanston, IL: Northwestern University Press, 1988).

17. The most famous fictional treatment of this concept occurs in Nikolai Chernyshevskii's novel *What Is to Be Done*. On the cultivation of such establishments as a means of educating women and liberating them from economic dependence on their families, see Stites, *Women's Liberation in Russia*, 118–21; also Engel, *Mothers and Daughters*, 88–90.

18. One reviewer, Natal'ia Ivanova, goes so far as to characterize Sof'ia as a twentieth-century version of Gogol's copy clerk, Akakii Akakievich. "Khranit' vechno," 87. Although I think this analogy is ultimately inaccurate, it does recognize Sof'ia's continuation of the "little man" role, a point I highlight in the chapter's conclusion.

19. It could be argued that Chukovskaia is parodying elements of Chernyshevskii's *What Is to Be Done*, although many of these had already been thoroughly absorbed into socialist realist models. My hypothesis is that Chukovskaia is playing off the gamut of nineteenth-century radical fiction and its socialist realist offspring.

20. In an unpublished review of *Sof'ia Petrovna* (recommending its publication in *Novyi mir* in the early 1960s), the critic Stepan Zlobin remarks that the novel presents the "little man" and his "little tragedy" ("melkii chelovek" and "melkaia tragediia") within the Stalinist context. Located in fund 2175, opis 5 in TsGALI—the Central State Archive of Literature and Art in Moscow.

21. The critic Michał Głowiński draws a distinction between the first-person novel and the diary on the basis of their "global awareness"; he maintains that the diary does not manifest any consciousness of a potentially large audience. "Powieść i dziennik intymny," in *O prozie polskiej XX wieku*, edited by A. Hutnikiewicz and Helena Zaworska (Warsaw: IBL PAN, 1971), 375–94.

22. All citations taken from Lidiia Chukovskaia, *Going Under*, translated by Peter M.

Weston (Barrie and Jenkins, 1972) with my revisions based on the Russian edition *Sof'ia Petrovna. Spusk pod vodu. Povesti* (Moscow: Moskovskii rabochii, 1988).

23. It is intriguing that for all her similarity to Chukovskaia, Nina Sergeevna never ascribes her poetic sensibility to another figure. She treats this belief as a given, not a parental legacy.

24. According to Hirshon, this place may also reflect a real-life sanatorium (Litvinovka outside of Moscow) that Chukovskaia loved to visit (135).

25. This critique negatively reflects certain values encouraged and expressed in official postwar culture. As Vera Dunham states in her innovative book, *In Stalin's Time: Middle-class Values in Soviet Fiction*, introduced by Jerry F. Hough (Cambridge: Cambridge University Press, 1976): "Material craving engulfed postwar society from top to bottom. Coiffures, cosmetics, perfume, clothes—the trappings of enhanced femininity—gained social significance" (43). Dunham describes how the regime promoted and rewarded the material values of the *meshchanstvo* (the petty bourgeoisie) to members of its cultural intelligentsia. Intellectuals of Nina Sergeevna's mindset generally countered this privilege with a defiant asceticism; her prejudice against materialistic women also seems to be widely shared. In her article, " 'Middle Class Values' and Soviet Life in the 1930s," in *Soviet Society and Culture*, Sheila Fitzpatrick suggests an interesting revision of Dunham's thesis—that this new *intelligentsia* was composed of both *arrivistes* from lower-class backgrounds *as well as* "members of the old 'bourgeois' intelligentsia" (35–36).

4. Notes on Anna Akhmatova

1. Lidiia Chukovskaia, *Zapiski ob Anne Akhmatovoi* (Notes on Anna Akhmatova), T. 2, 1952–1962 (Paris: YMCA Press), 1980, 448.

2. Chukovskaia disavowed any models in our conversation of 25 September 1989.

3. Henry Gifford, "A Poet for Her People," *The Times Literary Supplement*, 18 November 1977, 1352.

4. It is interesting that Chukovskaia herself attributes special importance to Eckermann—not as a great writer, but as an interlocutor who was "in love with literature." See *V laboratorii redaktora* (In the editor's workshop), 218.

5. Chukovskaia has recorded impressions of other great contemporaries—in particular, Marina Tsvetaeva and Boris Pasternak—but to a much more limited extent (the Pasternak impressions are actually contained in *Notes*), and interestingly enough, only at the point of their greatest crises—i.e., the days before Tsvetaeva's suicide and the last years of Pasternak when he endured the scandal of *Doctor Zhivago*. Cf. "Predsmertie" in *Sobesednik*, 3 (1988): 41–64 on Tsvetaeva; *Notes on Anna Akhmatova*, T. 2, 1952–62 (Paris: YMCA Press, 1980), 245–79, 314–32 on Pasternak.

6. In one of the very few extant analyses of *Notes*, Stephanie Sandler perceptively reads this self-effacement as a product of the Stalinist terror, when the very concept of an independent self was undermined. "Reading Loyalty in Chukovskaia's *Zapiski ob Anne Akhmatovoi*," in *The Speech of Unknown Eyes: Akhmatova's Readers on Her Poetry*, vol. 2, edited by Wendy Rosslyn (Nottingham: Astra Press, 1990), 269. It may have been that Chukovskaia's diary was also other-directed; we cannot compare the two, for the diary no longer exists. Chukovskaia told me that she had kept the diary from age thirteen until 1937 and thereupon entrusted it to a female friend, at the same time giving the friend permission to destroy it if she felt she was in danger. Unfortunately (or fortunately, as Chukovskaia insists), the friend managed to burn the diary about a month before she was arrested. Since the completion of *Notes*, Chukovskaia has also ventured to write her own memoirs, but, significantly, she refuses to publish them because she says she doubts their quality and feels that in them she is too exposed. Even this unpublished text was first conceived as an account of another. She had wanted to dedicate a book to her second

husband, Matvei Bronshtein, but before she could write about him, she had to write about herself in the years preceding their marriage.

7. All quotes from the first volume of *Notes* taken from *Notes on Anna Akhmatova*, T. 1, 1938–1941, 2d ed. (Paris: YMCA Press, 1984); all quotes from the second volume are taken from *Notes on Anna Akhmatova*, T. 2, 1952–1962 (Paris: YMCA Press, 1980); translations mine. In her *Notes*, Chukovskaia frequently uses the Russian form of address, referring to Akhmatova by her first name and patronymic—Anna Andreevna.

8. Gifford, "A Poet for Her People."

9. Chukovskaia recalled that after each meeting with Akhmatova she rushed home and wrote down memorized dialogue and impressions, attempting to preserve the accuracy and immediacy of her experience. There exist a large number of memoir-records of Akhmatova, although none of them match Chukovskaia's painstaking technique. These include Nataliia Roskina, *Chetyre glavy* (Paris: YMCA Press, 1980); Sophie Kazimirovna Ostrovskaya, *Memoirs of Anna Akhmatova's Years: 1944–1950*, with an appendix of memoirs by Margarita Aliger, translated by Jessie Davis (Liverpool: Lincoln Davies, 1988); and the collection *Ob Anne Akhmatovoi: Stikhi, esse, vospominaniia, pis'ma*, compiled by M. M. Kralin (Leningrad: Lenizdat, 1990).

10. For a discussion of this consonance between personae and person, see chapter 2 in Wendy Rosslyn's *The Prince, the Fool and the Nunnery: Religion and Love in the Early Poetry of Anna Akhmatova* (Amersham, England: Avebury, 1984), 73–81. See also Amanda Haight, *Anna Akhmatova: A Poetic Pilgrimage* (New York: Oxford University Press, 1976), 21.

11. In his book *The Theme of Time in the Poetry of Anna Akhmatova* (The Hague: Mouton, 1971), Kees Verheul traces this tendency in Akhmatova's work, begun before her serious persecution, as the development of a "public, historical dimension."

12. Describing his acquaintance with Akhmatova in the late 1950s, the poet Anatolii Naiman claims that "the authenticity of her fate" most attracted him. *Rasskazy o Anne Akhmatovoi* (Moscow: Khudozhestvennaia literatura, 1989), 10. For a translation of his work, see *Remembering Akhmatova*, introduction by Joseph Brodsky, translated by Wendy Rosslyn (London: Halban, 1991).

13. Lidiia Ginzburg, "Akhmatova. Neskol'ko stranits vospominanii," in *Literatura v poiskakh real'nosti. Stat'i, esse, zametki* (Leningrad: Sovetskii pisatel', 1987), 124–25. In our conversation, Chukovskaia made a related observation, remembering a strong resemblance between Akhmatova's spoken word and written verse.

14. Chukovskii's essay, entitled "Anna Akhmatova," is included in his *Sobranie sochinenii v 6 tomakh*, vol. 5 (Moscow: Khudozhestvennaia literatura, 1967), 725–55. Ostrovskaya composes this description of Akhmatova at their second meeting: "On the platform was Akhmatova—medieval, dark and beautiful, sedate and noble in her bearing, and in her mature years still maintaining her feminine charm and the strange fascination of an old statue and a snake" (3).

15. Cf. Natal'ia Il'ina's record of their first meeting in "Anna Akhmatova v poslednie gody ee zhizni," *Oktiabr'*, 2 February 1977, 111.

16. See this passage from the letters of one of Akhmatova's early mentors, Nikolai Nedobrovo (quoted in Haight, 29): "'One can't exactly call her beautiful, but she is so interesting to look at that it would be worth while making a Leonardo drawing of her; a Gainsborough portrait in oil; an icon in tempera; or best of all, to place her in the most important position in a mosaic illustrating the world of poetry. . . .'"

17. Haight, 130. Vitalii Vilenkin's book, *V sto pervom zerkale*, 2d ed. (Moscow: Sovetskii pisatel', 1990), includes a marvelous appendix of photographed Akhmatova "artifacts." For another collection of portrait-photographs, see *Anna Akhmatova: Stikhi, perepiska, vospominaniia, ikonografiia*, compiled by E. Proffer (Ann Arbor: Ardis, 1977).

18. Chukovskaia actually interrupts Akhmatova's sitting for the artist Osmerkin in July 1940 (I, 142). Akhmatova has attracted an impressive number of amateur collectors

("akhmatovtsy")—private citizens who, out of a kind of passion for her work, gathered all manner of related materials (books, albums, autographs, pictures, artwork) and established private archives in their own homes. These collectors were attempting a wholly private corrective to the government's legislation and selective preservation of art. For an account of one such Akhmatova collection, see Leonid Vysheslavskii's "Poema nevedomykh drug," *Al'manakh bibliofila*, vyp. 18 (Moscow: Kniga, 1985), 221–27.

19. See Helena Goscilo's introduction to *Balancing Acts: Contemporary Stories by Russian Women*, xv, where she comments on "the ubiquity of the Feminine Ideal . . . and the immemorial Madonna/Whore dichotomy" in the writings and conceptions of many Russian modernists.

20. Akhmatova's famous "Epigramma" echoes the same attitude in poetic form: "Could Beatrice fashion such a work as Dante's/Or Laura praise love's fever and love's chill?/I showed woman her voice and how to use it,/But, God, how can one teach her to be still?" Translation taken from *Modern Russian Poetry: An Anthology in Verse*, translated, edited and with an introduction by Vladimir Markov and Merrill Sparks (Indianapolis: Bobbs-Merrill, 1967), 280–81. In *Terrible Perfection*, Heldt examines how Liubov' Blok attempts to reclaim her image from her husband's mythologizing (93–98).

21. See Heldt's discussion of Akhmatova's early relationship with her audience in *Terrible Perfection*: "Anna Akhmatova, early in her career, mastered the public use of a private persona to great popular effect. She dramatized a weak self, a concessive self, a 'female' self. Her readers identified with it, and her appeal both to scholars and to the poetry-reading public was immediate. A guarded strength emerged from Akhmatova's lines, a gathering together of parts of the divided self—the strategies of the lyric heroine who would become in a harsher era a symbol of Russia" (124).

22. Il'ina notes the distinctive aphoristic quality of the poet's speech (123). The critic Emma Gershtein, a close friend of both Akhmatova and Chukovskaia, offers a fascinating observation on the poet's role-playing: ". . . I often noticed that among women, Anna Andreevna posed, adopted an unapproachable air, uttered chiselled phrases and overwhelmed everyone with important silences. But when I found her in the company of men, especially if they were prominent people, I was always impressed anew by the simple, intelligent, and sad expression of her face. In the company of men she joked gaily and companionably." "Iz vospominanii. Pis'ma Anny Akhmatovoi," *Voprosy literatury*, 6 (1989): 249. If we accept Gershtein's generalization, then it would seem that Akhmatova felt most compelled by women to play her own scripted role as poet, to distinguish herself from them through her ability and poetic vocation. We will see that, in other respects, Akhmatova demonstrates an ambiguous (and occasionally misogynist) attitude toward women, struggling to avoid the cultural devaluation of her sex and to assert her place as great artist among the "prominent" men.

23. Liubimova's complete memoir "Dnevnikovye zapisi o vstrechakh s Annoi Andreevnoi Akhmatovoi (1944–1965)," is held in manuscript form in the Gosudarstvennyi Literaturnyi Muzei, fond 40, opis 1, no. 17. Part of this memoir has been excerpted and published as "Kak ia pisala Akhmatovu," *Nauka i zhizn'*, 2 (1978): 94–96. A fuller version appears as "Zapisi o vstrechakh," in *Ob Anne Akhmatovoi*, 231–59.

24. In her article "Iz rukopisnogo naslediia A. A. Akhmatovoi," *Neva*, 6 (1979): 196–200, L. A. Mandrykina describes Akhmatova's halting progress on a prose autobiography; by the time of her death, Akhmatova had left laconic factual sketches of her early years, with no coverage of the last three decades of her life.

25. Il'ina, dismayed by what she considered Akhmatova's excessive attention to Haight, later amends her judgment: "I did not understand then that by helping this young Englishwoman, Akhmatova hoped at last to see the truth about herself in print. Let it appear in the western press—certainly there was no hope for this in her own country." "Eshche ob Akhmatovoi," *Ogonek*, 38, 19–26 September 1987, 30. For the result of Akhmatova's and Haight's joint effort, see Amanda Haight, *Anna Akhmatova: A Poetic Pilgrimage* (New York: Oxford University Press, 1976).

26. Mikhail Polivanov develops these astute observations in his foreword to the Soviet edition of Nadezhda Mandelstam's *Hope Abandoned*: N. Ia. Mandel'shtam, *Vtoraia kniga: vospominaniia*, edited and with a foreword by M. K. Polivanov (Moscow: Moskovskii rabochii, 1990), 5.

27. Ostrovskaya makes this telling observation in her diary: "Once again Akhmatova lives her biography—and (quite consciously) transfers her days to the posthumous. She is very concerned (truly and in a business-like way) about what will be written about her 'then' and how this or that will be reflected in the biographies—say, of 2047" (64).

28. In our September 1989 conversation Chukovskaia remarked that Akhmatova generally seemed unaware of her *Notes*.

29. Nadezhda Mandelstam coins this phrase in the first version of *Hope Abandoned*, parts of which were published as "[Ob Akhmatovoi]," in *Literaturnaia ucheba*, 3 (1989): 134–51. It appears on page 148 of the Russian original of *Vtoraia kniga* (Second book), 4th ed. (Paris: YMCA Press, 1987); in the English version, *Hope Abandoned* (New York: Atheneum, 1974) this phrase is translated as "a marked tendency to . . . self-renunciation" (129).

30. Emma Gershtein recalls how Akhmatova was sometimes misperceived by the people as a *"baryshnia"* (a woman of gentry family) (254). It is interesting that the authorities committed the same clumsy, sexist mistake when they expelled Akhmatova from the Union of Soviet Writers in 1946, declaring her to be (in an unintentional parody of the Symbolists) "half nun and half whore."

31. This impression is echoed in Roskina's account, among others. She meets the poet in 1945 and is struck by the juxtaposition of her personal grandeur and her physical poverty. *Chetyre glavy*, 5–6.

32. Cf. the entry for 21 June 1961: "She is sick and tormented. Homeless old age. And really nothing is so essential in old age as a home. . . . Homelessness is yet another method of fate to drive her from the world" (II, 386).

33. See Chukovskaia's lament in the entry for 14 July 1939: "A tram like any other. People like people. And no one saw that it was her" (I, 29). See also 14 May 1953 (II, 23).

34. See, for example, I, 151 where Chukovskaia complains about the presumptions of Akhmatova's female readers who think Akhmatova "writes about women, about some special female sorrows." The concept of "poetess" in Russian, contrasted with that of "poet," carries a pejorative meaning, implying a female poet of limited thematic range and inferior ability. For a good elaboration on the Russian cultural myth of the "poetess," see Boym, *Death in Quotation Marks*, 192–200: "The word 'poetess' is derived from 'poet'; poet plus a feminine suffix, an excess, a mark of 'bad taste,' a sign of cultural inferiority" (192).

35. In his review of the first volume of the *Notes*, Gifford makes a similar claim: "So not hearing about Yezhov, Stalin and Vyshinsky, the presence of whom was so palpable during those days, we might have assumed, but for her warning, that literature absorbed them more than anything else.//In a way this was true" ("A Poet for Her People," 1351). It bears mentioning here, too, that although Chukovskaia enjoyed a much freer hand in transcribing the material for her second volume of *Notes*, her text still reflects a preponderant emphasis on literature.

36. At one point Akhmatova remarks that one should be able to like a poet without liking his/her verses; Chukovskaia notes parenthetically that she very often cannot manage this distinction (II, 181). In general, Akhmatova balks at any direct association of a writer's life and work; as she insists, a writer "should not give herself *au naturel*" in any text (I, 79).

37. Chukovskaia cites a striking example of this connection in her remarks on Akhmatova's Pushkin criticism. Akhmatova insists that in one of the unfinished fragments of his masterpiece *Eugene Onegin* Pushkin is referring to the grave of the Decembrists, a group of officers who rebelled against the tsar in 1825. Chukovskaia insists that Akh-

matova is able to spot this intersection of ethics and art "on the strength of her similar biography" and sense of moral responsibility (II, 8).

38. Sandler outlines the complex moral defense of Chukovskaia's *Notes*—its attempt "to restore to public literary discourse a sense of ethical norms and honest speech" and its function as "a public record of Akhmatova's words, an alternative account of her views about poetry, political allegiances, and, above all, honourable behavior." "Reading Loyalty in Chukovskaia's *Zapiski ob Anne Akhmatovoi*," 267, 272. Akhmatova and Chukovskaia share another common feature in their approach to literature. Both evince a dislike for self-important and/or jargonistic literary scholarship. Writing about her beloved Pushkin, Akhmatova felt a particular hostility for a certain breed of Soviet/Russian scholar—the Pushkin specialist. Both chose, in their own critical efforts, to assume the role of intelligent, sensitive observer of the artist's work.

39. As the critic Henry Gifford asserts: "[i]t was in talking about literature, and about Akhmatova's relation to other poets past and present, that they kept alive a sense of the living culture which had been so rich in the Russia of Akhmatova's early years" ("A Poet for Her People," 1351).

40. I am using the most complete extant version of *Notes* for my analysis—i.e., the most recent *tamizdat* publication of the text by YMCA Press in Paris. Chukovskaia is currently in the process of revising and reissuing the text for Russian publication. At the point of this book's publication, only the first volume has appeared in print, issued by the Moscow publishing house "Kniga" in 1989.

41. Hirshon remarks on the substantive change in the second volume, pointing out the greater freedom and detail of the texts and commentary (161–62).

42. See her 13 July 1940 entry where, after just learning that she requires a serious operation, Chukovskaia responds to Akhmatova's peremptory call and tries to check her publication proofs while suffering from a migraine headache (I, 146–48).

43. It is interesting to compare Chukovskaia's reaction with that of Natal'a Il'ina, who perceives Akhmatova's dependence on her admirers and, with a certain amount of self-regard, eventually distances herself from the source, deciding to let others carry out the poet's bidding. "Anna Akhmatova v poslednie gody ee zhizni," 131.

44. Chukovskaia describes this enigmatic break in their friendship in the preface to the second volume. In her words, Akhmatova's rancor came "out of the blue" as she began to criticize everything Chukovskaia said as "incorrect, inappropriate, and irrelevant" (*"neverno, neumestno, nekstati"*) (II, xvi). Because she felt no guilt, Chukovskaia, with characteristic moral certitude, refused to ask what she had done wrong or who had slandered her and eventually stopped visiting the poet. She reinitiated their friendship in 1952, when Akhmatova was staying near her home in Moscow (II, xxxi-xxxii).

45. Cf., for example, Chukovskaia's 5 September 1939 meeting with Vysotskaia, who has just brought Akhmatova lunch because the poet "does not prepare anything for herself, and the cleaning woman shows up only on her day off" (I, 43). See also Chukovskaia's expression of solicitude in her 13 January 1940 entry: "I began to speak about the apartment. I so wanted her to have a human place to live! Without these footsteps and phonograph records next door, without these constant humiliations!" (I, 61)

46. See the entry for 20 October 1957, where Ol'shanskaia admonishes Akhmatova for neglecting her health: "Anna Andreevna was silent, lowering her eyes like a little girl being reprimanded, and I admired Nina's caustic rage" (II, 212). Chukovskaia earlier recognizes the benefit of this arrangement: "It is much more comfortable for [Akhmatova] to live in Moscow as a guest than as her own housekeeper" (II, 32).

47. This behavior perhaps most clearly differentiates Akhmatova from Chukovskaia's father.

48. Cf. the observation of Elizabeth Abel in her article "(E)merging Identities: The Dynamics of Female Friendship in Contemporary Fiction by Women," *Signs*, 6, no. 3 (1981): "Friendship becomes a vehicle of self-definition for women, clarifying identity

through relation to an other who embodies and reflects an essential aspect of the self" (416). For a more general discussion about female relationships in writing by women, see Judith Kegan Gardiner, "Mind mother: psychoanalysis and feminism," in *Making a Difference*, 134–39.

49. Akhmatova makes another general attack on the wife of the famous nineteenth-century essayist and activist, Aleksandr Herzen: "I cannot stand women (here the Russian pejorative term for woman—*baba*) who get their husbands entangled in their love affairs" (II, 82).

50. Characteristically, Chukovskaia considers Akhmatova's attacks on Pasternak unworthy of her. See, for example, II, 334. Just as she refrains from criticizing a sometimes contrary Akhmatova, so she refuses to find fault with her fellow poet. When she suspects Ol'ga Ivinskaia, Pasternak's mistress, of stealing goods she is sending through her to a friend in a labor camp, Chukovskaia refuses, against Akhmatova's insistence, to inform Pasternak (II, 154, 551–52).

51. As we shall see, Akhmatova "approves" one sort of wife—the "Decembrist wife" she finds exemplified in Nadezhda Mandelstam (II, 438). This noble wife renounces all thought of her own welfare for the sake of her husband and, like the wives of the Decembrists, voluntarily shares his persecution. Despite her approval, however, Akhmatova would never limit herself to that role.

52. In both these cases, Chukovskaia hesitates over what is essentially a question of ranking. She refuses to claim women's superiority over men and Akhmatova's superiority (in suffering) over Pasternak.

53. For one pioneering discussion of the customary association of women with the long-term effort of raising children, see Sherry B. Ortner's "Is Female to Male as Nature Is to Culture?" in *Women, Culture, and Society*, edited by Michele Zimbalist Rosaldo and Louise Lamphere (Stanford: Stanford University Press, 1974), 67–87. Contemporary biologists and anthropologists are questioning more and more the "naturalness" of this association.

54. In June of 1960, when Akhmatova angrily complains about her torn copy of Gumilev's poetry (what she presumes was the work of the secret police), Chukovskaia remarks: "What could I reply to her? Evidently the preservation of verses, even in our new age, is possible only through one long-proven method . . ." (II, 349–50). Chukovskaia notes in June 1961 that Akhmatova carries her manuscript in a makeshift "archive"—a little beat-up suitcase tied with rope (II, 385).

55. Remarking on her fading ability to remember, Chukovskaia nonetheless claims that what she "memorized then [she] remembers firmly up to the present day" (II, 414).

56. N. Ia. Mandel'shtam, *Vtoraia kniga* (Second book), 55, 73.

57. See the 18 October 1939 entry where Akhmatova comments: "'Have you ever seen a poet who relates so indifferently to her verses? . . . And all the same nothing will come of this enterprise. . . . No one will publish anything'" (I, 52).

58. Once again, Akhmatova renders herself the helpless child or, speaking symbolically, a temporarily "unfit mother." In drawing these analogies, I do not presume to judge Akhmatova's performance as a mother; I am calling attention to certain similarities which she herself cultivates between her life and art. Her relationship with her son seemed basically loving, but terribly complicated and especially painful after his release from the camps, when he mistakenly held her accountable for his imprisonment. Chukovskaia comments directly on this later misunderstanding; she concludes that Lev is retaliating for the pain of his early childhood, when he sensed that he wasn't primary in his mother's affections (II, 402). But it is interesting that Akhmatova, for complex reasons, left her young son for long intervals in the care of his paternal grandmother and, in her poetry of that period, projected a female persona who has abandoned her child (Rosslyn, 126). Her treatment of her art seems at least superficially to echo this self-inscribed pattern of giving birth and initially abandoning her child.

59. In her journal, the critic Lidiia Ginzburg also wonders at Akhmatova's incredible

lack of professional training. See her "Zapisi 1920–1930-kh godov," in *Chelovek za pis'mennym stolom. Esse: iz vospominanii: chetyre povestvovaniia* (Leningrad: Sovetskii pisatel', 1989), 166.

60. When Akhmatova is forced to write her work, as is the case with the translations she must undertake to earn money, she relies more specifically on Chukovskaia's editorial skill. See the entry for 24 May 1955 (II, 78–80).

61. Haight, 148–49; Verheul, 180–81. See also Jeanne van der Eng-Liedmeier, "Poèma bez Geroja," *Two Poems by Anna Axmatova: Essays by Jeanne van der Eng-Liedmeier and Kees Verheul with Unpublished Poems by Anna Axmatova* (The Hague: Mouton, 1973), 63–114.

62. The entry for 29 May 1962 is characteristic. Finding that her readers have misunderstood the latest variant of the *Poem*, Akhmatova complains: "'But I am an Acmeist, not a Symbolist. I am for clarity. The secret of poetry is in its inspiration and depth, not in the fact that the reader does not understand the action. I redid it again'" (II, 417). Akhmatova commissions Kornei Chukovskii himself to write an historical preface to the *Poem* (II, 427, 445–46).

63. The English version of these two lines of verse (which occur in Part One, Section Three, 440–41 of the *Poem*) are taken from Anna Akhmatova, *Requiem and Poem without a Hero*, translated by D. M. Thomas (London: Paul Elek, 1976), 53. The Cameron Gallery is a building in Tsarskoe Selo, now the town of Pushkin outside Leningrad, where Akhmatova lived during the years of her early fame and turbulent romantic life.

64. Akhmatova asks her to write down her thoughts on the *Poem*—a commentary that Chukovskaia relegates to a lengthy footnote (II, 314–15). Presenting these thoughts, Chukovskaia explains that they are unsatisfactory, but she deems it "necessary to include here what I gave to Anna Andreevna."

65. Verheul offers this interesting information: "Moreover, it is significant that a large proportion of the various notes in prose from Axmatova's later years—only a very small number of which has been published so far—is devoted to reflections on *Poèma bez geroja*. In these notes the author considers her *poèma* and her work on it from varying points of view, and she carefully takes down those remarks of others about it which strike her as significant" (181).

66. It is striking that Chukovskaia also submits her poetry for Akhmatova's perusal—a much riskier business—but she relegates this account to a short passage in the preface of volume two (xvi). She notes that at least one of her poems pleased Akhmatova because the poet bothered to memorize it; Akhmatova responded to the whole collection with a tactfully cryptic comment: "Time is writing your book" ("*Vremia pishet vam knigu*").

67. In the footnotes to the first volume, Chukovskaia explains that she returned from the sanatorium where she wrote *Sof'ia Petrovna* in January 1940. Her reading of the novel takes place on 4 February 1940.

68. In fact, at the end of this entry, Akhmatova confirms what Chukovskaia "seemed" to see. When Chukovskaia thanks her for patiently listening, the poet protests: " 'You ought to be ashamed of yourself! I wept, but you say—patiently' " (I, 70).

69. Chukovskaia relates the complete story of this preservation to Alla Latynina. She rediscovers the manuscript only after Glikin's sister has died; she finds her notebook hidden in the bottom of a basket among the odds and ends Glikin's sister left with their relatives. See "Pisat'-èto bylo spasenie."

5. Husband and Wife

1. N. E. Shtempel', "Mandel'shtam v Voronezhe," *Novyi mir*, 10 (1987): 230.
2. Emma Gershtein, *Novoe o Mandel'shtame* (Paris: Atheneum, 1986), 27.
3. All citations listed as "II" refer to the English translation of the second volume,

entitled *Hope Abandoned*, translated by Max Hayward (New York: Atheneum, 1974) with my revisions based on the Russian original, *Vtoraia kniga*, 4th edition (Paris: YMCA Press, 1987).

4. See, for example, II, 136, 232–33. On Nadezhda Mandelstam as "Europa," see II, 116.

5. Nadezhda Mandelstam offers an interesting version of the syndrome Carolyn Heilbrun identifies in *Writing a Woman's Life* (New York: Ballantine Books, 1988). Heilbrun points out that, in the absence of stories recapitulating their very different lives and vantage point, women have had to make do with the often highly circumscribed narratives and roles men have assigned to them (37–40).

6. During the fall of 1989, I was privileged to conduct interviews with a number of Nadezhda Mandelstam's circle in Moscow—psychiatrist and Mandelstam scholar Iurii Freidin; Varvara Shklovskaia (daughter of Viktor and Vasilisa Shklovskii—close friends of the Mandelstams) and her husband, the poet Nikolai Panchenko; the poet Nina Belosinskaia; Liudmila Sergeeva, an editor for the publishing house *Sovetskii pisatel'*; and Mikhail Polivanov, a physicist and Mandelstam scholar. I have also relied on Carl Proffer's account of his relationship with Nadezhda Mandelstam, included in his collection *The Widows of Russia*, 13–61.

7. From his reading of *Kniga tret'ia* (Third book), Donald Fanger gleans the same valuable information: For all her claims to be "made" by Mandelstam, she "was not quite a tabula rasa" when the couple first met. Review of Nadezhda Mandelstam's *Kniga tret'ia* in *The Russian Review*, 48, no. 2 (April 1989): 219–20. These three sketches appear in *The Third Book (Kniga tret'ia)* (Paris: YMCA Press, 1987), 79–91. All citations are taken from this collection; the translations are mine.

8. Despite her indignation at Nadezhda Mandelstam for certain "slanderous" remarks in the second volume, the critic Emma Gershtein recalls much positive information about her character in her own *Memoirs*. She remarks, for example, on Nadezhda Mandelstam's strong family feeling and fondness for memories of her childhood. See her account in *Novoe o Mandel'shtame*, 26.

9. Liudmila Sergeeva, one of her close friends in later years, remembered that Nadezhda Mandelstam would often compare the current poor food situation with the wonderful meals she relished in childhood. Interview conducted in Moscow, 14 October 1989.

10. Although Nancy Chodorow's research on mothering is based on Western examples of family life, her account of a more fluid relationship between mother and daughter certainly coincides with Nadezhda Mandelstam's family experience. *The Reproduction of Mothering: Psychoanalysis and the Sociology of Gender* (Berkeley: University of California Press, 1978), e.g., 166–67. There is no precisely correspondent research on the Russian family, but for an account of how sex roles and sex differences in personality have been addressed in the Soviet Union, see Lynne Attwood, *The New Soviet Man and Woman: Sex-role Socialization in the USSR*.

11. Nadezhda Mandelstam refers to this impressive fact obliquely in *Hope against Hope*: "My mother, who as a doctor was mobilized after the Revolution to help with famine relief in the Volga region, told me that the peasants just lay quite still in their houses, even in parts where there was already something to eat and people were not totally exhausted by hunger." *Hope Against Hope*, translated by Max Hayward, with an introduction by Clarence Brown (New York: Atheneum, 1970), 185. Nadezhda Mandelstam's legal heir, Iurii Freidin, confirmed this information in our interview on 15 October 1989 in Moscow.

12. For a brief introduction to Ekster's life and work, see John Bowlt's "Biography, Bibliography" and Jean-Claude Marcade's "Alexandra Exter or the Search for the Rhythms of Light-Colour" in *Kunstlerinnen der Russischen Avantgarde, 1910–1930* (Cologne: Galerie Gmurzynska, 1979), 112, 124–28.

13. Gershtein remembers the stories Nadezhda Mandelstam told of her years as a "lively, mischievous girl" in Kiev (*Novoe o Mandel'shtame*, 26).
14. Gershtein makes a corresponding observation—that Nadezhda Mandelstam "scorned 'primitive' people and preferred any deviations from the norm" (12).
15. In its clear-eyed view of a man's condescension to his female lover, Nadezhda Mandelstam's description is reminiscent of Akhmatova's early poem *"Vecherom"*: "So they caress cats or birds,/And gaze at shapely circus-riders . . . / There is only laughter in his calm eyes / Behind the light gold of his lashes."
16. See his fine essay "The Rhetoric of *Hope Against Hope*," in *Autobiographical Statements in Twentieth-Century Russian Literature*, 193–206: "The situation is paradoxical: the writer arraigns Stalinism for its destruction of the possibility of an ordinary life, yet her text risks implying that the special pressure exerted by the state upon the Mandelstams has the effect of saving their marriage from the usual fate of such marriages" (198). For an earlier version of this essay, see Charles Isenberg, "The Rhetoric of Nadezhda Mandelstam's *Hope Against Hope*," in *New Studies in Russian Language and Literature*, edited by Anna Lisa Crone and Catherine V. Chvany (Columbus, OH: Slavica, 1987), 168–82.
17. Nadezhda Mandelstam notes that, after Mandelstam's death, she "was sustained by the memory of his words 'Why do you think you ought to be happy?' and by the passage in the *Life* of the Archpriest Avvakum when his exhausted wife asks him: 'How much further must we go?' and he replies: 'Until the very grave, woman.' Whereupon she gets to her feet and walks on" (I, 57).
18. *Notes on Anna Akhmatova*, II, 438.
19. Isenberg generally observes how Nadezhda Mandelstam is empowered by the tradition of women's memoirs (*"the* central genre of female writing in Russia" [197]), although he does not distinguish between different types of memoirs.
20. In my joint interview with Varvara Shklovskaia, her husband Nikolai Panchenko, and the poet Nina Belosinskaia, they mentioned that Nadezhda Mandelstam liked to read about "women's essence" (*"zhenskaia sushchnost'"*) and, in this connection, had read the memoirs of Princess Dolgorukaia. Interview conducted 3 October 1989 in Peredelkino.
21. See also her characterization in II, 142, where she maintains that Mandelstam preferred a younger, dependent partner and "was angered by the least display of [her] independence."
22. Gershtein recognizes the terrible burden of Mandelstam's neediness and the tension of their daily lives (25, 89). Iurii Freidin remarked that Nadezhda Mandelstam frequently helped her husband with his purely "money-making" translations. Interview 15 October 1989.
23. For example, in April 1937, Vera Khazina writes to her daughter from Voronezh where she is staying with Osip while Nadezhda is off in Moscow on some business. She complains, in a joking way, about her son-in-law's improvidence: "In domestic matters we do not agree. But Osia is convinced that he is as good a household manager as he is a poet." Quoted from fond 2833, n. 7, ed. khran. 544 in TsGALI, the Central Archive of Literature and Art in Moscow. Natasha Shtempel' remembers the Voronezh visits of Vera Khazina—a "small, thin little old lady, very lively and sharp-witted" who treats the poet like a sick child. "Mandel'shtam v Voronezhe," *Novyi mir*, 10 (1987): 219.
24. For one of her discussions of Mandelstam's *joie de vivre*, see II, 239; here she remembers how his "love of life grew stronger" even during the most terrible period.
25. The "man-who-would-understand" refers to a character type elaborated by Marianne Hirsch, who, in turn, borrows the term itself from Adrienne Rich. Hirsch identifies this recurring figure in nineteenth-century realist writing by women: "the male object in this transformation of the marriage plot takes the form of a 'brother' who can be nurturing even as he provides access to the issues of legitimacy and authority central to plot-

ting. Most importantly, perhaps, his fraternal/incestuous status can protect the heroine from becoming a mother and can thereby help her, in spite of the closure of marriage, to remain a subject, and can help her not to disappear from the plot as the object of her child's fantasy" (58).

26. "Even in the smallest things he was always to expect the same from me as from himself, and he could make no distinction between my life and his own: if I am given a permit to live in Moscow, then so will you be; what happens to me will happen to you; you will read this book, if I read it . . ." (II, 233).

27. In his reminiscences about Nadezhda Mandelstam, Carl Proffer comments on her salty language and sexual candor. "Nadezhda Mandelstam," in *The Widows of Russia and Other Writings*, 17, 23.

28. As indicated in one of the epigraphs to this chapter, Gershtein also traces much of her charm to her "bold language," "self-assuredness," and "daredevil tricks" (27).

29. Isenberg identifies her aim to "unmask" in *Hope against Hope*, although he does not go so far as to connect this aim with her development of a distinctive and (for many readers) problematic persona. He interprets her "unmasking" as largely effective social commentary, the strategy of "an acute field anthropologist." "The Rhetoric of *Hope Against Hope*" (205).

30. Isenberg remarks on this important sequence: " . . . the death of the poet Mandelstam is represented as the originary act that brings the writer Nadezhda Mandelstam into being" (201).

6. *Hope against Hope*

1. Complete text of the letter in Box III, m. 91–92 of Osip Emilyevich Mandelshtam Papers held in Firestone Library, Princeton University. Published with permission of Princeton University Library.

2. I hasten to point out, however, that Nadezhda Mandelstam *was* interested in publishing her memoirs. Tvardovskii's letter to her indicates that he is responding to her request; in the opening he thanks her for the chance to read the text.

3. Both Iurii Freidin and Varvara Shklovskaia made this point in our respective interviews. Like Akhmatova, Nadezhda Mandelstam was highly irritated by the distorted memoirs of émigré writers such as Georgii Ivanov and Irina Odoevtseva, the more so because their work was freely disseminated in the West and they could fear no disclaimer from their silenced subjects in the Soviet Union.

4. In his introduction to the journal publication of her *Vospominaniia* in the Soviet Union, Mikhail Polivanov names the various towns where Nadezhda Mandelstam was forced to work and "disappear"—places like Ul'ianovsk, Chita, Cheboksary, Pskov. See *Iunost'*, 8 (1988): 34–35.

5. In his letter of 27 March 1951 (?), B. M. Zhirmunsky, her advisor, specifically praises her academic ability. Box III, m. 149–54, Mandelshtam Papers, Firestone Library, Princeton University. Published with permission of Princeton University Library.

6. Joseph Brodsky, "Nadezhda Mandelstam (1899–1980): An Obituary," in *Less Than One: Selected Essays* (New York: Farrar Straus Giroux, 1986), 145–56.

7. Interview with Shklovskaia, Panchenko, and Belosinskaia, 3 October 1989.

8. Shklovskaia, Freidin, and Sergeeva interviews.

9. Freidin interview, 15 October 1989.

10. Richard Pevear posits the connection between *Hope against Hope* and the Greek epic in "On the Memoirs of Nadezhda Mandelstam," *The Hudson Review*, 24, no. 3 (Autumn 1971): 426–40. Iurii Freidin offered the comparison to *Tristram Shandy* in our interview; Liudmila Sergeeva suggested the likeness to Herzen.

11. Isenberg, "The Rhetoric of *Hope Against Hope*," 201.

12. Isenberg notes the growing number of memoirists and scholars (a list that includes Lidiia Chukovskaia and Emma Gershtein) who have questioned the truthfulness of Nadezhda Mandelstam's work (198–99). In many cases, these critics fault her for glossing over her husband's and her own less attractive and sometimes ignoble behavior. See, for example, Gregory Freidin's re-examination and revaluation of Mandelstam's "Ode to Stalin," a poem Nadezhda Mandelstam denigrates as unsuccessful and alien to Mandelstam's creative gift. This analysis appears in Freidin's *A Coat of Many Colors: Osip Mandelstam and His Mythologies of Self-Presentation*, 250–71; an earlier version was printed as "Mandelstam's 'Ode to Stalin,'" *Russian Review*, 41, no. 4 (1982): 400–26.

13. Freidin, *A Coat of Many Colors*, 271.

14. All quotations taken from *Hope Against Hope*, translated by Max Hayward, with an introduction by Clarence Brown (New York: Atheneum, 1970), with my revisions based on *Vospominaniia*, fourth edition (Paris: YMCA Press, 1982). The English titles of both volumes of Nadezhda Mandelstam's memoirs are not direct translations of the Russian, but plays on the author's given name Nadezhda (Russian for "Hope"). For reasons that are not altogether clear (perhaps the discrepancy between translator's license and standard usage), the title of the first volume is variously capitalized in citations and reviews; unless the citation indicates otherwise, my text adheres to standard capitalization procedure with the English title *Hope against Hope*.

15. Clarence Brown, *Mandelstam*, 49–52.

16. For eyewitness accounts of Mandelstam's charismatic poetry readings, see Freidin, *A Coat of Many Colors*, 6–7.

17. Nadezhda Mandelstam specifically complains of this difficulty in *Hope Abandoned*.

18. See Nadezhda Mandelstam's essay *Mozart and Salieri*, translated by Robert A. McLean (Ann Arbor: Ardis, 1973), 11.

19. Freidin, *A Coat of Many Colors*, 270–71.

20. For a further discussion of Mandelstam's self-image as a *raznochinets*-writer, see Jane Gary Harris, *Osip Mandelstam*, 49–50, 58–59.

21. It is noteworthy that both Akhmatova and Mandelstam, writing from different positions on the margins of high Russian culture (as a woman and as a Jew), utilize this sense of difference as a creative benefit.

22. See Carl Proffer's observation on her general habits: "As for twentieth-century writers, she was usually acerbic and witty in her opinions. Often it seemed that something O.M. once said had inclined her permanently in one direction or another" (*The Widows of Russia*, 38).

23. Bednyi objects to the greasy fingerprints Stalin leaves on the books he lends him (*Hope against Hope*, 25–27).

24. In this, Nadezhda Mandelstam's approach contains an interesting paradox: While underscoring Mandelstam's symbolic biography as the "last Helleno-Christian poet" she distinguishes his "message" from that of other great poets who exercise a quasi-religious appeal.

25. Carl Proffer considers Nadezhda Mandelstam's ambiguous relationship with Pasternak, particularly in the light of this call: "There had been friendly times; she recalled 'madly curious' O.M., Pasternak, and herself walking the crowded streets together right after Lenin's death. When we knew her, she still had warm and frequent relations with some members of his family. But there were definitely episodes from the past that still rankled" (*The Widows of Russia*, 41).

26. Jane Gary Harris makes this point about Mandelstam's reworking of autobiography in *Shum vremeni (The Noise of Time)*. *Osip Mandelstam*, 49–50.

27. Her lengthy diatribe here about Sergei Rudakov, a poet who attempted to work with her husband while they were exiled in Voronezh, serves not only as warning but also as a subtle reinforcement of her own primary position as Mandelstam's personal and professional caretaker. I discuss this strategy further in the chapter on *Hope Abandoned*.

28. Isenberg, too, notes her device of "generaliz[ing] her own widowhood" by citing parallel examples. Nadezhda Mandelstam will refer periodically in her text to other truly heroic women who preserve their loved ones. For an extensive example, see her portrait of Alisa Gugovna Usova, a linguist stranded in Tashkent after she followed her husband into exile (364–66). I will comment more on this strategy in the chapter on *Hope Abandoned*.

29. In the first chapter of *A Coat of Many Colors*, Freidin considers the charismatic bond existing between Russian poets and their reader/listeners in the early twentieth century: "It is a truth universally acknowledged that the famous poets of modern Russia, Mandelstam among them, have a personal following that borders on a cult. No doubt a complex phenomenon, it involves a strong tendency toward identification with the poet on the part of the reader, both individually and en masse. Such identification is implied in the very idea of intensity, which denotes a relation of quantity between qualitatively similar entities, and without this underlying similitude the notion of intensity will not make any sense" (12–13).

30. For a sample of the literature exploring the connection between persona and person in autobiography, see Philippe Lejeune's *Le pacte autobiographique* (Paris: Editions du Seuil, 1975); Elizabeth Bruss's *Autobiographical Acts: The Changing Situation of a Literary Genre* (Baltimore: Johns Hopkins University Press, 1976); Michael Sprinker's "Fictions of the Self: The End of Autobiography," *Autobiography: Essays Theoretical and Critical*, edited by James Olney (Princeton: Princeton University Press, 1974), 321–42; and Paul Jay's *Being in the Text: Self-Representation from Wordsworth to Roland Barthes* (Ithaca, NY: Cornell University Press, 1984).

31. Interview with Freidin (10/15/89); interview with Mikhail Polivanov (10/21/89) in Moscow.

32. Isenberg notes that "she both undercuts and authenticates her own account, inviting us to believe her because she admits the inevitability of error, while strongly implying that we should also disbelieve her" ("The Rhetoric of *Hope Against Hope*," 199).

33. ". . . these young intellectuals have appeared and the process is now irreversible — it cannot be stopped even by the physical destruction which the representatives of the past would love to visit on them. Nowadays the repression of one intellectual creates dozens more . . . The birth of our new intelligentsia is now accompanied by an unprecedented craving for poetry" (333). See also the passage on page 328 where she admits to being an "incorrigible optimist" and says that she is "convinced that we will soon witness a complete victory of humanism and high-minded humanity."

34. *Iunost'*, 8 (1988): 35.

35. Polivanov, Freidin, and Sergeeva all made this point in my interviews with them.

36. Isenberg asserts that the structure of *Hope against Hope* is dependent on synecdoche and metonymy (203–204).

37. Hayden White has conducted the boldest (although by no means the first) inquiry into the literary reflex of history writing. See *Metahistory: The Historical Imagination in Nineteenth-Century Europe*, 3rd ed. (Baltimore: Johns Hopkins University Press, 1980). For another interesting typology, see Ellen Hurwitz and Donald Ostrowski, "The Many Varieties of Historical Writing," in *Okeanos: Essays Presented to Ihor Ševčenko on His Sixtieth Birthday by His Colleagues and Students* (Cambridge, MA: Harvard Ukrainian Studies, 1983), 296–308. Hurwitz and Ostrowski propose a typology that ranges from fontology ("analyses of a source *qua* source") to historical fiction.

38. Roy A. Medvedev, *Let History Judge: The Origins and Consequences of Stalinism*, translated by Colleen Taylor, edited by David Joravsky and Georges Haupt (New York: Vintage Books, 1973), xxxiii. Even in the revised and updated version of his book, Medvedev asserts that he "did not make use of or have access to any closed archives, 'special collections,' or any other limited-access depositories" and instead lists a whole host of *people* who have supplied him with "documentary materials, testimony, advice,

and critical commentary." *Let History Judge: The Origins and Consequences of Stalinism*, revised and expanded edition edited and translated by George Shriver (New York: Columbia University Press, 1989), xvii-xviii.

39. Alexander Solzhenitsyn, *The Gulag Archipelago, 1918–1956: An Experiment in Literary Investigation*, translated by Thomas P. Whitney (New York: Harper & Row, 1974).

40. Robert Conquest, *The Great Terror: Stalin's Purge of the Thirties* (London: Macmillan, 1968), 563–71.

41. Her deictic "advantage" echoes Mikhail Bakhtin's claims for the *chronotope* of the road: By associating with the time-space of the road, a hero can expand and concretize his or her experience. M. M. Bakhtin, *The Dialogic Imagination: Four Essays*, edited by Michael Holquist, translated by Caryl Emerson and Michael Holquist (Austin, Texas: The University of Texas Press, 1981), 120.

42. Nadezhda Mandelstam remarks how she was "saved by chance"—more specifically, by the fact that she was not able to register as a Moscow resident (285).

43. Cf. *The Dialogic Imagination*, 124–26. These roles are reviewed and considered in connection with Bakhtin's own historical context by Gary Saul Morson and Caryl Emerson in *Mikhail Bakhtin: Creation of a Prosaics* (Stanford, CA: Stanford University Press, 1990), 388–92. Morson and Emerson suggest how Soviet literature has reconceived this private/public division in response to the "public" emphasis of socialist realism.

44. Emma Gershtein appreciates the storytelling ability that seems to run in the Khazin family: "both she and Evgenii Iakovlevich [her brother] had a particular relish for events and people. 'That's good,' they'd say to each other, repeating some well-turned phrase" (*Novoe o Mandel'shtame*, 26).

45. See, for example, this passage from page 289: "People who were silent or closed their eyes to what was happening also try to justify the past. They usually accuse me of subjectivism: you only see one side of the picture, but there were good things besides—the building up of the country, Meyerhold's stage productions, the Cheliuskin expedition and lots more . . . I could add that the sky and the stars also existed, but it is necessary to make sense of what happened."

46. For an example of another negative portrait, see her chapter on the "Russian revolutionary woman," Larisa Reisner (108–12).

47. Osip Mandelstam, "The End of the Novel," in *The Complete Critical Prose and Letters*, 199–200.

48. As Iurii Freidin suggests in his redaction of the first volume for Soviet publication, Nadezhda Mandelstam may have intended to conclude with the chapter *"Moe zaveshchanie"* ("My Testament"), which describes how she construes her execution of Mandelstam's will. *Iunost'*, 9 (1989): 62. This change in order in no way detracts from the pattern, however; it merely underscores Nadezhda Mandelstam's assumption of personal responsibility for the biography and art of a person who has been officially effaced.

49. George Steiner, "Death of a Poet," *The New Yorker*, 26 December 1970, 61.

50. Mikhail Polivanov, *Vtoraia kniga*, 6.

51. Irving Howe, "Books," *Harper's Magazine*, 243, no. 1454 (July 1971): 90.

52. Saul Maloff, "Poetry and Power," *Commonweal*, 43, no. 14 (8 January 1971): 352. See also Ludmilla Thorne's comment in *The New Leader*, 16 November 1970, 16: "I can think of no other book that so graphically illustrates the disarming effects of a totalitarian regime on its people—particularly the intelligentsia."

53. See, for example, Christopher Read's list of sources for the "historian of twentieth-century Russia" in *History Today*, 33 (April 1983): 41. Noting that "access to sources is relatively limited and that the subject is highly politicized," he specifically recommends the memoirs of Victor Serge, Nadezhda Mandelstam, and Evgeniia Ginzburg as important references.

54. Richard Pevear, "On the Memoirs of Nadezhda Mandelstam," 431.

7. Hope Abandoned

1. Mikhail Polivanov, introduction to Nadezdha Mandelstam's *Vospominaniia*, *Iunost*, 8 (1988): 35.
2. Carl R. Proffer, *The Widows of Russia*, 19.
3. Sergeeva interview, 14 October 1989.
4. These commentaries are published in her *Kniga tret'ia* (Third book) (Paris: YMCA Press, 1987), 139–263. Hedrick Smith recalls one instance of this kind of instruction in his book *The Russians* (New York: Ballantine Books, 1976), 539.
5. While noting her substantial help, Proffer describes her sometimes testy relations with visiting scholars and her aversion to "modern schools of criticism" and "all kinds of syllable counting" (27). Freidin recalls her concern that scholars not interpret Mandelstam as a deliberately esoteric writer. Interview, 15 October 1989.
6. Hedrick Smith records this characteristic description: "Young Russian intellectuals hovered around her like acolytes, attending to her housekeeping, while she preached or lectured as long as energy held out" (539).
7. In her memoirs, Emma Gershtein notes the Mandelstams' happy sociability after they managed to obtain an apartment in Moscow; they enjoyed repaying all the friends who showed them hospitality (71). In her later years, when Polivanov's wife asks her how she can stand the steady stream of visitors, Nadezhda Mandelstam answers: "If you had lived as I did, when I didn't see anybody for twenty years, you wouldn't ask that question." *Iunost'*, 8 (1988): 35.
8. In one interview, Nadezhda Mandelstam claims that her new friends are primarily young people. Frank Diamond, "Dva interv'iu s Nadezhdoi Iakovlevnoi Mandelshtam," in Nadezhda Mandelstam, *Moe zaveshchanie i drugie esse*, with a foreword by Joseph Brodsky (New York: Serebrianyi vek, 1982), 116.
9. Protoierei Aleksandr Men', review of the first volume of Nadezhda Mandelstam's memoirs, *Literaturnoe obozrenie*, 5 (1990): 68. Iurii Freidin identifies this atmosphere as one of Nadezhda Mandelstam's greatest achievements.
10. Panchenko states her need most eloquently: "After her [first] book was finished, she felt the need to talk more." Interview at Peredelkino, 3 October 1989.
11. Writing about women's attraction to the diary in *Centuries of Female Days: Englishwomen's Private Diaries* (New Brunswick, NJ: Rutgers University Press, 1988), Harriet Blodgett maintains that this form served effectively as a "sanatorium" for its writers (80): "Both widows and wives may rely on their diaries for some sort of emotional sustenance and unburdening" (85). In her introduction to *A Quilt of Words: Women's Diaries, Letters and Original Accounts of Life in the Southwest, 1860–1960* (Boulder: Johnson Books, 1988), Sharon Niederman compares the keeping of a journal to quilting: Both are forms of self-expression which are continuous, accessible, and (often) created for the use of future generations of family and friends (3). For a more wide-ranging study of women's use of the journal form, see Joanne E. Cooper's "Shaping Meaning: Women's Diaries, Journals, and Letters—the Old and the New," *Women's Studies International Forum*, 10, no. 1 (1987): 95–99.
12. Nina Belosinskaia recalls that Nadezhda Mandelstam wanted to write a book about Gor'kii, among other things. Iurii Freidin says that she hoped to write a *Third Book* "about herself only, about her wandering, and about all the disgusting things she observed in the years she lived alone." In a published interview with Nadezhda Mandelstam in the fall of 1972, Jack Ludwig quotes yet another project: "'I want very much to write a third book. It will be about Soviet education and Soviet washrooms. It will be a historical book. I traveled very much from 1934 to 1965 and I saw different kinds of washrooms. It will be a work of art if I can write it. It is strange. I never thought of writing such a book before. Now it seems almost necessary." In *Partisan Review*, 41, no. 3 (1974): 460.

13. "[Ob Akhmatovoi]," *Literaturnaia ucheba*, 3 (1989): 151.

14. All quotes of this text taken from Nadezhda Mandelstam, *Mozart and Salieri*, translated by Robert A. McLean (Ann Arbor: Ardis, 1973).

15. Here again Nadezhda Mandelstam specifically condemns the Symbolists, who accorded themselves "the position of the elect" and attempted to serve as "priests" (73).

16. Nadezhda Mandelstam reports to others as well about Akhmatova's conduct. Emma Gershtein recalls how Nadezhda Mandelstam would tell her the juicy details of Akhmatova's unusual romantic situations. *Novoe o Mandel'shtame*, 24.

17. All quotations taken from Nadezhda Mandelstam, "[Ob Akhmatovoi]," *Literaturnaia ucheba*, 3 (1989): 134–51. Translations mine.

18. Isenberg, "The Rhetoric of *Hope Against Hope*," 197.

19. This does not mean, however, that women do not join in this cult of force. We have only to refer to Nadezhda Mandelstam's portrait of Larisa Reisner in *Hope against Hope*: "She had no time for those who sighed into their pillows, bemoaning their helplessness—in her circle the cult of force flourished" (109).

20. It is interesting that Nadezhda Mandelstam first tries to attribute the poet's character to her regional environment. Comparing Akhmatova with another great female poet—the selfless, generous, Great Russian Tsvetaeva—she implies that her friend's "self-absorption" ("*samopogloshchennost*") may derive from her south Russian origins overlaid with her Petersburg experience.

21. Nadezhda Mandelstam claims that when Russian émigré women write in their memoirs that Akhmatova was not pretty, the poet naturally protests (why must a female writer be held to standards inapplicable to male writers?), but at the same time begins to collect photos of herself as if to provide evidence to the contrary (149).

22. In the first variant, Nadezhda Mandelstam plays with the notion of a "real woman"—confessing that she cannot be classified as one (142) and relating elsewhere that she lacks the "womanly" trait of jealousy (for which Mandelstam, Akhmatova, and others censure her) (143).

23. Nerler ascribes this supposition to several of Nadezhda Mandelstam's old friends in his comments on the first variant ("[*Ob Akhmatovoi*]," 151).

24. Mikhail Polivanov, "Predislovie" to Nadezhda Mandelshtam's *Vtoraia kniga* (*Hope Abandoned*), 6. Polivanov claims that, in part, Nadezhda Mandelstam's sharp criticism of older writers like Briusov, Ivanov, and Voloshin reflects more the opinions of Akhmatova than Mandelstam.

25. Nerler also argues for a broader impulse, hypothesizing that Nadezhda Mandelstam's intentions changed in the course of writing. Her work comes to "foreground the figure of the author, her tense reflections about her own life and about the tragic link between her biography and the pain and horror of her epoch . . ." (151).

26. I am quoting the dates Iurii Freidin remembers. In his foreword to *Vtoraia kniga* (*Hope Abandoned*), Polivanov asserts that the text was written in 1970 (4–5).

27. Iurii Freidin interview. Simon Karlinsky makes the same point in his review of *Hope Abandoned*: "The emphasis is now not on Mandelstam and on his wife's heroic and successful struggle to save his manuscripts from destruction, but rather on the author herself, her views and her opinions." *The New York Times Book Review*, 20 January 1974, 11.

28. Mikhail Polivanov, "Predislovie," *Vtoraia kniga*, 8.

29. All quotations of the second volume taken from *Hope Abandoned*, translated by Max Hayward (New York: Atheneum, 1974) with my revisions based on the 4th edition of the Russian original published by YMCA Press in Paris in 1985.

30. In his famous open letter to Nadezhda Mandelstam, the writer Veniamin Kaverin reads this last association as mere arrogance: "You decided to prove nothing less than that we have had no literature for the last fifty years. There was only Mandelstam, Akhmatova, and you—who hadn't written a single line." I am citing from Faina Ranevskaia's

copy of his letter dated 23 March 1973 and held in fond 2788, op. 1, ed. khr. 625 in TsGALI.

31. On page 56 Nadezhda Mandelstam mentions, in an offhand way, that she is "neither a historian nor a literary scholar."

32. For an opposing version of the Rudakov episode, see Gershtein's account in *Novoe o Mandel'shtame*.

33. In her review of the English-language editions of *To the Memory of Childhood* and Leonid Andreev's *Photographs by a Russian Writer*, Claudia Roth Pierpont notes Nadezhda Mandelstam's attack on Chukovskii and argues that it is "psychologically acute": "In falsifying scraps of heroism and humanity for the sake of a powerful writer, she finds, Chukovskii was acting in the name of a larger belief; that is, nothing less than the 'good name of literature,' the necessity of maintaining its cult and honor" (131). "Childhoods," *The New Yorker*, 17 December 1990, 124–32.

34. Her attack on the persona emphasizes her dismissal of certain textual complexities; just as she ignores any distinction between her own voice and her presence in the text, so she claims the same unity for the artists she most esteems.

35. At one point she herself anticipates the impression her "settling accounts" might make: "I don't like memoirists like Georgii Ivanov, but I resemble them in this chapter because it is so full of ill will—more toward Voloshin than the freakish Briusov. It's clear that, as the saying goes, there's folly in every old woman" (86).

36. Joseph Brodsky, "Beyond Consolation," *New York Review of Books*, 7 February 1974, 14. In his discussion of her memoirs, Robert Hughes suggests an interesting analogy between her technique and that of her husband in his "scintillating and caustic 'Fourth Prose' (1930), a restorative and self-liberating counterattack on his vilifiers and ideological opponents." Robert P. Hughes, "Another Work of 'Unpermitted Literature,'" *The Nation*, 16 November 1974, 501.

37. Nadezhda Mandelstam is careful to make this distinction: "When I speak of an indivisible whole, I am far from advocating that there be a single, standardized culture throughout the world . . ." (276).

38. Proffer remarks on her religious beliefs: "As she grew older, her Christianity became stronger and more important." (*The Widows of Russia*, 51.)

39. It bears mention here that Nadezhda Mandelstam's blend of religious and artistic views partly echoes the modernist "religion" of Kornei Chukovskii.

40. It is important to note that Nadezhda Mandelstam rarely passes judgment on these cases. Her response to one such story is typical: "It is clear to me that my friend entered into relations of a kind it is absolutely wrong to enter into. However I blame not him but his tormentors. I have known other people who went regularly to meetings in 'private apartments' and signed forms promising not to talk. Some of them were the purest people imaginable, but they could not decide to condemn themselves and their families to destruction. One cannot demand heroism from ordinary people" (567).

41. Nadezhda Mandelstam even posits that if she could convey all her bad dreams for the last thirty years, no one "would even want to kill" (608).

42. In *The Reproduction of Mothering*, Nancy Chodorow presents these synopses: "From the retention of preoedipal attachments to their mother, growing girls come to define and experience themselves as continuous with others; their experience of self contains more flexible or permeable ego boundaries. Boys come to define themselves as more separate and distinct, with a greater sense of rigid ego boundaries and differentiation. The basic feminine sense of self is connected to the world, the basic masculine sense of self is separate" (169). In her pioneering study *In a Different Voice: Psychological Theory and Women's Development* (Cambridge, MA: Harvard University Press, 1982), Carol Gilligan observes similar patterns: "For men, the moral imperative appears rather as an injunction to respect the rights of others and thus to protect from interference the rights to life and self-fulfillment. . . . For women, the integration of rights and responsibilities takes place through an understanding of the psychological logic of relationships" (100).

43. Again, Nadezhda Mandelstam never makes the simplistic claim that all women are inherently better than men. See, for example, her statement on page 168: "Women can be even more horrible than men in such administrative posts."

44. The spiritual-cultural opposition she posited in the first variant is asserted here with a slightly different emphasis. She credits the women with strength and sees no men who can undertake the courageous, active, "manly" part Mandelstam had divined for them (89); the role of "weak" men is implicit.

45. With her references to these "beauties," Nadezhda Mandelstam may also be alluding to Akhmatova's bisexuality, a disclosure that would be sure to outrage many of the poet's supporters. Proffer recognizes this provocation: "Therefore it was no surprise that N.M.'s picture of Anna Akhmatova shocked many of the great poet's admirers. To such enthusiasts it was impossible to allow a talented artist such normal human traits as querulousness, egotism, or pettiness—let alone the veiled suggestion that she was occasionally attracted to beautiful women" (35). It is interesting, however, that Nadezhda Mandelstam condemns Akhmatova for playing the lady in any sort of erotic relationship, not for her sexual preference. Incidentally, the diarist Sophie Ostrovskaya is much more explicit and judgmental in identifying the poet's bisexuality. See her *Memoirs of Anna Akhmatova's Years*, 33, 49, 53.

46. She also complains about Akhmatova's sense of "incomparable rightness" ("*nesravnennaia pravota*")—a trait she attributes to women in the first variant of *Hope Abandoned*: "It is well known that women do not like to admit that they are wrong. . . . However much I love women, it is still terrifying that they are as sinless as the pope" (142).

47. Her observation does not endear her to many of the poet's devoted followers. See, for example, the defensive counterattack in the memoirs of Anatolii Naiman, *Rasskazy o Anne Akhmatovoi* (Moscow: Khudozhestvennaia literatura, 1989): "After the death of Akhmatova, Nadezhda Mandelstam also wrote and published her *Second Book*. Her main device was a subtle, well-dissolved dosage of untruth in truth—often on a grammatical level where there was no way to extract the malignant molecule without damage to the whole. . . . Akhmatova is presented as a capricious old woman who has lost touch with reality. Here the only truth is that Akhmatova was an old woman. . . . In later years Nadezhda Mandelstam sincerely believed that she had surpassed [both Mandelstam and Akhmatova] in intelligence and was not much inferior to them (if she was inferior at all) in talent. It is possible that she needed this compensation for the pain, horror, and humiliation of her former life" (83). Naiman quotes Akhmatova as saying that she had not read Nadezhda Mandelstam's first volume: " 'She, fortunately, didn't propose it, and I didn't ask.' "

48. Nadezhda Mandelstam declares that she is "disarmed by her license" and remarks that N.N. simply has no language to account for her behavior (577).

49. See also Nadezhda Mandelstam's portrait of the "vivacious, talkative," and altruistic Susanna Mar (143, 149). Compared with N.N., Mar appears to be more sympathetic than influential, but it is important that Nadezhda Mandelstam pays tribute to another "wild and frivolous woman"—one "who never became 'a somebody' in Soviet literature and was not worried by such 'disruptive' acts as the publication of Mandelstam" (149).

50. Chukovskaia's response is cited by Nina Christesen in her introduction to Hirshorn's *Lydia Korneevna Chukovskaya* (ix). Christesen maintains that "Chukovskaya later wrote a book of her own to counter Nadezhda Matveevna's [sic] second volume and called it *Misfortune*: whether it will ever be published is hard to tell."

51. Emma Gershtein, *Pod"em*, 7 (1988): 89.

52. Cited from Ranevskaia's copy of the letter—fond 2788, op. 1, ed. khr. 625 in TsGALI.

53. See also Kaverin's reaction to her treatment of Akhmatova: "I note that in *Hope against Hope* you write about Akhmatova as if she were an elder sister and in *Hope Abandoned* as if she were younger and could occasionally be put in her place."

54. One of her few understanding readers is Joseph Brodskii, who defends Nadezhda Mandelstam's sweeping judgment: "Her book is relentless, it breathes typical Judaic devotion to justice. What Mme. Mandelstam does in its 621 pages is nothing other than hold a Day of Judgment on earth for her age and its literature—a judgment administered all the more rightfully since it was this age that had undertaken the construction of paradise on earth" (*The New York Review of Books*, 7 February 1974, 13).

8. The Widows' Might

1. For the English translation of these memoirs, see Liubov' Mendeleeva-Blok, "Facts and Myths about Blok and Myself," in *Blok: An Anthology of Essays and Memoirs*, edited and translated by Lucy Vogel (Ann Arbor: Ardis, 1982,) 8–63. See also Barbara Heldt's perceptive analysis of her case in *Terrible Perfection*, 93–98.

2. For an intriguing discussion of Tsvetaeva's achievement, see Boym, *Death in Quotation Marks*, 192–240.

3. Sigrid McLaughlin, "Introduction," in *The Image of Women in Contemporary Soviet Fiction: Selected Short Stories from the USSR*, edited and translated by Sigrid McLaughlin (London: Macmillan, 1989), 10. McLaughlin provides an excellent synopsis of this gender-blind orientation: "When asked about their themes or about admired predecessors and influences on them, they usually place themselves in the tradition of nineteenth-and twentieth-century Russian and Western prose and emphasize the universality and humanistic orientation of their themes. Focusing on women's problems would be too narrow ('men suffer too'), and so would writing for primarily a female audience. They also insist that they are not feminists and do not want to further the cause of emancipation. Feminism, to most of them, is the outlook of extremists, unhappy outsiders, troublemakers or ethical nihilists. Emancipation—defined as the right to equal opportunity in education and employment—is considered to have been achieved, and found of doubtful merit: it has brought women a double burden, they argue, and masculinized them" (10).

4. One recent example: After polemicizing with the notion of "women's prose" and faulting women writers for second-rate literary achievement, the critic Evgeniia Shcheglova concludes her article by praising the distinctive merits of *Sof'ia Petrovna*: "Think how our national tragedy achieved a new penetrating resonance when Chukovskaia's novel *Sof'ia Petrovna* appeared. A woman's voice in literature does not have to be a superlative work. But it should be its own, distinctive, not imitative, on the one hand free of a sense of bitterness and, on the other, free of bravado and shock value" (26). "V svoem krugu: polemicheskie zametki o 'zhenskoi proze,' " *Literaturnoe obozrenie*, 3 (1990): 19–26.

5. Vladimir Shlapentokh, *Public and Private Life of the Soviet People: Changing Values in Post-Stalin Russia* (New York: Oxford University Press, 1989).

6. Ludmila Alexeyeva, *Soviet Dissent: Contemporary Movements for National, Religious, and Human Rights*, translated by Carol Pearce and John Glad (Middletown, CT: Wesleyan University Press, 1985), 284.

7. Ludmila Alexeyeva and Paul Goldberg, *The Thaw Generation: Coming of Age in the Post-Stalin Era* (Boston: Little, Brown, 1990), 83.

8. Alexeyeva, *The Thaw Generation*, 83.

9. In her *Memoirs*, translated by Samuel Cioran (New York: Random House, 1983), Raisa Orlova remembers Chukovskaia's visits to the dacha she and her family shared with the family of Frida Vigdorova (263); she also writes of Chukovskaia's involvement in the group that tried to defend Joseph Brodskii when he went on trial (281–82).

10. See Hedrick Smith's description of an evening at Chukovskii's "home museum": "Lidiya Chukovskaya, determined that the remembrance should be not only for the man

but more significantly the cultured spirit and an era of cultural elegance, had arranged for some readings" (536).

11. These texts, which first appeared in *samizdat*, have been collected in *Otkrytoe slovo* (New York: Izdatel'stvo "Khronika," 1976).

12. In yet another act of "monumentalization," Hedrick Smith develops this portrait of Chukovskaia as dissident. He observes her at her father's graveside: "But unbowed and straightbacked, Lidiya Chukovskaya stood by the grave, tall, white-haired and erect, like some New England Calvinist heroine. Of her, another writer remarked, 'When there is a flood in the countryside, there is usually a stick which stands upright in the stream and shows the level of the flood. Lidiya Korneyevna is like that. Always the same. Rigid. Uncompromising.' And for that unbending independence—her novels published in the West about the Stalinist period, her public defense of dissident physicist Andrei Sakharov when he was under severe attack in the fall of 1973 and her giving shelter to Solzhenitsyn in his final months in the Soviet Union—she was expelled from the Writers' Union in 1974" (536). Smith also remembers how Chukovskaia agonized over the fate of "little people" convicted for possession of *samizdat* texts (615–16).

13. Alexeyeva, *Soviet Dissent*, 15–16, 285–87.

14. Alexeyeva, *The Thaw Generation*, 200–201.

15. Orlova, 268, 279.

16. Alexeyeva, *Soviet Dissent*, 288–89; see also Alexeyeva, *The Thaw Generation*, 140–41.

17. Alexeyeva, *Soviet Dissent*, 451.

18. For a brief history of this important human rights movement, see John Simpson and Jana Bennett, *The Disappeared and the Mothers of the Plaza: The Story of the 11,000 Argentinians Who Vanished* (New York: Saint Martin's Press, 1985), 152–70.

19. Alexeyeva, *The Thaw Generation*, 206. See Dina Kaminskaia's memoirs, *Zapiski advokata* (New York: Khronika Press, 1984).

20. For documentation of this event (and the consequent prosecution of its participants), see Natalia Gorbanevskaya, *Red Square at Noon*, with an introduction by Harrison E. Salisbury, translated by Alexander Lieven (New York: Holt, Rinehart & Winston, 1970).

21. Alekseeva calculates that "for the fifteen-year period from 1968 to 1983, about half a million Soviet citizens have publicly declared their dissident opinions." But she is quick to point out that "this is not a small number considering Soviet conditions" (*Soviet Dissent*, 453).

22. Alexeyeva, *Soviet Dissent*, 385. These groups formed around the publications *Zhenshchina i Rossiia* (*Women and Russia*) and *Mariia*.

23. See Chukovskaia's moving obituary for her friend, included in *Otkrytoe slovo*; also her introduction to Vigdorova's book *Doroga v zhizn'*. Hirshon notes this testimony and comments that Chukovskaia and Vigdorova were lifelong friends.

24. It would be a fascinating project to examine how different family generations of women are depicted and assessed in the post-Stalin memoirs of female dissidents, to provide a much-needed sequel to Alpern Engel's mother-daughter study of nineteenth-century women revolutionaries. Both Orlova and Alekseeva, for example, try to place themselves in a line of maternal descent, pondering the figures of their mothers and, in Alekseeva's case, paying tribute to her grandmother's powerful influence. Another excellent subject for this study would be Elena Bonner's recent memoir of her mother's family, *Mothers and Daughters*, translated by Antonina W. Bouis (New York: Alfred A. Knopf, 1992).

25. Ratushinskaia demonstrates a particularly traditional prejudice in her condescending pity for lesbians in the camps.

26. Irina Ratushinskaya, *Grey Is the Color of Hope*, translated by Alyona Kojevnikov (New York: Alfred A. Knopf, 1988), 73.

27. Alexeyeva, *The Thaw Generation*, 19–20.

28. Alexeyeva, *The Thaw Generation*, 62–63.

29. Alekseeva truly generalizes the influence of Bogoraz in her history (*Soviet Dissent*, 278).

30. Alexeyeva, *The Thaw Generation*, 179.

31. In her "Separate Spheres, Female Worlds, Woman's Place: The Rhetoric of Women's History," Linda K. Kerber offers a final analysis which seems to me to be illuminating for this particular moment in Russian history: "The reconstruction of gender relations, and of the spaces that men and women may claim, is one of the most compelling contemporary social tasks. It is related to major social questions: the feminization of poverty, equal access to education and the professions, relations of power and abuses of power in the public sector and in the family. On a wider stage, the reconstruction of gender relations is related to major issues of power, for we live in a world in which authority has traditionally validated itself by its distance from the feminine and from what is understood to be effeminate" (39).

32. In *Hope Abandoned*, Nadezhda Iakovlevna refers to the "brotherhood" of *sobornost'*. Chukovskaia uses this term in *Going Under* as well as in her nonfictional *Process of expulsion* where she states that "[e]ach of us has a brother—a loving, truthful, stern, brave brother. He did not abandon us and will not abandon us if we remain worthy. Let's forget about the halls of the Writers' Union. We'll learn to see in the darkness: our brotherhood is all around us" (192).

WORKS CITED

Note: Because of delays in the publication of unofficial Soviet works, I have chosen to list the works of Lidiia Chukovskaia and Nadezhda Mandelstam in the chronological order of their writing or their preparation for *tamizdat/samizdat* publication rather than by date of official publication.

Abel, Elizabeth. "(E)merging Identities: The Dynamics of Female Friendship in Contemporary Fiction by Women." *Signs*, 6, no. 3 (1981): 413–35.
Akhmatova, Anna. *"Requiem" and "Poem without a Hero"*. Translated by D. M. Thomas. London: Paul Elek, 1976.
Alexeyeva, Ludmila. *Soviet Dissent: Contemporary Movements for National, Religious, and Human Rights*. Translated by Carol Pearce and John Glad. Middletown, CT: Wesleyan University Press, 1985.
Alexeyeva, Ludmila, and Paul Goldberg. *The Thaw Generation: Coming of Age in the Post-Stalin Era*. Boston: Little, Brown, 1990.
Anna Akhmatova: Stikhi, perepiska, vospominaniia, ikonografiia. Compiled by E. Proffer. Ann Arbor: Ardis, 1977.
Armstrong, Nancy. *Desire and Domestic Fiction: A Political History of the Novel*. New York: Oxford University Press, 1987.
Attwood, Lynne. *The New Soviet Man and Woman: Sex-Role Socialization in the USSR*. Bloomington: Indiana University Press, 1990.
Aucouturier, Michel. "The Legend of the Poet and the Image of the Actor in the Short Stories of Pasternak (1966)." In *Boris Pasternak: Modern Judgements*, edited by Donald Davie and Angela Livingstone, with verse translations by Donald Davie, pp. 220–30. Nashville: Aurora, 1970.
Baines, Jennifer. *Mandelstam: The Later Poetry*. Cambridge: Cambridge University Press, 1976.
Bakhtin, M. M. *The Dialogic Imagination: Four Essays*. Edited by Michael Holquist, translated by Caryl Emerson and Michael Holquist. Austin: The University of Texas Press, 1981.
Barratt, Andrew. *Between Two Worlds: A Critical Introduction to "The Master and Margarita."* Oxford: The Clarendon Press, 1987.
Belosinskaia, Nina. Interview with author. Peredelkino, USSR, 3 October 1989.
Blodgett, Harriet. *Centuries of Female Days: Englishwomen's Private Diaries*. New Brunswick, NJ: Rutgers University Press, 1988.
Bonnell, Victoria E. "The Representation of Women in Early Soviet Political Art." *The Russian Review*, 50 (1991): 267–88.
Bonner, Elena. *Mothers and Daughters*. Translated by Antonina W. Bouis. New York: Alfred A. Knopf, 1992.
Bowlt, John. "Biography, Bibliography." In *Kunstlerinnen der Russischen Avantgarde, 1910–1930*, p. 112. Cologne: Galerie Gmurzynska, 1979.
Boym, Svetlana. *Death in Quotation Marks: Cultural Myths of the Modern Poet*. Cambridge, MA: Harvard University Press, 1991.
――――. "Dialogue as 'Lyrical Hermaphroditism': Mandel'shtam's Challenge to Bakhtin." *Slavic Review*, 50, no. 1 (1991): 118–26.
Brain, James L. "An Anthropological Perspective on the Witchcraze." In *The Politics of Gender in Early Modern Europe*, edited by Jean R. Brink, Allison P. Coudert, and Maryanne C. Horowitz. *Volume 12, Sixteenth Century Essays and Studies*, pp. 15–27. Kirksville, MO: Sixteenth Century Journal, 1989.
Brodsky, Joseph. "Beyond Consolation." *New York Review of Books*, 7 February 1974, 13–16.

———. "Nadezhda Mandelstam (1899–1980): An Obituary." In *Less Than One: Selected Essays*, pp. 145–56. New York: Farrar Straus Giroux, 1986.
Brown, Clarence. *Mandelstam*. London: Cambridge University Press, 1973.
Brown, Edward J. "The Mobilization of Culture." In *The Stalin Revolution: Foundations of Soviet Totalitarianism*, 2d ed., edited and with an introduction by Robert V. Daniels, pp. 128–37. Lexington, MA: D. C. Heath, 1972.
———. *Russian Literature since the Revolution*. Revised and enlarged edition. Cambridge, MA: Harvard University Press, 1982.
Brown, Gillian. *Domestic Individualism: Imagining a Self in Nineteenth-Century America*. Berkeley: University of California Press, 1990.
Bruss, Elizabeth. *Autobiographical Acts: The Changing Situation of a Literary Genre*. Baltimore: Johns Hopkins University Press, 1976.
Buckley, Mary. *Women and Ideology in the Soviet Union*. New York: Harvester Wheatsheaf, 1989.
Bulgakov, Mikhail. *The Master and Margarita*. Translated by Mirra Ginzburg. New York: Grove Press, 1978.
Bulgakova, Elena. *Dnevnik Eleny Bulgakovoi*. Moscow: Izdatel'stvo "Knizhnaia palata," 1990.
Caldwell, Lesley. "Reproducers of the Nation: Women and the Family in Fascist Policy." In *Rethinking Italian Fascism: Capitalism, Populism and Culture*, edited by David Forgacs, pp. 110–41. London: Lawrence and Wishart, 1986.
Chodorow, Nancy. *The Reproduction of Mothering: Psychoanalysis and the Sociology of Gender*. Berkeley: University of California Press, 1978.
Chudakova, Marietta. "Tvorcheskaia istoriia M. Bulgakova *Master i Margarita*." *Voprosy literatury*, 1 (1976): 218–53.
———. "Vzglianut' v litso." In *Vzgliad. Kritika. Polemika. Publikatsiia*, compiled by A. Latynina and S. Lesnevskii, pp. 376–404. Moscow: Sovetskii pisatel', 1988.
———. "Arkhivy v sovremennoi kul'ture." *Nashe nasledie*, 3 (1988): 141–47.
Chukovskaia, Lidiia. *Sof'ia Petrovna*. In *Povesti*. Moscow: Moskovskii rabochii, 1988. English version: *Sofia Petrovna*, translated by Aline Worth (revised and amended by Eliza Kellogg Klose). Evanston, IL: Northwestern University Press, 1988. (Manuscript completed in February 1940.)
———. *Slovo predostavliaetsia detiam*. Tashkent, 1942.
———. *Dekabrist Nikolai Bestuzhev: Issledovatel' Buriatii*. Moscow: Geografgiz, 1950.
———. *Dekabristy: Issledovateli Sibiri*. Moscow: Geografgiz, 1951.
———. *Spusk pod vodu*. In *Povesti*. Moscow: Moskovskii rabochii, 1988. English version: *Going Under*, translated by Peter M. Weston. London: Barrie and Jenkins, 1972. (Manuscript completed in 1957.)
———. *V laboratorii redaktora*. 2d ed. Moscow: Iskusstvo, 1963.
———. "*Byloe i Dumy*" *Gertsena*. Moscow: Khudozhestvennaia Literatura, 1966.
———. *Zapiski ob Anne Akhmatovoi*, T. 1, 1938–1941, 2d ed. Paris: YMCA Press, 1984. Soviet publication: Moscow: "Kniga," 1989. (Manuscript prepared for *tamizdat* publication by June 1966.)
———. *Otkrytoe slovo*. New York: "Khronika," 1976.
———. *Po ètu storonu smerti: iz dnevnika 1936–1976*. Paris: YMCA Press, 1978.
———. *Protsess iskliucheniia*. Paris: YMCA Press, 1978.
———. *Zapiski ob Anne Akhmatovoi*, T. 2, 1952–1962. Paris: YMCA Press, 1980. (Manuscript prepared for *tamizdat* publication in 1979.)
———. *Pamiati detstva*. With an afterword by Efim Etkind. New York: Chalidze Publications, 1983. English version: *To the Memory of Childhood*. Translated by Eliza Kellogg Klose. Evanston, IL: Northwestern University Press, 1988. (Manuscript appears to have been prepared for Soviet publication by 1972, but at that time only excerpted chapters published.)
———. "Predsmertie." *Sobesednik*, 3 (1988): 41–64.
———. Letter to the author. 7 July 1989.

Chukovskii, Kornei. "Anna Akhmatova." *Sobranie sochinenii v 6 tomakh*, vol. 5, pp. 725–55. Moscow: Khudozhestvennaia literatura, 1967.
———. *From Two to Five*. Revised edition, translated and edited by Miriam Morton, with a foreword by Frances Clarke Sayers. Berkeley: University of California Press, 1968.
Clark, Katerina. "Little Heroes and Big Deeds: Literature Responds to the First Five-Year Plan." In *Cultural Revolution in Russia, 1928–1931*, edited by Sheila Fitzpatrick, pp. 189–206. Bloomington: Indiana University Press, 1978.
———. *The Soviet Novel: History as Ritual*. 2d ed. Chicago: University of Chicago Press, 1985.
Clements, Barbara Evans. "Later Developments: Trends in Soviet Women's History 1930 to the Present." In *Russia's Women: Accommodation, Resistance, Transformation*, edited by Barbara Evans Clements, Barbara Alpern Engel, and Christine D. Worobec, pp. 262–78. Berkeley: University of California Press, 1991.
Cohn, Dorrit. *Transparent Minds: Narrative Modes for Presenting Consciousness in Fiction*. Princeton: Princeton University Press, 1978.
Conquest, Robert. *The Great Terror: A Reassessment*. New York: Oxford University Press, 1990. Also first edition, *The Great Terror: Stalin's Purge of the Thirties*. London: Macmillan, 1968.
Cooper, Joanne E. "Shaping Meaning: Women's Diaries, Journals, and Letters—the Old and the New." *Women's Studies International Forum*, 10, no. 1 (1987): 95–99.
Curtis, J. A. E. *Bulgakov's Last Decade: The Writer as Hero*. Cambridge: Cambridge University Press, 1987.
Daniels, Robert V. "The Struggle with the Right Opposition." In *The Stalin Revolution: Foundations of Soviet Totalitarianism*, 2d ed., edited and with an introduction by Robert V. Daniels, pp. 22–39. Lexington, MA: D. C. Heath, 1972.
de Grazia, Victoria. *How Fascism Ruled Women: Italy, 1922–1945*. Berkeley: University of California Press, 1992.
Deutscher, Isaac. *Stalin: A Political Biography*. 2d ed. New York: Oxford University Press, 1966.
Do dnes' tiagoteet. Compiled by Semen Samuilovich Vilenskii. Moscow: Sovetskii pisatel', 1989.
Dunham, Vera. *In Stalin's Time: Middle-class Values in Soviet Fiction*. Introduced by Jerry F. Hough. Cambridge: Cambridge University Press, 1976.
Durova, Nadezhda. *The Cavalry Maiden: Journals of a Russian Officer in the Napoleonic Wars*. Translation, introduction, and notes by Mary Fleming Zirin. Bloomington: Indiana University Press, 1989.
Engel, Barbara Alpern. "From Feminism to Populism: A Study of Changing Attitudes of Women of the Russian Intelligentsia 1855–1881." Ph.D. diss., Columbia University, 1974.
———. "Mothers and Daughters: Family Patterns and the Female Intelligentsia." In *The Family in Imperial Russia: New Lines of Historical Research*, edited by David L. Ransel, pp. 44–59. Urbana: University of Illinois Press, 1978.
———. *Mothers and Daughters: Women of the Intelligentsia in Nineteenth-Century Russia*. Cambridge: Cambridge University Press, 1983.
Etkind, Efim. "Otets i doch'." Afterword to *Pamiati detstva*. New York: Chalidze, 1983.
Fanger, Donald. Review of Nadezhda Mandelstam's *Kniga tret'ia*. *The Russian Review*, 48, no. 2 (April 1989): 219–20.
Fitzpatrick, Sheila. "'Middle Class Values' and Soviet Life in the 1930s." In *Soviet Society and Culture: Essays in Honor of Vera S. Dunham*, edited by Terry L. Thompson and Richard Sheldon, pp. 20–30. Boulder: Westview Press, 1988.
Fleishman, Lazar. *Boris Pasternak: The Poet and His Politics*. Cambridge, MA: Harvard University Press, 1990.
Foucault, Michel. "What Is an Author?" Reprinted in *Textual Strategies: Perspectives in*

Post-Structuralist Criticism, edited and with an introduction by Josue Harari, pp. 141–60. Ithaca, NY: Cornell University Press, 1979.

Freidin, Gregory. "Mandelstam's 'Ode to Stalin.'" *Russian Review*, 41, no. 4 (1982): 400–26.

———. *A Coat of Many Colors: Osip Mandelstam and His Mythologies of Self-Presentation*. Berkeley: University of California Press, 1987.

Freidin, Iurii. Interview with author. Moscow, USSR, 15 October 1989.

Friedman, Susan Stanford. "Women's Autobiographical Selves: Theory and Practice." In *The Private Self: Theory and Practice of Women's Autobiographical Writings*, edited by Shari Benstock, pp. 34–62. Chapel Hill: University of North Carolina Press, 1988.

Frye, Marilyn. *The Politics of Reality: Essays in Feminist Theory*. Trumansburg, NY: The Crossing Press, 1983.

Frye, Northrop. *Anatomy of Criticism: Four Essays*. Princeton: Princeton University Press, 1957.

Gardiner, Judith Kegan. "Mind mother: psychoanalysis and feminism." In *Making a Difference: Feminist Literary Criticism*, edited by Gayle Green and Coppelia Kahn, pp. 113–45. London: Routledge, 1985.

Gasiorowska, Xenia. *Women in Soviet Fiction, 1917–1964*. Madison: University of Wisconsin Press, 1968.

Gershtein, Emma. *Novoe o Mandel'shtame*. Paris: Atheneum, 1986.

———. "Mandel'shtam v Voronezhe." *Pod"em*, 6 (1988): 112–23; 7 (1988): 84–105; 8 (1988): 112–29; 9 (1988): 108–29; 10 (1988): 104–24.

———. "Iz vospominanii. Pis'ma Anny Akhmatovoi," *Voprosy literatury*, 6 (1989): 248–70.

Gifford, Henry. "A Poet for Her People." *The Times Literary Supplement*. 18 November 1977, 1351–52.

Gilbert, Sandra M., and Susan Gubar. *The Madwoman in the Attic: The Woman Writer and the Nineteenth-Century Literary Imagination*. New Haven: Yale University Press, 1979.

Gilligan, Carol. *In a Different Voice: Psychological Theory and Women's Development*. Cambridge, MA: Harvard University Press, 1982.

Ginzburg, Evgeniia. *Krutoi marshrut*, volumes one and two. With a foreword by Vasilii Aksenov. New York: Possev, 1985. English translation: *Journey into the Whirlwind*. Translated by Paul Stevenson and Max Hayward. 1st ed. New York: Harcourt, Brace and World, 1967. *Within the Whirlwind*. Translated by Ian Boland, with an introduction by Heinrich Boll. 1st ed. New York: Harcourt Brace Jovanovich, 1981.

Ginzburg, Lidiia. "Akhmatova. Neskol'ko stranits vospominanii." In *Literatura v poiskakh real'nosti. Stat'i, esse, zametki*, pp. 124–29. Leningrad: Sovetskii pisatel', 1987.

———. "Zapisi 1920–1930-kh godov." In *Chelovek za pis'mennym stolom. Esse: iz vospominanii: chetyre povestvovaniia*, pp. 4–182. Leningrad: Sovetskii pisatel', 1989.

Głowiński, Michał. "Powieść i dziennik intymny." In *O prozie polskiej XX wieku*, edited by A. Hutnikiewicz and Helena Zaworska, pp. 375–94. Warsaw: IBL PAN, 1971.

Gorbanevskaya, Natalia. *Red Square at Noon*. With an introduction by Harrison E. Salisbury, translated by Alexander Lieven. New York: Holt, Rinehart & Winston, 1970.

Goscilo, Helena. "Introduction." *Balancing Acts: Contemporary Stories by Russian Women*, pp. xiii-xxvii. Bloomington: Indiana University Press, 1989.

Greene, Gayle, and Coppelia Kahn. "Feminist scholarship and the social construction of woman." In *Making a Difference: Feminist Literary Criticism*, edited by Gayle Green and Coppelia Kahn, pp. 1–36. London: Routledge, 1985.

Grois, Boris. "Stalinizm kak esteticheskii fenomen." *Sintaksis*, 17 (1987): 98–110.
———. *The Total Art of Stalinism: Avant-Garde, Aesthetic Dictatorship, and Beyond.* Translated by Charles Rougle. Princeton: Princeton University Press, 1992.
Haight, Amanda. *Anna Akhmatova: A Poetic Pilgrimage.* New York: Oxford University Press, 1976.
Haraszti, Miklos. *The Velvet Prison: Artists under State Socialism.* Foreword by George Konrad, translated by Katalin and Stephen Landesmann with the help of Steve Wasserman. New York: Basic Books, 1987.
Harris, Jane Gary. *Osip Mandelstam.* Boston: Twayne, 1988.
———. "Diversity of Discourse: Autobiographical Statements in Theory and Praxis." In *Autobiographical Statements in Twentieth-Century Russian Literature*, edited by Jane Gary Harris, pp. 3–35. Princeton: Princeton University Press, 1990.
Heilbrun, Carolyn. *Writing a Woman's Life.* New York: Ballantine Books, 1988.
Heldt, Barbara. *Terrible Perfection: Women and Russian Literature.* Bloomington: Indiana University Press, 1987.
Hingley, Ronald. *Pasternak: A Biography.* New York: Alfred A. Knopf, 1983.
Hirsch, Marianne. *The Mother/Daughter Plot: Narrative, Psychoanalysis, Feminism.* Bloomington: Indiana University Press, 1989.
Hirshon, Bella. *Lydia Korneevna Chukovskaya: A Tribute by Bella Hirshon.* Melbourne: University of Melbourne, 1987.
Homans, Margaret. *Bearing the Word: Language and Female Experience in Nineteenth-Century Women's Writing.* Chicago: University of Chicago Press, 1986.
Howe, Irving. "Books." *Harper's Magazine*, 243, no. 1454 (July 1971): 89–91.
Hughes, Robert P. "Another Work of 'Unpermitted Literature.' " *The Nation*, 16 November 1974, 501–502.
Hurwitz, Ellen, and Donald Ostrowski. "The Many Varieties of Historical Writing." In *Okeanos: Essays Presented to Ihor Ševčenko on His Sixtieth Birthday by His Colleagues and Students*, pp. 296–308. Cambridge, MA: Harvard Ukrainian Studies, 1983.
Il'ina, Natal'ia. "Anna Akhmatova v poslednie gody ee zhizni." *Oktiabr'*, 2 February 1977, 107–31.
———. "Eshche ob Akhmatovoi," *Ogonek*, 38 (19–26 September 1987): 28–30.
Ioffe, Mariia. *Odna noch': Povest' o pravde.* New York: Izdatel'stvo "Khronika," 1978.
Isenberg, Charles. *Substantial Proofs of Being: Osip Mandelstam's Literary Prose.* Columbus, OH: Slavica, 1987.
———. "The Rhetoric of Nadezhda Mandelstam's *Hope Against Hope*." *New Studies in Russian Language and Literature.* Edited by Anna Lisa Crone and Catherine V. Chvany, pp. 168–82. Columbus, OH: Slavica, 1987.
———. "The Rhetoric of *Hope Against Hope*." In *Autobiographical Statements in Twentieth-Century Russian Literature*, edited by Jane Gary Harris, pp. 193–206. Princeton: Princeton University Press, 1990.
Ivanova, Natal'ia. "Khranit' vechno." *Iunost'*, 7 (1988): 86–90.
Ivinskaia, Olga. *V plenu vremeni: gody s Borisom Pasternakom.* Paris: Fayard, 1978. English translation: *A Captive of Time.* Translated by Max Hayward. New York: Doubleday, 1978.
Jay, Paul. *Being in the Text: Self-Representation from Wordsworth to Roland Barthes.* Ithaca, NY: Cornell University Press, 1984.
Jelinek, Estelle. *The Tradition of Women's Autobiography: From Antiquity to the Present.* Boston: Twayne, 1986.
Kaminskaia, Dina. *Zapiski advokata.* New York: Khronika Press, 1984.
Karlinsky, Simon. Review of *Hope Abandoned. The New York Times Book Review*, 20 January 1974, 1–16.
Kaverin, Veniamin. Letter to Nadezhda Mandelstam. Held in fond 2788, op. 1, ed. khr. 625 in TsGALI Moscow, USSR.

Kerber, Linda K. "Separate Spheres, Female Worlds, Woman's Place: The Rhetoric of Women's History." *The Journal of American History*, 75 (June 1988): 9–39.
Khan-Magomedov, Selim O. *Pioneers of Soviet Architecture: The Search for New Solutions in the 1920s and 1930s*. Translated by Alexander Lieven and edited by Catherine Cooke, pp. 341–98. New York: Rizzoli, 1983.
Koonz, Claudia. *Mothers in the Fatherland: Women, the Family, and Nazi Politics*. New York: St. Martin's Press, 1987.
Korallov, M. "Nado zhit' dolgo." *Novyi mir*, 11 (1988): 248–50.
Kovalevskaia, Sofia. *A Russian Childhood*. Translated by Beatrice Stillman. New York: Springer-Verlag, 1978.
Kreps, Mikhail. *Bulgakov i Pasternak kak romanisty: Analiz romanov "Master i Margarita" i "Doktor Zhivago"*. Ann Arbor: Hermitage, 1984.
Lapidus, Gail. *Women in Soviet Society: Equality, Development, and Social Change*. Berkeley: University of California Press, 1978.
Latynina, Alla. "Pisat'-èto bylo spasenie: Vstrecha s Lidiei Chukovskoi." *Moskovskie Novosti*, 17, 12 April 1988, 7.
Lejeune, Philippe. *Le pacte autobiographique*. Paris: Editions du Seuil, 1975.
Levy, Anita. *Other Women: The Writing of Race, Class, and Gender, 1832–1898*. Princeton: Princeton University Press, 1991.
Lewin, Moshe. "Society, State, and Ideology during the First Five-Year Plan." In *Cultural Revolution in Russia, 1928–1931*, edited by Sheila Fitzpatrick, pp. 41–77. Bloomington: Indiana University Press, 1978.
Liubimova, A. "Dnevnikovye zapisi o vstrechakh s Annoi Andreevnoi Akhmatovoi (1944–1965)." In the Gosudarstvennyi Literaturnyi Muzei, fond 40, opis 1, n.17. Parts published as "Kak ia pisala Akhmatovu." *Nauka i zhizn'*, 2 (1978): 94–96.
Ludwig, Jack. "Hope Without Hope." *Partisan Review*, 41, no. 3 (1974): 455–62.
Maloff, Saul. "Poetry and Power." *Commonweal*, 43, no. 14 (8 January 1971): 352–54.
Mandelstam, Nadezhda. *Vospominaniia*. 4th ed. Paris: YMCA Press, 1982. English translation: *Hope Against Hope*. Translated by Max Hayward, with an introduction by Clarence Brown. New York: Atheneum, 1970. (Manuscript was circulating in *samizdat* in 1965.)
———. "[Ob Akhmatovoi.]" *Literaturnaia ucheba*, 3 (1989): 134–51. (Manuscript completed by March 1967.)
———. "Moe zaveshchanie." *Iunost'*, 9 (1989): 62. (Manuscript submitted for *tamizdat* publication in 1971.)
———. *Vtoraia kniga*. 4th ed. Paris: YMCA Press, 1987. Soviet edition: *Vtoraia kniga*. Moscow: Moskovskii rabochii, 1990. English translation: *Hope Abandoned*. Translated by Max Hayward. New York: Atheneum, 1974. (Manuscript completed 1970–71.)
———. *Mozart and Salieri*. Translated by Robert A. McLean. Ann Arbor: Ardis, 1973. (Manuscript was presented to *tamizdat* publisher in 1972.)
———. *Moe zaveshchanie i drugie esse*. With a foreword by Joseph Brodsky. New York: Serebrianyi vek, 1982. Includes Frank Diamond, "Dva interv'iu s Nadezhdoi Iakovlevnoi Mandelshtam."
———. *Kniga tret'ia*. Paris: YMCA Press, 1987.
Mandelstam, Osip. *Voronezhskie tetradi*. Edited and with an introduction by Viktoriia Shveitser. Ann Arbor: Ardis, 1980.
———. Correspondence and materials from fond 2833, n. 7, ed. khran. 544 in TsGALI, Moscow, USSR.
———. Correspondence contained in Box III, m. 91–92 of Osip Emilyevich Mandelshtam papers held in Firestone Library, Princeton University.
———. *The Complete Critical Prose and Letters*, edited by Jane Gary Harris, translated by Jane Gary Harris and Constance Link. Ann Arbor: Ardis, 1979.
Mandrykina, L. A. "Iz rukopisnogo naslediia A. A. Akhmatovoi." *Neva*, 6 (1979): 196–200.

Marcade, Jean-Claude. "Alexandra Exter or the Search for the Rhythms of Light-Colour." In *Kunstlerinnen der Russischen Avantgarde, 1910–1930*, pp. 124–28. Cologne: Galerie Gmurzynska, 1979.
Martyna, Wendy. "Psychology of the Generic Masculine." In *Women and Language in Literature and Society*, edited by Sally McConnell-Ginet, Ruth Borker, and Nelly Furman, pp. 69–78. New York: Praeger, 1980.
Masculinity/Femininity: Basic Perspectives, The Kinsey Institute Series, vol. 1. Edited by June Machover Reinisch, Leonard A. Rosenblum, and Stephanie A. Sanders. Oxford: Oxford University Press, 1987.
McLaughlin, Sigrid. "Introduction." In *The Image of Women in Contemporary Soviet Fiction: Selected Short Stories from the USSR*, edited and translated by Sigrid McLaughlin, pp. 1–17. London: Macmillan, 1989.
Medvedev, Roy A. *Let History Judge: The Origins and Consequences of Stalinism*. Revised and expanded edition, edited and translated by George Shriver. New York: Columbia University Press, 1989. Also 1st ed., translated by Colleen Taylor, edited by David Joravsky and Georges Haupt. New York: Vintage Books, 1973.
Men', Aleksandr. Review of first volume of Nadezhda Mandelstam's memoirs. *Literaturnoe obozrenie*, 5 (1990): 67–68.
Mendeleeva-Blok, Liubov'. "Facts and Myths about Blok and Myself." In *Blok: An Anthology of Essays and Memoirs*, edited and translated by Lucy Vogel, pp. 8–63. Ann Arbor: Ardis, 1982.
Morson, Gary Saul, and Caryl Emerson. *Mikhail Bakhtin. Creation of a Prosaics*. Stanford: Stanford University Press, 1990.
Moyle, Natalie K. "Mermaids (*Rusalki*) and Russian Beliefs about Women." In *New Studies in Russian Language and Literature*, edited by Anna Lisa Crone and Catherine V. Chvany, pp. 221–38. Columbus, OH: Slavica, 1987.
Naiman, Anatolii. *Rasskazy o Anne Akhmatovoi*. Moscow: Khudozhestvennaia literatura, 1989. English translation: *Remembering Akhmatova*. Introduction by Joseph Brodsky, translated by Wendy Rosslyn. London: Halban, 1991.
Nash, Carol S. "Educating New Mothers: Women and the Enlightenment in Russia." *History of Education Quarterly* (Fall 1981): 301–16.
Niederman, Sharon. *A Quilt of Words: Women's Diaries, Letters and Original Accounts of Life in the Southwest, 1860–1960*. Boulder: Johnson Books, 1988.
Ob Anne Akhmatovoi: Stikhi, esse, vospominaniia, pis'ma. Compiled by M. M. Kralin. Leningrad: Lenizdat, 1990.
Orlova, Raisa. *Memoirs*. Translated by Samuel Cioran. New York: Random House, 1983.
Ortner, Sherry B. "Is Female to Male as Nature Is to Culture?" In *Women, Culture, and Society*, edited by Michele Zimbalist Rosaldo and Louise Lamphere, pp. 67–87. Stanford: Stanford University Press, 1974.
Ostrovskaya, Sophie Kazimirovna. *Memoirs of Anna Akhmatova's Years: 1944–1950*. With an appendix of memoirs by Margarita Aliger, translated by Jessie Davis. Liverpool: Lincoln Davies, 1988.
Panchenko, Nikolai. Interview with author. Peredelkino, USSR, 3 October 1989.
Pasternak, Boris. *Doktor Zhivago*. Société d'Edition et d'Impression Mondiale, 1959. English edition: *Doctor Zhivago*. Translated by Max Hayward and Manya Harari. New York: Ballantine, 1986.
Pevear, Richard. "On the Memoirs of Nadezhda Mandelstam." *The Hudson Review*, 24, no. 3 (Autumn 1971): 426–40.
Pierpont, Claudia Roth. "Childhoods." *The New Yorker*, 17 December 1990, 124–32.
Polivanov, Mikhail. Interview with author. Moscow, USSR, 21 October 1989.
———. Introduction to Nadezhda Mandelstam's *Vospominaniia* in *Iunost'*, 8 (1988): 34–35.
———. "Predislovie." In N. Ia. Mandel'shtam, *Vtoraia kniga*, pp. 3–9. Moscow: Moskovskii rabochii, 1990.
Proffer, Carl. *The Widows of Russia and Other Writings*. Ann Arbor: Ardis, 1987.

Ratushinskaya, Irina. *Grey Is the Color of Hope*. Translated by Alyona Kojevnikov. New York: Alfred A. Knopf, 1988.
Read, Christopher. "Stalin's Russia." *History Today*, 33 (April 1983): 41–43.
Richardson, Alan. "Romanticism and the Colonization of the Feminine." In *Romanticism and Feminism*, edited by Anne K. Mellor, pp. 13–25. Bloomington: Indiana University Press, 1988.
Roskina, Nataliia. *Chetyre glavy*. Paris: YMCA Press, 1980.
Rosslyn, Wendy. *The Prince, the Fool and the Nunnery: Religion and Love in the Early Poetry of Anna Akhmatova*. Amersham, England: Avebury, 1984.
Sandler, Stephanie. "Reading Loyalty in Chukovskaia's *Zapiski ob Anne Akhmatovoi*." In *The Speech of Unknown Eyes: Akhmatova's Readers on Her Poetry*, vol. 2, edited by Wendy Rosslyn, pp. 267–82. Nottingham: Astra Press, 1990.
Sergeeva, Liudmila. Interview with author. Moscow, USSR, 14 October 1989.
Shcheglova, Evgeniia. "V svoem krugu: polemicheskie zametki o 'zhenskoi proze.'" *Literaturnoe obozrenie*, 3 (1990): 19–26.
Shklovskaia, Varvara. Interview with author. Peredelkino, USSR, 3 October 1989.
Shlapentokh, Vladimir. *Public and Private Life of the Soviet People: Changing Values in Post-Stalin Russia*. Oxford: Oxford University Press, 1989.
Shtempel', N. E. "Mandel'shtam v Voronezhe." *Novyi mir*, 10 (1987): 207–34; *Pod"em*, 5 (1989): 194–229; *Pod"em*, 6 (1989): 179–213.
Shumikhin, S. V. *Istoriia Gosudarstvennogo Literaturnogo Muzeia (1931–1941 gg.)* Unpublished dissertation. Moscow, 1988.
Simpson, John, and Jana Bennett. *The Disappeared and the Mothers of the Plaza: The Story of the 11,000 Argentinians Who Vanished*. New York: St. Martin's Press, 1985.
Siniavskii, Andrei/Abram Tertz. *The Trial Begins and On Socialist Realism*. Translated by George Denis, with an introduction by Czeslaw Milosz. Berkeley: University of California Press, 1960.
———. "Boris Pasternak (1965)." In *Boris Pasternak: Modern Judgements*, edited by Donald Davie and Angela Livingstone, with verse translations by Donald Davie, pp. 154–219. Nashville: Aurora, 1970.
———. "Literaturnyi protsess v Rossii." *Kontinent*, 1 (1974): 143–90; English-language edition: 77–118.
———. "Stalin—geroi i khudozhnik stalinskoi epokhi." *Sintaksis*, 19 (1987): 106–25.
———. *Soviet Civilization: A Cultural History*. Translated by Joanne Turnbull with the assistance of Nikolai Formozov. New York: Little, Brown, 1990.
Smith, Dorothy E. *The Everyday World as Problematic: A Feminist Sociology*. Boston: Northeastern University Press, 1987.
Smith, Hedrick. *The Russians*. New York: Ballantine Books, 1976.
Smith, Sidonie. *A Poetics of Women's Autobiography: Marginality and the Fictions of Self-Representation*. Bloomington: Indiana University Press, 1987.
Sokol, Elena. *Russian Poetry for Children*. Knoxville: University of Tennessee Press, 1984.
Solzhenitsyn, Alexander. *The Gulag Archipelago, 1918–1956: An Experiment in Literary Investigation*. Translated by Thomas P. Whitney. New York: Harper & Row, 1974.
Sprinker, Michael. "Fictions of the Self: The End of Autobiography." *Autobiography: Essays Theoretical and Critical*, edited by James Olney, pp. 321–42. Princeton: Princeton University Press, 1974.
Stanton, Domna. "Autogynography: Is the Subject Different?" *The Female Autograph: Theory and Practice of Autobiography from the Tenth to the Twentieth Century*, edited by Domna Stanton, pp. 3–20. Chicago: University of Chicago Press, 1984.
Steiner, George. "Death of a Poet." *The New Yorker*, 26 December 1970, 59–63.
Stites, Richard. *The Women's Liberation Movement in Russia: Feminism, Nihilism, and Bolshevism 1860–1930*. Princeton: Princeton University Press, 1978.

———. *Revolutionary Dreams: Utopian Vision and Experimental Life in the Russian Revolution*. New York: Oxford University Press, 1989.
Thorne, Ludmilla. "Horseshoes at the Head." *The New Leader*, 16 November 1970, 16–17.
Tolstaia, Tat'iana. "Soviet Women: Walking the Tightrope." *The New York Review of Books*, 31 May 1990, 3–7.
Tovrov, Jessica. "Mother-Child Relationships among the Russian Nobility." In *The Family in Imperial Russia: New Lines of Historical Research*, edited by David L. Ransel, pp. 15–43. Urbana: University of Illinois Press, 1978.
Tsvetaeva, Marina. *A Captive Spirit: Selected Prose*. Edited and translated by J. Marin King. Ann Arbor: Ardis, 1980.
Tucker, Robert C. *Stalin in Power: The Revolution from Above, 1928–1941*. New York: W. W. Norton, 1990.
Ulam, Adam B. *Stalin: The Man and His Era*. New York: The Viking Press, 1973.
van der Eng-Liedmeier, Jeanne. "Poèma bez Geroja." *Two Poems by Anna Akhmatova: Essays by Jeanne van der Eng-Liedmeier and Kees Verheul with Unpublished Poems by Anna Axmatova*, pp. 63–14. The Hague: Mouton, 1974.
Verheul, Kees. *The Theme of Time in the Poetry of Anna Akhmatova*. The Hague: Mouton, 1971.
Vilenkin, Vitalii. *V sto pervom zerkale*. 2d ed. Moscow: Sovetskii pisatel', 1990.
Vysheslavskii, Leonid. "Poèma nevedomykh drug." *Al'manakh bibliofila*, vyp. 18. Moscow: Kniga, 1985, 221–27.
Waters, Elizabeth. "The Female Form in Soviet Political Iconography, 1917–1932." In *Russia's Women: Accommodation, Resistance, Transformation*, edited by Barbara Evans Clements, Barbara Alpern Engel, and Christine D. Worobec, pp. 225–42. Berkeley: University of California Press, 1991.
White, Hayden. *Metahistory: The Historical Imagination in Nineteenth-Century Europe*. 3rd ed. Baltimore: Johns Hopkins University Press, 1980.
Zlobin, Stepan. Unpublished review of *Sofia Petrovna* for *Novyi mir*. Located in fund 2175, opis 5 in TsGALI, Moscow, USSR.

INDEX

Acmeists, 15, 117, 121, 122, 144, 156, 157
Akhmatova, Anna, 1, 2, 4, 14, 25, 47, 65, 108, 109, 111, 117, 118, 119, 121, 123, 124, 125, 130, 131, 137, 141–42, 143, 149, 150, 152, 153, 156, 157, 159, 166, 171, 172, 173, 176, 198n58; as model for Lidiia Chukovskaia, 68, 69–70, 72, 75–76, 81, 85, 91, 93–94; as model for Nadezhda Mandelstam, 122, 142, 144–48, 160–62; as physical icon, 71–76, 81, 122; biography of, 23–24; conflation of her life and art, 70–72. *See also* Chukovskaia; *Requiem*
Alekseeva, Liudmila, 174, 175, 178
Anikieva, Vera, 83
Armstrong, Nancy, 9
Art of Translation, The, 39
Authorship: conditions for official writers, 7; conditions for unofficial writers, 7–8; in nineteenth-century Russia, 7–8. *See also* Literary process
Autobiography and memoirs: as accessible genres for women, 2; as response to Stalinist repression, 1; comparison of Russian and Western European women's autobiographies, 29–30; functions of, 25; implicit conventions of memoirs, 166. *See also* Women
Averbakh, Leopold, 120
Avvakum, Archpriest, 108, 168

Babel', Isaac, 132
Bakhtin, Mikhail, 131
Bednyi, Demian, 120, 135
Belosinskaia, Nina, 200n6
Belyi, Andrei, 121
Berdiaev, Nikolai, 121
Bestuzhev, Nikolai, 41
Blok, Aleksandr, 71, 110, 121
Blok, Liubov', 71, 173
Bogoraz, Larisa, 175, 176, 178
Borisov brothers, 41
Boswell, James, 69
Brik, Osip, 121
Briusov, Valerii, 121
Brodskii, Joseph, 42, 115, 155, 159
Bronshtein, Matvei, 40, 191n29
Brown, Clarence, 118
Brown, Gillian, 9
Bulgakov, Mikhail, 14, 17, 18, 19, 20, 22, 23, 24, 26, 59, 81, 142, 147, 172; biography of, 17, 23
Bulgakov, Sergei, 155, 156
Bulgakova, Elena. *See* Shilovskaia

Cement, 13
Chernyshevskii, Nikolai, 7–8

Chicherin, Georgii, 119
Chronicle of Current Events, 174
Chudakova, Marietta, 8, 181n3
Chukokkala, 68
Chukovskaia, Elena, 40, 174, 191n29
Chukovskaia, Lidiia, 2, 12, 14, 23, 25, 49, 51, 55, 58, 60, 61, 62, 63, 64, 65, 66, 71, 98, 99, 101, 102, 103, 108, 109, 116, 118, 120, 124, 125, 126, 130, 131, 137, 142, 145, 146, 148, 152, 153, 154, 164, 166; biography of, 29–30, 37, 40–42; description of Akhmatova, 72–76; development as writer, 3–4, 26, 29, 33–34, 41, 42–43, 44–47, 56–57, 59, 67, 68–70, 72, 85, 88, 91–94, 171–72; legacy of literary works, 171–73; legacy of other works, 174–79; relationship with Akhmatova, 79–94; relationship with father, 29–30, 31–34, 35, 36–40, 42–43; transcription of Akhmatova, 76–79
Chukovskaia, Mariia, 31, 38
Chukovskii, Kornei, 3, 26, 31, 32, 33, 37, 41, 46, 71, 92, 94, 101, 102, 140, 153, 174; biography of, 29n, 30, 34–36, 38–39; "religion" of art, 35–36, 42, 43; works of, 39, 45, 68–69
Chukovskii, Nikolai, 30, 189n6
Clark, Katerina, 13, 182n12
Coat of Many Colors: Osip Mandelstam and His Mythologies of Self-Presentation, A, 16
Cohn, Dorrit, 47
Conquest, Robert, 130

Daniel', Iulii, 175, 178
Davidenkov, Kolia, 83
de Beauvoir, Simone, 107
de Vega, Lope, 104
Doctor Zhivago, 17, 18, 19–20, 21, 22, 23, 79, 81, 83, 84, 107, 108, 123
Dolgorukaia, Princess Natal'ia, 108
Domestic sphere: as compared with domestic sphere in fascist Germany and Italy, 10; as domain of Soviet women, 9–10; as site of unofficial culture, 2, 10, 26, 173–74; in *Doctor Zhivago,* 18, 22, 23; in *Going Under,* 57, 58; in *Hope against Hope,* 126, 130–31; in Mandelstam's poetry, 15; in *The Master and Margarita,* 18–19, 22, 23; in *Notes on Anna Akhmatova,* 73, 74; in *Requiem,* 24; in socialist realist literature, 14; in *Sofia Petrovna,* 47, 48, 50, 52, 53; in *To the Memory of Childhood,* 30, 42; state policies on, 9–10
Dostoevskii, Fiodor, 76, 82, 155, 156, 157, 158
Durova, Nadezhda, 30

Eckermann, Johann, 69
Egyptian Stamp, The, 119

Index

Ehrenburg, Il'ia, 104, 153, 163
Ekster, Aleksandra, 103, 104
Engel, Barbara Alpern, 11
Etkind, Efim, 45

"Family," 99, 102–103
"Father," 99, 101–102
Faust, 22
Foucault, Michel, 7
Fourth Prose, 119
Freidin, Gregory, 16, 119
Freidin, Iurii, 200n6, 205n48, 207n27
From Two to Five, 39
Funteovejuna, 104, 105

Gabbe, Tamara, 90
Gandhi, Mahatma, 175
Garshin, Vladimir, 74, 79, 85
Gasiorowska, Xenia, 13–14
Gender roles: in Chukovskaia's "poetic education," 31–33, 34, 35, 36, 38, 39; in *Doctor Zhivago,* 19–20, 21, 23; in *Going Under,* 60–62, 66–67; in *Hope Abandoned* (both variants), 146–48, 158–65, 172–73; in Mandelstam's poetry, 16–17; in *The Master and Margarita,* 19, 20, 21, 22, 23; in Nadezhda Mandelstam's authorship, 107–109, 111–12; in *Notes on Anna Akhmatova,* 80–84, 85, 87, 93, 94; in *Requiem,* 24–25; in socialist realist literature, 12–14; in *Sofia Petrovna,* 49, 51, 55, 56, 66–67
Georgievskaia, Susanna, 41
Gershtein, Emma, 97, 166, 195n22
Ginzburg, Evgeniia, 26
Ginzburg, Lidiia, 70–71, 85
"Girls and a Boy," 99, 100
Gladkov, Fiodor, 13
Glebova-Sudeikina, Olga, 160
Glikin, Isidor, 92–93, 199n69
Gogol', Nikolai, 76, 155
Going Under, 56–67, 68, 78, 79, 82, 86, 92, 94, 172, 176; genesis of, 44–47
Gorbanevskaia, Natal'ia, 174, 175, 176
Gor'kii, Maksim, 121, 153
Great Terror, The, 130
Grey is the Color of Hope, 177
Grigorieva, Tania (the "non-Party Bolshevik"), 135
Grois, Boris, 6
Gulag Archipelago, The, 129–30
Gumilev, Lev, 69, 70, 83, 84
Gumilev, Nikolai, 70, 122, 156

Haight, Amanda, 71–72
Harris, Jane Gary, 16–17
Herzen, Aleksandr, 41–42, 116, 168
Hope Abandoned, 103, 105, 109, 111, 113, 122, 128, 134, 145–68; first variant of, 141, 145–48; genesis of, 141–42; reception of, 165–67

Hope against Hope, 109, 113, 114–38, 140, 141, 143, 145, 146, 149, 151, 155; genesis of, 114–17; reception of, 114, 136–38
Howe, Irving, 137

Illiad, The, 116
Ioffe, Mariia, 26
Isenberg, Charles, 107, 116–17, 131, 137, 145
Ivanov, Viacheslav, 153, 155
Ivinskaia, Olga, 17, 26, 82

"Journey to Armenia," 15

Kallistratova, Sofia, 176
Kaminskaia, Dina, 176
Kaverin, Veniamin, 166–67
Khardzhiev, Nikolai, 151
Khazin, Aleksandr, 99
Khazin, Evgenii, 126
Khazin, Iakov, 26, 99, 100, 101, 102, 103, 104, 112
Khazina, Vera, 99, 100, 101, 109, 201n23
Khlebnikov, Velimir, 157
Khodorovich, Tat'iana, 176
King, Martin Luther, Jr., 175
Kniazev, Vasilii, 73–74
Kniazev, Vsevolod, 160
Kompanii, 174
Kosmodemianskaia, Zoia, 178
Kovalevskaia, Sofia, 30

Lazareva, Natal'ia, 177
Lenin, Vladimir, 48
Let History Judge, 129
Levy, Anita, 9
Life of Samuel Johnson, 69
Literary process: for socialist realist writers, 7; for unofficial writers and their readers, 2, 8–9; in *Doctor Zhivago,* 20, 21, 23; in *Going Under,* 58–60; in *Hope Abandoned,* 152; in *Hope against Hope,* 124–26; in *The Master and Margarita,* 20, 22, 23; in *Mozart and Salieri,* 142–44; in *Notes on Anna Akhmatova,* 84–93
Little Princess, The, 32
Little Women, 32
Liubarskaia, Aleksandra, 83
Liubimova, A., 71
Livshits, Ekaterina, 146
Lofty Art, The, 39

Maiakovskii, Vladimir, 121
Mandelstam, Nadezhda, 2, 3, 12, 14, 23, 25, 166; as literary critic, 124–27, 142–45, 150–55; as social critic, 129–36, 155–65; biography of, 98–104, 105, 106, 108–109, 114–15, 140; development as writer, 4, 26, 97, 98, 108, 111–13, 114–18, 127–29, 130–32, 133, 134–35, 137–38, 141–42, 148–50, 155, 164–65, 167–68, 172–73; legacy of literary works,

171–73; legacy of other works, 174–79; relationship with Osip Mandelstam, 104–13; "salon" of, 140–41, 149, 168, 174. *See also* Akhmatova
Mandelstam, Osip, 3, 14, 15–17, 19, 20, 23, 24, 25, 26, 70, 87, 97, 98, 113, 114, 115, 116, 119, 128, 131, 132, 133, 135, 136, 137, 138, 140, 141, 147, 150, 151, 152, 153, 154, 156, 157, 159, 160, 162, 163, 165, 166, 172; as model for Nadezhda Mandelstam, 117–25, 137, 142–45; biography of, 15, 106–107. *See also* Mandelstam, Nadezhda
Mandelstam, Tatka, 135
Mariia, 177
Marshak, Samuil, 40, 153–54, 155
Master and Margarita, The, 17–18, 19, 20, 21–23, 79, 81, 84, 107, 108
Meck, Galina, 159–60
Medvedev, Roy, 129
Miklukho-Maklai, Nikolai, 41
Mothers and Daughters: Women of the Intelligentsia in Nineteenth-Century Russia, 11
"Mothers of the Plaza de Mayo," 175, 176
Mozart and Salieri, 142–45, 149, 150, 153
My Past and Thoughts, 41, 116

Narbikova, Valeriia, 173
Narbut, Vladimir, 156
Neigauz, Zinaida, 17, 82–83
Nekrasov, Nikolai, 36, 37, 45, 87
Nerler, P., 141
Noise of Time, The, 152
Notes on Anna Akhmatova, 29, 44, 46, 68–94, 116, 117, 118, 122, 123, 126, 127, 130, 137, 145, 148, 172, 175; genesis of, 68–72

Ol'shanskaia, Nina, 80
"On the Nature of the Word," 15
Orlova, Raisa, 177, 178
Osipova, Tat'iana, 177

Panchenko, Nikolai, 116, 200n6
Panova, Vera, 185n44
Pasternak, Boris, 14, 17, 19, 20, 21, 23, 24, 26, 59, 62, 63, 70, 81, 82–83, 122, 123–24, 142, 143, 144, 147, 172; biography of, 17, 23
Petrushevskaia, Liudmila, 173
Pevear, Richard, 137
Po ètu storonu smerti, 192n6
"Poem without a Hero," 89–91, 92, 160
Polivanov, Mikhail, 128, 137, 139, 148–49, 200n6
Prison lines: in *Going Under*, 46, 58, 59–60, 66, 176; in *Hope Abandoned*, 159, 164; in *Notes on Anna Akhmatova*, 69–70, 74; in *Requiem*, 24; in *Sof'ia Petrovna*, 46, 52–53, 55, 56, 66

Proffer, Carl, 139, 140, 165, 166, 171, 172, 181n4
Prologue, 153
Protsess iskliucheniia, 191n2
Punin, Nikolai, 69, 70, 73, 74, 81, 82, 131
Pushkin, Aleksandr, 21, 76, 143, 144

Ratushinskaia, Irina, 177, 178
Requiem, 1, 24–25, 47, 65, 72, 85, 86, 88
Rozanova, Mariia, 175
Rudakov, Sergei, 151, 203n27

Sakharov, Andrei, 42, 177
Sartre, Jean-Paul, 107
Semenko, Irina, 140
Sergeeva, Liudmila, 140, 200n6
Shalamov, Varlam, 146
Shilovskaia, Elena, 17, 26
Shklovskaia, Varvara, 116, 200n6
Shklovskaia, Vasilisa, 109
Shklovskii, Viktor, 134
Shlapentokh, Vladimir, 173
Shtempel', Natasha, 16–17, 97, 126, 159
Siniavskii, Andrei (Abram Tertz), 6–7, 174, 175, 178, 182–83n14
Sobornost', 158, 164
Socialist realism, 1, 7, 12–14, 19, 64, 122; echoes in *Sof'ia Petrovna*, 47, 48, 49, 50, 51
Sof'ia Petrovna, 44, 47–56, 66–67, 68, 91–92, 94; genesis of, 44–47
Solomakha, Tat'iana, 178
Solzhenitsyn, Aleksandr, 42, 55, 129–30, 168, 174, 177
Stalin, Joseph, 1, 5, 6, 7, 9, 10, 12, 15, 17, 23, 26, 41, 44, 48, 76, 77, 85, 114, 123, 124, 129, 130, 137, 149, 173; aesthetic properties of his dictatorship, 6–7
Steiner, George, 137
Stoliarova, Natasha, 157, 163–64, 176
Sviatopolk-Mirskii, Dmitrii, 73–74

Tertz, Abram. *See* Siniavskii
Third Book, 141, 200n7
Tikhonov, Nikolai, 120
To the Memory of Childhood, 29, 30, 31–40, 42–43, 45, 68, 100, 102, 172
Tolstoi, Aleksei, 119
Tolstoi, Lev, 7, 76, 155
"Toward the empty earth," 16–17
Tristia, 15–16, 107
Tristram Shandy, 116
Trotskii, Lev, 119
Tsvetaeva, Marina, 30, 70, 122–23, 124, 159, 162, 172, 173, 191n35
Tvardovskii, Aleksandr, 114
Tynianov, Iurii, 154–55, 167

V laboratorii redaktora (In the editor's workshop), 40

Index

Vaksel, Olga, 106
Velikanova, Tat'iana, 176, 177
"Verse on the Unknown Soldier," 150
Vigdorova, Frida, 159, 175, 177, 178
Voloshin, Maximilian, 153
Volpe, Tsezar, 15, 191n29
Voznesenskaia, Iuliia, 173
Vysotskaia, Ol'ga, 83

"What Is an Author?" 7
What Is Socialist Realism? 6
Widows of Russia, The, 171
Wife: the "blessed wife," 16–17, 20, 22–23, 25, 87, 107–108, 147, 165; the "literary widow," 2, 171–72; the materialistic wife, 61, 62, 81–83, 93, 109–10, 111

Women: as heroic caretakers, 2, 12, 26, 62–63, 67, 83–84, 93, 109, 146, 160; as memoirists and diarists, 2, 25–26, 56, 69, 131, 138, 141, 206n11; as mourners and witnesses, 2, 25, 65, 66–67, 87, 108, 126, 165; in the post-Soviet state, 179; involved in political oppositions, 10–12, 174–78. *See also* Prison lines; Wife

Zenkevich, Mikhail, 156
Zhitkov, Boris, 41
Zoo, 134

BETH HOLMGREN is Assistant Professor of Slavic Languages and Literatures at the University of North Carolina. She has authored articles on Russian and Polish literary history.